THE LAW OF
PARTNERSHIPS AND
CORPORATIONS

Other books in *Essentials of Canadian Law* Series

Criminal Law

The Law of Evidence

Statutory Interpretation

Media Law

The Law of Trusts

Intellectual Property Law

Income Tax Law

ESSENTIALS OF
CANADIAN LAW

THE LAW OF PARTNERSHIPS AND CORPORATIONS

J. ANTHONY VANDUZER

Faculty of Law
The University of Ottawa

THE LAW OF PARTNERSHIPS AND CORPORATIONS
© Publications for Professionals, 1997

Published in 1997 by
Irwin Law
1800 Steeles Avenue West
Concord, Ontario
L4K 2P3

ISBN: 1-55221-008-1

Canadian Cataloguing in Publication Data

VanDuzer, J. Anthony (John Anthony), 1958–
    The law of partnerships and corporations

(Essentials of Canadian law)
Includes bibliographical references and index.
ISBN 1-55221-008-1

1. Business enterprises – Law and legislation – Canada.
2. Partnership – Canada.   3. Corporation Law – Canada.
4. Sole proprietorship – Canada.   I. Title.   II. Series.

KE1345.V36 1997   346.71'065   C96-932183-X
KF1355.V36 1997

Printed and bound in Canada.

    2   3   4   5   00   99

SUMMARY
TABLE OF CONTENTS

DETAILED
TABLE OF CONTENTS

CHAPTER 7:
MANAGEMENT AND CONTROL OF THE CORPORATION   *182*

FOREWORD

Canadian corporate law is messy. The federal government has its own corporate law statute, as does each of the ten provinces. Although there are similarities among these statutes, there are also substantial differences. Not only that, but provincial securities regulation also regulates corporate governance, and needs to be accounted for in any treatment of the Canadian corporate law regime. Further complicating matters are the many liabilities and duties, based on a range of statutes and common law doctrines, that regulate corporate behaviour.

Tony VanDuzer has written an indispensable book on the structure and operation of Canadian partnership and corporate law. Ever mindful of the complexities of the legal regime, he skilfully navigates his treatise through a number of doctrinal areas and gives the reader an appreciation of how the system works. He does so in a way that is sensitive to the distinct market and regulatory environment in which Canadian corporations operate.

All in all, this book is a distinguished piece of scholarship, and I commend it to both practitioners and students of corporate law.

Ronald J. Daniels
Dean, Faculty of Law
University of Toronto

ACKNOWLEDGMENTS

I would like to thank the following people for their assistance in reviewing earlier drafts of this book: Jeremy Farr, Marc LeBlanc, Jeffrey MacIntosh, Douglas Scott, Sean Wise, and Jacob Ziegel. Any errors, of course, remain my sole responsibility. I acknowledge the support of the Common Law Section at the University of Ottawa, the University of Toronto, Faculty of Law, where most of this book was written, the Law Foundation, and Macleod Dixon.

I also wish to thank my children, Taylor and Eli, for their patience, and my wife, Jodie Karpf, without whose constant indulgence and support this book would not have been possible.

J. Anthony VanDuzer

LIST OF STATUTES, REGULATIONS, AND ABBREVIATIONS

Statutes

ABCA	*Business Corporations Act*, S.A. 1981, c. B-15
BCCA	*Company Act*, R.S.B.C. 1979, c. 59
CBCA	*Canada Business Corporations Act*, R.S.C. 1985, c. C-44
MBCA	*The Corporations Act*, R.S.M. 1987, c. C-225
NBBCA	*Business Corporations Act*, S.N.B. 1981, c. B-9.1 as amended by *An Act to Amend the Business Corporations Act*, S.N.B. 1984, c. 17
NCA	*Corporations Act*, R.S.N. 1990, c. C-36
NSCA	*Companies Act*, R.S.N.S. 1989, c. 81, as amended by *Investors Protection Act*, S.N.S. 1990, c. 15
NwtBCA	*Companies Act*, R.S.N.W.T. 1988, c. C-12
OBCA	*Business Corporations Act*, R.S.O. 1990, c. B.16
OBNA	*Business Names Act*, R.S.O. 1990, c. B.17
OEPCA	*Extra-Provincial Corporations Act*, R.S.O. 1990, c. E.27
OLPA	*Limited Partnerships Act*, R.S.O. 1990, c. L.16
OPA	*Partnerships Act*, R.S.O. 1990, c. P.5
OSA	*Securities Act*, R.S.O. 1990, c. S.5
PEICA	*Companies Act*, R.S.P.E.I. 1988, c. C-14
QCA	*Companies Act*, R.S.Q. 1977, c. C-38
SBCA	*The Business Corporations Act*, R.S.S. 1978, c. B-10
UKCA	*Companies Act* (U.K.), 1985, c. 6
YBCA	*Business Corporations Act*, R.S.Y. 1986, c. 15

Regulations

CBCA Regulations	SOR/79-316
OBCA Regulation	R.R.O. 1990, Reg. 62
OSA Regulation	R.R.O. 1990, Reg. 1015

CHAPTER 1

INTRODUCTION

A. INTRODUCTION TO THIS BOOK

This book provides an overview of the essential features of the law governing business organizations in Canada. It is intended to be an accessible and practical reference for law and business students, lawyers, accountants, and others concerned with business organizations.

The three legal arrangements most commonly used for carrying on business in Canada are the sole proprietorship, the partnership, and the corporation. The law governing these forms of business organization touches all of us, in a variety of diverse and overlapping ways, as employees, managers, customers, creditors, and, most significantly, investors. Although only some of us may invest our money directly in businesses, almost all of us have some stake as investors, since our deposits in our bank account, the premiums we pay to our insurance company, and our contributions to our pension fund are all reinvested by these financial intermediaries in businesses.[1]

Every business carries on some commercial activity that involves certain risks. Although the specific sources of risk will vary from one business to the next, in every business the fundamental nature of the risk is the same: there will be those who benefit if the business prospers

---

1   Some money deposited in bank accounts, of course, is not invested in business, but loaned to consumers.

and those who lose if it does not. As investors and in our other relationships with business enterprises, the main way business organizations law affects us is by allocating the risks associated with carrying on the business. In general, business organizations law strikes a balance between the interests of investors and the other stakeholders, including employees, managers, customers, creditors, and the public, by establishing rules that assign liability in connection with business activities. For example, business organizations law determines when individual investors are personally liable for the debts and other obligations of the business. By affecting the allocation of the risks of doing business in this way, business organizations law influences the incentives for entrepreneurs to engage in business. Business organizations law is concerned also with providing an organizational structure for the operation of businesses.[2]

This book examines the balance struck between the interests of investors and other stakeholders in the sole proprietorship, the partnership, and the corporation and the particular kind of organizational structure provided by each. Throughout the book, emphasis is placed on the practical application of legal rules in an everyday context, including, in particular, in a lawyer's practice.

This chapter continues with an examination of the nature of a business and the interests of its stakeholders, and then takes a first look at how the law governing business organizations mediates among these interests. Next, the basic characteristics of the sole proprietorship, the partnership, and the corporation, as well as some other forms and methods of carrying on business, such as joint ventures, franchises, and co-ownership arrangements, are described. Both legal and practical considerations are discussed, and some of the advantages and disadvantages of each are identified.

In the remainder of the book, partnerships and corporations, respectively, are addressed in detail. In relation to each, the following areas are covered:

- How is the business organization formed?
- What are the relationships among the people who own and manage the business and how are they governed?

---

2   Business organizations in Canada, as elsewhere, were developed and are peculiarly adapted to facilitate the operation of a market-based capitalist economy. This book does not address the relative merits of such an economy, but accepts it as a given.

- What are the relationships between the business organization and those it deals with, such as creditors, customers, and tort[3] victims, and how are they governed?

The discussion of partnerships in chapter 2 also covers two special kinds of relationships: limited partnerships and joint ventures.

Chapters 3 through 12 on corporations make up the largest section of the book, reflecting the pervasive use of the corporate form to carry on business. Although the content of these chapters follows the model outlined above, the discussion is much more detailed. Most of the discussion focuses on smaller private corporations, the most common type of corporation in the marketplace. Nevertheless, some of the distinctive issues relevant to large public corporations, such as corporate governance, insider trading, and takeover bids, will be addressed in passing throughout the book and are the focus of chapter 11.

Unlike the other forms of business organization, the corporation is an entity separate in law from the people who own it, the shareholders, and those who manage it, the directors and officers. Chapter 3 introduces the corporation by tracing the historical development of corporate law in Canada and examining the constitutional competence of the federal and provincial governments to incorporate and regulate corporations. This chapter also looks at the nature of the corporation's separate personality. Chapter 4 outlines the process of and considerations relating to incorporation. Chapter 5 discusses some of the operational issues arising in the context of the corporation's external relationships which are created by the corporation's separate legal existence, such as how the corporation becomes liable in contract and for torts and crimes.

The rest of the book is devoted largely to the internal relationships in the corporation. The legal scheme set out in Canadian corporate statutes is explained and some of the current issues of corporate governance in practice are discussed. Chapter 6 deals with the nature of shares, the ownership interests in the corporation. Chapter 7 deals with the division of powers to manage and control the corporation among the shareholders, who are the owners of the corporations; the directors, who are elected by the shareholders to manage the corporation; and the officers who are appointed by the directors and to whom the directors delegate management authority. Chapter 8 deals with the duties of directors and

---

3   A tort is an act or omission giving rise to civil liability. The most important tort is negligence. If a person can prove that the act or omission of another meets the legal standard for negligence, that person will be entitled to compensation from such other person for any loss suffered as a result.

officers. The focus is on corporate law duties designed to ensure that directors and officers manage competently in the corporation's best interests, though the burgeoning statutory duties of directors and officers imposed to ensure the attainment of other public policy objectives, such as compliance with environmental legislation, are also considered. Chapter 9 looks at the remedies available to shareholders when directors and officers fail to meet their legal obligations. In Chapter 10 the technical and practical aspects of fundamental corporate changes, such as the amalgamation of two corporations and the dissolution of the corporation, are considered. Chapter 11 addresses some of the technical and practical issues of specific relevance to larger public corporations, such as takeover bids and insider trading. A brief introduction to securities law is included as well.

The final chapter of the book, chapter 12, introduces some of the current issues in business organizations law. It looks at possible future developments in areas such as corporate governance and the responsibilities of corporations to be accountable to non-shareholder stakeholders, including employees and the public.

In putting the book together, several features have been added to facilitate its use. Each chapter contains a chapter summary and a list of further readings, as well as a number of examples. At the end, a glossary of important terms has been provided, along with a comprehensive index.

B. WHAT IS A BUSINESS AND HOW DOES LAW GOVERN BUSINESS ORGANIZATIONS?

All businesses carry on some commercial activity and, in doing so, become the focus of a variety of relationships (see figure 1.1).[4] One of the major concerns of business organizations law is the relationship of owners and managers to the business and to each other. For this reason, in this book we look at what rights and obligations the sole proprietor, the partner, and the shareholder have to manage the business themselves and to monitor and control others who manage. We also look at what remedies are available to owners where management is acting in a manner inconsistent with the best interests of the business. We will stray into securities law, to the extent that it addresses some of these same concerns.

---

4   The idea for presenting stakeholder interests in this way came from E.E. Palmer & B. L. Welling, *Canadian Company Law: Cases, Notes and Materials*, 3d ed. (Toronto: Butterworths, 1986) at 2–5.

Figure 1.1   Stakeholders in Business Organizations

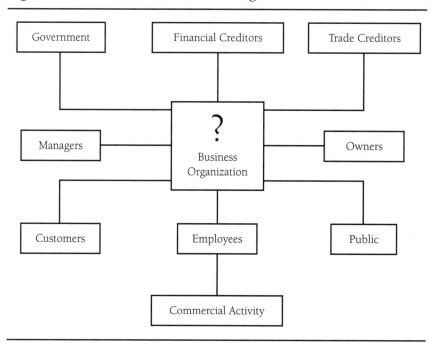

The second major concern of business organizations law is the responsibility of the business, the owners, and the managers to other stakeholder groups. The focus of business organizations law in this regard, however, is narrow. For the most part, relations between non-shareholder stakeholders and business organizations, their owners, and their managers is governed by other types of laws.

The rights and obligations of employees in relation to the business are governed by their contracts of employment, subject to a range of regulatory laws including employment standards and occupational health and safety legislation. There are a small number of discrete kinds of protection for employees in business organizations law, but its main impact on employees is to determine who bears responsibility for obligations to employees: Is it the owners, the managers, or the organization itself that is responsible? In chapter 12 we discuss briefly the extent to which business organizations law permits or requires managers to take employees' interests into account in making business decisions.

The particular relationships between a business and its trade creditors (e.g., suppliers of goods and services to the business), financial creditors (e.g., banks), and customers are not the subject of business organizations law but are dealt with under various other categories of law, such as contract, tort, property, commercial, and criminal law. Business organizations law is concerned with the narrower issue of when the business organization is liable for the obligations created under these other categories of law. In other words, we will not look at the substantive basis of a claim that a crime or a tort, for example, has been committed, but rather at the circumstances in which a business organization can be said to have committed the crime or the tort. As with employees, business organizations law does provide certain limited protection for creditors and customers, and addresses the extent to which management is permitted or required to take their interests into account.

Business organizations have a complex and multifaceted relationship with the public. Decision making by business organizations has an enormous impact on the public interest in relation to such areas as employment, the environment, and tax revenues. The consequence, of course, is that businesses are subject to a variety of forms of direct regulation in these areas. Such regulation is not the subject of business organizations law. We are concerned in this book only to address the limited ways in which business organizations law permits or requires management to take public interests into account.

Businesses operate, then, within a web of relationships involving a number of stakeholders which are regulated by a wide variety of laws designed to achieve a range of public policy objectives. Business organizations law focuses primarily on a subset of these relationships — those between owners, managers, and the business. It is important to remember, however, that the other relationships and the rules which govern them not only constitute the context in which business organizations law operates but have a significant impact on the behaviour of management and owners.

C. BASIC FORMS OF BUSINESS ORGANIZATIONS

1) Sole Proprietorships

The sole proprietorship is the simplest form of business organization. A sole proprietorship comes into existence whenever an individual starts to carry on business for her own account without taking the steps necessary to adopt some other form of organization, such as a corporation. Although the sole proprietor may enter into contracts of employment with others and, in this way, allocate certain functions in the business to them, the sole proprietor is the sole owner of the business and the only person entitled to manage it. Indeed, both legally and practically, there is no separation between the sole proprietorship business organization and the person who is the sole proprietor. One consequence is that the sole proprietor may not be an employee of the business. There is no one with whom she can contract.

All benefits from the business accrue to the sole proprietor, and all obligations of the business are his responsibility. In terms of the relationships between the business and the other stakeholders in the business, the sole proprietor's complete responsibility has several important implications.

- The sole proprietor is exclusively responsible for performing all contracts entered into in the course of the business, including, for example, sales contracts with customers, financial commitments, contracts with suppliers, and employment contracts.
- The sole proprietor is exclusively responsible for all torts committed by her personally in connection with the business, and she is vicariously liable for all torts committed by employees in the course of their employment.
- All the sole proprietor's personal assets, as well as those contributed to the business, may be seized in fulfilment of the obligations of the sole proprietor's business.
- For income tax purposes, the income or loss from the business is included with the income or loss from other sources in calculating the sole proprietor's personal tax liability.

The chief attraction of the sole proprietorship is its simplicity and ease of creation. It is equally easy to dissolve; the sole proprietor simply ceases to carry on business. Ceasing to carry on business, however, has no effect on liabilities incurred in connection with the business while it was being carried on. The chief disadvantage of the sole proprietorship is unlimited personal liability. All the sole proprietor's personal assets, not just those of the business, may be taken by third parties in satisfaction of obligations of the business. As the scale of the business and the concomitant liabilities increase, this exposure to personal liability becomes an increasingly important disincentive to using this form of business organization. By comparison, the corporation, but not the partnership, provides protection against personal liability. Another problem with sole proprietorships is raising money. Every business needs additional investment to grow. It is not possible to divide up ownership of the sole proprietorship, so the only method of financing is for the sole proprietor to borrow money directly. As will be discussed below, an advantage of both the partnership and especially the corporation is that they permit a wider range of investment possibilities. For both these reasons, sole proprietorships are used only for relatively small businesses.

One of the legal requirements in connection with the use of a sole proprietorship is that the name of the sole proprietorship must be registered under the business name legislation in each province in which the proprietorship is carrying on business if it is using a name other than simply the name of the proprietor. In Ontario, registration is governed by section 2(2) of the *Business Names Act* (*OBNA*). So, for example, Janet Smith would not have to register if she were carrying on a convenience store business under the name Janet Smith Milk and Nuts, but would if she chose instead to use the name World's Best Milk and Nuts. A sole proprietor may also register voluntarily (*OBNA*, s. 4).

The *OBNA* and other provincial names legislation contain certain inducements to register. In Ontario, if you do not register when required to, without reasonable cause, you are committing an offence and are liable for a fine of up to $2000 (*OBNA*, s. 10(2)). Also, you may not sue in Ontario for an obligation incurred in connection with the business except with leave of the court (*OBNA*, s. 7). The court must grant leave if the failure to register was inadvertent, there is no evidence that the public has been deceived or misled, and, at the time of application to the court, you have filed a registration (*OBNA*, s. 7(2)). The main reason for these incentives is to ensure that there is a public record for creditors and others to search to find out the identity of the person behind the business name who will bear responsibility for any obligation of the business. The registration of the name of a sole proprietorship also has the effect of discouraging others from using the name and so reducing the likelihood of confusion in the marketplace. This is one reason to register even if you are not obliged to.

Another sort of advantage to registration is the right to statutory damages up to $500 against any person who registers a name that is deceptively similar to another registered name and that causes injury (*OBNA*, s. 6). It is important to note that this right is in addition to any other legal right an aggrieved person may have in connection with someone using a confusingly similar name. For example, you may have a claim against such a person under the common law tort of passing-off.

Where a plaintiff in an action brought under *OBNA*, section 6, is successful, the court must also order the cancellation of the offending registration. The availability of statutory damages and cancellation encourages sole proprietors to police the names register themselves and so protects the integrity of the public record. Registration does not, however, create any proprietary interest in a name. Such interests are protected only under provincial passing-off laws and federal trade-marks law. These laws are discussed in relation to corporate names in chapter 4.

The only other category of requirement for sole proprietorships, one that applies equally to all forms of business organization as well, is business licences. In order to commence certain types of businesses, a sole proprietor must obtain a licence from one of the levels of government. For example, most municipalities in Ontario require the proprietors of taxi-driving businesses and restaurants to obtain a licence. Provincial governments have enacted licensing requirements for many types of businesses, such as real estate agents, car dealers, and securities dealers. In areas of federal legislative competence, licensing requirements may also be imposed. Anyone starting up a business should check the relevant licensing requirements.

2) Partnerships

a) Introduction

The law of partnerships was developed by the courts in England and was codified in the English *Partnership Act* of 1890.[5] All provinces, other than Quebec, have legal systems based on the English common law approach,[6] and all have partnership legislation based on this English statute. The Ontario *Partnerships Act* (OPA) is typical. Quebec also has partnership legislation that has many similarities to the legislation in the common law provinces. Because the Acts are quite short and have never been revised substantially, they often do not provide a satisfactory scheme for organizing a partnership. For this reason, partners will frequently supplement or modify the rules governing their relationship in a contract commonly referred to as a partnership agreement. Some of the ways in which this is done are described below and in chapter 2. In order to deal with any issue involving a partnership, one must have regard both to the relevant partnership statute and to any partnership agreement.

b) Characteristics

In a manner similar to sole proprietorships, partnerships come into being as a matter of law when two or more persons carry on business together with a view to a profit (OPA, s. 2). We will examine the criteria for determining whether such a relationship exists in chapter 2. In this introductory discussion, we will simply describe the general characteristics of partnerships.

By definition, partnerships involve more than one person, so there is a need for rules to govern the relationships among partners. Issues

---

5   See chapter 2.
6   The English common law system is discussed in chapter 2.

such as who will do what in managing the partnership business and how responsibility is allocated if things go wrong need to be addressed. The Ontario *Partnerships Act* sets out a framework of such rules in sections 20–31. These rules are not mandatory (*OPA*, s. 20). They may be and typically are modified, supplemented, and replaced by rules agreed on by the partners in their partnership agreement. The rules of the *Partnership Act* provide a kind of standard form agreement or set of default rules that apply unless the partners agree to something else. This approach gives partners great flexibility to design an internal structure customized to their particular needs.

Like sole proprietorships, partners directly carry on business themselves. The partnership is not a legal entity separate from the partners. One consequence is that a partner cannot enter into a contract of employment with the partnership, for such arrangement would require him to contract with himself. Another consequence with greater significance is that all benefits of the partnership business accrue directly to the partners, and all partners are personally liable for the obligations of the business. Each partner is liable to perform all contractual obligations agreed to by other partners in connection with the partnership business, even if the partner did not consent to the obligation. Partners are liable for each other's torts committed in connection with the business and are vicariously liable for the torts of employees of the partnership committed in the course of their employment.

We will discuss the rules governing how partnerships incur obligations to third parties later in this section, but, once liability for an obligation has been established, each partner is liable to the full extent of the obligation. All her personal assets, not just assets the partner has committed to the business, may be seized to satisfy it. As among the partners, the partnership statutes provide that each is liable to contribute equally to any obligation owed by the partnership to a third party (e.g., *OPA*, s. 24) unless they agree to some other allocation. Any such agreement has no effect on third parties. A creditor or a tort victim may proceed against and recover from any partner or all partners. Once a partner pays a partnership obligation, he may seek to recover a contribution from the others under the partnership statute or their agreement.

For the purpose of determining the liability of partners for income tax in connection with the partnership business, the income (or loss) of the business is calculated for the partnership by adding up all revenues of the partnership business and deducting expenses. Each partner's share is allocated in accordance with the partner's entitlement under the partnership statute or the partnership agreement and is included in her personal income tax calculation. The partner's share of the income or loss from the partnership business must be included even if all profits are reinvested in the business and no cash is actually paid to the partner.

The partnership statutes create a code governing when a partnership is liable to third parties (e.g., *OPA*, ss. 6–19). Unlike the provisions just discussed governing the internal relationships among partners, these rules are mandatory. They will be discussed in detail in chapter 2. The basic principle is that each partner is the agent of the partnership, meaning that each of the partners may bind the partnership when acting in the usual course of the partnership business (*OPA*, s. 6). A third party will be unable to rely on the ability of a partner, acting in the usual course of the partnership business, to bind the partnership only if the partner in fact does not have authority, perhaps because of a restriction in the partnership agreement, and the third party is aware of the limit on the partner's authority.

This principle of "mutual agency" effectively allocates the risk of unauthorized behaviour by an individual partner to the partners. It creates an organizational concern: How can the partners ensure that individual partners do not enter into obligations that, collectively, the partnership does not want? Given the unlimited personal liability of each partner, this concern is significant. Both legal and practical protection are available to partners.

First, the courts have held that each partner owes a fiduciary duty to the others.[7] This duty obliges each partner at all times to act honestly and in good faith in relation to his partners. A partner must never put her personal interests ahead of those of the partnership. Though this duty is not specifically expressed in the partnership statutes, there are several provisions that create specific obligations which are consistent with this general fiduciary duty (eg., ss. 28, 29, & 30, *OPA*).

The second legal method of providing protection is to expressly limit a partner's powers by allocating responsibility and establishing formal control and monitoring mechanisms in the partnership agreement. For example, it might be desirable to provide that all expenditures on behalf of the partnership above a certain dollar amount require the approval of all partners. Although any such measure will not be effective to defeat the claim of any third party, it will work to prevent unauthorized liabilities to the extent that it is followed operationally. Also, it may form the basis for a contractual claim by the innocent partners to be indemnified by the partner who made the unauthorized expenditure for any amount they are required to pay.

---

7   *Hitchcock v. Sykes* (1914), 49 S.C.R. 403 at 407.

There are also practical protections against unauthorized activity in most partnerships which are likely to be even more effective than the legal protections mentioned above. Most partnerships involve only a small number of individuals, each being vitally involved in the business and affairs of the partnership on a daily basis. There is no separation of ownership and management. Also, typically, there is a relationship of trust and confidence among partners because they know each other well. In such circumstances, the likelihood of unauthorized activity is reduced at the same time as the opportunity to monitor the activities of one's fellow partners is increased.

As a partnership gets bigger, involving more and more people as partners and employees, these practical protections break down. In the large law and accounting firms, for example, few partners are actively involved in all aspects of the business of the partnership, and formal monitoring mechanisms must be established. The law of partnerships was developed to address small businesses and so has little in the way of specific provisions designed to address the needs of the large modern partnership.

In the United States, the absence of these practical protections in large modern partnerships, combined with an explosion in professional liability, has encouraged professionals to lobby for changes to the laws governing them to permit them to carry on business using a corporation, which, as will be discussed in the next section, has the effect of limiting the liability of the owners of the business. It is important to note that the use of a corporation does not reduce the risk associated with carrying on a business. Instead, it has the effect of shifting risk to non-owners dealing with the business. We pursue this point in some detail in chapter 3.

A partnership must register its name under provincial business names legislation unless it is carrying on business under a name that is composed only of the names of the partners (e.g., *OBNA*, s. 2(3)).[8] The other provisions of names legislation described above in relation to sole proprietorships apply equally to partnerships, as does the previous discussion of business licences.

c) Limited Partnerships

In addition to the kind of partnership described above, sometimes called a general partnership, the law of Ontario and each other province recognizes limited partnerships. We discuss these partnerships in chapter 2. For the purposes of this introductory chapter it is sufficient to note three essential distinctions between limited partnerships and general partnerships. First, in limited partnerships at least one of the partners,

---

8   The rules in this regard vary somewhat from province to province.

called a general partner, has unlimited liability, and at least one other, called a limited partner, has limited liability. The liability of the limited partner is limited, typically, to the amount that she has contributed to the limited partnership. In general partnerships, all partners are general partners, in the sense that they all have unlimited personal liability. Second, limited partnerships come into existence only with a filing made with the appropriate government authority under provincial limited partnership legislation, whereas a general partnership comes into existence as soon as the partners start carrying on business. Third, limited partners cannot take part in the management of the business of the partnership without losing their limited liability.

3) Corporation

a) Formation

Unlike the sole proprietorship and the general partnership, corporations do not come into existence simply by virtue of one or several people starting a business. Creation, called incorporation, occurs upon making a filing with the appropriate government authority and paying the requisite fee. Incorporation may be under the federal *Canada Business Corporations Act* (*CBCA*) or under corporate statutes in each of the provinces and territories. In chapter 4 we will talk about how incorporation is accomplished in some detail, but it is sufficient to note here that the corporation is entirely a statutory creature. As with partnerships, it is possible for shareholders in a corporation to customize their relationship to the corporation. Subject to some limits, they may augment the statutory scheme through the provisions of the various components of the corporate constitution, the articles, by-laws, and resolutions of directors and shareholders, as well as through agreements among shareholders.

Upon incorporation, the filing made by the corporation becomes a matter of public record. Accordingly, no registration under provincial business names legislation is required for corporations unless they use a name different from their corporate name. The complex issues associated with corporate names are taken up in chapter 4. The discussion above concerning the business licences needed by sole proprietorships applies equally to corporations.

b) Characteristics

i) Separate Legal Existence

Unlike the sole proprietorship and the partnership, the corporation is an entity endowed with a separate legal existence. The corporation itself carries on business, owns property, possesses rights, and incurs liabilities. Shareholders have a bundle of rights in relation to the corporation through their ownership of shares, but they do not own the business carried on by the corporation or the property belonging to the corporation.[9] The rights and liabilities of the corporation are not the rights and liabilities of the shareholders. In contrast, sole proprietors and partners carry on the business, own its property, possess its rights, and are directly responsible for its liabilities.

Separate legal existence has three other important implications. First, a shareholder can be an employee and a creditor of the corporation because there is a legal entity, separate from the shareholder, to be the other party to the employment contract or the credit obligation. Second, because it is distinct from the people who are the shareholders, the corporation has perpetual existence; it is not dependent in any way on the continuation of its shareholders. The corporation is not affected if a shareholder dies or withdraws from the corporation by selling her shares. Third, for income tax purposes, the corporation is taxed separately. Income or loss from the business carried on through the corporation is determined and taxed at the corporate level. Shareholders pay tax only when they receive something from the corporation, such as a dividend or some other form of distribution.

It is often said that shareholders have limited liability for the obligations of the corporation, but this is misleading. In order to obtain shares, shareholders provide the corporation with money, property, or services that then belong to the corporation. Shareholders are said to have limited liability because their maximum loss in connection with the business operated by the corporation is limited to the value of the money, property, or services they have transferred to the corporation in return for their shares. Creditors, employees, and other claimants against the corporation can demand to be paid out of the assets of the corporation, but once the corporation's assets are exhausted the creditors cannot claim to be paid by the shareholders personally. In the worst case, if all the assets of the corporation are taken by creditors, the shareholder's shares will be worth nothing. They will have lost all their investment, but that is all they will lose. In other words, shareholders are not directly liable for the obligations of the corporation, but their maximum potential loss is limited to the amount they have invested. As will be discussed in chapter 3, this limitation on shareholder liability shifts some of the risk associated with the commercial activity in which the corporation is engaged from the shareholders to other stakeholders.

---

9   *Kosmopoulos v. Constitution Insurance Co. of Canada*, [1987] 1 S.C.R. 2.

Finally, even though the corporation is a separate legal entity, it can act only through individuals, often referred to generically as "agents" of the corporation. In this sense, agents include directors, officers, and anyone else who may act on behalf of the corporation in relation to outsiders. In chapter 5 we look at the law governing the circumstances in which a corporation will be bound by the acts of its agents. In general, like a partnership, a corporation will be bound by a contractual commitment to a third party entered into on its behalf when the agent is actually authorized to do so or appeared to have such authority. Similarly, the law imposes liability on the corporation for crimes and torts committed by its agents when the agent can be said to be acting on behalf of the corporation, unless some particular mental state must be shown as an element of the tort or crime, such as an intention to commit the tort or crime. In such a case, the courts have determined that the corporation is liable only if the agent who has this mental state can be considered to be acting as the corporation itself for the purposes of committing the tort or crime. The difference between an agent acting on behalf of a corporation and one acting as the corporation is discussed in chapter 5.

ii) Separation of Ownership and Management

The rights and obligations of managers and those with interests represented by shares of the corporation are legally distinct. Under the organization imposed by statute federally and in each province and territory, corporations are managed by a board of directors, which is elected by shareholders by majority vote, and by officers, who are appointed and delegated responsibilities by the directors. Shareholders do not participate, as shareholders, in the management of the corporation.[10] In many corporations, especially small ones, however, these legally distinct roles are played by the same people, because the shareholders are also the directors and officers. As the business gets larger, directors and officers are less likely to hold all the shares of a corporation, though often they do hold shares. Large corporations like Bell Canada Enterprises Inc. have thousands of shareholders, including the officers and directors.

The separation of ownership and management creates a number of issues regarding internal relationships in the corporation which must be addressed by corporate law. Perhaps the most important relationship is the one between shareholders, on the one hand, and officers and direc-

---

10   Under the *Canada Business Corporations Act* and provincial statutes modelled after it, shareholders may assume the powers of the directors when they use a unanimous shareholder agreement (*CBCA*, R.S.C. 1985, c. C-44, s. 146(2)). This device is discussed in chapter 6.

tors (referred to in this section collectively as "management"), on the other. From the shareholders' point of view, the key issue in this relationship is how shareholders can control management and ensure that management acts in their interests.

One of the challenges faced by corporate law in addressing this issue is that the nature of the appropriate response will be different depending on a number of variables, including, in particular, the scale of the corporation. For example, in corporations involving only a few shareholders, where each is actively engaged in the business, the need for formal accountability mechanisms, as in the small partnership discussed above, may be minimal. Not only will the shareholders likely be very aware of what is going on in the corporation but they may be the directors and officers themselves.

By contrast, in a large corporation with thousands of geographically dispersed shareholders, each having only a small financial interest in the corporation, shareholders will not be able to monitor, much less control, management in these informal ways. At the same time, management is in a position where its interests may be thought to diverge from those of shareholders. As soon as a manager has less than 100 percent of the shares of a corporation, she can benefit by indulging in perquisites at the expense of the corporation. She may be tempted to pay herself an excessive salary or shirk her duties, resulting in a diminution in the value of the shareholders' investment in the corporation.[11] Even if the manager has some shares in the corporation, the loss on her investment is more than compensated by her opportunistic behaviour, since she receives the full amount of the benefit from it, whereas her loss as a shareholder is limited to the proportion that her shareholding represents of all shares issued by the corporation. Also, there is risk that, because management receives most of its income from the corporation's activities, it will be reluctant to cause the corporation to take risks. Shareholders, by contrast, are more likely to want the corporation to take appropriate risks, since their exposure to loss from the corporation's activities is much less.[12] As discussed

---

11   The costs of such opportunistic behaviour and expenditures by shareholders to guard against it are referred to as "agency costs" and are discussed in chapter 7.

12   The assertion that shareholders are likely to have a higher risk tolerance than managers is based on portfolio theory, which holds that by holding a large diversified portfolio of investments, much of the business-specific risk of poor returns on individual investments will be offset by higher returns on other investments in the portfolio. Shareholders, at least in public corporations, typically will have a variety of investments, of which their shareholding in a particular corporation will be only one. Managers, by contrast, will have a large investment in the corporation for which they work. It will be their major source of income. See, generally, P. Halpern, J.F. Weston, & E.F. Brigham, *Canadian Managerial Finance,* 3d ed. (Toronto: Holt, Rinehart & Winston, 1989).

in Chapter 7, there are some market-based mechanisms that encourage management to be accountable to shareholder interests. These market mechanisms are supplemented with a variety of legal mechanisms designed to provide accountability, without unduly constraining the freedom of action management needs if it is to be able to do its job of running the business in the most effective way. The four major kinds of accountability mechanisms provided by corporate law are set out in figure 1.2.

Figure 1.2   Corporate Law Mechanisms Providing Management Accountability to Shareholders

---

- **Corporate democracy**: Shareholders have the collective power to determine who the directors are and so to influence the directors' choice of officers and what decisions the directors make. Certain fundamental changes cannot be made to the corporation without shareholder approval.

- **Directors' and officers' duties**: Management has a duty to act for the benefit of the corporation, thereby protecting shareholders' interests.

- **Shareholder rights to information**: Shareholders have certain rights of access to information which help to ensure that management's duties are performed.

- **Shareholder remedies**: Shareholders have certain remedies in the event that management's duties are not performed.

The primary power of shareholders is to elect directors in the first place, to refuse to re-elect them, and to remove them. As discussed in chapter 7, the effectiveness of corporate democracy may be limited in some circumstances, such as where there are large numbers of shareholders who may find it difficult to exercise their will collectively or in corporations of any scale where there is a majority shareholder who can determine the outcome of any shareholder vote.

Given these sorts of problems with corporate democracy, the effectiveness of the other accountability mechanisms is very important to shareholders. The standards of behaviour to which management must conform and the ability of shareholders to monitor management performance — and, ultimately, to seek relief where those standards have not been complied with — are critical issues in corporate law, and they are addressed in chapters 7 through 11. At this point, however, it may be useful to illustrate more specifically some of the concerns shareholders may have about managers and how the duties imposed on managers are responsive to these concerns. In some ways, shareholders' concerns are similar to those of partners in partnerships where management responsibilities have been delegated to one of the partners or to someone else. The degree of separation of ownership and management in large corporations, however, makes shareholders' concerns more pressing. Also, because the corporation is almost universally the form chosen to carry on businesses of any size in Canada, how these concerns are resolved is a much more important matter of public policy. For both these reasons, the provisions of corporate law to address these concerns are much more developed than those in partnership law.

The first kind of concern shareholders may have is that they do not want managers of the corporation to be negligent in managing the corporation's business. To address this concern, the common law, the CBCA (s. 123), and most provincial corporate statutes impose a duty of care on managers.

Second, shareholders do not want management to be engaged in activities that put the interests of management ahead of those of the corporation and its shareholders. For example, shareholders would be justifiably unhappy if management was diverting business from the corporation to themselves or exercising their management powers to maintain themselves in office rather than for the benefit of the corporation. The latter concern might arise where a takeover bid is made for the corporation and the bidder has announced that he will replace management if the bid is successful. In such a situation, management's personal interest in maintaining their jobs may be in conflict with the interests of the corporation, which might benefit from the new management.

Similarly, shareholders would not want management to favour one group of shareholders over another. As a democratically elected body, directors may feel they have a mandate to act in accordance with the wishes of the majority; after all, they hold their jobs because of the goodwill of the holders of a majority of shares. But this should not give them the right to ignore — or, worse, trample on — the interests of the minority.

To address these types of problems, the common law, the CBCA, and most provincial corporate statutes impose on management obligations to act in the best interests of the corporation and prohibit managers from favouring the interests of one group of shareholders over another (CBCA, s. 122(1)(a)). This fiduciary duty requires managers to act in the best interests of the corporation as a whole. Corporate statutes in most Canadian jurisdictions also provide that minority shareholders may obtain relief if the majority shareholder causes the corporation to act in a manner that is unfair or oppressive to the interests of the minority or if management acts in such a way (e.g., CBCA, s. 241).

4) Other Methods of Carrying on Business

Several other forms or methods of carrying on business are commonly referred to and, although they are not the focus of this book, deserve mention.

a) Joint Venture

Joint ventures are not a distinct form of business organization, nor a relationship that has any precise legal meaning. The term "joint venture" is used loosely to refer to a wide variety of legal arrangements in which one or more parties combine their resources for some limited purpose, for a limited time, or both. A joint venture may be established, for example, by a contract in which the joint venturers agree they will do certain things to carry out their common purpose; by two people carrying on business together, in which case the joint venture is a partnership; or by two people forming a corporation to carry out their common purpose. Although the legal consequences of a joint venture that is a corporation or a partnership are clear, the legal consequences of a joint venture relationship that is not a partnership or a corporation are not. Joint ventures will be discussed at the end of chapter 2.

b) Co-ownership

Co-ownership is a relationship among persons under which they hold title to some property, usually real property, together in some way — for example, as tenants in common. The principal feature of this relationship which distinguishes it from partnership is that the parties' property interests remain separate; each co-owner is free to dispose of her interest. In chapter 2 we will explore this distinction.

c) Licence

A licence is also a purely contractual relationship under which one party, the licensor, agrees to permit the other, the licensee, to use something, usually some form of intellectual property such as a patent, trademark, or copyright, in return for compensation, usually in the form of a royalty. One example of a licence would be an agreement by a trademark owner, such as McDonald's, to permit someone else, such as one of its franchisees operating a McDonald's restaurant in Calgary, to use its trademark in the franchisee's business. In this example the licence was agreed to in the context of a franchise agreement, but licences may also be part of other business arrangements such as joint ventures or partnerships, as well as stand-alone contractual arrangements.

d) Franchise

A franchise is a purely contractual relationship under which the franchisor gives the franchisee the right to operate a "system" in return for a set of fees. The parties typically provide in their agreement that their relationship does not constitute a partnership or a joint venture. The basic terms of the relationship consist of a licence in which the franchisor gives the franchisee the right to use its trade-marks and promises to provide certain assistance in running the franchised business, including training. In return, the franchisee agrees to operate the franchised business in accordance with the standards of the franchisor and to pay certain fees based, in part, on the sales of the business.

e) Strategic Alliance

Like joint venture, the term "strategic alliance" has no precise legal meaning and is used to refer to a wide variety of relationships involving more or less legal formality and greater and lesser degrees of working together among the alliance partners. A joint venture or a partnership may be referred to as a strategic alliance. The terms may also be used to describe, for example, an agreement to do research and development together, to market products jointly, or simply to share information.

D. CHAPTER SUMMARY

We began this chapter by describing the scope and coverage of this book as the most common types of business organizations: the sole proprietorship, the partnership, and the corporation. Next, we described the nature of business as the nexus of a variety of stakeholder relationships and defined the limits of business organizations law in this context. Business organizations law is primarily concerned with the relationships between owners and managers of business organizations. The interests of other stakeholders are addressed primarily under other kinds of laws. The rest of the chapter was devoted to introductory discussions of the sole proprietorship, the partnership, and the corporation.

The sole proprietorship is the simplest form of business organization; it comes into existence whenever a person begins to carry on a business. A sole proprietor has unlimited personal liability for the obligations of the business and is solely entitled to its benefits. The only legal requirements are name registration under provincial business names legislation and, in some cases, a business licence.

A partnership comes into existence when two or more people start to carry on business together with a view to a profit. Partnerships are governed by special statutes in each province that provide default rules governing the relations of partners to each other, which apply in the absence of an agreement to the contrary, and mandatory rules that govern the relationship of the partnership to persons dealing with the partnership. Like the sole proprietor, the partners in a partnership are personally responsible for the obligations of the business and are entitled to the benefits from it. Each partner is considered the agent of the partnership for the purpose of creating partnership obligations within the course of the partnership business. The risks associated with unlimited personal liability and the ability of all partners to bind the partnership are addressed legally by the fiduciary duty owed by each partner to the partnership and by provisions in partnership agreements. In smaller partnerships, these legal protections are supplemented by informal monitoring of each other by the partners who work in the business.

A limited partnership is a special form of partnership that is created by filing a declaration with the appropriate government authority. Limited partners' liability is limited to the amount of their investment in the partnership, and they are prohibited from taking part in the management of the business.

A corporation is formed upon making a prescribed filing with the appropriate government authority. Unlike the other forms of business organization, a corporation is a legally separate entity from its shareholders and managers. The corporation alone is responsible for the obligations of the business it carries on and is solely entitled to the benefits from the business. Although, in small corporations, shareholders and managers may be the same people, their roles are legally distinct. Shareholders have a financial interest in the corporation represented by their shares; they vote to elect directors who have responsibility for the management of the business and the affairs of the corporation. The directors may delegate some of their management responsibility to officers. Where management and shareholders are not the same people, the potential exists for managers to engage in opportunistic behaviour favouring their own interests over those of the corporation, such as excessively indulging in perquisites and shirking work. Corporate law encourages management accountability through corporate democracy, management's fiduciary duty and duty of care, shareholder rights to information, and shareholder remedies.

There are other forms and methods of carrying on business, such as joint ventures, co-ownership, franchises, licences, and strategic alliances. Of these, only joint ventures and co-ownership are dealt with in this book.

FURTHER READINGS

BUCKLEY, F.H., M. GILLEN, & R. YALDEN, *Corporations: Principles and Policies*, 3d ed. (Toronto: Emond Montgomery, 1995)

CARY, W.L., & M.A. EISENBERG, *Cases and Materials on Corporations*, 6th ed. (Mineola, N.Y.: Foundation Press, 1994)

CLARK, R., *Corporate Law* (Toronto: Little Brown & Co., 1986)

DANIELS, R.J., & J.G. MACINTOSH, "Toward a Distinctive Canadian Corporate Law Regime" (1991) 29 Osgoode Hall L.J. 863

FLANNIGAN, R., "The Economic Structure of the Firm" (1995) 33 Osgoode Hall L.J. 105

GOWER, L.C.B., *Principles of Modern Company Law*, 5th ed. (London: Stevens, 1993)

HADDEN, T., R.E. FORBES, & R.L. SIMMONDS, *Canadian Business Organizations Law* (Toronto: Butterworths, 1984)

IACCOBUCCI, F., M.L. PILKINGTON, & J.R.S. PRICHARD, *Canadian Business Corporations* (Agincourt: Canada Law Book, 1977)

LAW SOCIETY OF UPPER CANADA, *Bar Admission Course Reference Materials: Business Law* (Toronto: Law Society of Upper Canada, 1995)

MANZER, A.R., *A Practical Guide to Canadian Partnership Law* (Aurora: Canada Law Book, 1995) (looseleaf)

MORSE, G., ed., *Palmer's Company Law*, 25th ed. (London: Sweet & Maxwell, 1992)

SCAMMELL, E.H., & R.C. BANKS, eds., *Lindley and Banks on the Law of Partnership*, 17th ed. (London: Sweet & Maxwell, 1995)

SIMMONDS, R.L., & P.P. MERCER, *An Introduction to Business Associations in Canada: Cases, Notes and Materials* (Toronto: Carswell, 1984)

SUTHERLAND, H., ed., *Fraser's Handbook on Canadian Company Law*, 8th ed. (Toronto: Carswell, 1994)

WELLING, B., *Corporate Law in Canada: The Governing Principles*, 2d ed. (Toronto: Butterworths, 1991)

ZIEGEL, J.S., ed., *Studies in Canadian Company Law*, vol. 2 (Toronto: Butterworths, 1973)

ZIEGEL, J.S., et al., *Cases and Materials on Partnerships and Canadian Business Corporations*, 3d ed. (Toronto: Carswell, 1994)

PARTNERSHIPS

A. WHAT IS A PARTNERSHIP?

1) Introduction

Originally, partnership law was developed by the English common law courts. In a common law system, the law, in areas not governed by statute, consists of the accumulation of rules made in judicial decisions. Once a rule is applied in a particular case, it becomes a precedent: all courts are bound to decide all subsequent cases in a manner consistent with this rule.[1] The application of the rule from the precedent case to different facts in subsequent cases clarifies and refines the rule. As a result of this binding character of precedent cases, it is often said that common law is made by judges. Prior to the enactment of partnership legislation, the English courts, in deciding individual cases, had developed rules of their own to determine when a partnership relationship existed and what its legal consequences were. In the late nineteenth century the judge-made rules for partnerships were codified in the English *Partnerships Act* of 1890.

In Canada, the provinces have constitutional jurisdiction to enact laws regulating partnerships under section 92(13) of the *Constitution*

---

1   To be precise, only courts lower in the hierarchy of courts than the court rendering a decision are bound to follow the decision. So, for example, a decision of the Ontario Court of Appeal is binding on the Supreme Court of Ontario (General Division), but not on the Supreme Court of Canada.

Act, 1867, which gives the provinces jurisdiction in relation to "Property and Civil Rights." All the provinces except Quebec are common law jurisdictions, like the United Kingdom, and all have enacted essentially identical statutory regimes based on the English *Partnerships Act* of 1890. Few changes have been made to these provincial statutes since their enactment, and there is an extensive body of judicial decisions interpreting these partnership statutes. These decisions are also precedents binding on courts in subsequent cases. The common law continues to apply to the extent not inconsistent with the provincial legislation.[2]

In Quebec, Canada's only civil law jurisdiction, partnerships are governed by the *Civil Code* of *Quebec*[3] (*Civil Code*). In civil law jurisdictions, judges do not make the law in the common law sense. All law has its source in the *Civil Code*. Although previous decisions are used to argue in favour of a particular interpretation of the *Civil Code*, they are not binding on courts in future cases.

Under the *Civil Code*, the nature of a partnership is different, in some respects, from partnerships under the laws in the other provinces. A partnership in Quebec takes on different characteristics depending on the manner in which the partnership is formed. Under the *Civil Code*, partnerships are either "declared" or "undeclared." Declared partnerships are those registered under the *Code*, while undeclared partnerships are similar to partnerships in the common law jurisdictions in that no registration is required for them to exist. An important difference is that only those partners who are known by a third-party creditor doing business with an undeclared partnership are liable to the third party. In a declared partnership, all partners are liable whether the third party knew about them or not. Declared partnerships may be limited partnerships, very like limited partnerships in the common law jurisdictions, or general partnerships, which have characteristics similar to common law partnerships.[4]

The statutory law in Quebec and the other provinces deals with the nature of the partnership, the relationship of the partners to each other and to outsiders dealing with the partnership, and the dissolution of the partnership. In no jurisdiction, however, do these provisions provide a complete code to regulate the affairs of partnerships, with the result that agreements among partners, along with the substantial body of judicial decisions dealing with partnerships, constitute important sources of the law governing partnerships.

This chapter focuses on the partnership law of the common law provinces, emphasizing the Ontario *Partnerships Act*, though some com-

2   See, for example, Ontario *Partnerships Act*, R.S.O. 1990, c. P.5, [*OPA*].
3   Arts. 2186–266 C.C.Q.
4   Arts. 2252–54 C.C.Q.

parisons with the Quebec law are included. It also discusses some of the considerations relevant to drafting partnership agreements. Limited partnerships and joint ventures are considered at the end of this chapter.

2) The Legal Nature of Partnership

If a relationship exists which meets the requirements of section 2 of the Ontario *Partnerships Act*, a partnership exists. Section 2 provides as follows:

> Partnership is the relation that subsists between persons carrying on a business in common with a view to profit, . . .[5]

As noted in chapter 1, a partnership is like a sole proprietorship in that partners directly carry on business themselves; the partnership is not a legal entity separate from its partners. The chief consequence is that each partner is liable to the full extent of his personal assets for debts and other liabilities of the partnership business as provided in the *Partnerships Act* (ss. 10–13). A further consequence of the partnership being no more than the partners is that, in the absence of an agreement to the contrary, the continued existence of the partnership depends on the continuing participation of the partners who make it up.[6] Another is that a partner may not be an employee of the partnership business. Similarly, except in several discrete situations contemplated by statute, a partner cannot also be a creditor of the partnership. There is not a legal person, separate from the partner, with whom she may contract.[7] Nevertheless, there are several ways in which a partnership is treated as a collective entity.

5　The remainder of the definition (*OPA*, above note 2) reads as follows:
　　. . . but the relation between the members of a company or association that is incorporated by or under the authority of any special or general Act in force in Ontario or elsewhere, or registered as a corporation under any such Act, is not a partnership within the meaning of this Act.

6　See the discussion of the dissolution of partnerships and partnership agreements in sections D and E of this chapter and *OPA*, ss. 19, 26, 32, & 33.

7　*Thorne v. New Brunswick (Workmen's Compensation Board)* (1962), 33 D.L.R. (2d) 167 (N.B.C.A.); *Craig Brothers v. Sisters of Charity*, [1940] 4 D.L.R. 561 (Sask. C.A.). It is, however, possible to structure the relationship of a partner to resemble that of an employee. A provision may be made for fixed periodic payments like wages to be paid to a partner, and the other partners may agree to indemnify this partner against any losses in the business. In such cases it may be difficult to determine if the person is actually a partner or simply an employee being compensated out of profits. See section 3.3(b) of the *OPA*, *ibid.*, and Interpretation Bulletin No. IT-138R, "Computation and Flow-Through of Partnership Income" (29 January 1979), items 10 and 11, in which Revenue Canada indicates its acceptance, for tax purposes, of a partnership where one partner receives a fixed salary. Under the Quebec *Civil Code*, a partnership may be a separate legal person (Art. 2188 C.C.Q.).

- Section 5 of the Ontario *Partnerships Act* provides that, for the sake of convenience, a partnership is called a "firm" and the name under which the partnership carries on business is called the firm name.
- For income tax purposes, the income from the partnership business is calculated at the firm level. The partnership is not taxed as a separate entity on this income, however. It is allocated out to the partners and must be included in their individual returns.[8]
- Actions against a partnership may be commenced and must be defended using the firm name.[9] Any order made against a partnership may be enforced against the property of the partnership as well as against the property of any person who was served personally and either did not deny being a partner or was adjudged to be a partner.[10]

As will be discussed below, the possibility that partnership assets may be subject to claims means that the interest in a partnership of a person who became a partner after an obligation of the partnership was incurred, but prior to enforcement of a judgment based on the obligation, could be diminished as a result of the seizure of partnership property in satisfaction of the obligation. That a partner's interest may be affected as a consequence of an obligation incurred prior to his joining the partnership seems clearly inconsistent with the notion that the partnership is no more than the partners, from time to time.[11]

It is important to recognize that this legal conception of the partnership as no more than the partners is typically quite different from the view that many business people have of the partnership. Often they will think of the business and its assets and liabilities as separate from their personal assets and liabilities.

The policy that the common law courts express for imposing unlimited liability on anyone found to be a partner is a fundamental principle of the law of agency: if a business is being carried on by someone, the agent, on behalf of someone else, the principal, the principal should be responsible for the obligations of the business. In accepting a commitment on behalf of the partnership, a third party should be able to rely on the personal creditworthiness of each person who is, or appears to be, carrying on the business.

---

8   *Income Tax Act*, R.S.C. 1985 (5th supp.), c. 1, s. 96 [*ITA*].

9   In *Unical Properties v. 784688 Ontario Ltd.* (1990), 75 O.R. (2d) 284 (Gen. Div.), an action in the name of a partnership against one of the partners was dismissed on the basis that the partnership was not a legal entity separate from the defendant partner.

10   Ontario Rules of Civil Procedure.

11   See section C, "Liability of the Partnership to Third Parties" in this chapter.

The practical problem for business people and the lawyers who advise them is to know when a partnership relationship will be found to exist. Persons carrying on a business may be willing to accept the risk of unlimited liability because of other benefits of the partnership form, such as the ability to deduct losses from the partnership business against income from other sources for tax purposes or because they can manage the risk in some way. Other persons involved with a business — lenders, for example — will want to avoid this risk and will not have arranged their affairs so they are either compensated for or protected against this risk. For such a person, being found to be a partner may have disastrous, unanticipated financial consequences. In the case law, the issue of whether a person is a partner usually arises where the partnership business has become insolvent and a creditor is looking for someone to claim against who has assets. The creditor then argues that a particular person should be liable for the obligations of the business because he is a partner. Lawyers need to be aware of the circumstances in which a partnership will be found to exist in order to ensure that their clients do not become involved in a relationship where they will be found to be a partner or that they take appropriate steps to manage the risk of being a partner.

3) Definition of Partnership

a) General
The focus in this section is to explain when a partnership relationship exists, by reference to the elements of the definition in section 2 of the Ontario *Partnerships Act*. Partnership statutes in other common law provinces contain similar definitions.

"**Carrying on a Business**": Giving meaning to "carrying on a business" is the least difficult challenge in the section 2 definition. "[B]usiness" is defined in section 1 as including "every trade, occupation and profession." These broad, non-exhaustive words have been defined as any ongoing activity or even a single transaction.[12]

"**View to a Profit**": The words "view to a profit" simply mean that the undertaking is not for the purpose of carrying out charitable, social, or cultural purposes. A partnership need have only a view to profit. There is no need actually to make profits. The meaning of profits is discussed later in this section.

---

12   *Thrush v. Read*, [1950] O.R. 276 (C.A.).

"In Common": These words mean that the putative partners are carrying on business together, based on some kind of agreement. The agreement may be written, oral, or implied. Whether an agreement exists is determined objectively, in the sense that persons may be characterized as partners without their knowledge[13] and even contrary to their express intention[14] so long as the court decides that the circumstances show the existence of an agreement. What the agreement must relate to is an intention to participate in a relationship that fits within the definition set out in section 2 of the Ontario *Partnerships Act*. Similarly, as in other areas of law, whether the parties describe themselves as partners or not is not conclusive. Even an express provision in an agreement denying that the parties intended to be partners is not conclusive. Such provisions may help to clarify the intended effect of other clauses of the parties' agreement where such clauses are not clear, but, in every case, regard must be had to all the facts, the rights and obligations created by the parties' agreement, their conduct, and any other relevant circumstances.[15]

Section 3 of the *Partnerships Act* sets out some guidelines to assist in determining whether persons are carrying on a business together. Common ownership of property does not make the co-owners partners (*OPA*, s. 3.1). Similarly, the sharing of gross returns, meaning business revenues without deduction of related expenses, does not create a partnership (*OPA*, s. 3.2). Since the old decision of *Waugh* v. *Carver*,[16] the principal indicia of carrying on a business in common has been whether profits were shared. This rule is set out in section 3.3 of the Ontario *Partnerships Act*:

> Receipt by a person of a share of the profits of a business is proof, in the absence of evidence to the contrary, that the person is a partner in the business, but the receipt of such a share or payment, contingent on or varying with the profits of a business, does not of itself make him or her a partner in the business[.]

Unsnarling the difficult construction of this provision does not yield a rebuttable presumption. Section 3.3 does not say that sharing profits alone is conclusive that a person is a partner in the absence of evidence to the contrary, though it very nearly says so. Although something more is required, it is not clear what this is, though it seems to be very little. In order to flesh out what is required it is necessary to consider the case law.

---

13   *Robert Porter & Sons Ltd.* v. *Armstrong*, [1926] S.C.R. 328 [*Porter*].
14   *Weiner v. Harris (1909)*, [1910] 1 K.B. 285 (C.A.).
15   *Adam v. Newbigging* (1888), 13 App. Cas. 308 at 315, (H.L.), Lord Halsbury.
16   (1793), 2 Hy. Bl. 235, 126 E.R. 525 (C.P.).

In *Cox* v. *Hickman*[17] it was established that the fundamental characteristic of the relationship of partnership is mutual agency: a partnership exists where each person alleged to be in partnership carries on the business on behalf of the other alleged partners. The issue often arises in situations where there is a partnership, and the question is whether a particular person is a partner in the partnership. In such a case the test is whether the business is being conducted on behalf of that person. In this regard, one of the most important indicia of partnership is the sharing of profits (see figure 2.1).

Figure 2.1 Definition of Profits

Profits	**=**	**Revenues**	**less**	**expenses**
		[all monies received in connection with the business]		[all monies paid to earn the revenue: e.g., for acquiring the goods or services sold; wages to employees, etc.]

The rationale for this focus on profits can be easily explained. If a person was to be compensated out of revenues, she would have a stake only in how much the business could sell. On the other hand, if a person is sharing profits, that person must also be concerned about how the business is managed, including, in particular, how expenses are managed. This stake in the effectiveness of management means that the sharing of profits is more suggestive of being in business together. Similarly, agreements to share losses as well as profits are strongly indicative of partnership, though partnership can exist even though the agreement between the parties contains a provision indemnifying one of them against losses from the business.

Prior to *Cox* v. *Hickman*, several cases, including the leading case of *Waugh* v. *Carver*, had held that sharing of profits was conclusive of partnership. The sharing of profits test was found to be too broad however, because, in part, there are a variety of relationships in which profits may be shared, but it is not accurate to say that the parties are carrying on business together. An illustrative list of relationships which should not give rise to an inference of partnership even though there is sharing of profits, or one party is receiving a return on an investment that varies with or is contingent on profits is set out in section 3.3(a) to (e) of the Ontario

---

17   (1860), 8 H.L. Cas. 268.

Partnerships Act. A relationship is not that of partners carrying on business together, but some other relationship in the following circumstances:

- one party receives repayment of a debt or some other fixed amount out of profits;
- an employment contract where the remuneration of the employee varies with profits;
- a loan where the lender's compensation is to be a share of profits or an interest rate varying with profits;
- an annuity paid out of profits to a spouse or child of a deceased partner; and
- receipt of a share of profits of a business paid to a vendor as consideration for the sale of the business.

This list identifies relationships that are not partnerships. It does not assist with the more difficult and fundamental question of whether any given relationship is, in law, one of these relationships or a partnership. The following section deals only with what distinguishes partnerships from the first relationship in this list: that between debtor and creditor. Determining when a person is a partner as opposed to a creditor of a business has proven difficult, whereas distinguishing employment relationships, annuities paid to spouses or children of deceased partners, and vendor and purchaser relationships from partnerships has proven to be relatively straightforward.

b) Debtor/Creditor Relationships

Both cases discussed in this section deal with claims by a creditor of an existing partnership against persons the creditor alleges are partners. In each case the reason the creditor pursued the claim in this way is that the acknowledged partners were insolvent.

Cox v. *Hickman* provides an excellent example of a sharing of profits where a partnership relationship was not found to exist. It also illustrates the difficulty of drawing a clear distinction between creditors and partners in many situations. In this case an ironworks business in financial difficulty entered into an arrangement with its creditors under which the property of the business was transferred to certain trustees who were appointed by the creditors to operate the business. The debtors retained beneficial ownership in that, if and when all the debts were paid, they would receive anything left over. The creditors were given the right to make rules for the conduct of the business, including winding it up. Profits earned were paid to the creditors. Several creditors, including Cox and Wheatcroft, were appointed trustees. While the business was being operated by the trustees, it became indebted to Hickman. Hickman sued Cox and Wheatcroft alleging that they, along with the other creditors, were partners in a partnership carrying on the ironworks business.

The House of Lords held that Cox and Wheatcroft were not partners. The basis of the decision was that the sharing of profits, in this case, was not sufficient for a finding of partnership. To find a partnership involving Cox and Wheatcroft, the business had to be carried on by others as agents for the benefit of Cox and Wheatcroft as principals. Here the true relationship was debtor and creditor. The trustees were carrying on business on behalf of the debtors. The debtors received the benefit of the profits, but had agreed to have the profits applied for the exclusive purpose of paying off their creditors. Some of the judges in the Court of Appeal[18] had agreed that the true basis of partnership was not simply sharing of profits. They had found Cox and Wheatcroft to be partners, however, because they characterized the facts differently. On the basis of the extensive involvement of the creditors in the business, including their access to the books and their ability to control who were the trustees and to make rules for the business, these judges determined that the business was being carried on for the benefit of the creditors, and so they should be considered partners.

This case shows that, even accepting the agency basis of partnership, it will often be difficult, on particular facts, to determine if a partnership exists or, given the existence of a partnership, if certain persons are partners in it. It also raises the question of the relevance of the involvement of an alleged partner in the partnership business to a determination of partnership. The discussion of *Pooley* v. *Driver*[19] addresses how the rights belonging to a partner alleged to be involved in and even to control the partnership business, as well as the behaviour of alleged partners in connection with the business, are relevant to determining whether she is a partner.

In *Pooley* v. *Driver,* Borrett and Hagan were partners carrying on a grease, pitch, and manure business. They entered into a partnership agreement that provided, among other things, that the "capital"[20] of the partnership would be split between Borrett and Hagan and persons "advancing money by way of loan" (referred to here as the "Lenders");

---

18 In the English judicial hierarchy, the House of Lords hears appeals from decisions of the Court of Appeal.

19 (1876), 5 Ch. D. 458 [Pooley].

20 "Capital" is a slippery term whose meaning may vary depending on the context in which it is used. Often it is used to refer to the total amount contributed to a business by owners and lenders. See the definition in the glossary.

and that profits from the partnership business were to be paid out in accordance with the interests of Borrett, Hagan, and the Lenders in the capital. The partners promised to do the following:

- to carry on the business to the best of their ability;
- not to distribute the property of the business to the partners;
- to prepare annual accounts;
- to have a valuation of the business done every year;
- not to borrow or hire employees without the consent of the other partners; and
- not to permit assets of the business to be seized by creditors to satisfy the debts of the business.

Within six months of the termination of the partnership, the amounts owed to all the creditors of the business would be determined and the creditors paid. Then the partnership would repay the money advanced by way of a loan, less any amount needed to satisfy the creditors. The Lenders could also be asked to repay profits paid out to them if this was necessary to pay off the creditors. The Lenders were also supposed to enter into a loan or "contributorship" agreement that repeated many of these provisions and also provided as follows:

- The covenants in the partnership agreement were incorporated in the loan agreement and so were enforceable by the Lenders. These covenants included a right to compel Borrett and Hagan to use the invested capital in carrying on the business of the partnership.
- Each Lender's entitlement to profits would be determined annually, based not just on the profits made but also on the amount invested by all Lenders in aggregate. For example, if Lenders bought all 20 units available to them out of the 60 units of ownership in the partnership, each unit would have an entitlement to 1/60th of the profits. If only 10 were purchased, each unit would have an entitlement to 1/50th of profits.
- The bankruptcy of a Lender meant that the Lender's relationship with the partnership was terminated subject only to an obligation of the partnership to repay the amount the Lender had invested.
- Repayment of Lenders' investments was expressed to come out of the assets of the partnership.

The term of both the partnership agreement and the loan agreement was fourteen years.

This rather complex relationship was expressly designed to ensure that the Lenders were not found to be partners. The English law at the time contained a provision virtually identical to section 3.3(d) of the Ontario *Partnerships Act*. Section 3.3(d) provides as follows:

[T]he advance of money by way of a loan to a person engaged or about to engage in a business on a contract with that person that the lender is to receive a rate of interest varying with the profits, or is to receive a share of the profits arising from carrying on the business, does not of itself make the lender a partner with the person or persons carrying on the business or liable as such, provided that the contract is in writing and signed by or on behalf of all parties thereto[.]

By identifying the Lenders as persons "advancing money by way of loan" and giving them a return that depended on the profits of the partnership, Borrett and Hagan sought to fit the Lenders within this provision. In looking at the whole relationship between the Lenders and the partnership as described in the partnership and loan agreements, however, the court concluded that the Lenders were partners.

In support of this conclusion, the court cited the following factors:

- The fact that the alleged partners had an interest in capital is more indicative of an ownership interest in the business than a creditor's claim against the business.
- The Lender's ability to enforce the covenants of the partnership agreement gives them a degree of participation and control that would be unusual for lenders, though not for partners.
- Having the return on the Lender's investment vary with the aggregate amount invested in the business is highly unusual for a lender, but not for a partner.
- The provision terminating the relationship of any Lender who goes bankrupt might not be unusual for a partnership in which the solvent partners would not want the trustee in bankruptcy of the bankrupt partner succeeding to the rights of a partner, but would be highly unusual for a lender.
- It would be highly unusual for a lender to be required to pay back all profits received as well as its original investment if there were insufficient partnership assets otherwise to pay off all other creditors. Such an obligation is more like partnership liability.
- Coincidence of the loan and partnership terms suggests that the Lenders were partners.

The court's analysis also demonstrates the very limited operational effect of paragraphs (a) to (e) of section 3.3. The court made it clear that these provisions are examples only of relationships that are not partnerships. In the case of section 3.3(d), the relationship referred to is that of debtor and creditor. In every case the court must decide if, based on all the circumstances, the most accurate characterization of the relationship is one of partnership or some other relationship. In this case the court had to decide if the relationship was partnership or that of debtor and creditor. That the return to the alleged partner is dependent on profits, as described in section 3.3(d), does not, in any way, mean that the relationship is therefore deemed not to be a partnership. It simply means that the sharing of profits in these circumstances does not, by itself, give rise to a presumption of partnership. Indeed, the court went on to say that it was not sure that section 3.3(d) has any effect; since the court must determine that there has been "an advance by way of loan," which requires that a determination must be made that the relationship is one of debtor and creditor, and not partnership. Once such a determination has been made, however, there is no need to rely on section 3.3(d).[21]

This discussion of the *Cox* and *Pooley* cases reveals that there are various factors that a court will take into account in determining whether any given relationship is a partnership or a debtor and creditor relationship. None is conclusive.[22] These factors are also those that have been relied on in other contexts to determine if a partnership exists, such as where the parties own property together. The following section discusses cases dealing with co-ownership relationships.

c) Co-ownership

Section 3.1 of the Ontario *Partnerships Act* provides that holding property in some form of common ownership does not, of itself, create a partnership in relation to the property, even if the co-owners share profits made from the use of the property. Co-ownership may arise in a variety of circumstances where the relationship should not be considered a partnership. Significantly, while a partnership is always the result of agreement, co-ownership may arise by operation of law, such as on the passing of title from one person to several on death.

Being able to distinguish relationships that are partnerships from those involving only co-ownership is important because co-ownership relationships have different legal consequences. Unlike partners, co-owners are not agents of each other. One co-owner is at liberty to deal with his

---

21 In light of this conclusion, it is perhaps surprising that if one does have a relationship falling within section 3.3(d), section 4 of the *OPA*, above note 2, provides that repayment of such lender is postponed until all other creditors have been paid in the event that the business becomes insolvent.

22 See other cases in which a loan repaid out of profits has been combined with some control over the business and no partnership found: *Mollwo, March & Co.* v. *Court of Wards* (1872), L.R. 4 P.C. 419 (no profits received); *Re Young, ex p. Jones*, [1896] 2 Q.B. 484; *Canada Deposit Insurance Corp.* v. *Canadian Commercial Bank*, [1992] 3 S.C.R. 558 (repayment out of profits is not equivalent to sharing profits).

interest in the common property as his own without the consent of the others. As will be discussed below, the transfer of a partner's interest in the partnership is limited. In the absence of the agreement of all partners, a partner cannot transfer her interest, though she can transfer her right to receive profits. Also, in a partnership, there is an agreement that the property is to be held jointly as an asset of the business. No partner has the right to deal with the property separately. The partner's right is to a division of profits, not to any particular property of the partnership business.[23]

Where, in addition to co-owning property, the co-owners share profits from the use of the property, the relationship approaches a partnership, but there must be something more than simply owning property and sharing the profits from it to create a partnership; some management or other business activity must exist. How much activity is required, however, is elusive. The mere fact that co-owners intend to acquire, hold, and sell property does not make them partners. One way of formulating the question to ask is, Was "the intention of the co-owners . . . 'to carry on a business' or simply to provide by an agreement for the regulation of their rights and obligations as co-owners of a property"?[24]

Several cases have addressed the circumstances in which a partnership may be found to exist where there is co-ownership. In *A.E. LePage Ltd. v. Kamex Developments*,[25] for example, the co-owners of some real property were held not to be partners, even though, in addition to co-ownership, the parties had put in place the following arrangements:

- profits were to be paid to each co-owner in proportion to her interest and each was liable to pay any deficiency in the same proportions;
- no co-owner could sell her interest without offering it first to the other co-owners (a "right of first refusal"); and
- any sale or other dealing with the property required approval by majority vote of the co-owners.

The court held that the ability of the co-owners to deal with their individual interests is incompatible with an intention that the property become

---

23   Partners have no right in partnership property *in specie* (i.e., in its existing form), nor to compel the sale of partnership property while the partnership exists. Upon dissolution, however, a partner has the right to have the partnership property sold and the proceeds divided: *Porter,* above note 13 at 330. For a more complete review of the differences between co-ownership and partnership, see E.H. Scammell & R.C. Banks, eds., *Lindley and Banks on the Law of Partnership*, 17th ed. (London: Sweet & Maxwell, 1995) at 75–78.

24   *A.E. LePage Ltd. v. Kamex Developments Ltd.*, (1977), 16 O.R. 193 at 195 (C.A.), aff'd (*sub nom. A.E. Lepage Ltd. v. March*) [1979] 2 S.C.R. 155.

25   *Ibid.*

part of a partnership, since partners have no right to do so. The right of first refusal was not considered to be inconsistent with the co-owners' basic right to deal with their respective interests. The co-owners' intention to keep their property separate was confirmed by their individual treatment of their respective interests for income tax purposes. They made individual decisions regarding the capital cost allowance relating to the property[26] to deduct against their income. Because the court did not find the co-owners to be partners, the action by one of them who purported to enter an exclusive listing agreement for the sale of the property without the authorization of the others was not binding on the co-owners.

Where, in addition to co-ownership and sharing profits, there is substantial participation in the activities associated with the management of the co-owned property, a partnership will likely be found. While it is clear that a person need not have any control over management in order to be found a partner,[27] it is difficult to be precise regarding how much activity is required to be added to co-ownership in order to create a partnership. Use of a common bank account, signing cheques in connection with the management of the assets, an agreement to share the costs of developing the business, and common participation in financing the business and in dealing with tenants' concerns were all held to be indicative of a partnership between co-owners in *Volzke Construction* v. *Westlock Foods Ltd.*[28] Practically speaking, determining when a partnership will be found in real estate co-ownership cases will be difficult since, in almost all real estate holdings, some management will be required.

d) Managing the Risk of Being Found a Partner

In the cases considered so far, the courts dealt with claims against persons who wanted to avoid the liabilities arising out of being found a partner. In *W.* v. *M.N.R.*,[29] the court considered a claim by some widows and daughters of deceased lawyers that they *were* partners in a law firm partnership. The widows and daughters of the deceased did not contribute or participate in the business of the firm in any way. Revenue Canada had challenged the status of the widows and daughters as partners because it objected to the taxation of the partnership profits allocated to the widows and daughters. In its view, the partners working in the busi-

---

26   Capital cost allowance is the equivalent of depreciation for income tax purposes. See the examples of capital cost allowance deduction at the end of this chapter.

27   *Volzke Construction* v. *Westlock Foods Ltd.* (1986), 70 A.R. 300 (C.A.).

28   *Ibid.* in this case, a contributing factor to the finding of partnership was a finding in another proceeding that the parties were partners.

29   [1952] Ex.C.R. 416.

ness, who were paying tax at a higher marginal rate, should have been liable for the tax. The court held that it was sufficient that the widows and daughters had entered into an agreement in which they were identified as partners and they had acknowledged, albeit not in the operative part of the agreement but in a recital, that they were liable for losses as well as entitled to receive profits. The court also noted that they had acted in accordance with the agreement.[30] Accordingly, Revenue Canada's challenge was defeated.

This case illustrates an important aspect of partnership law: responsibility for management may be delegated however the partners decide in the partnership agreement. It also dramatically underlines the impossibility of precisely defining the circumstances in which a partnership may be found to exist (see figure 2.2). Both have important implications for lawyers advising their clients. In general, if a client wants to be a partner, thereby assuming all the liabilities associated with the business, the courts are likely to accommodate his wishes. If, on the other hand, a client wants to avoid being a partner, the lawyer will have to give careful consideration to the relationship her client intends to enter to see if there is a risk of a partnership being found based on the extent to which the factors discussed above are present, especially the sharing of profits. If there is a risk of partnership being found, a client must be advised to take whatever steps are available to avoid this consequence, including contractual provisions stating the nature of the relationship[31] and structural changes to the relationship itself, taking into account the factors discussed. Steps may also be taken to minimize the consequences of

---

30   This case is also noteworthy because it shows that, in general, the court will apply the principles of partnership law to determine the appropriate tax treatment of a particular relationship (see Interpretation Bulletin IT-90), "What Is a Partnership?" (17 February 1973). The possibility of allocating partnership income to persons who do not participate in the partnership has been expressly eliminated by amendment to the *ITA*, above note 8. Now, under section 103(1.1) of the Act, where partners do not deal at arm's length, the allocation of income must be reasonable, having regard to the capital invested in or work performed for the partnership by the partners or other relevant factors. This has no effect on whether, as a matter of partnership law, there is a partnership. In *Schettler v. M.N.R.* ((1994), 7 C.C.E.L. (2d) 213 (T.C.C.)), it was held that the absence of any effective control means that a person is unlikely to be found a partner. See to similar effect A.R. Manzer, *A Practical Guide to Canadian Partnership Law* (Aurora: Canada Law Book, 1995) (looseleaf) at 2-23.

31   Though, of course, stating that the parties are not partners will not be enough in itself (*I.R.C. v. Williamson* (1928), 14 T.C. 335 at 340 (Ct. Sess., Scot.); *Dickenson v. Gross (Inspector of Taxes)* (1927), 11 T.C. 614 (K.B.). Regard must be had to what is done under the agreement.

being found a partner, such as holding the partnership interest in a corporation and creating indemnification provisions in the agreement establishing the relationship.[32] Finally, the client will need to consider if he is being appropriately compensated for any residual risk of partnership liability.

Figure 2.2   Some Factors Suggesting a Partnership Relationship

---

- Sharing profits
- Sharing responsibility for losses, including guaranteeing partnership debts
- Jointly owning property
- Controlling partnership business
- Participating in management
- Stating intention to form partnership in contract
- Making government filing showing partnership (e.g., registration under business names legislation, tax returns)
- Access to information regarding the business
- Signing authority for contracts, bank accounts
- Holding oneself out as a partner
- Contributing money, services, or property as capital (especially if contribution is complementary to the contribution of others for the purpose of running a business)
- Full-time involvement in the business
- Use of a firm name, perhaps in advertising
- Firm having its own personnel and address

B. THE RELATIONSHIP OF PARTNERS TO EACH OTHER

1) General

In most cases the relations of partners to each other will be specified in their partnership agreement. Like other provincial statutes, the Ontario *Partnerships Act* (ss. 20–31) provides a set of default rules to govern the parties' relations to the extent that they have not been addressed by agreement. These provisions have been created by statute as a sort of standard form contract to make it easier to set up a business as a part-

---

32   These strategies will be discussed in section E in this chapter under "Partnership Agreements."

nership by reducing the need for the parties to create a set of rules from scratch. The rules operate only in default of agreement because different partnerships will need different rules. The flexibility in possible internal structures afforded by the use of default rules is one of the major advantages of partnerships. The value of the default rules will depend on how closely they approximate what prospective partners will want. Unfortunately, the partnership legislation in most provinces has never been amended significantly and does not respond to the needs of modern partnerships. This section describes the framework of default rules in the *Partnership Act*. In section E on "Partnership Agreements" below, the kinds of changes often made to these rules will be discussed. Finally, the remainder of this section describes the fiduciary duty each partner owes to his fellow partners as well as the nature of a partner's interest in partnership property.

2) Default Rules

The default rules governing partners' relations are based on certain presumptions about the nature of partnership. The archetypal partnership contemplated by the Ontario *Partnerships Act* and other provincial statutes is one in which all partners are equal, both in terms of their financial interest in the partnership and their rights to participate in the business of the partnership. In practice, such equality rarely occurs. Typically, partners make unequal contributions of capital and services to the business. Each partner's interest in the partnership and the returns to each partner on her contributions will vary accordingly. Also, in all but the smallest partnerships, the partners will delegate certain management functions to particular partners or committees of partners because the participation of all partners in all decisions will be unduly cumbersome. Because there are likely to be significant differences between what partnership legislation provides in its default rules and what the parties' expectations and intentions are, it is essential to know what the default rules are and to ensure that they are changed by agreement where appropriate. The most important default rules are set out in figure 2.3.

3) Fiduciary Duty

In addition to the default rules described in the previous section, partners owe each other a fiduciary duty: they must deal with the partnership and with their partners in the utmost good faith. Partners must never put their personal interests ahead of the interests of the partnership.

Figure 2.3   Default Rules in the Ontario *Partnerships Act*

- Each partner shares equally both in the capital of the partnership and in any profits distributed, and must contribute equally to any losses incurred (s. 24.1).
- Each partner is entitled to be indemnified in respect of payments made or liabilities incurred in the ordinary course of the partnership business, or to preserve the business or property of the firm (s. 24.2).
- A partner is not entitled to interest on capital contributed (s. 24.4).
- If a partner makes a contribution to the partnership in excess of the amount that he has agreed to contribute, he is entitled to interest at 5 percent per year on the excess contribution (s. 24.3).
- Each partner has a right to participate in the management of the partnership business (s. 24.5).
- Decisions regarding ordinary matters connected with the partnership business may be decided by a majority of the partners in number (s. 24.8).
- Each partner has equal access to the partnership books (s. 24.9).
- Admission of a new partner (s. 24.7) and any change in the nature of the partnership business (s. 24.8) require unanimous consent.
- No majority of partners may expel a partner (s. 25).
- Any person who takes an assignment of a partner's interest, whether as a purported transfer or for the purposes of giving security for some obligation of the partner, has no rights as a partner, except to receive the share of the partnership profits to which the assigning partner would otherwise be entitled (s. 31).
- Any partner may terminate the partnership by giving notice (ss. 26 & 32).
- Any variation of the default rules requires unanimous consent (s. 20)

Although there is no general expression of this duty in the Ontario *Partnerships Act*,[33] it is well established in the common law that the fiduciary duty is a guiding principle of partnership law.[34]

There are several provisions in the Ontario *Partnerships Act* which create specific obligations consistent with this general duty. Each partner is obliged to render to each other partner "true accounts and full information" regarding all matters affecting the partnership (*OPA*, s. 28). In

---

33   Section 22(1) of the British Columbia *Partnership Act*, R.S.B.C. 1973, c. 312 [BCPA] expresses a general duty in the following terms: "[A] partner shall act with the utmost fairness and good faith towards the other members of the firm in the business of the firm."

34   For example, *Hitchcock v. Sykes* (1914), 49 S.C.R. 403 at 407.

one recent case it was held that each partner has a right to access to documents prepared by and for the partnership.[35] Each partner must also account to the partnership for certain benefits obtained without the consent of the other partners. These benefits include those derived by her from "any transaction concerning the partnership or from any use by the partner of the partnership property, name or business connection" (*OPA*, s. 29(1)) and any profits made by competing with the partnership business (*OPA*, s. 30). In *Olson* v. *Gullo*[36] it was held that the profits received by one partner who sold part of the real property owned by the partnership had to be paid over to the partnership based on section 29(1) as well as common law principles of fiduciary duty. One of the difficult features of cases like this is that the partner in breach of his duty receives a benefit from the breach because, as a partner, he shares in the profits when they are paid over to the partnership.

4) Partnership Property

Partnership property consists of all property contributed to the partnership as well as all property acquired on its behalf or for the purpose and in the course of the partnership business (*OPA*, s. 21(1)). In particular, where property is bought with money belonging to the partnership, it is deemed, in the absence of evidence to the contrary, to have been bought on behalf of the partnership (*OPA*, s. 22). Where property is treated as partnership property, it becomes partnership property even if title is retained by an individual partner. Once property becomes partnership property, it must be held and used exclusively for the purposes of the partnership and in accordance with the terms of the partnership agreement (*OPA*, s. 21(1)).[37] A partner loses his individual beneficial interest in property contributed to a partnership.

There can be a partnership as to profits from property, but not the property itself, if the partners have agreed that they will continue as co-owners. Section 21(3) of the Ontario *Partnerships Act* creates this rule for real property, but it probably applies also to personal assets.

---

35   *Dockrill* v. *Coopers & Lybrand Chartered Accountants* (1994), 129 N.S.R. (2d) 166 (C.A.).
36   (1994), 17 O.R. (3d) 790 (C.A.).
37   Partnership property is treated as personal property (*OPA*, above note 2, s. 23).

C. LIABILITY OF THE PARTNERSHIP TO THIRD PARTIES

1) Basic Rules

Unlike the default rules governing the internal relations of partners, the rules governing the relationships between partnerships and third parties are mandatory in the interests of ensuring that persons dealing with partnerships are protected. Nevertheless, provisions that address the risks associated with liabilities to third parties may be included in the partnership agreement. These provisions include internal monitoring and control mechanisms to reduce the likelihood of unauthorized liabilities and arrangements to allocate risk among partners.[38]

In general, all partners are liable for all liabilities of the partnership.[39] Who is liable as a partner, however, is an issue that has frequently been the subject of litigation. As evidenced by the cases discussed under "What Is a Partnership?" above, typically the litigation is initiated by an unpaid creditor when the partnership, if there is one, or the business otherwise being carried on is insolvent. The creditor will argue that a person with assets is a partner as a way of seeking to have its claim paid. The main subject of this section, however, is how a partnership becomes liable to third parties.

Partnerships become liable to third parties in contract when, based on principles of agency, someone who is an agent of the firm enters into a contract on its behalf. Under the Ontario *Partnerships Act* and other provincial statutes, each partner is constituted an agent of the firm. Section 6 provides that the acts of a partner for carrying on the business of the firm in the usual way bind the firm. The rule does not apply only where the partner in fact has no authority and the person with whom the partner is dealing either knows that the partner has no authority or does not know or believe her to be a partner.[40] What the usual scope of the business is will depend on the nature of the business activity in which the partnership is actually engaged.

A partnership is liable for the torts of its agents or employees, based on general principles of tort law. Liability arises where the partnership authorized the tort, ratified it after it was committed or it was committed by the agent or employee in the course of his duties. Where any tort is committed by a partner in the ordinary course of the firm's business or with the authority of the other partners, the firm is liable for all damages

---

38 See section E, "Partnership Agreements," in this chapter.
39 Under the Quebec *Civil Code*, a partner in an undeclared partnership becomes liable only if the third party knows that the person is acting as a partner (Art. 2253 C.C.Q.).
40 See also *OPA*, above note 2, section 9.

to the same extent as the partner herself (*OPA*, s. 11).[41] As well, partners may be jointly and severally liable for fraudulent acts of partners. In *Ernst & Young Inc. v. Falconi*[42] the estate of a partner in a law firm was held jointly and severally liable for the acts of another partner in assisting persons who were adjudged bankrupt to make fraudulent dispositions of their property contrary to the *Bankruptcy Act*. The fraudulent activity was held to be in the ordinary course of the law firm's business. The court said that the test is "whether the unlawful acts are of the sort that would be within the scope of the partnership if done for legitimate, as opposed to illegitimate, purposes as seen from the perspective of the overall business of the partnership."[43] It was sufficient that the partner used the assets and facilities of the law firm to perform services normally performed by a law firm in carrying out the transactions, as a result of which the creditors of the firm's clients suffered loss.

All obligations of the firm are obligations of every partner who was a member of the firm at the time the obligation arose.[44] It does not matter whether any partner sought to be held liable by a third party actually approved the obligation entered into.[45] This liability is independent of any right of contribution or indemnity that the partner may have against the partner who incurred the obligation for the firm. Indemnification where a partner has paid a partnership obligation is provided for in the

---

41   *OPA*, above note 2, section 12, specifically imposes liability on the firm for certain misapplications of funds received from a third party by a partner or by the firm. Liability for these wrongs may also be found under section 10 or section 11.

42   (1994), 17 O.R. (3d) 512 (Gen. Div.).

43   *Ibid.* at 516–17.

44   Liability of individual partners for torts under *OPA*, above note 2, section 11 is joint and several pursuant to section 13, while liability for "debts and obligations of the firm" is only joint under section 10. The distinctions between these two kinds of liability have been all but eliminated under modern rules of civil procedure. The original common law rule was that, where liability was only joint, a creditor of a partnership who obtained a judgment against one partner would not be able to take action against any other partner, even if he was unable to recover the judgment amount from the partner he originally sued (*Kendall v. Hamilton* (1879), 4 App. Cas. 504 (H.L.)). If liability was joint and several, the creditor would not lose her rights against the other partners. This rule has been abolished in Ontario by section 139(1) of the *Courts of Justice Act* (R.S.O. 1990, c. C-43). Also, as noted above, it is possible under the Ontario Rules of Civil Procedure to sue a firm using the firm name (R. 8.01). A creditor who obtains an order against a partnership in such an action may apply to the court for leave to enforce it against any partner who has not previously been a party to the suit.

45   For an example of the imposition of liability on a lawyer for breaches by his partner of his fiduciary duty and duty as a solicitor, where the lawyer did not participate in the wrongful activity, see *Korz v. St. Pierre* (1987), 61 O.R. (2d) 609 (C.A.). See also *Bet-Mur Investments Ltd. v. Spring* (1994), 20 O.R. (3d) 417 (Gen. Div.) [*Bet-Mur*].

Ontario *Partnerships Act* and is often dealt with specifically in partnership agreements.[46]

As noted, the time at which the liability arises is critical for determining who is responsible for it. In general, partners are only liable for obligations incurred while they were partners in the firm.

This liability continues after the partner leaves the firm (*OPA*, s. 18(2)) and binds her estate (*OPA*, s. 10). A partner is not responsible for liabilities of the firm which arose prior to his becoming a partner (*OPA*, s. 18). The only exception to this rule arises where partnership assets are seized after a person becomes a partner in satisfaction of an obligation which arose prior to that person joining the partnership. As mentioned above, such proceedings are expressly permitted by the Ontario Rules of Civil Procedure. Except as described below, a partner is not liable for obligations of the partnership incurred after she leaves (see figure 2.4).

Figure 2.4   Example of Effect of Pre-partnership Liability

In 1992 ABC partnership incurred a debt of $5000 to a supplier which it did not pay. The supplier sued the partnership in 1992. X joined ABC partnership in 1993, paying $10,000 for a 10 percent interest in the partnership. The $10,000 was invested in acquiring assets for use in the partnership business.

In 1994 the supplier obtained judgment against the partnership and obtained an order of seizure and sale against the partnership. Certain assets were sold and the proceeds used to pay the supplier's judgment. Even though the obligation to the supplier was incurred prior to X joining the partnership, and X was not responsible for it, the value of X's interest in the partnership has been diminished as a result of satisfying the judgment resulting from the debt.

2) Holding Out

A person may be held liable for obligations even though he was never a partner or was not a partner at the time the partnership incurred the obligation, if he was held out as a partner. Section 15 of the Ontario *Partnerships Act* imposes liability on persons held out as partners:

> Every person, who by words spoken or written or by conduct represents himself or herself or who knowingly suffers himself or herself to be represented as a partner in a particular firm, is liable as a partner to any per-

---

46   See section E, "Partnership Agreements," in this chapter.

son who has on the faith of any such representation, given credit to the firm, whether the representation has or has not been made or communicated to the persons so giving credit by or with the knowledge of the apparent partner making the representation or suffering it to be made.

Examples of representations that may give rise to liability under this provision include use of a person's name in the firm name, on a sign at the premises of the firm, or on its invoices or letterhead. An essential element of the holding out is that it be with the knowledge of the person held out. It is not sufficient, for example, if the person was negligent or careless by failing to ensure that she was not held out as a partner.[47] It should be noted also that the person held out does not have to know that the holding out was to the person who advanced credit to the firm. Knowledge of a general holding out is sufficient. The person who advanced credit to the firm must have relied on the holding out in doing so.[48]

One of the most common situations in which holding out may arise is when a partner retires. In such a case there may be various conflicting interests at stake. The retiring partner is generally interested in limiting her liability after retirement. Persons who dealt with the firm prior to the retirement and who innocently continue to rely on the creditworthiness of the retired partner will expect to be able to attach liability to the retired partner even in the absence of some post-retirement holding out as contemplated in section 15. On the other hand, those who deal with the firm for the first time after the retirement should not be able to hold the retiring partner liable to them in the absence of some representation to them that she is a partner. Finally, in many cases, the retiring partner's name will be part of the firm name and the continuing partners will have an interest in the continuity of the firm name to ensure that any goodwill associated with it is not lost after the retirement.[49] The Ontario *Partnerships Act* has several provisions that strike a sort of balance between these various interests.

A retired partner is liable to every person who has dealt with the firm *prior* to his retirement for obligations of the firm incurred after retirement unless

- actual notice of the retirement is given to the person (*OPA*, s. 36(1)),
- the person never knew that the retiring partner was a partner (*OPA*, s. 36(3)), or

---

47 *Tower Cabinet Co. Ltd.* v. *Ingram*, [1949] 2 K.B. 397 [*Tower*].
48 *Bet-Mur*, above note 45.
49 This was the case, for example, in *Dominion Sugar Co.* v. *Warrell* (1927), 60 O.L.R. 169 (C.A.).

- the partner left the firm because he became insolvent or died (*OPA*, s. 36(3).

Section 15(2) specifically, though seemingly unnecessarily, provides that a partner who dies is not liable for obligations of the firm after death even if the partner's name continues to be used in the firm name.

Persons who deal with the firm for the first time after a retirement are entitled to hold liable any person who is an apparent member of the firm (*OPA*, s. 36(1)). A person will be an "apparent member" if, for example, her name is used in the firm name, on letterhead, invoices, or signs at the business premises, or by an express representation that a person is a partner. A person may be an apparent partner if her name appears as a partner in a registration under provincial business names legislation, such as the Ontario *Business Names Act,* or if her membership in the partnership is notorious because, for example, her name was used in the firm name. "Apparent" means "apparent to the person dealing with the firm" so as to give that person the impression that the person is a partner.

Although it may seem reasonable that someone dealing with the firm for the first time should be able to rely on a person being an apparent partner, the law makes it imprudent to do so. Section 36(2) provides that a retired partner is not liable to such persons if a notice that the partner has retired has been published in the *Ontario Gazette.*[50] In effect, new clients of a firm are deemed to have notice of any retirement so advertised. Also, even in the absence of a notice in the *Ontario Gazette,* the retired partner will be liable for any obligation incurred by the partnership after retirement only if the actions making her an apparent partner constitute a holding out within the meaning of section 15. In other words, she must hold herself out or knowingly permit herself to be held out as a partner. This was the conclusion reached in *Tower* v. *Ingram,*[51] based on the stipulation in section 36(3). As noted above, this section provides that a retiring partner is not liable to any person who deals with a partnership after the retirement who did not know that the person was a partner. In *Tower,* a partner's name was used on firm letterhead after his retirement, but without his permission and contrary to his express instructions. The court held that a third party who dealt with the firm for the first time after the partner's retirement and received the letterhead could not hold the retired partner liable because there had been no holding out for the purposes of section 15. Section 36(3) has the effect, in the absence of a holding out, of insulating retiring partners

---

50   The *Ontario Gazette* is the official publication of the Ontario legislature.
51   Above note 47; *Coatsworth & Cooper Ltd.* v. *Schotanus,* [1962] O.R. 1118 (H.C.J.).

from all liability for obligations of the partnership incurred after their retirement to all persons who did not know them to be partners at the date of retirement. The plaintiff could have succeeded only if he had knowledge that the retired partner was a partner prior to his retirement.

Two practical questions must be addressed based on this thorny analysis. First, what should a retiring partner do to minimize her liability for obligations of the partnership after her retirement? Second, what should a person contemplating dealing with a partnership do to assess the creditworthiness of a partnership?

In answer to the first question, the retiring partner should ensure that all persons who had dealings with the firm prior to the date of her retirement have actually received notice of her departure. She should also ensure that she documents her instructions to the remaining partners that notice is to be given to ensure that liability based on holding out cannot be claimed. As well, she should ensure that notice of her retirement is published in the *Ontario Gazette* and that the partnership's registration under the *OBNA* is amended.

For persons dealing with the partnership, if the creditworthiness of a particular person is to be relied on, it would be desirable to obtain some form of specific representation or acknowledgment of that person's membership in the partnership. Checking the *Ontario Gazette* would also be prudent.

Figure 2.5 Liabilities of Partner D to Third Parties Dealing with Partnership under the Ontario *Partnerships Act*

D is a member of the partnership		
1994	1995	1996
No liability (s. 18(1))	**Unlimited liability** (ss. 6 & 10–13) • continues after retires (s. 18 (2)) • binding on estate (s. 10)	No liability (implicit in ss. 10 & 36(3)) UNLESS • creditor dealt with firm before retirement (unless they did not know **D** a partner prior to retirement, s. 36(3)) or are given actual notice
Except 1. Obligation arises $\rightarrow$ 2. Holding out (s. 15 (1)) • must be knowing	execution against partnership property: Ontario Rule of Civil Procedure 8.06 (1)	• creditor dealt with the partnership for the first time after **D** retires, no notice in *Ontario Gazette* (s.36(2)) and is holding out by **D** under s. 15(1) • BUT IN ANY CASE no liability after D dies, or becomes insolvent (ss. 15(2) & 36(3)).

D. DISSOLUTION OF THE PARTNERSHIP

Because the partnership is not a legal entity separate from its partners, it is inherently fragile. This is reflected in the many ways in which it may be dissolved, as provided in the Ontario *Partnerships Act* and the partnership laws of other provinces. Many of these provisions may be varied by agreement and typically are changed to render the partnership more stable. These aspects will be discussed further in section E below on Partnership Agreements.

Unless the partners have agreed otherwise, the partnership is terminated in the following circumstances:

- if formed for a fixed term, on the expiry of the term (*OPA*, s. 32(a));
- if not formed for a fixed term, on notice by one partner to all the others (*OPA*, ss. 26 & 32(c));[52]
- if formed for a single adventure or undertaking, on termination of the adventure or undertaking (*OPA*, s. 32(b));
- on the death or insolvency[53] of any partner (*OPA*, s. 33 (a)).

The partners may also provide for any other events that will result in the termination of the partnership, such as the inability of a partner to continue to work in the partnership. Section 33(b) contemplates that partners may agree that dissolution should occur if any partner permits his share of the partnership property to be charged for his personal debts.

The Ontario *Partnerships Act* provides for termination regardless of any agreement by the partners if it becomes illegal for the business of the partnership to be carried on at all or illegal to be carried on by the members of the partnership (*OPA*, s. 34). The disbarment of all the lawyers in a legal partnership is an example of a situation that would trigger dissolution under this section. The Act also provides that a court may order dissolution on a wide variety of grounds, including mental incapacity of a partner, persistent breaches of the partnership agreement,

---

52   See, for example, *Blundon v. Storm*, [1972] S.C.R. 135.

53   PWA Corporation recently sought to have a limited partnership it had entered into with Air Canada for the operation of an airline reservation system terminated on the grounds of the insolvency of the general partner, Gemini Group Automated Distribution Systems Inc., although the claim was based on a reference to insolvency in the partnership agreement and not section 32, *OPA*, above note 2. PWA also sought dissolution on the ground set out in section 35(f) that it was just and equitable to do so. The action failed on both grounds. *PWA Corp. v. Gemini Group Automated Distribution Systems Inc.* (1993), 101 D.L.R. (4th) 15 (Ont. Gen. Div.), aff'd (1993), 15 O.R. (3d) 730 (C.A.) [*PWA*].

and a catch-all ground: a court may order dissolution when, in the opinion of the court, it is just and equitable to do so.[54] Examples of situations in which the court might be disposed to order dissolution would be the refusal by a group of partners to permit a partner to exercise her rights to participate in the management of the partnership as provided in section 24.5 of the Ontario Act or irreconcilable differences among the partners.[55]

Section 44 of the Ontario Act provides a skeleton of a process to deal with the settlement of the many claims needing to be dealt with on dissolution. Debts and liabilities to persons who are not partners are paid first, then debts to partners (other than advances of capital), and then capital is returned. The statutory scheme may be fleshed out in a partnership agreement.

E. PARTNERSHIP AGREEMENTS

1) General

The foregoing discussion provides an outline of the law of partnership. But the law, as indicated in many places in this chapter, provides only the barest skeleton of rules for the regulation of the relations among partners and the conduct of the business of a partnership. Also, for particular partnerships, the rules may be inappropriate. For both these reasons it is commonplace for partners to enter into a partnership agreement to flesh out their relationship, though in many cases no written agreement may be prepared. In this section we will discuss some of the considerations that should go into drafting a partnership agreement, with emphasis on how the agreement interacts with the law of partnership. The purpose of this section is not, however, to provide a comprehensive guide to all the provisions needed in partnership agreements.[56]

The main purposes of partnership agreements are as follows.

- To modify the default provisions of the Ontario *Partnerships Act* (ss. 20-31 & 32), either to replace them or to supplement them by extending and tailoring them to the particular needs of the partners. In part, the partners will need to provide a structure for operating the

---

54 See the discussion on dissolution in chapter 10.
55 See also *PWA*, above note 53.
56 A useful discussion of the considerations for drafting a partnership agreement and a good precedent are set out in the Ontario *Bar Admission Course Reference Materials: Business Law* (Toronto: Law Society of Upper Canada, 1995), c. 2.

partnership where the legislation is silent or where the partners want something different from what it provides.

- To respond to the mandatory provisions of the *Partnerships Act,* especially those providing for liability to third parties, by structuring the relations among partners to address liability among partners, and to create reporting, monitoring, and control mechanisms to manage liability risk.
- To reproduce *Partnerships Act* provisions for partners' information.

2)   Selected Elements of Partnership Agreements and Commentary

a) Name

A partnership may carry on business using any name it likes. Professional partnerships often use the names of individual partners in the firm name, though many large firms in the interests of continuity use the names of deceased partners. The name of the partnership raises a number of issues in addition to the practically important and often sensitive question of whose name appears in the firm name. Some of the more important issues are identified below. Names are a complex subject, and a comprehensive treatment of issues associated with them is far beyond the scope of this book.

Ownership Issues The name of the partnership forms part of the goodwill of the business and belongs to the partners. In the absence of some provision in the partnership agreement, each may be entitled to use the name on the dissolution of the firm. The partnership agreement should address who is entitled to use the firm name in the event that there is a change in membership or dissolution of the partnership. To avoid conflict, the partners may agree that on the withdrawal of a partner, neither the withdrawing partner nor the remaining partners may use the firm name. The remaining partners will have to adopt a different name. Where a "name" partner is retiring from the business or profession or dies, the firm may want to continue to use the name, perhaps because of the prestige associated with it. In such a case the partnership agreement may provide for the continued use of the name. If so, the agreement should address the risk of liability described below.

Liability Issues The use of a person's name as part of the firm name with his knowledge constitutes holding that person out as a partner within the meaning of *OPA*, section 15, and makes him an apparent partner for the purposes of section 36(2). Any person so held out after he leaves the partnership will be liable to persons dealing with the firm after his departure.[57] Accordingly, if a person's name is going to be used

---

57   See section C, "Liability of the Partnership to Third Parties," in this chapter.

after she leaves, the remaining partners of the firm should agree to indemnify her against any such liabilities. This agreement will have no effect on her liability to third parties, but it gives her a right to recover any amount she has to pay from her former partners. Since a deceased partner's estate is not liable for obligations of the partnership after she leaves the partnership, there is no need for an indemnity in cases where a partner dies and the firm continues to use the deceased partner's name in the firm name (*OPA*, s. 15(2) & 36(3)).

Registration Issues Under the Ontario *Business Names Act,* partners must register their firm name unless they are "carrying on business or identifying themselves to the public under a name that is composed of the names of the partners." The Ministry of Consumer and Commercial Relations considers that this provision means that at least a first name and the surname of each partner must be used in the firm name to avoid the obligation to register. Partners named Yves Leduc and Sherry Scott would have to register their firm name if it was "Leduc and Scott," but not if it was "Yves Leduc and Sherry Scott."[58]

In any case, it may be desirable to register even if it is not required, since registration provides notice to anyone who searches the public file that the name is being used; it also has certain other advantages.[59] In some cases, trade-mark registration should also be considered.

In choosing a name, it is advisable to search the register maintained in the province as well as trade directories and other sources of information to ensure that the name chosen or a similar name is not already being used by someone else. Use of a name that conflicts with someone else's name may expose the partnership to loss of goodwill, if it subsequently has to change its name, and to possible liability for passing-off, trade-mark infringement, and contravention of the Ontario *Business Names Act* (s. 6).

b) Description of Business

As agents of the partnership, each partner's authority is limited by the nature of the business undertaken (*OPA*, s. 6). The scope of each partner's authority to bind the partnership to a third party will be determined by what the partnership does rather than on any limits in the partnership agreement, unless the third party has knowledge of the

---

58 It is not obvious that this is the correct interpretation of the Ontario *Business Names Act*, R.S.O. 1990, c. B.17, but it is the interpretation the Ministry uses for its administrative purposes, including imposing fines for failing to register.

59 See chapter 1.

limit (*OPA*, ss. 6 & 9). Nevertheless, there are several reasons to describe the business in the partnership agreement.

Describing the business makes clear what activities are to be considered to be carried on for the benefit of the partnership. This description will help to avoid disagreements in the future about what income earned by the partners must be paid to the firm. In a law firm partnership, for example, the partners may want to expressly provide that the business includes teaching a law school course or writing papers, so any fees or honoraria received are income of the partnership. Such a provision gives specific content to section 29 of the Ontario *Partnerships Act*, which obliges partners to account for all benefits derived from any use by a partner of the partnership property, name, or business connection. Broadening the scope of the business, however, extends the range of potential liability for the partnership.

Describing the business also gives substance to partners' noncompetition obligations. Recall that a partner's fiduciary obligation obliges him not to compete with the partnership business and that section 30 of the Ontario *Partnerships Act* requires him to account to the partnership for all profits made if he does.[60] Many partnership agreements also contain provisions prohibiting partners from competing with the business for a period of time and in a limited geographic area after they leave the partnership.[61] Describing the business of the partnership helps to define what constitutes competition with the partnership business for all these purposes. To avoid conflicts over what is personal and what is partnership income, many partnership agreements provide that each partner will devote her full time and attention to the business of the partnership and will not engage in any other business without the consent of the other partners.

Finally, describing the scope of the partnership business provides the basis for the firm to claim against a partner for liabilities imposed on the firm as a result of unauthorized actions by the partner outside the firm's defined business.

---

60   There is some old authority for the proposition that simply using information acquired in the course of one's involvement as a partner for purposes outside the scope of the partnership business does not give rise to the obligation to account (*As v. Benham*, [1891] 2 Ch. 244 (C.A.)).

61   Non-competition provisions of this type must be reasonable in area and time, not contrary to the public interest, and no more restrictive than necessary to protect the business interests of the partnership in order to be enforceable (*Bassman v. Deloitte, Haskins and Sells of Canada* (1984), 4 D.L.R. (4th) 558 (Ont. H.C.J.); *Baker v. Lintott* (1983), 141 D.L.R. (3d) 571 (Alta. C.A.)).

c) Membership of Partnership

The admission of a new partner is one of the most important decisions for a partnership and often one of the most difficult. Section 24.7 of the Ontario *Partnerships Act* provides that, in the absence of an agreement to the contrary, all partners must consent to the admission of a new partner. For the reasons discussed above, the requirement for unanimity is often changed to some lesser degree of agreement, often weighted by each partner's economic interest in the partnership. It is also common to articulate some of the criteria for admission, such as years of experience.

The Ontario *Partnerships Act* is silent on the arrangements for admission to partnership. Issues such as capital contribution and the new partner's interest in capital and share in profits should be addressed in the agreement.

The expulsion of a partner is prohibited under the default rules of the Ontario *Partnerships Act* (s. 25), so many agreements provide for expulsion on the vote of some specified majority. The partnership agreement may set out certain other rules governing the circumstances in which partners must leave the partnership. For example, withdrawal may be mandatory on reaching a stipulated retirement age or on a partner becoming incapable of working full time in the business. For each kind of withdrawal, it should be provided that the partnership is not dissolved and some formula should be established for how the departing partner is to be paid out his share of capital, profits, and any work in progress to which he has contributed but which has not yet been billed.

d) Capitalization

The amount contributed by the partners to the firm is called its capital. Capital contributions and partners' entitlements to capital should be dealt with in the partnership agreement.

Every partnership needs money to pay the costs of setting up the partnership business and to cover ongoing operating expenses, such as salaries and rent, while work is being done and before it is billed and paid for.[62] Money may be needed at various other times in the life of a business, such as to buy new equipment or to expand the business. Money may be raised from the partners or from a third party, such as by borrowing it from a bank. The partners will need to agree on what will be the initial contributions of capital by the partners, including contributions by partners who join the firm in the future. They may also want to provide for the basis on which additional amounts of capital will be

---

62 This second type of capital is called "working capital."

contributed by the partners in the future. For example, it may be provided that when additional capital is required, each partner must contribute an amount calculated by reference to her percentage entitlement to profits of the firm. The circumstances in which capital may be withdrawn are often addressed as well. It is common in law firm partnerships for capital contributions of new partners to be used to return capital contributions of more senior partners. The agreement may also provide for some way to keep track of each partner's aggregate contributions over time. In the absence of a specific agreement as to what is each partner's share in capital, all partners share equally (*OPA*, s. 24.1). Each partner will be entitled to the return of capital contributed by him when he leaves the partnership, so the partners may want to agree on the process by which this will be done.[63]

Under the Ontario Act, no interest is paid on capital advanced, and partners who make loans to the partnership are entitled only to 5 percent interest unless the partners otherwise agree (*OPA*, ss. 24.3 & 24.4).

e) Arrangements Regarding Profits and Their Distribution

Pursuant to the Ontario *Partnerships Act,* all profits are to be divided equally among the partners (s. 24.1). This provision is almost invariably changed to allocate to each partner a share commensurate with his contribution to the firm. There are many kinds of contributions to the business of a firm, both direct and indirect. Each partnership must decide what kinds of contributions to take into account and what weight to give to each for the purpose of allocating profits. This division will vary from business to business, but the following are some kinds of contributions typically considered in law firm partnerships:

- capital contributions;
- billable hours worked;
- hours worked on matters that were not billable;
- fees billed and collected;
- total billings to new clients introduced to the firm by the partner;
- total billings to clients of which the partner is in charge; and
- business development.

As is evident from this list of factors, each partner's entitlement will change each time the factors are evaluated. Most firms make an evaluation on an annual basis.

---

63   Section 42 of the *OPA*, above note 2, provides that if an outgoing partner is not paid her share of capital, she is entitled, in the absence of any agreement to the contrary, to receive either a share of profits attributable to the use of her capital since she left the firm or interest of 5 percent per year on the capital.

It is also necessary to provide for how the profits are to be distributed. Typically, partners are permitted to draw against their anticipated share of the profits, based on forecast profits and their previous year's entitlement, subject to an adjustment at the annual review.

f) Management
The default rules in section 24.5 and 24.8 of the Ontario *Partnerships Act* provide that all partners are entitled to participate in management and that decisions on ordinary matters are to be made by a majority of partners, but decisions relating to the nature of the partnership business require the consent of all partners. Management relations vary tremendously in their nature and complexity depending on partnership size and other variables. As a result, it is usual to change these rules to some extent and it is hard to generalize about partnership management structures. Nevertheless, some comments may be made.

Usually the requirements in the Ontario *Partnerships Act* for a numerical majority and unanimous consent for decisions are replaced by a decision-making structure reflecting the typically unequal economic interests of the partners. Also, as the partnership becomes larger, more of the decision making, particularly of a routine nature, is delegated to a committee of partners, a single partner, or, in some very large firms, a professional manager who is not a partner.[64]

The Ontario Act contains no procedures for partnerships to act collectively. Rules about meeting procedures, such as notice and quorum requirements for meetings of the partnership, will usually be included in a partnership agreement.

Management arrangements are an important way in which the risk created by mutual agency may be addressed. Restrictions on who may sign contracts, who may write cheques, authorization, and reporting requirements for particular activities (e.g., giving legal opinions) are examples of how the risk of unauthorized or otherwise undesirable activity having the consequence of creating liability for the firm and for the partners may be reduced. As a result, there are often provisions for such internal monitoring and control mechanisms in partnership agreements. It is important to remember that these mechanisms will have no effect on avoiding liability to a third party where they are contravened, but, to the extent that they are implemented in practice, they will tend to prevent liability from arising. Also, where one partner fails to observe

---

64 Delegation of powers in a partnership is expressly recognized in the Quebec *Civil Code* (Art. 2213 C.C.Q.).

requirements imposed in the partnership agreement, the other partners will have a claim for breach of contract and perhaps grounds for dissolution (*OPA*, s. 35(d)).

g) Dissolution

As noted, the Ontario Act permits partnerships to be dissolved easily and in a variety of ways. Typically, in the interests of ensuring the continuity of the business, the partners will agree that the partnership shall not be dissolved in many of the circumstances contemplated in the *Partnerships Act*. Dissolution on the death or insolvency of a partner and on notice from one of the partners are usually excluded and replaced by a provision requiring unanimous or some majority consent for dissolution. Partners may agree on certain other specified events that will result in dissolution.

Section 44 of the Ontario *Partnerships Act* provides a skeleton of a process to deal with the settlement of the many claims needing to be dealt with on dissolution. Debts and liabilities to persons who are not partners are paid first, then debts to partners (other than advances of capital), and then capital is returned. The statutory scheme may be fleshed out in an agreement.

F. JOINT VENTURES

Joint ventures are not a distinct form of business organization, nor a relationship that has any precise legal meaning. Functionally, the term "joint venture" is used to describe a relationship among persons who agree to combine their money, property, knowledge, skills, experience, time, or other resources for some common purpose. Usually the joint venturers agree to share the profits and losses from the venture, and each has some degree of control over it. The distinguishing feature of a joint venture is that it is an arrangement set up for a limited time, for a limited purpose, or both. "Joint venture" is used loosely to refer to all sorts of legal arrangements given effect in corporations, partnerships, and in relationships based exclusively on contract.

For example, a small mineral exploration business that has rights in certain claims might combine its resources with those of a larger business with the financial strength and experience to develop the claims. This activity could be described as a joint venture and could be carried on through a corporation in which each business was a shareholder; a partnership, in which each was a partner; or by the parties together, with the parties' respective rights and obligations governed only by a contract between them.

While the legal consequences of a joint venture that is a corporation or a partnership are clear, the legal consequences of a joint venture relationship that is not a partnership or a corporation are not. The main question is to what extent are there legal consequences associated with the joint venture outside those specifically provided for in the agreement creating the relationship?

Central Mortgage & Housing Corp. v. *Graham*[65] suggests that in a joint venture with the following characteristics, each of the joint venturers is responsible for all obligations of the joint venture, just as each partner is responsible for all obligations of the partnership:

- contribution by both parties of money, property, skill, or knowledge to a common undertaking;
- joint interest in the subject matter of the joint venture;
- mutual control and management;
- arrangement limited to one project;
- expectation of profit; and
- mutual sharing of profit.

In this case, Canadian Mortgage and Housing Corporation (CMHC) initiated a relationship with a builder, Bras D'Or, under which it provided the financing for Bras D'Or to build some houses to specifications provided by CMHC on property owned by Bras D'Or. The financing was secured by a mortgage on the property in favour of CMHC. CMHC was consulted during construction and had the right to approve the purchasers. With each sale, the purchaser would assume a portion of the debt owed by Bras D'Or to CMHC and assume a corresponding portion of the mortgage. Bras D'Or would be released to the same extent. Graham bought one of the houses from Bras D'Or and, after taking possession, stopped making payments on the mortgage because of some defects in the house. CMHC commenced foreclosure proceedings, and Graham counterclaimed for damages based on the defects, alleging that CMHC was liable for the defects because it was in a joint venture with Bras D'Or. The court, relying exclusively on American authority, held that the relationship in this case satisfied the factors identified above sufficiently that there was a joint venture. Consequently, CMHC was liable for the obligations of its fellow venturer Bras D'Or.

CMHC v. *Graham* has never been overruled and recently was cited as an accurate statement of the law in *Bow Valley Husky (Bermuda) Ltd.* v. *Saint John Shipbuilding Ltd.*[66] Nevertheless, neither in that case nor in other subsequent Canadian cases has a joint venture been found to have

---

65   (1973), 13 N.S.R. (2d) 183 (S.C.T.D.).
66   (1995), 130 Nfld. & P.E.I.R. 92 at 103 (Nfld. C.A.).

partnership-like legal characteristics.[67] This may be because, if all the incidents of a joint venture listed above are present, a partnership will be found in most cases. It is important to remember that what is often cited as the key identifying feature of a joint venture, limitation to a specific project, can also occur in partnerships. It is expressly contemplated in section 32(b) of the Ontario *Partnerships Act,* and such a limit has been present in other cases in which a partnership was found (e.g., *Pooley* v. *Driver*[68]).

Even if their legal position is not appropriately analogized to partnership, in many cases joint ventures will have more limited legal consequences. Most significantly, parties to a joint venture owe a fiduciary to each other in relation to the activities of the joint venture.[69] As with partners,[70] this duty means that joint venturers cannot put their individual interests ahead of the interests of the joint venture.

A striking example of one joint venturer attempting to enrich itself at the expense of the other occurred in *Wonsch Construction Co.* v. *Danzig Enterprises Ltd.*[71] Wonsch had entered into a joint venture agreement with Danzig to build and operate an apartment and office complex. In constructing the building, Wonsch had incurred substantial indebtedness to the National Bank of Canada. Danzig took an assignment of the debt owed by Wonsch, paying significantly less than the full amount, and immediately sued Wonsch for the full amount. The court held that Danzig owed a fiduciary duty to Wonsch which precluded it from, in effect, trying to make a profit from dealing in Wonsch's debt incurred for the purposes of the joint venture.

Another aspect of the fiduciary duty is the obligation not to disclose confidential information disclosed by one joint venturer to the other for the purposes of the joint venture.[72]

---

67 See cases cited in J.S. Ziegel, *et al., Cases and Materials on Partnerships and Business Corporations,* 3d ed. (Toronto: Carswell, 1994) at 81–83.

68 Above, note 19.

69 *Hogar Estates Ltd.* v. *Shebron Holdings Ltd.* (1979), 25 O.R. (2d) 543 (H.C.J.).

70 See above under "Fiduciary Duty."

71 (1990), 1 O.R. (3d) 382 (C.A.).

72 This duty of confidentiality may be imposed even in the absence of a fiduciary duty between parties who are only negotiating to establish a joint venture where the "circumstances of a relationship are such that one party is entitled to expect that the other will act in his interests in and for the purposes of the relationship" (P.D. Finn, "The Fiduciary Principle" in T.G. Youdan, ed., *Equity, Fiduciaries and Trusts* (Toronto: Carswell, 1988), at 46, cited in *LAC Minerals Ltd.* v. *International Corona Resources Ltd.,* [1989] 2 S.C.R. 574 at 644). See *Fines* v. *Vanderveen* ((1994), 55 C.P.R. (3d) 61 (Ont. Gen. Div.)) for a recent example of an unsuccessful attempt to invoke this protection.

G. LIMITED PARTNERSHIPS

1) General

A limited partnership is a specialized vehicle designed to fulfil the needs of particular investors who want to be able to share in partnership profits, but limit their liability for partnership losses. In most cases, limited partners are not interested in participating in management. Their investment is passive in nature. In Ontario, limited partnerships are governed by the *Limited Partnerships Act* (*OLPA*) and, to the extent that the Act is silent, by the *Partnerships Act* and the common law.[73] Each province has legislation dealing with limited partnerships.

Every limited partnership must consist of at least one general partner with unlimited liability and one limited partner with limited liability (*OLPA*, s. 2(2)). Unlike general partnerships, however, limited partnerships do not come into existence simply by virtue of persons in such a relationship carrying on business; a declaration must be filed with the Registrar appointed under the *Business Names Act* (*OLPA*, s. 3). The declaration expires after five years unless renewed. Expiry does not terminate the limited partnership, but an additional fee must be paid for renewal (*OLPA*, s. 3(3)).

The general partner has all the rights and powers and is subject to the same restrictions and unlimited personal liability as a partner in a general partnership, subject to certain additional constraints designed to protect the limited partners (*OLPA*, s. 8). By contrast, limited partners have certain fairly narrowly defined rights and their liability is limited to the extent of their contribution (*OLPA*, s. 9).

Limited partners have the right to share in profits and to have their contribution returned (*OLPA*, ss. 11 & 15). In addition, section 10 of the Ontario Act provides that a limited partner has the same rights as a general partner to

- inspect books and make copies;
- get full and true information regarding the limited partnership and to be given a complete and formal account of the partnership affairs; and
- to obtain dissolution by court order.

Where the units of the limited partnership are to be distributed to the public for the purposes of provincial securities laws, all investors

---

73   *OPA*, above note 2, ss. 45 & 46.

must have received a disclosure document (called a prospectus or offering memorandum) and have a civil claim for any misrepresentation in it. The regulation of the distribution of securities to the public is discussed in chapter 11.

A limited partner may transact business with the partnership, but cannot hold a security interest in the assets of the partnership and cannot receive anything from the partnership if it is insolvent. Unlike a general partner, a limited partner may be an employee of the partnership (*OLPA*, s. 12).

Participation by limited partners in management is subject to significant restrictions. A limited partner may "enquire into the state and progress of the limited partnership business and may advise as to its management" (*OLPA*, s. 12(2)(a)), but if the limited partner "takes part in the control of the business" (*OLPA*, s. 13(1)) or allows her name to be used in the firm name (*OLPA*, s. 6(2)), she loses her limited liability. In practice, drawing a distinction between advising as to management and taking part in control has been difficult. The few decided cases disclose no consistent principle.

One of the more difficult issues in this regard arises in the common situation where the general partner is a corporation and individual limited partners are involved as directors, officers, employees, and/or shareholders in the corporation. In these circumstances, the person who acts in his capacity as an employee, officer, or director of the general partner very often may be taking part in the control of the limited partnership. When does this role result in the loss of the limited partner's limited liability? The answer is not clear. In *Haughton Graphics Ltd.* v. *Zivot*,[74] Zivot was a limited partner in a limited partnership as well as the controlling shareholder and president of the corporation that was the general partner. In this capacity, he acted as the manager of the limited partnership. The court held that he was liable as a general partner on the basis that he took part in the control of the limited partnership business. In interpreting the *Partnerships Act* of Alberta,[75] the court made clear that there was no requirement in the section for the person who was claiming against the limited partnership to have believed, based on the limited partner's conduct, that she was a general partner, rejecting a line of U.S. authority to this effect. As a consequence, it would not have mattered if the limited partnership structure had been made known to the claimant.

The court expressed the view that any time a limited partner was an employee, officer, or director of a corporate general partner and, in that

74   (1986), 33 B.L.R. 125 (Ont. H.C.J.).
75   R.S.A. 1980, c. P-2.

capacity, took part in the control of the business, he would be liable personally as a general partner for the obligations of the partnership.[76] This position seems unduly broad, since it systematically disregards the separate existence of the corporation[77] and has not been followed in subsequent cases. In *Nordile Holdings Ltd.* v. *Breckenridge*[78] the court specifically held that where individual limited partners act only in their capacities as directors and officers of a corporate general partner, they are not liable as general partners. Since Zivot was also the controlling shareholder in *Haughton,* it may be possible to argue that the right approach is that limited partners may act as employees, officers, and directors of corporate general partners and take part in control without losing their limited liability, unless they also control the corporate general partner.

A limited partner's interest is transferable, but the transferee only has the full rights of the transferor (i.e., becomes a substituted limited partner) if all partners consent, or the transfer is in accordance with the partnership agreement (*OLPA,* s. 18). It is common in most limited partnerships, especially those in which the limited partnership units are publicly traded, to provide that transfers may occur in some simpler fashion, such as with the consent of the general partner.

A limited partner has a right to receive repayment of her investment in these circumstances:

- on dissolution of the limited partnership;
- at the time specified in the partnership agreement;
- on six months notice, if no time is specified in the limited partnership agreement; and
- on the unanimous consent of all partners (*OLPA,* s. 15(1)).

No return of a limited partner's investment may occur if there are not enough assets to pay all prior claims (*OLPA,* s. 15(2)).[79]

---

76 Above note 74 at 134.

77 See "Disregard of Separate Corporate Personality," in chapter 3.

78 (1992), 66 B.C.L.R. (2d) 183 (C.A.) aff'g (21 February 1991), (B.C.S.C.) [unreported] [case summarized at [1991] B.C.W.L.D. 860. In this case, the court also held that liability of the limited partners could be excluded by a contractual provision that the obligations were solely those of the limited partnership and not the limited partners, thus appearing to permit the alteration of the rules set out in the BCPA, above note 33. See, generally, L. Philipps, "The Amazing Three-Headed Limited Partner: Reflections on Old Loopholes and New Jurisprudence" (1993) 21 Can. Bus. L.J. 410.

79 There is a similar provision restricting distributions to shareholders of corporations in Canadian corporate statutes (e.g., *Canadian Business Corporations Act,* R.S.C. 1985, c. C–44, s. 42). See chapter 6.

Dissolution of a limited partnership occurs in the same circumstances as for a general partnership — death, incompetence, and retirement of a general partner — unless at least one general partner remains and the partnership agreement provides for continuation or all the partners agree (*OLPA*, s. 21). Dissolution also occurs on the withdrawal of all limited partners (*OLPA*, s. 23) or if (a) a limited partner's contribution is not returned when it is required to be or (b) the liabilities of the limited partnership are not paid or the assets of the limited partnership are not enough to pay the liabilities (*OLPA*, s. 15(4)). Finally, just as in any general partnership, dissolution may occur by court order under section 35 of the *Partnerships Act*.

Two final points may be made. A person can be both a general and a limited partner (*OLPA*, s. 5(1)). A general partner's liability can only be unlimited, and becoming a limited partner has no effect on this liability. A general partner may nevertheless want to be a limited partner in order to participate with the limited partners in distributions of losses, profits, and on dissolution to the extent of the units owned in the limited partnership. Finally, limited partnerships formed under the laws of one province must register if they carry business on in another (e.g., *OLPA*, s. 25), and they are subject to penalties if they do not (e.g., *OLPA*, s. 35). Limited partners do not, however, lose their limited liability if they fail to register (e.g., *OLPA*, s. 27).[80]

2) Tax Effects

One of the most common reasons for investing in limited partnerships is to receive a share of tax losses generated by the limited partnership business. Sharing losses may be very attractive to individuals with high incomes from other sources. The losses will be deductible against that income, with the effect of reducing the individual's overall tax liability.

Figures 2.6A and 2.6B are examples of how the federal government may use the tax treatment of limited partners to encourage investment in an identified industry. By increasing the rate at which capital cost allowance may be taken on assets acquired for use in identified industries, such as the film, mineral exploration, and manufacturing industries, the federal government can make investment in those

---

80   In general, the effectiveness of limited liability will be governed by the law of the jurisdiction in which the limited partnership was created (Manzer, above note 30 at 9-45 & 9-46).

Figure 2.6A Taxation of Limited Partnerships: Case 1

Assume
(a) A business acquires film equipment for $1,000,000 in 1995, its first year of operation.
(b) The business has revenue of $100,000 in 1995.
(c) The tax rate for the business is 50 percent.
(d) The only expense deductible from revenue for tax purposes is capital cost allowance (CCA) (i.e., an amount that may be deducted from income to reflect the reduction in the remaining useful life of an asset).
(e) Under the *Income Tax Act*, CCA may be deducted in each year at the rate of 5 percent of the acquisition cost of the film equipment (reflecting an expected useful life of twenty years).

If Corporation-Owned Business

Tax paid by corporation for 1995 would be

Revenue	$100,000	
less CCA	50,000	(5% of $1,000,000)
Taxable income	50,000	
less tax of 50%	25,000	
After tax income	$ 25,000	

There would be no tax consequences for shareholders unless the corporation pays a dividend to shareholders.

If Limited Partnership–Owned Business

The taxable income of $50,000 would be allocated to the limited partners in accordance with their respective interests in the limited partnership and added to their other income for the purposes of calculating their personal taxes owing for 1995.

---

industries through limited partnerships attractive to investors with high taxable incomes. Businesses in these industries will be able to create tax losses in their first years of operation by taking large deductions for CCA. By investing in limited partnerships that are engaged in these businesses, investors will be able to deduct the losses resulting from CCA deductions against their other income to reduce their overall tax liability. Figure 2.6B provides an example of the effect of such "accelerated" CCA.

Figure 2.6B Taxation of Limited Partnerships: Case 2

Assume the same facts as in Case 1, except that the permitted CCA deduction is not 5 percent but 100 percent in the year of acquisition. The calculation of taxable income for the business for 1995 would change as follows:

Revenue	$ 100,000	
less CCA	1,000,000	(100% of 1,000,000)
Loss	(900,000)	

For the Corporation: This loss will mean that no taxes are payable for 1995. The loss will be deductible, subject to certain limitations, against income in future years. There are no tax consequences for shareholders. Much of the benefit to the corporation is deferred.

For the Limited Partners: Subject to certain limitations, this loss may be deducted by limited partners against their other income to reduce their overall tax liability for 1995.

H. CHAPTER SUMMARY

This chapter provides a brief overview of the law of partnership and a practical discussion of the considerations for structuring partnerships in the context of this legal framework.

A partnership has no existence separate from the partners who make it up. A number of significant consequences flow from this fact, the most important of which are that partners have unlimited personal liability for the obligations of the partnership business and, in the absence of an agreement to the contrary, partnerships may be dissolved by any of the partners. Partnerships come into existence without any formality; it is sufficient if one or more persons begin to carry on business together with a view to a profit. In each case, the existence of a partnership will be determined by whether the parties intended to enter into such a relationship. The fundamental test for such an intention is whether the business is being carried on for the benefit of the alleged partners. The most significant indicia of such an intention is sharing profits from the business activity, though one must be careful to distinguish other relationships in which profits are shared, such as some creditor and debtor and co-ownership relationships. Other important indicia include participation in the management and control of the partnership and common ownership of property. No single factor is conclusive. Whether a partnership exists depends on the circumstances of each case.

The relationship of partners to each other is governed by default rules in the partnership legislation which operate unless the parties agree on some other arrangement. The relationship between partners and third parties dealing with the partnership is governed by a set of mandatory rules. In general, all partners are liable for all obligations incurred in the course of the partnership business while they are partners. After a person dies or becomes bankrupt, he ceases to be liable for obligations occurred afterwards. If he leaves the partnership in other circumstances, he may continue to be liable for new obligations of the partnership unless he was never known to be a partner or notice is given that he has ceased to be a partner. Persons who are not partners will nevertheless be liable as partners if they knowingly allow themselves to be held out as partners.

Partnership agreements are a critical supplement and complement to the law of partnerships. The default provisions of partnership legislation governing the relations among partners provide an inadequate and out-of-date skeleton of a structure not suitable for most partnerships. The default rules governing the relations among partners, including those dealing with management, interests in profits and capital, membership in the partnership, and dissolution, typically will need to be changed. It will also be desirable, in most circumstances, to create monitoring and control arrangements for the purpose of reducing the likelihood of unauthorized behaviour, as well as provisions to deal with how liability imposed under partnership law will be allocated as among the partners.

Finally, we looked at contractual joint ventures and limited partnerships. Joint ventures, although they are not partnerships, have some lesser partnership-like legal consequences. Joint venturers owe each other a fiduciary duty not to put their personal interests ahead of the interests of the venture and, in some circumstances, may have liability for obligations incurred in connection with the venture. Limited partnerships are like general partnerships except that the liability of at least one partner is limited to the amount she invested in the partnership. Such limited partners also have restrictions on their ability to participate in management. If a limited partner violates the restrictions, he loses his limited liability and becomes a general partner.

FURTHER READINGS

BROMBERG, A.R., *Crane and Bromberg on Partnership* (St. Paul: West, 1968)

ELLIS, M.V., *Fiduciary Duties in Canada* (Don Mills: De Boo, 1988)

FLANNIGAN, R.D., "The Control Test of Investor Liability in Limited Partnerships" (1983) 21 Alta. L. Rev. 303

FLETCHER, K.L., *The Law of Partnership in Australia and New Zealand*, 6th ed. (Sydney: Law Book Co., 1991)

GOWER, L.C.B., ed., *Pollock on the Law of Partnership*, 15th ed. (London: Stevens, 1952)

HEPBURN, L.R., & W.J. STRAIN, *Limited Partnerships* (Toronto: Carswell, 1983) (looseleaf)

KARP, A., "The Professional Partnership: Withdrawal of Partners and Dissolution of Partnership" [1977] Spec. Lect. L.S.U.C. 329

KELLOUGH, H.J., "The Business of Defining a Partnership under the Income Tax Act" (1974) 22 Can. Tax. J. 189

LAW SOCIETY OF UPPER CANADA, *Bar Admission Course Reference Materials: Business Law* (Toronto: Law Society of Upper Canada, 1995) c. 2

MANZER, A.R., *A Practical Guide to Canadian Partnership Law* (Aurora: Canada Law Book, 1995) (looseleaf)

PHILIPPS, L., "The Amazing Three-Headed Limited Partner: Reflections on Old Loopholes and New Jurisprudence" (1993) 21 Can. Bus. L.J. 410

SCAMMELL, E.H., & R.C. BANKS, eds., *Lindley and Banks on the Law of Partnership*, 17th ed. (London: Sweet & Maxwell, 1995)

WARE, J.G., & P.W. FARWELL, "The Professional Partnership: The Tax Position of the Partnership and the Partners" [1977] Spec. Lect. L.S.U.C. 171

WATEROUS, R.N., "Some Problems in the Formation and Function of the Small Professional Partnership" [1977] Spec. Lect. L.S.U.C. 19

ZIEGEL, J.S., et al., *Cases and Materials on Partnerships and Canadian Business Corporations*, 3d ed. (Toronto: Carswell, 1994)

CHAPTER 3

INTRODUCTION TO CORPORATE LAW

A. INTRODUCTION

In this chapter we introduce the corporation from a variety of perspectives. After a historical overview of the development of corporate law in Canada, we will briefly introduce the current form of corporate law in terms of the following questions:

- What is the constitutional competency of the federal government and the provinces in relation to corporations?
- What is the current process of incorporation and organization of corporations in Canada?
- What is the function of corporate law and what policy underpins it?
- What is the relationship between corporate law and securities law?
- What are the implications of the separate legal existence of the corporation?
- To what extent is the *Charter of Rights and Freedoms* applicable to corporations?

B. A BRIEF HISTORICAL NOTE ON CANADIAN CORPORATE LAW

Before the nineteenth century, only two types of incorporation were provided for in English and Canadian law. First, a corporation could be created by exercise of the royal prerogative. This was done by the Crown issuing letters patent sometimes referred to as a "Royal Charter." Second, incorporation could also be effected by special or general Act of the legislature. Incorporation by an enactment of the legislature rarely occurred, though Canadian legislatures passed special Acts to permit incorporation for special purposes. A small number of royal charters were granted, such as the charter of the Hudson's Bay Company granted by the English Parliament in 1670.

In 1849, statutes were passed in Upper and Lower Canada allowing for the incorporation of companies for the purpose of building roads and bridges.[1] These companies were not business organizations resembling modern business corporations. They were organizations set up for a limited purpose, and did not provide limited liability. Incorporation did not require the exercise of the royal prerogative, but was obtained by the registration of certain documents in the county in which work was to be done.

In 1850 the United Provinces of Canada enacted a general statute for incorporation.[2] Following the American approach, the new Act permitted incorporation for mining, shipbuilding, manufacturing, and chemical businesses through an expeditious process that did not depend on the exercise of the royal prerogative. Like the 1849 Acts, incorporation was obtained by the registration of certain documents. Unlike those incorporated under the 1849 Acts, however, corporations under this Act had two of the defining characteristics we associate with the modern corporation: separate legal personality and limited liability. In contrast to modern corporations, their life was limited to fifty years.

In 1862 the English *Companies Act* was passed. It, too, was based on a registration approach; the Act provided for incorporation on the filing of the documents required by statute: a memorandum of association and articles of association. Unlike earlier legislation, however, this Act permitted incorporation for any commercial purpose.

For some reason, the United Provinces of Canada reverted to a model based on the exercise of royal prerogative in a new general incorporation statute passed in 1864.[3] Under this Act, letters patent were

---

1   *An Act to Authorize the Formation of Joint Stock Companies for the Construction of Roads' and Other Works in Upper Canada*, S.C. 1849, c. 84; and *An Act to Authorize the Formation of Joint Stock Companies in Lower Canada for the Construction of Macadamized Roads, and of Bridges and Other Works of Like Nature*, S.C. 1849, c. 56.

2   *An Act to Provide for the Formation of Incorporated Joint Stock Companies, for Manufacturing, Mining, Mechanical or Chemical Purposes*, S.C. 1850, c. 28.

3   *An Act to Authorize the Granting of Charters of Incorporation to Manufacturing, Mining, and Other Companies*, S.C. 1864, c. 23.

issued on application to the Governor-in-Council. The letters patent approach was followed in the federal incorporation statute enacted in 1869[4] and in provincial legislation in Prince Edward Island, New Brunswick, Quebec, Ontario, and Manitoba. In contrast, by 1900 Nova Scotia, Newfoundland, Saskatchewan, Alberta, and British Columbia had enacted corporate legislation providing for incorporation through filing a memorandum and articles of association following the English registration approach.[5]

Certain conceptual differences between the two approaches should be borne in mind. As mentioned above, the creation of a corporation under letters patent statutes is a discretionary act of the Crown. Under a registration approach, incorporation must be granted by the state so long as the documents filed satisfy the statutory requirements. Also, a letters patent corporation is deemed to have the rights and powers of a natural person, whereas a corporation under an English model registration system (referred to here as a "memorandum corporation") only has the powers provided for expressly or by implication in its articles. In effect, this meant that actions of memorandum corporations frequently were attacked as outside their corporate powers or *ultra vires*. Also, under English registration model statutes, the incorporators have to provide a set of rules in the memorandum of association governing how the corporation is to function internally: who is authorized to act for the corporation; how the shareholders and directors exercise power; and so on. With letters patent corporations, these rules are set out in the corporation's by-laws or in the statute. The significance of this distinction is that letters patent corporations do not have to file their by-laws with the state, so much less information concerning such corporations becomes a matter of public record. Also, prior to the enactment of modern corporate statutes, persons dealing with a corporation were deemed to have notice of what was on the public record, so that if the requirements of the memorandum or articles were not satisfied in connection with the creation of an obligation to such a person, the obligation could not be enforced. Such a *constructive* notice meant, therefore, that the greater public disclosure required in relation to memorandum corporations had implications beyond the simple fact of disclosure.[6]

---

4   *Canadian Joint Stock Companies Letters Patent Act*, S.C. 1869, c. 13.
5   *Companies Act* (U.K.), 1862, c. 89.
6   See "Liability of Corporations in Contract" in chapter 5.

Perhaps most important, the memorandum and articles of association of memorandum corporations constitute a contract between the members and between the corporation and the members.[7] This contract has two major consequences. First, the memorandum and articles of association are the primary source of the allocation of powers between the directors and the shareholders. Second, the directors act as delegates of the shareholders, and any power not granted to the directors in the memorandum and articles or the statute remains in the shareholders. Under letters patent statutes, by contrast, directors derive their powers from the statute, though some derogation in favour of shareholders is permitted. It is at best unclear whether shareholders in letters patent corporations have a residual authority. This distinction becomes relevant where, for example, a dispute has arisen between a shareholder and the corporation to determine whether relief may be available to the shareholder, what that relief might consist of, and how the claim for relief should be framed.[8] The members of a registration corporation can sue civilly for a breach of the memorandum or articles, though their entitlement to damages is limited[9], whereas shareholders of letters patent corporations must rely, primarily, on statutory remedies.

Throughout most of this century, Canadian registration and letters patent model statutes changed very little. Then, in 1970, Ontario engaged in a wholesale amendment of its corporate law.[10] Based on the Lawrence Committee Report[11] in 1967, the Ontario legislature finally abandoned the letters patent system in favour of a registration system. Unlike the English-style memorandum and articles of association statutes, however, under the new Ontario Act incorporation was effected by filing a simple document called "articles of incorporation." This approach followed the Model Business Corporations Act drafted by a committee of the American Bar Association.

---

7   See British Columbia *Company Act*, R.S.B.C. 1979, c. 59, s. 13, [*BCCA*]; *Companies Act*, (U.K.), 1985, c. 6, s. 14; *Hickman v. Kent or Romney Marsh Sheep-Breeders' Association*, [1915] 1 Ch. 881.

8   See, generally, B. Welling, *Corporate Law in Canada: The Governing Principles*, 2d ed. (Toronto: Butterworths, 1991) at 38–40 & 48–73, for a discussion of the confused state of the law on the nature of this "Statutory Contract."

9   J. Ziegel *et al.*, *Cases and Materials on Partnerships and Canadian Business Corporations*, 3d ed. (Toronto: Carswell, 1994).

10   *The Business Corporations Act*, R.S.O. 1970, c. 53.

11   Ontario, *Interim Report of the Select Committee on Company Law* (Toronto: Queen's Printer, 1967).

In 1975, based on the recommendations of the Dickerson Committee,[12] the federal government implemented its own new corporate law statute: The *Canada Business Corporations Act* (the *CBCA*). The *CBCA* adopted an articles of incorporation approach along the same general lines as the new Ontario Act, but went much farther in the protection of minority shareholders.

Most corporate statutes in Canada now follow the *CBCA* model. In 1982 Ontario enacted legislation which, for the most part, mirrors the federal legislation (S.O. 1982, c. 4). The *CBCA* was also adopted without substantial changes in Alberta (*Business Corporations Act*, S.A. 1981, c. B-15 (*ABCA*)), Saskatchewan (*The Business Corporations Act*, R.S.S. 1978, c. B-10 (*SBCA*)), Manitoba (*The Corporations Act*, R.S.M. 1987, c. C225 (*MBCA*)), and, to a lesser extent, Newfoundland (*Corporations Act*, R.S.N. 1990, c. C-36 (*NCA*)) and New Brunswick (*Business Corporations Act*, S.N.B. 1981, c. B-9.1 (*NBBCA*)). The *CBCA* has also influenced major reforms of corporate law in Quebec[13] and Nova Scotia (S.N.S. 1982, c. 17; S.N.S. 1990, c. 15 (*NSCA*)). British Columbia reformed its corporate law in 1973 (now the *Company Act*, R.S.B.C. 1979, c. 59 (*BCCA*)) and, although many of the same changes brought about by the *CBCA* were introduced, such as the remedy for minority shareholder oppression, the B.C. legislation remains distinct, still following the English *Companies Act* in significant respects. Prince Edward Island retains its letters patent model statute (*Companies Act*, R.S.P.E.I. 1988, c. C-14 (*PEICA*)). Currently the federal, Ontario, and British Columbia governments are working on significant amendments to their corporate law.

While both the memorandum and articles of association model for corporate statutes, like British Columbia's, and the articles of incorporation model now dominant elsewhere in Canada provide for incorporation on the registration of certain documents, there are several differences between them. Essentially, the articles of incorporation model, like the letters patent model, creates a statutory allocation of powers, rights, and responsibilities among shareholders, directors, and officers. Much of the structure of the corporation is provided by the corporate statute, though, to some extent, this structure may be changed by the parties in the articles or by other means, such as a unanimous shareholders' agreement.[14] The directors are directed to "manage the business and affairs of

---

12 R.V.W. Dickerson, J.L. Howard, & L. Getz, *Proposals for a New Business Corporations Law for Canada*, 2 vols. (Ottawa: Information Canada, 1971).
13 Quebec now has two corporate laws: *Companies Act*, R.S.Q. 1977, c. C-38 (*QCA*), and S.Q. 1980, c. 28.
14 See chapter 4.

a corporation" (*CBCA*, s. 102(1)). The Act provides that these powers may be delegated subject to certain limitations (*CBCA*, s. 115), and it grants certain limited rights for shareholders to have a say in how the corporation is managed.[15] By contrast, under the memorandum and articles of association model, many of the basic rights and obligations of the shareholders are provided for in the memorandum and articles of association, and the memorandum and articles are considered to be a contract between the corporation and the shareholders as discussed above.[16] One must be careful to keep these differences in mind when considering the applicability of judicial decisions rendered in relation to a corporation created under one model to a situation involving a corporation created under the other. Perhaps the most important practical implication of these differences is that, in most cases, shareholders of corporations incorporated under articles of incorporation statutes may not commence a civil suit for breach of the articles but must rely on the statutory remedies provided.[17] In practice, the remedies introduced in the *CBCA* have provided much better protection of shareholders' interests than exists in memorandum corporation jurisdictions.[18] Improved shareholder remedies also distinguish *CBCA* model statutes from letters patent statutes, such as the current *PEICA*.

The *CBCA* made several other significant changes to corporate law in Canada: the new Act provided significantly greater flexibility in structuring the corporation by changing mandatory rules into rules that applied except to the extent that the incorporators agreed to change them; constructive notice and the doctrine of *ultra vires* were abolished and shareholders were permitted, by unanimous agreement, to assume some or all of the powers of the directors, thus altering the statutory division of powers. Because of the pre-eminence of the *CBCA* as a model for corporate law in Canada, this book focuses on the *CBCA*, noting the differences between it and the provincial regimes where relevant.

---

15   See chapter 7.

16   See, for example, section 13 of the *BCCA*, above note 7:

> [T]he memorandum and articles, when registered, bind the company and its members to the same extent as if each had been signed and sealed by the company and by every member and contained covenants on the part of every member, his heirs, executors and administrators to observe the memorandum and articles.

17   Although the *Canada Business Corporations Act*, R.S.C. 1985, c. C-44 [*CBCA*] does provide that a shareholder, or a creditor, may seek to enforce compliance with the Act, the articles, the by-laws, or any unanimous shareholder agreement (s. 247).

18   *Ibid.* See also J.G. MacIntosh, "Minority Shareholders Rights in Canada and England: 1860–1987" (1989) 27 Osgoode Hall L.J. 561.

In the discussion of Canadian corporate law that follows, extensive references will be made to both English and American authorities. Notwithstanding the differences between the articles of incorporation and memorandum and articles of association models, there continues to be a strong English influence present in the Canadian cases dealing with the basic concepts and doctrines we share with the United Kingdom arising out of our common legal traditions. As noted, however, the predominant model for corporate law statutes in Canada is American. For this reason and because of the wealth of U.S. case law and scholarship on corporate law issues as well as the increasingly close business ties between the two countries, the influence of American precedents is strong and increasing. There are, however, significant differences between the form and content of the regulation of corporate behaviour and the business contexts in the two countries in which corporations operate, differences that must be borne in mind.[19]

C. CONSTITUTIONAL MATTERS: DIVISION OF POWERS

1) Introduction

As discussed in the foregoing historical overview, both the federal and the provincial governments have enacted corporate law statutes from time to time. In this section we will discuss their respective jurisdictions to incorporate and to regulate corporations.

2) Jurisdiction to Incorporate

a) Provincial Incorporation

Under section 92(11) of the *Constitution Act, 1867*, the provinces have jurisdiction over the "Incorporation of Companies with Provincial Objects." The limitation imposed by the reference to provincial objects has been interpreted narrowly. It has nothing to do with the nature of the corporation's business operations, nor does it impose an effective limitation on the territory within which the corporation operates. All it means is that a province is not capable of endowing a corporation with the right to carry on business in any other jurisdiction, including any other province. A province can, however, grant a corporation the capacity

---

19 See below this chapter. For an excellent discussion of these issues see R.J. Daniels & J.G. MacIntosh, "Toward a Distinctive Canadian Corporate Law Regime" (1991) 29 Osgoode Hall L. J. 863.

to do so subject to its obtaining the permission of the other jurisdiction to carry on business.[20]

Practically speaking, within Canada, such permission is routinely granted under extraprovincial licensing regimes set up by each province.[21] Under these regimes, corporations incorporated under the laws of another province or territory, or a foreign jurisdiction, may obtain a licence to carry on business on the filing of certain basic information and a fee. Although the decision to grant such a licence is discretionary, licences are rarely refused, except where the name of the corporation seeking to do business in a province is likely to be confusing with the name of a business already being carried on in the province.[22] As a result, the mobility of a provincial corporation, at least within Canada, is almost unrestricted.

b) Federal Incorporation

The *Constitution Act* grants the federal government limited powers to incorporate in certain areas, such as the incorporation of banks, but contains no express general power of incorporation. In *Citizens Insurance Co. of Canada* v. *Parsons*,[23] however, it was held that this power was implicit in the federal government's residual jurisdiction to "make Laws for the Peace, Order and good Government of Canada, in relation to all Matters not coming within the Classes of Subjects by this Act assigned exclusively to the Legislatures of the Provinces."[24] The Privy Council reasoned that since the provinces had been given the jurisdiction to incorporate corporations with provincial objects, the federal government must have jurisdiction to legislate in relation to the incorporation of corporations with objects to be carried out in more than one province. The validity of federal incorporation, however, is not dependent on the corporation, in fact, carrying on business in more than one province.

---

20   *Bonanza Creek Gold Mining Co. Ltd.* v. *R.*, [1916] 1 A.C. 566 (P.C.). The nature of provincial jurisdiction is reflected in section 16 of the Ontario *Business Corporations Act*, R.S.O. 1990, c. B.16 [*OBCA*]: "A corporation has the capacity to carry on its business, conduct its affairs and exercise its powers in any jurisdiction outside Ontario to the extent that the laws of such jurisdiction permit."

21   For example, Ontario *Extra-Provincial Corporations Act*, R.S.O. 1990, c. E.27.

22   See chapter 4.

23   (1881), 7 App. Cas. 96 (P.C.).

24   The preamble to section 91 of the *Constitution Act, 1867* (U.K.), 30 & 31 Vict., c. 3 [*CA 1867*], grants to the federal government the jurisdiction to legislate "in relation to all Matters not coming within the Classes of Subjects by this Act assigned exclusively to the Legislatures of the Provinces."

Unlike provincially incorporated corporations, federally incorporated corporations have a right to carry on business in each province. There is no risk that a federally incorporated corporation will be barred from carrying on business in a province as a result of its name being confusing with one already in use in the province or for any other reason.[25] Federal corporations are required, however, to file information similar to that required of a provincial corporation in an application for an extraprovincial licence on commencing business in a province; so, in practice, there is often little difference in the treatment of federal and provincial corporations.

3) Jurisdiction to Regulate

a) Provincial Regulation of Federal Corporations
To what extent can a provincial government regulate a federally incorporated corporation? This is an important question in light of the extensive provincial regulation of various business activities. The answer is based on traditional division of powers jurisprudence and is effectively reviewed by Professor Peter Hogg in *Constitutional Law of Canada*.[26] The following outline is simply a cursory overview.

Provinces cannot legislate solely in relation to the status or powers of a federal corporation. In other words, provinces cannot legislate restrictions on the powers of federal corporations, such as, for example, removing limited liability.[27] Provinces cannot directly regulate intracorporate relations, such as those between directors and shareholders,[28] or require a federal corporation to use a name other than its corporate name for business purposes in the province because of the risk of confusion in the provincial marketplace between the corporation's name and the name used by a business already being carried on in the province.[29]

---

25   This is one reason that the federal government conducts a much more careful review of names proposed for corporations to be incorporated than the provinces. See "Names" in chapter 4.

26   3d ed. (Toronto: Carswell, 1992), chapter 23.

27   Ontario legislation preventing unlicensed corporations, including federal corporations, from holding freehold property was upheld as not being in relation to the status or powers of a federal corporation (*Great West Saddlery Co. v. R.*, [1921] 2 A.C. 91 (P.C.)).

28   Though, as will be discussed below in this chapter, provincial securities law has a significant impact in this area.

29   *Reference Re Constitution Act*, 1867, ss. 91 & 92 (1991), 80 D.L.R. (4th) 431 (Man. C.A.) [*Reference Re Constitution Act*].

Provinces can legislate to affect directly the way in which federal corporations exercise their powers if two requirements are met:

- the legislation can be justified as primarily in relation to a provincial head of jurisdiction in section 92 of the *Constitution Act, 1867*; and
- the legislation is not inconsistent with federal law.

If the second requirement is not met, the provincial law will be ineffective to the extent of the inconsistency based on the doctrine of paramountcy.[30] So, for example, provincial securities legislation designed to protect Ontario investors may be validly enacted under the province's jurisdiction to legislate in relation to property and civil rights under section 92(13) of the *Constitution Act* so long as it is not inconsistent with federal corporate law. Provincial securities legislation that regulates the way in which securities of a federal corporation are sold in the province by requiring sales through provincially registered dealers has been upheld as validly enacted and not inconsistent with federal law.[31] By contrast, legislation purporting to prohibit the sale of securities in certain circumstances for the protection of investors has been held to be inconsistent with federal corporate law, which gives corporations the right to issue securities.[32]

Name registration statutes are another example of valid provincial legislation. Such legislation, which exists in every province, requires registration of the business name of all corporations carrying on business in the province using a name other than their corporate name. Its purpose is to provide the public with a means of ascertaining the legal identity of the person legally responsible for a business that is conducted under a name other than the corporate name. This is a matter of civil rights in the province, and such registration requirements can be imposed on federal corporations.[33]

Provinces can enact laws that are solely within one of the enumerated heads of section 92 of the *Constitution Act, 1867,* such as labour law, contract law, and much industry specific-legislation, even if the effect is, indirectly, to sterilize the federal corporation by prohibiting it from

---

30 *Multiple Access Ltd.* v. *McCutcheon*, [1982] 2 S.C.R. 161. In that case, separate insider trading legislation enacted by the federal government and Ontario which was largely duplicative was upheld on the basis that there was no actual conflict between the two schemes. Paramountcy does not restrict the regulation of foreign extraprovincial corporations.

31 *Lymburn v. Mayland*, [1932] A.C. 318 (P.C.).

32 *Manitoba (A.G.)* v. *Canada (A.G.)*, [1929] A.C. 260 (P.C.).

33 *Reference Re Constitution Act*, above note 29.

carrying on business. An example of this sort of provincial legislation was the British Columbia legislation setting up a provincially operated automobile insurance scheme that precluded private insurance companies from offering automobile insurance in the province. The Supreme Court of Canada upheld this legislation as validly enacted in relation to property and civil rights in the province even though one of its effects was to preclude federal insurance companies from carrying on business in British Columbia.[34]

To summarize, a province cannot enact legislation that operates directly to affect some essential aspect of a federal corporation, but provinces have jurisdiction to regulate most businesses and their activities, including their ability to sell securities, their relations with their employees, and the contracts they enter into. A federal corporation is subject to provincial regulation to the extent that it is involved in these businesses or activities.[35]

b) Federal Regulation of Provincial Corporations

Since most business areas are within the jurisdiction of the provinces, federal regulation of provincial corporations may be thought of as somewhat less important than the provincial regulation of federal corporations and it has generated little jurisprudence. There are, however, several critically important areas within federal regulatory competence, such as telecommunications and interprovincial transportation.[36]

Professor Hogg's view is that the federal government may not regulate provincial corporations directly in relation to their corporate status or characteristics. It may, however, may directly affect the way in which provincial corporations exercise their powers if the legislation can be justified as primarily in relation to an area of jurisdiction assigned to the federal government.[37]

c) Regulation of Extra-provincial Corporations

In principle, both provincial and federal governments should have broader jurisdiction to regulate corporations incorporated outside a province in which it is doing business, whether incorporated in another

---

34   *Canadian Indemnity Co. v. British Columbia (A.G.)* (1976), [1977] 2 S.C.R. 504.

35   Welling, above note 8 at 20.

36   Such matters fall within federal jurisdiction under the residual jurisdiction created by the Peace, Order and Good Government clause or the jurisdiction under section 91(29) and section 92(10) over interprovincial undertakings (*CA 1867*, above note 24).

37   Hogg, above note 26 at chapter 23, 20–1.

province or in a foreign jurisdiction. Each provincial government is competent to legislate in relation to the status and characteristics of such an extraprovincial corporation. Similarly, the federal government may legislate in relation to a corporation operating outside its jurisdiction of incorporation.[38] Neither level of government has enacted legislation that imposes a heavier regulatory burden on such extraprovincial corporations incorporated in Canada, though some statutes discriminate against foreign incorporated corporations.[39]

D. INCORPORATION AND ORGANIZATION

1) What Is a Business Corporation?

The corporate statutes we will be looking at govern business corporations. Charitable and other not-for-profit entities are governed under separate statutory regimes.[40] Similarly, the corporate statutes do not apply to certain entities carrying on businesses subject to their own scheme of regulation. The *CBCA* does not apply to banks, which are governed by the *Bank Act*, insurance companies governed by the *Insurance Companies Act,* or trust and loan companies governed by the *Trust and Loan Companies Act* (*CBCA*, s. 3).[41]

2) The Incorporation Process

The process of incorporation will be discussed in more detail in chapter 4, but it is useful as part of this chapter to outline the basic elements as a way of introducing the sources of the rules governing the relationships among directors, shareholders, and officers as well as some basic vocabulary.

When one or more people or corporations decide that they want to carry on business using a corporation, they must file certain prescribed material with the branch of the federal government or one of the provincial governments having responsibility for incorporations.[42] Under the *CBCA*, it is necessary to file the following:

---

38   *Ibid.* at 23-20 to 23-21.

39   For example, the *Income Tax Act*, R.S.C. 1985, (5th Supp.), c. 1 [*ITA*].

40   Federally non-profit and charitable corporations may be incorporated under the *Canada Corporations Act*, R.S.C. 1970, c. C-32. In Ontario, incorporation is under the *Corporations Act*, R.S.O. 1990, c. C.38. Incorporation under these Acts is by letters patent.

41   See *OBCA*, above note 20, s. 2.

42   See below for a discussion of consideration relevant to choosing the jurisdiction under which to incorporate.

- articles of incorporation (s. 6, Form 1);
- notice of registered office (s. 19(2), Form 3);
- notice of directors (s. 106, Form 6);
- a name search report on the proposed name of the corporation; and
- the fee of $500.

The articles are by far the most important of these documents because they set out the fundamental characteristics of the corporation: the name of the corporation, the class and number of shares authorized to be issued, the number of directors, any restrictions on transferring shares, and any restrictions on the business the corporation may carry on.

Once these documents are properly filed along with the fee, the director appointed to administer the *CBCA* issues a certificate, to which the articles are attached (Form 2), certifying that the corporation was incorporated on the date of the certificate (*CBCA*, ss. 8 & 9). The corporation comes into existence on the date of the certificate (*CBCA*, s. 9). The directors named in the notice of directors hold office until the first meeting of shareholders at which an election of directors is held (*CBCA*, s. 106(2)). The provisions in the articles may only be changed by articles of amendment filed with the director after approval by a special resolution of shareholders.[43]

The actual process of filing the requisite documents with the fee and receiving a certificate of incorporation is very expeditious and may be engaged in by anyone. Lawyers routinely incorporate corporations for their clients, but there are a variety of commercial services offering to do incorporations more quickly and cheaply. Individuals may also obtain incorporation kits to permit do-it-yourself incorporations. As will be discussed below, there are a variety of issues and potential pitfalls associated with incorporation, which, in any case, is usually only the first step in organizing a business. Consideration should be given to the desirability of professional advice in connection with incorporations.

On incorporation, the corporation may commence carrying on a business. The business may be a new one, or an existing business may be transferred to the corporation. Unlike a partnership, there is no need for a corporation to carry on business; its existence derives exclusively from issuance of the certificate under the statute. Several more steps are required, however, before the corporation is fully organized. First, the

---

43   A special resolution is a resolution signed by all shareholders or passed at a meeting of shareholders by a majority of not less than two-thirds of the votes cast by shareholders present and voting at the meeting (*CBCA*, above note 17, s. 2), see below.

directors should have a meeting and pass a resolution to issue shares to the shareholders. This is essential since, until the shares are issued, the only persons who may act for the corporation are the directors named in the notice of directors. Should anything happen to them, the corporation would be unable to act.

Typically, also at the first meeting, the directors will adopt arrangements for carrying on the formal legal business of the corporation, including how notice is given of meetings of directors and shareholders, what constitutes a quorum, who may sign contracts on behalf of the corporation, and what the offices of the corporation will be. These arrangements are usually set out in a by-law. To take effect, a by-law must be passed by the directors, but it continues in effect only if it is passed by the shareholders at their next meeting following the approval by the directors (*CBCA*, s. 103). Because making, amending, and repealing by-laws ultimately requires shareholder approval, including these arrangements in a by-law serves to entrench them as part of the corporation's constitution.[44]

At the first meeting, directors will pass resolutions dealing with other organizational matters, such as appointing officers and an auditor, and making banking arrangements, such as authorizing certain people to sign cheques on behalf of the corporation. Once the shares are issued it is common, though not necessary, to have a shareholders' meeting at which any by-laws approved by the directors are voted on.

A final organizational step that often occurs in corporations with few shareholders is that the shareholders enter into an agreement to govern their relationship with each other. Shareholders may wish to customize the way in which the corporation is governed by agreeing to alter the rights and obligations provided for in the *CBCA*. For example, all shareholders may agree to vote their shares for certain people as directors, or to have certain matters, which would otherwise require approval only by the directors, put to a shareholder vote. Shareholder agreements also often deal with the circumstances in which shares may be transferred, such as by giving each shareholder a right to be offered first any shares a shareholder proposes to sell to a third party.[45]

In order to determine what rules govern a corporation, its shareholders, directors, and officers, it is necessary to take into account not just the governing corporate statute and the case law but also the elements of the corporate constitution identified above: the articles of incorporation, the

---

44   See below.

45   Shareholders' agreements are discussed in section H in chapter 7.

by-laws, directors' resolutions, shareholders' resolutions, and any share-holders' agreement. These documents are agreed to by the directors or shareholders, or both, and represent, in that sense, private arrangements between them. They are private arrangements which are bounded by various mandatory provisions of the corporate statutes and are, to a greater or lesser extent, enforceable through statutory mechanisms.

All these documents must be maintained by the corporation at its registered office (*CBCA*, s. 20), usually in something called a "minute book," and shareholders and creditors must be given access to them (*CBCA*, s. 21). Articles and any other document filed with the Director appointed under the *CBCA*, such as the notice of directors and notice of registered office, are placed in a publicly accessible record.

E. FUNCTION OF CORPORATE LAW

1) Introduction

A business organization is used to run a business, and various classes of people, including, in particular, the shareholders, have an interest in that business. In chapter 1 we described the business organization as a nexus of relationships among stakeholders. In the corporation, these stakeholders are the shareholder/owners; the managers, consisting of the officers and directors; employees; creditors, both trade and financial; customers; the public; and government. In this section we deal with what function corporations and corporate law fulfil in relation to these stakeholders.

In general, corporate law operates to encourage people to invest money in starting, maintaining, and expanding businesses. To understand how it does so, it is necessary first to consider how people make decisions about investing. The basic corporate finance model for investment decision making holds that people make decisions to invest based on an evaluation of the returns expected from the investment and the risk associated with those returns. The returns are what the investor will receive from the investment. They may take the form of interest on a loan, dividends on shares, an increase in the price of shares, or something else. Risk may be thought of as the likelihood that the expected returns will be received in light of the range of possible returns the investor could receive. The rational investor will invest only if the expected returns are sufficient, given the risks associated with those returns. The riskier the investment, the higher must be the expected returns because the investor will require compensation for bearing the additional risk. In choosing between two investments promising the same returns, the rational investor should invest in the one promising returns that are less risky. Figure 3.1 demonstrates the implications of the relationship of risk and return for investment decision making.

Figure 3.1   Example of How Risk and Expected Returns
Affect Investment Decision Making

Canada Savings Bonds (CSBs) are a low-risk investment because the payment obligation is undertaken by the federal government. Indeed, since there is virtually no other possible return than the stated interest rate, the range of possible returns and the risk is 0.

Because CSBs are a "no risk" investment, you might be prepared to buy them when they promise a return in the form of interest of, say, 8 percent.

By contrast, investing in the shares of a diamond exploration business is much riskier. If the business finds diamonds, your shares may skyrocket in value such that the best possible return may be, say, 500 percent. On the other hand, it is certainly possible that no diamonds will ever be found, in which case not only will you receive no positive return but your shares may be worthless. This worst case represents a negative return, or a loss of 100 percent. So the range of possible outcomes is from a 500 percent gain to a 100 percent loss. Given the risk that this range of possible outcomes represents, an investor would not invest in the diamond exploration business unless she expected returns substantially higher than the returns on the no-risk CSBs.

It should be clear that, other things being equal, a business opportunity will become more attractive for investors as the returns increase or as the risk associated with those returns diminishes, or both. Corporate law does both and so operates to encourage investment. As will be discussed below, corporate law also contains certain provisions that provide protection for other stakeholders,[46] though this is very much a secondary purpose of corporate law. The main legal ways in which the interests of other stakeholders are protected are through regulation in other areas (e.g., commercial law, labour law, and products liability law).

2) Corporate Law Increases Returns

Like partnership law, corporate law provides certain presumptive or default rules that apply to govern the relationship between the corporation and its shareholders in the absence of some other rule being agreed

---

46   See sections E(3) and (4) in this chapter.

on by the corporation and its shareholders as expressed in the articles, by-laws, or a shareholders' agreement. In this way, corporate law provides a sort of standard form contract that parties setting up a corporation may adopt, in whole or in part, or may replace with their own arrangements. To the extent that this standard form contract is a good approximation of what most parties would have worked out for themselves if they had the time and money to do so, the availability of the standard form will save the parties money. In economists' jargon, it reduces the transaction costs of setting up a corporation. Some examples of these default rules are the rules regarding the calling and conduct of shareholders' and directors' meetings (*CBCA*, ss. 94–114 & 117–119). These kinds of default rules are called "enabling rules," and increase returns to shareholders by reducing the costs of setting up a corporation.

As discussed in more detail in the next section, corporate law also reduces costs by providing limited liability. Although there are alternative ways of reducing liability, such as contractual provisions and insurance, they are not usually as inexpensive or comprehensive as incorporation.

3) Corporate Law Decreases Shareholder Risk

a) Limited Liability
As discussed below, though shareholders are often said to have limited liability for the obligations of the corporations, this is really only a somewhat inaccurate way of saying that the most a shareholder can lose in connection with the business of the corporation is the amount of his investment. Corporate law provides that a shareholder is not liable for the debts and obligations of the corporation at all.

By providing a simple cost-effective mechanism to limit shareholders' potential loss, corporate law reduces the risk associated with investing. It caps the worst possible return at 100 percent of a shareholder's investment. This may be contrasted with a partnership in which the maximum loss is all of a partner's business and personal assets. Capping the risk encourages investment. The size of the incentive created by corporate law will depend on the cost effectiveness of corporate limited liability as compared with other ways of limiting risk, such as through insurance or contractual provisions as well as how effectively it protects shareholders. We will discuss some of the limits of limited liability below.

It is important to note that limited liability does not eliminate risk, but shifts it to other stakeholders, such as employees and creditors. Limiting the pool of assets that creditors and employees may claim against to the assets of the corporation, while a benefit to shareholders, increases the likelihood that there will be insufficient assets to pay the creditors and employees. By providing limited liability, corporate law represents an intervention in the marketplace that strikes a particular balance between the interests of shareholders and other claimants against the corporation which favours shareholders.

b) Mandatory Rules Protecting All Shareholders

Corporate law reduces the risk of investing in a corporation by imposing certain mandatory rules designed to protect shareholders from abuse by management. We will discuss the problem of management misbehaviour in more detail below,[47] but for the purposes of this introduction it is sufficient simply to note that to the extent that management is carried out by different people from those who own the corporation, the shareholders, there is a risk that managers will act to benefit their own interests instead of those of the corporation and the shareholders. Corporate law imposes standards of behaviour on managers, such as their fiduciary duty to act in the best interests of the corporation (*CBCA*, s. 122(1)(a)), facilitates shareholder monitoring of managers, such as by requiring disclosure of financial information (*CBCA*, s. 155(1)), and provides a variety of remedial procedures for shareholders to obtain relief in the event that management misbehaves (e.g., providing for an application to obtain compliance with the corporate statute, *CBCA*, s. 247). In all these ways, corporate law decreases risk. These rules also increase expected returns for shareholders to the extent that they prevent managers from enriching themselves at the expense of the corporation.

c) Mandatory Rules Protecting Minority Shareholders

Finally, corporate law contains a variety of mandatory rules to protect the interests of minority shareholders from exploitation by the majority. Since corporations operate based on majority rule, any person or group of persons who has control of a majority of the votes attached to the corporation's shares has control of the corporation. A majority shareholder may exert its power in ways beneficial to itself at the expense of the corporation and minority shareholders, such as by causing the corporation to enter into a favourable contract with itself. To guard against this risk, some of these mandatory rules impose two-thirds majority requirements for shareholder approval of certain fundamental changes to the corporation, such as the sale of "all or substantially all the property of a corporation" (*CBCA*, s. 189(3)), and rights for minority shareholders to

---

47   See chapters 7 and 8.

be bought out if they disagree with the outcome of such a vote (*CBCA*, s. 190). Also, since directors are elected by majority vote, there is a risk that management activity will favour the interests of majority shareholders over those of the minority. As a result, the protection referred to in the previous section are more important to minority shareholders than majority shareholders. All these shareholder protection devices decrease the risk associated with minority shareholder investment and are likely to increase expected returns. Because they impose limits on control by majority shareholders, they correspondingly increase the risks and decrease the returns for majority shareholder investors.

4) Balancing Mandatory Rules Protecting Non-shareholder Stakeholders

As mentioned above, protection of the interests of stakeholders other than shareholders typically is provided by legislation outside the corporate law area. Nevertheless, corporate law does contain certain mandatory rules in favour of such stakeholders. For example, a corporation may not pay dividends to shareholders if it is insolvent, or would be after making the payment, (*CBCA*, s. 42). The courts have also developed certain rules that permit them to disregard corporate law's limited liability rule and to impose personal liability on shareholders.[48] These mandatory rules represent a further intervention in the marketplace to shift the risk associated with business activities carried on by a corporation back to the corporation and the shareholders.

Throughout this book we will be looking at how corporate law operates to encourage investment through the combination of mandatory and enabling rules described above as well as the extent to which it balances these incentive measures with rules protecting the interests of other stakeholders.

F. THE RELATIONSHIP BETWEEN CORPORATE LAW AND SECURITIES LAW

Each province has a law concerned with regulating the marketplace for the trading of securities,[49] with a view to ensuring that participants in

---

48   See "Disregard of Separate Corporate Personality" below.

49   Securities are shares or debt obligations, like bonds, or other claims on a corporation or other business organization. See the definition in section 1(1) of the Ontario *Securities Act*, R.S.O. 1990, c. S.5.

the market act honestly and that buyers and sellers have sufficient information to make decisions about investing in securities. These laws, referred to as securities laws, generally seek to accomplish this objective by requiring securities dealers and other participants in the securities industry to be registered and supervised, and by requiring disclosure of information regarding securities to be sold to the public both at the time the securities are issued and on an ongoing basis.

In this way securities laws have a significant effect on the manner in which corporations may raise funds by selling shares and other securities. To this extent, securities laws overlap very little with corporate law, since the latter is not concerned with the operation of markets. In the interests of investor protection on an ongoing basis, however, securities laws have evolved in ways that overlap with corporate law in important ways. For example, both securities and corporate law govern the disclosure that must be made to shareholders in connection with meetings, and both are concerned with ensuring that corporate decisions are made in ways which are fair to minority shareholder interests. As a result, many corporations, especially those with shareholders in more than one province, are subject of multiple, sometimes inconsistent, requirements. This complexity has caused corporations to lobby for a single set of requirements or, at least, acceptance of the requirements of one jurisdiction as meeting the other jurisdictions.[50]

A number of distinctions can be made between corporate and securities laws:

- *Scope of Application* The scope of application of corporate and securities law are different. The corporate laws of a jurisdiction are concerned only with corporations incorporated in that jurisdiction. Corporate laws apply to the corporation and its shareholders whether or not the corporation operates in that jurisdiction or the shareholders are resident there. The securities laws of a jurisdiction, by contrast, are concerned with all business organizations selling securities to investors within that jurisdiction regardless of the jurisdiction of incorporation of the business organization. Because securities laws are directed to the operation of markets, they are concerned with prospective investors as much as current shareholders, whereas, for the most part, corporate law affects only current shareholders.

---

50   In response to this pressure, federal corporate regulators have issued a policy statement which provides that annual meeting material prepared in accordance with certain provincial securities laws will be accepted as conforming to the *CBCA* requirements. Securities regulators are continually engaged in a process of harmonizing their requirements. See chapter 11.

- *Enforcement* Under many provincial securities regimes, securities regulators, such as the Ontario Securities Commission, have broad discretionary powers to ensure that participants in the securities markets are acting in the public interest. In some provinces, especially Ontario, the securities commission has actively used its administrative and quasi-judicial powers to regulate corporate activity. Although corporate statutes provide that the government official responsible for corporations may play a role in enforcing the law,[51] in practice they rarely do. The enforcement of corporate law rules is generally left to the parties affected.
- *Substantive Law* Corporate law addresses a significant number of areas not dealt with in securities laws. The nature of the corporation, the detailed enabling rules for the incorporation and operation of corporations, and the rules regarding the nature of shares are not addressed at all by securities law.

G. THE NATURE OF THE CORPORATION

1) Separate Legal Existence and Limited Liability

Incorporation brings into existence a new legal person whose rights and obligations may be thought of as analogous to those of a human person.[52] Section 15(1) *CBCA* provides that a corporation "has the capacity and, subject to this Act, the rights, powers and privileges of a natural person." In this section we discuss what this definition means in legal and practical terms.

The separate legal existence of the corporation was authoritatively confirmed by the House of Lords in *Salomon* v. *Salomon & Co.*[53] In that case, Aron Salomon transferred a leather boot business carried on by him as a sole proprietor to a corporation in which he and six of his family members were shareholders. As part of the consideration paid for transfer of the business, the corporation issued debentures to him

---

51   See, for example, *CBCA*, above note 17, s. 239, which allows the Director appointed to administer the *CBCA* to commence oppression actions. Under the *OBCA*, above note 20, the Ontario Securities Commission is charged with the enforcement of the Act.

52   The current corporate law as described in this section is based on the notion that the corporation is solely a creation of the statute. There are, however, other theoretical constructions of the nature of corporate personality. For a brief discussion of these alternate constructions, see Ziegel, above note 9 at 138–39.

53   [1897] A.C. 22 (H.L.) [*Salomon*].

which represented a claim against the corporation for £10,000, secured against the assets of the business now owned by the corporation. It also issued shares to him. As a result, after the transfer, he held the vast majority of the shares and was in effective control of the corporation as well as being a secured creditor. Shortly after the business was transferred to the corporation, it ran into serious financial difficulty, despite Salomon's best efforts. Ultimately, a liquidator was appointed to gather in the assets of the corporation, pay off the debts, and transfer any remaining assets to the shareholders. If the secured claim of Salomon were paid first, as it normally would be, there would have been no assets left out of which to pay the unsecured creditors.

The liquidator claimed that the corporation was a sham in that it was merely Salomon carrying on business in another name. It was argued that Salomon was personally carrying on the business; the corporation was merely his agent for doing so. Since the corporation was only an agent, Salomon's claim under the debentures was really a claim against himself and so unenforceable. The result of this argument, in effect, was that there would be sufficient assets to ensure that the unsecured creditors would be paid.

The House of Lords rejected the liquidator's claim. It held that what Salomon had done was exactly what was contemplated in the *Companies Act* of 1862 and that all the requirements of the Act had been complied with. In these circumstances, there was no reason not to give effect to the separate legal existence of the corporation and to permit Aron Salomon's claim to be paid ahead of the unsecured creditors. It did not matter that Aron Salomon was in effective control of the corporation, the other six shareholders being family members under his control and, as such, in the words of Lord MacNaughton, "mere nominees of Mr. Salomon — mere dummies." The House of Lords said there was no requirement in the Act that the shareholders each have a mind of his own.[54] Just because the business was precisely the same after it was transferred to the corporation as it was before, and the same persons were the managers and the same hands ultimately received the financial rewards associated with the business, this did not make the corporation the agent of the shareholder.

---

54   This apparently was not the intention of the English Parliament. The purpose for requiring seven shareholders was to avoid incorporation of small partnerships (P. Ireland, "The Triumph of the Company Legal Form, 1856–1914" in J. Adams, ed., *Essays for Clive Schmitthoff* (London: Professional Books, 1983) at 29, cited in Ziegel, above note 9 at 122). Incorporation by a small number or even a single person is expressly permitted under Canadian corporate statutes.

This case is almost universally cited for the proposition that the corporation is a separate legal entity. Notwithstanding the strong position taken in this case and the substantial influence it has had on the development of Canadian corporate law, we will discuss below the various ways in which the courts have eroded the separateness of legal personality.[55] In the remainder of this section we will flesh out the consequences of the separate legal personality of the corporation.

As indicated in Salomon, the separate legal existence of the corporation means that a shareholder may also be a creditor, even a secured creditor of the corporation. This is permitted under Canadian corporate law. The only restriction is that the creation of a debt or the granting of a security interest may not be effected if the purpose is to defeat the claims of other creditors.[56] Another consequence of the separate existence of the corporation is that a corporation owns its own property. The shareholders have certain property-like rights in the corporation, but no property interest in the assets of the corporation.[57]

The specific bundle of rights that shareholders have will depend on the provisions set out in the articles, as discussed in chapter 6, and the corporate statute. In general, shares represent a claim on the residual value of the corporation after the claims of all creditors have been paid.[58] The value of this residual claim will be a function of the value of the corporation's business. Unfortunately, valuing a business is a complex and inevitably imprecise exercise because the value will depend on a variety of factors that will change over time. The value of a business will depend, in part, on the value of the tangible assets owned by the business, which themselves may be difficult to assess. How much is a piece of commercial real estate in downtown Toronto worth? It will also depend on intangible assets that are even harder to value. How much is Coca-Cola's "Coke" trade-mark worth? The value will also depend on what you intend to do with it. Most businesses are worth more as an operating unit or as a "going concern" than if the assets were sold piecemeal. The value of an

---

55   See "Disregard of Separate Corporate Personality," below.

56   See, for example, the Ontario *Fraudulent Conveyances Act*, R.S.O. 1990, c. F-29 [*FCA*], and the federal *Bankruptcy and Insolvency Act*, R.S.C. 1985, c. B-3.

57   *Army & Navy Department Store* v. *M.N.R.,* [1953] 2 S.C.R. 496, approved in *Bow Valley Husky (Bermuda) Ltd.* v. *Saint John Shipbuilding Ltd.* (1995), 130 Nfld. & P.E.I.R. 92 at 105 (Nfld C.A.) [*Bow Valley*].

58   Where there is only one class of shares, they must have this residual claim (s. 24(3), *CBCA*, above note 17). Where there is more than one class of shares, at least one must have this claim (*CBCA*, s. 24(4)). Typically, the others will have some other limited claim on assets, such as a claim to the return of the amount invested for those shares. See chapter 6.

ongoing business in excess of the value of the assets sold piecemeal is called "goodwill." The expected future growth of the business will also be a significant factor.[59]

The courts considered a claim to the residual value represented by shares of a corporation in *Kosmopoulos* v. *Constitution Insurance Co. of Canada*.[60] Mr. Kosmopoulos was the sole shareholder in and the only director of a corporation carrying on a leather-goods business. Mr. Kosmopolous was not careful to distinguish his personal rights and obligations from those of the corporation and, as a result, the insurance on the assets of the corporation's business was taken out in Mr. Kosmopoulos's name rather than in the name of the corporation. When a fire damaged assets of the business, the insurance company refused to pay on the ground that Mr. Kosmopoulos did not have an "insurable interest" in the assets. The Supreme Court ultimately determined that even though he had no property interest in the assets, his interest as the sole shareholder in the corporation gave him such a financial stake in the corporation that it could amount to an insurable interest.

Recall that with partnerships, a partner cannot be an employee of the partnership because the partnership is not a legal entity separate from the partners. Since a corporation is a separate entity, a shareholder may be an employee of the corporation in which he holds shares just as he may be a secured creditor. In *Lee* v. *Lee's Air Farming Ltd.*[61] a person was held to be capable of entering a contract of employment with a corporation of which he held all but one of the shares and was appointed "governing director . . . for life." The Judicial Committee of the Privy Council expressly held that it did not matter that he would be negotiating his employment contract as an employee, with himself acting on behalf of the corporation.[62]

---

59   For a discussion of business valuation from a lawyer's point of view, see V. Krishna, "Determining the 'Fair Value' of Corporate Shares" (1988) 13 Can. Bus. L.J. 132, and F.M. Buckley, M. Gillen, & R. Yalden, *Corporations: Principles and Policies*, 3d ed. (Toronto: Emond Montgomery, 1995) at 1–13.

60   (1983), 42 O.R. (2d) 428 (C.A.), aff'd [1987] 1 S.C.R. 2 [*Kosmopoulos*].

61   (1960), [1961] A.C. 12 (P.C.).

62   A final issue relating to the nature of the corporate personality arises in the context of criminal proceedings against the corporation when a director, officer, or senior employee is called to testify: Does a corporation have a right against self-incrimination and, if so, when is it violated? See the discussion of the right against self-incrimination guaranteed by section 11(d) of the *Charter of Rights and Freedoms*, Part I of the *Constitution Act, 1982*, being Schedule B to the *Canada Act 1982* (U.K.), 1982, c. 11, in section J in this chapter. See also S.A. Trainor, "A Comparative Analysis of a Corporation's Right against Self-Incrimination" (1995) 18 Fordham Int'l L.J. 2139.

One important implication for lawyers of the separation between the legal personality of the corporation and its shareholders is that lawyers must be careful to determine for whom they are acting when conflicts between the corporation and its shareholders or among shareholders arise.[63]

2) Balancing Rules Protecting Other Stakeholders

a) Limits on Limited Liability

Limited liability is a creation of the law designed to encourage entrepreneurship by shifting the risk of business activity from shareholders to other stakeholders. Although it is often said that the courts "rigidly adhere" to limited liability as a feature of separate corporate personality, there are a wide variety of circumstances in which they do not, with the result that personal liability is imposed on shareholders, directors, and officers. Liability is also imposed on directors and officers for torts committed in connection with the corporation's business as well as under certain statutory provisions. All these sources of personal liability are discussed in detail elsewhere in this book. The following discussion is intended simply to identify the sources of liability.

Despite the express statutory grant of limited liability (*CBCA*, s. 45),[64] the courts have arrogated to themselves the power to disregard the separateness of corporate personality. Unfortunately, the many cases in which this approach has been taken "illustrate no consistent principle."[65] Section H of this chapter deals with these cases under the heading "Disregard of Separate Corporate Personality."

Another source of personal liability is torts. Directors and officers of corporations may be held liable for torts committed in connection with the corporation's business where they have some involvement in the activity constituting the tort. It is important to keep in mind the conceptual distinction between imposing liability on corporate managers — the directors and officers — and on those putting their money at risk — the shareholders. In the former case, it is at least not precise to say that the corporation's existence is being disregarded and limited liability is

---

63 See Law Society of Upper Canada, *Professional Conduct Handbook* (Toronto: Law Society of Upper Canada, 1995), Rule 5.

64 The *CBCA*, above note 17, itself imposes liability on shareholders in certain limited circumstances: section 38 (distributions to shareholders contrary to the Act), section 146(5) (liabilities of directors when directors' powers assumed in unanimous shareholders' agreement), and section 226(5) (court may permit action against shareholders to recover distributions on dissolution of the corporation).

65 *Clarkson Co. v. Zhelka*, [1967], 2 O.R. 565 (H.C.J.) [*Clarkson*].

being destroyed. Liability is imposed based on the policy that individuals should be responsible for their torts. Nevertheless, imposing liability in cases where a director or an officer is acting in the course of her responsibilities clearly circumscribes the separateness of the legal person. Also, the practical effect may be much the same as disregarding separate legal existence since, at least in small corporations, the managers and the owners are likely to be the same people, such that imposing liability on managers is likely to create disincentives to engage in business activity of the same magnitude as if liability had been imposed on the shareholders. Tort liability is discussed in section I under "Liability of Corporate Managers for Torts."

To the extent that managers and shareholders are the same persons, all sources of personal liability for managers have the effect of eroding the effective protection of limited liability. A variety of other sources of management liability may be identified. Each involves a corresponding benefit to some non-shareholder stakeholder. Directors are liable, for example, under corporate statutes for unpaid wages in certain limited circumstances (e.g., *CBCA*, s. 119). Directors may also incur liability under other federal and provincial statutes for corporate obligations, such as liability for income tax withholdings on employee wages which the corporation has failed to remit to Revenue Canada.[66] Most other statutes imposing liability on management do not permit other stakeholders to recover against directors and officers directly. Instead, a finding of liability means that the manager is guilty of an offence and subject to a fine or even imprisonment,[67] thus discouraging actions contrary to the legislatively established public policy which such provisions protect.

Managers may be liable if they act in a manner that is "oppressive to or is unfairly prejudicial to or that unfairly disregards the interests of any security holder, creditor, director or officer" (*CBCA*, s. 241). This provision was intended primarily to protect shareholders in small corporations and has been used extensively for this purpose. The class of persons who may seek relief, however, includes "any other person who, in the discretion of the court, is a proper person to make an application." In an increasing number of cases, creditors and other types of claimants have been permitted to seek relief under this provision. The range of relief the court may grant is virtually unlimited, and liability has been imposed on directors and shareholders. As a result, liability for oppression is another way in which the protection of limited liability may be lost.

---

66   *ITA*, above note 39, s. 227.1.

67   For example, *Occupational Health and Safety Act*, R.S.O. 1990, c. 0.1.

Finally, there are also sources of liability for which the beneficiary is the corporation. Each director and officer has a fiduciary duty to act in the best interests of the corporation and a duty to exercise reasonable care, diligence, and skill in discharging his obligations (*CBCA*, s. 122(1)). In addition, directors have a specific liability to the corporation for issuing shares for inadequate consideration and authorizing certain payments contrary to the Act (*CBCA*, s. 118). These restrictions have an indirect benefit for other stakeholders in the sense that they protect the interests of the legal entity against which they have a claim.

As noted, in practice all these sources of liability for directors and officers reduce the benefit of limited liability, especially in the small corporation where the same person is a shareholder and a manager. In this introductory chapter we will deal only with the case law on two of examples: disregarding separate corporate personality and with it, limited liability, and liability in tort. The oppression remedy will be discussed in chapter 9, "Shareholder Remedies." Managers' liability for breach of fiduciary duty and duty of care and their statutory liabilities will be addressed in chapter 8, "Duties of Directors and Officers."

b) Other Rules Protecting Non-shareholder Stakeholders

Before we proceed to examine the disregard of corporate personality and liability in tort, we should note several other ways in which corporate law seeks to balance the shifting of risk to non-shareholder stakeholders caused by limited liability.

First, the *CBCA* requires all corporations to have as part of their name a word or abbreviation which indicates that the business is being carried on by an entity with limited liability. Every corporation's name must include one of the following: Corporation (or Corp.), Limited (or Ltd.), Incorporated (or Inc.), or the French equivalents of these expressions (*CBCA*, s. 10(1)). Usually, this "legal" part of the name follows the rest of the name. Each corporation must set out its full name on all "contracts, invoices, negotiable instruments and orders for goods or services made by or on behalf of the corporation" (*CBCA*, s. 10(6)). A corporation may use another name, but the other name must not include one of the listed legal elements, so people dealing with it do not believe they are dealing with two corporations. The full corporate name must appear as well. So, for example, a corporation's letterhead might say "123456 Canada Inc. doing business as Landco Real Estate Development." Failing to comply with the requirement to set out the full corporate name on the listed documents is an offence (*CBCA*, ss. 10(5) & 251; *Business Names Act* (Ontario),[68] ss. 2(6) & 10).

---

68 R.S.O. 1990, c. B.17 (*OBNA*).

Second, the corporate statutes have certain rules protecting the assets of the corporation for the benefit of creditors and others with claims against a corporation. Unlike some other jurisdictions, Canadian corporate statutes no longer require any minimum investment by shareholders (called "capitalization"); a corporation may issue one share for $1 and then start to carry on business. Although the absence of a requirement for some meaningful financial commitment on the part of shareholders is sometimes said to encourage frivolous incorporations, it is important to note that minimum initial capitalization requirements do little to protect non-shareholder stakeholders after incorporation. Money invested by shareholders does not create a pool against which creditors and others may claim. It will be used for the purposes of the business, such as to purchase assets or to pay expenses. There is no guarantee that shareholder's investment will not be squandered or lost. Also, there are a variety of ways to get around minimum capitalization requirements. For this reason the approach taken in Canadian corporate statutes is to impose rules designed to prevent certain uses of a corporation's assets which will render it unable to pay its obligations. For example, shares can only be issued for money or property that has a value not less than the fair equivalent of what the corporation could have got if it had issued shares for money. Shares cannot be issued on credit (*CBCA*, s. 25(3)).[69] The *CBCA* also contains restrictions on distributions to shareholders. The corporation cannot pay dividends, redeem or repurchase shares, or provide financial assistance to shareholders, directors, officers, or employees if the corporation is insolvent or would be made insolvent by the payment (*CBCA*, ss. 34, 35, 36, & 44). The *CBCA* restricts certain other payments, such as commissions paid in connection with the purchase of shares (s. 41), indemnities (s. 124), and payments on the exercise of certain shareholder remedies (ss. 190 & 241). For some of these payments certain financial tests, in addition to the solvency test, must be met. Directors are personally responsible for any payment made in contravention of these rules (*CBCA*, s. 118).

Finally, as noted above, the corporate statutes provide for certain public filings so that people dealing with a corporation will be able to find out something about it. The articles, notice of registered office, and notice of directors become matters of public record once filed.[70] Any time any of the information in any of these documents changes, a new filing must be made. As well, certain annual filings must be made. An

---

69   See chapter 6.
70   See chapter 4.

annual return with certain basic information must be filed under the *CBCA* (s. 263, Form 22). In Ontario, corporations doing business in the province must also file an initial return and an annual return (*Corporations Information Act* (Ontario),[71] ss. 3, 3.1). Corporations that have distributed their shares to the public must file their financial statements under the *CBCA* (s. 160). Additional filings for public corporations are typically required under provincial securities laws.

H. DISREGARD OF SEPARATE CORPORATE PERSONALITY

1) Introduction

Separate corporate personality is the principal way in which the risk of business activity is shifted from shareholders to other stakeholders.[72] Although courts "rigidly adhere"[73] to the separateness of corporate personality, they have refused to accept it in the three situations described below. In these cases the courts disregard the separate existence of the corporation in relation to some specific claim, usually the claim of a creditor of the corporation who would not be able to succeed against it because it has insufficient assets to satisfy the creditor's claim. Disregarding the corporation for such specific purposes does not destroy its separate existence for all other purposes, but only for the limited purpose of granting relief to the creditor directly against the shareholder. Unfortunately, the cases in this area "illustrate no consistent principle"[74] The courts typically refer to disregarding the personality of the corporation by the picturesque if somewhat antiquated and ultimately obscuring expression, piercing the corporate veil.[75]

2) It Is Just Not Fair

Courts have held that they have the power to ignore the separate existence of the corporation where to fail to do so would yield a result which is "flagrantly opposed to justice."[76] It is not clear what this means and

---

71   R.S.O. 1990, c. C.39.

72   See *CBCA*, above note 17, ss. 15 & 45, and *Salomon*, above note 53.

73   *Big Bend Hotel v. Security Mutual Casualty Co.* (1980), 19 B.C.L.R. 102 at 108 (S.C.) [*Big Bend Hotel*].

74   *Clarkson*, above note 65.

75   *Littlewoods Mail Order Stores Ltd.* v. *McGregor (Inspector of Taxes)*, [1969] 3 All E.R. 855 (C.A.).

76   *Kosmopoulos*, above note 60 at 10 (S.C.C.).

there is no easy way to predict when a court will be provoked to act on this basis. One can say that the courts are likely to be more sympathetic to claims by third parties, such as creditors and tort victims, than by shareholders who benefit from separate corporate personality.[77] There are, however, cases in which the courts have disregarded the separate existence of the corporation for the benefit of shareholders.[78] Also, the courts are more likely to disregard separate personality if doing so results in liability being imposed on another corporation rather than an individual.[79]

In many cases where separate corporate personality is disregarded, there is some element of unfairness in the way the corporation is being used, combined with one or more of the other bases described below.

3) Objectionable Purpose

Where a corporation has been incorporated in order to do something or to facilitate the doing of something that would be illegal or improper for the individual shareholders to do personally, or in order to reduce taxes paid to Revenue Canada, the courts have been willing to disregard separate legal personality in some circumstances.

The most common ground relied on by the courts is fraud. One set of circumstances in which fraud has been held to be a basis for disregarding separate corporate existence involves using the corporation to effect a purpose or commit an act that the shareholder could not effect or commit on her own. *Big Bend Hotel Ltd.*[80] is an example. A person who had had fire loss insurance cancelled as a result of a previous fire loss claim incorporated a corporation to own a hotel and to apply for fire insurance. When the hotel burned down, the insurance company refused to pay and the corporation sued. The court held that the corporation was being used to disguise a fraud and refused to permit the corporation's claim. *Gilford Motor Co. Ltd. v. Horne*[81] is another example. The defendant had entered into a non-competition agreement with his former employer. He incorporated a corporation to carry on the competing

---

77   *Ibid.; Rich v. Enns*, [1995] 6 W.W.R. 257 (Man. C.A.).
78   For example, *DHN Food Distributors Ltd. v. London Borough of Tower Hamlets,* [1976] 3 All E.R. 462 (C.A.) [*DHN*]; *Manley Inc. v. Fallis* (1977), 2 B.L.R. 277 (Ont. C.A.).
79   *De Salaberry Realties Ltd. v. M.N.R.* (1974), 46 D.L.R. (3d) 100 (Fed. T.D.) [*De Salaberry*]; *DHN, ibid.*
80   Above note 73.
81   [1933] Ch. 935 (C.A.).

business. The court held that the corporation could not be used to permit the defendant to avoid his contractual obligations.[82]

Another example of fraud arises where assets are transferred from a corporation that has some obligation to a third party to another corporation under the control of the same person or to a shareholder for the purpose of rendering the corporation incapable of performing its obligations. Although such a transaction may be attacked under provincial fraudulent conveyances legislation[83] or, as discussed below, using the tort of inducing breach of contract, it has also been held to be an appropriate case for disregarding the separate existence of the corporation.[84]

Sometimes the fraud will consist of a representation to a third party that the person the third party is dealing with is not the corporation but an individual or, perhaps, another corporation that has substantial assets.[85] In order for a court to disregard the separate existence of the corporation to impose liability on a shareholder, however, the fraud must be such as to misrepresent the identity of the corporation, not merely some attribute of the corporation, such as its assets. In *B.G. Preeco I (Pacific Coast) Ltd.* v. *Bon Street Holdings Ltd.*[86] the court refused to disregard the separate existence of the corporation in an obvious case of fraud. Two individual defendants acted on behalf of a corporation named Bon Street Developments Ltd. in negotiating the purchase of some property. To the knowledge of the vendors, the corporation had substantial assets. Just prior to the closing of the transaction the two individuals changed the name of the corporation to Bon Street Holdings and the name of a corporation without assets to Bon Street Developments Ltd. The contract was signed on behalf of the new Bon Street Developments Ltd. While the court found the individual defendants

---

82   Buckley calls this case an example of gapfilling (Buckley, above note 59). The employer failed to specifically provide that competition through a corporation was included in the defendant's non-competition promise. In refusing to recognize the corporation, the court was simply filling this gap in the contract (at 100–1).

83   For example, *FCA*, above note 56.

84   For example, *Fidelity Electronics of Canada Ltd.* v. *Fuss* (1995), 77 O.A.C. 34 (Div. Ct.). See J.S. Ziegel, "Creditors as Corporate Stakeholders: The Quiet Revolution — an Anglo-Canadian Perspective" (1993) 43 U.T.L.J. 511, regarding the trend towards imposing obligations to creditors on the directors of corporations that are insolvent or on the verge of insolvency. Ziegel notes that this trend is evidenced both legislatively and in the courts in other Commonwealth jurisdictions, but, with the exception of increasing access to the oppression remedy, is largely absent in Canada.

85   For example, *Pacific Rim Installations Ltd.* v. *Tilt-Up Construction Ltd.* (1978), 5 B.C.L.R. 231 (Co. Ct.).

86   (1989), 37 B.C.L.R. (2d) 258 (C.A.).

liable for fraud, it was not prepared to disregard the separate existence of the insolvent corporation to hold them or the original Bon Street Developments Ltd. liable under the contract because the fraud did not relate to the identity of the corporation, but only to its assets.

This case provides an interesting example of a practical difference between liability in tort for fraud and liability for breach of contract in terms of the damages available. The plaintiffs had pursued their claim that the separate existence of the corporation should be disregarded and liability for breach of contract imposed on the original Bon Street Developments Ltd. or on the individuals because the breach of contract claim against the new Bon Street Developments Ltd. was worthless and the measure of damages for the fraud judgment against the individuals was much less (about $500,000) than the damages that might have been obtained for breach of contract (about $1,400,000). Tort damages are intended to put the tort victim in the same position he would have been in if the tort had not been committed, whereas contract damages are intended to put the innocent party in the same position as if the contract had been fulfilled. As a result, only contract damages would have taken into account the substantial increase in the property's value after the breach.

As illustrated in *B.G. Preeco I (Pacific Coast)* v. *Bon Street Holdings Ltd.* and discussed in the following section, fraudulent representations by a director, officer, or shareholder that a corporation has sufficient assets to meet its obligations will result in personal liability for fraud for the director, officer, or shareholder.[87]

In several cases liability has been attached where the representation was not fraudulent and even in the absence of the usual contract law requirement that the representation be relied on.[88] In *Wolfe* v. *Moir*[89] an officer of a corporation that operated a roller skating rink was held personally liable for negligence in connection with an injury to a skater. The basis of the court's decision was that the business was advertised using the officer's name, and not the corporation's name, in contravention of the *ABCA*.[90]

---

87   *Baltimore Aircoil of Canada Inc.* v. *Process Cooling Systems Inc.* (1993), 16 O.R. (3d) 324 (Gen. Div.).

88   G.H.L. Fridman, *The Law of Contracts in Canada*, 2d. ed. (Toronto: Carswell, 1986) at 277.

89   (1969), 69 W.W.R. 70 (Alta. S.C.T.D.) [*Wolfe*].

90   See also *Tato Enterprises Ltd.* v. *Rode* (1979), 17 A.R. 432 (Dist. Ct.) [*Tato*].

Traditionally, courts have been sympathetic to arguments that the use of a corporation to reduce taxes is an improper purpose and a basis for disregarding separate corporate personality. The "interests of the Revenue" have been considered to be a special case.[91] In *De Salaberry*,[92] for example, the court disregarded the separate existence of one corporation in a large corporate group. It had been argued that a sale of land by the corporation was an isolated transaction such that the proceeds should be characterized as a capital gain. The court held that when one disregarded the separate existence of the corporation, it became clear that the sale was part of a business of buying and selling land being carried on by the whole group, so the proceeds from the sale were income from a business and taxed at higher rates.

With its decision in *Stubart Investments Ltd.* v. *M.N.R.*,[93] the Supreme Court of Canada signalled that the courts should be less willing to disregard the separateness of corporate personality in the interests of imposing tax liability on the use of corporations even where no business purpose for the corporation is shown. In 1988 the *Income Tax Act* was amended to introduce what has been called the "General Anti-avoidance Rule" (s. 245(2)). This provision allows the Minister of National Revenue to disregard transactions if they are abusive tax avoidance transactions. A transaction is a tax avoidance transaction if it is entered into without any real purpose other than obtaining a tax benefit. Such an avoidance transaction is abusive if it resulted in a misuse of some specific provision in the *Income Tax Act* or the provisions of the Act read as a whole. It remains to be seen to what extent the courts will disregard separate corporate personality now that power to address tax avoidance is expressly provided for in the General Anti-Avoidance Rule. In practical terms, the application of this provision is an important issue for tax planning.

The courts have also disregarded separate corporate existence in certain other circumstances where a corporation is being used to avoid other statutory requirements, though relatively rarely.[94]

---

91 *Kosmopoulos*, above note 60 at 10 (S.C.C.).
92 Above note 79.
93 [1984] 1 S.C.R. 536.
94 *Re A.E. Ames & Co.*, [1972] 3 O.R. 405 (C.A.) (securities law); *Nedco Ltd.* v. *Clark* (1973), 43 D.L.R. (3d) 714 (Sask. C.A.). There are also some cases in which statutes expressly provide that the separate existence of corporations shall be disregarded (e.g., *Employment Standards Act*, R.S.O. 1990, c. E.14, ss. 1(d) & 12), interpreted in 550551 *Ontario Ltd.* v. *Framingham* (1991), 4 O.R. (3d) 571 (Div. Ct.).

4) Agency

The third basis on which courts have purported to disregard separate corporate personality is by finding that the corporation is merely acting as the agent of someone else. Conceptually, the corporate form is not disregarded by a holding that it is an agent. Rather, the business of the corporation or whatever activity gives rise to the claim by a third party is determined to be carried on not by the corporation directly, but only as an agent of the controlling shareholder. The courts often use evocative but ultimately unhelpful language to describe the corporation — for example, "sham," "cloak," "conduit," or "alter ego."

The main test for the existence of this peculiar form of agency is whether there is extensive control by the shareholder over corporation. The factors referred to in *Smith, Stone and Knight Ltd.* v. *Birmingham Corp.*[95] are almost universally cited as those relevant to a determination whether agency exists:

- Were the profits treated as profits of the shareholder?
- Was the person conducting the business appointed by the parent company?
- Was the shareholder the head and brain of the trading venture?
- Did the shareholder govern the adventure and decide what should be done and what capital should be committed to the venture?
- Did the shareholder make the profits by its skill and direction?
- Was the shareholder in effectual and constant control?

Extensive and even complete control by a single person, however, is contemplated in the *CBCA*, so the existence of control satisfying the test in *Smith* cannot in any way be conclusive. Earlier in this chapter we noted that there may be various reasons a person might decide to carry on business through a corporation, including limited liability and tax planning. Similarly, there are legitimate reasons that corporations may carry business through a subsidiary corporation in which they hold all the shares. It may be, for example, that the parent corporation will carry on several businesses each through a separate subsidiary corporation in order to ensure that claims arising out of a particular business cannot be satisfied out of the assets of the others. Where subsidiaries are used, the degree of control by the parent corporation may range from absolute, such as where the same person owns 100 percent of the parent corporation and is the sole director and officer of the parent and the subsidiary, to minimal, such as where a subsidiary operates as if it were independent.

---

95   [1939] 4 All E.R. 116 (K.B.) [*Smith*].

There is nothing in any corporate statute which suggests that any particular degree of control is inappropriate or prohibited.

In *Alberta Gas Ethylene Co.* v. *M.N.R.,*[96] Madame Justice Reed observed that *Smith* does not stand for the proposition that one must ignore the separate existence of a subsidiary corporation when the six criteria are met. One must ask for what purpose the corporation was incorporated and used, and consider the overall context in which the obligation to the third party arose. This test was applied in *Sun Sudan Oil Co.* v. *Methanex Corp.*[97] In *Gregorio* v. *Intrans-Corp.,*[98] it was held that the policy behind holding a subsidiary liable is "to prevent conduct akin to fraud that would otherwise unjustly deprive claimants of their rights."[99] Where the court is able to find that a subsidiary had been set up for a legitimate business purpose, disregarding the separate existence of the subsidiary is inappropriate.[100]

5) Other Factors

Often courts are not very clear about whether they are talking about fairness, objectionable purpose, or agency as the basis on which they are disregarding the separate legal existence of the corporation, even though they are conceptually distinct.[101] Also, several other factors have been referred to by the courts as supporting decisions to disregard the corporation's existence, regardless of the basis for doing so. Lack of respect for the corporate form is cited in some cases as supporting the disregard of corporate personality.[102] In others, however, lack of respect, in the form of lack of proper corporate authorization for transactions and the use of shareholder funds to pay corporate obligations, has been found insufficient.[103] Inadequate or "thin" capitalization is also sometimes referred to as supporting the disregard of corporate personality.[104]

---

96   [1989] 41 B.L.R. 117 (Fed. T.D.), aff'd [1990] 2 C.T.C. 171 (Fed. C.A.).
97   (1992), 134 A.R. 1 at 15 (Q.B.); *Harris* v. *Nugent* (1995), 172 A.R. 309 (Q.B.) [*Harris*].
98   (1994), 18 O.R. (3d) 527 (C.A.).
99   *Ibid.* at 536.
100   *Harris*, above note 97; *Bow Valley*, above note 57.
101   For example, *Walkovszky* v. *Carlton*, 223 N.E.2d 6 (N.Y.C.A. 1966) [*Walkovszky*]; *De Salaberry*, above note 79.
102   For example, *Shibamoto & Co.* v. *Western Fish Producers Inc.* (*Trustee of*) (1991), 48 F.T.R. 176 (T.D.) [*Shibamoto*]; *Tato*, above note 90; *Wolfe*, above note 89.
103   For example, *Rockwell Developments Ltd.* v. *Newtonbrook Plaza Ltd.*, [1972] 3 O.R. (2d) 199 (C.A.).
104   For example, *De Salaberry*, above note 79, but rejected in *Walkovszky*, above note 101.

This situation occurs when the shareholders' investment in a corporation is inadequate to meet its anticipated obligations.

I.   LIABILITY OF CORPORATE MANAGERS FOR TORTS

In some cases, tort victims have been successful in claiming that individuals acting for corporations should be individually responsible for torts committed by them personally or by persons under their control. Imposing tort liability on people acting in the business in this way is inconsistent with separate corporate personality, at least to the extent that liability is imposed for actions on behalf of the corporation. For people acting outside the scope of their authority from the corporation, it would not do violence to the separateness of the corporation's existence to hold them liable. In the former case, however, where the people acting in the business are also the shareholders, holding them liable will threaten limited liability. In considering cases in which such liability has been sought, the courts have recognized the tension between the tort principle that each person should be responsible for her own wrongs and the principle of separate corporate personality.[105]

Unfortunately the courts have not been consistent in defining the circumstances in which personal liability will attach or how the tort and corporate law principles should be reconciled. In general, whether a director or officer or employee is responsible for tortious acts depends on the degree and kind of his personal involvement. Where he has performed, ordered, or procured the action constituting the tort, he is likely to be found liable.[106] It is not a defence to argue that the tort was committed for the benefit of the corporation.[107] On the other hand, where a person has only general management responsibilities in the area of the corporation's operations in which the tort was committed, but no knowledge or involvement in the actions constituting the tort, he is unlikely to be found liable.[108]

While these principles may be helpful in deciding whether to impose liability in the case of intentional torts, their application to negligence is more problematic. Welling has suggested that the liability for negligence

---

105   *Mentmore Manufacturing Co.* v. *National Merchandise Manufacturing Co. Inc.* (1978), 89 D.L.R. (3d) 195 at 202 (Fed. C.A.).
106   For example, *Shibamoto*, above note 102 (tort of conversion).
107   In *Shibamoto*, above note 102, the conversion was for the benefit of the corporation.
108   *C. Evans & Sons Ltd.* v. *Spritebrand Ltd.*, [1985] 2 All E.R. 415 (C.A.).

should only be imposed where the alleged tortfeasor has a duty towards the plaintiff arising out of a relationship to her, not simply by virtue of the corporation having a duty arising out of its relationship to the plaintiff and the tortious actions occurring in the general area of her responsibility. In the latter case, the tortfeasor should be considered merely the "human manifestation of the corporation" and, as such, not personally liable.[109]

However attractive this approach may be, it was not followed in *Berger* v. *Willowdale A.M.C.*[110] In that case, an employee slipped on the sidewalk while leaving work after a snowstorm. The *Workmen's Compensation Act*[111] barred her from suing the corporate employer in tort; she had to rely on the compensation scheme provided in the Act. Consequently, she sued the president personally, alleging negligence. The court found that the sidewalk had not been cleared adequately. It also found that the president had a general responsibility to ensure that the workplace was safe, a task he had failed to discharge. He was in a position to know about the danger and to remove it, but failed to do so. As a result, he was liable in negligence. The court indicated that a personal duty would not arise in every case, but would depend on a variety of factors, including[112] the size of the corporation, the number of employees, the nature of the business, and whether the danger should have been readily apparent to the manager, the manager had the authority and the ability to control the situation, and had ready access to the means to rectify the danger. Welling is critical of this case on the basis that the only relationship between the president and the employee arose by virtue of the president's position in the corporation. Few[113] subsequent cases have followed *Berger* and liability of corporate managers for negligence has been relatively rare.

Tort actions have also been used to claim against managers where there has been a breach of contract by the corporation they represent. The tort of inducing breach of contract is committed when a person,

---

109   Welling, above note 8 at 117.
110   (1983), 41 O.R. (2d) 89 (C.A.), leave to appeal refused (1983), 41 O.R. (2d) 89n (S.C.C.) [*Berger*].
111   R.S.O. 1970, c. 505.
112   *Berger*, above note 110.
113   This case was not followed in *Kavanagh* v. *Don Sloan Equipment Rentals Ltd.* (1988), 4 M.V.R. (2d) 34 (Ont. H.C.J.) or *Bradsil Ltd.* v. *602871 Ontario Ltd.*, [1996] O.J. No. 294 (Gen. Div.) (QL). One important result of this case was the imposition of tort liability where a claim against the corporation would have failed. *London Drugs Ltd.* v. *Kuehne & Nagel International Ltd.*, [1992] 3 S.C.R. 299 is another example. In that case, employees acting in the course of their duties were found to be liable in negligence. Their corporate employer escaped liability on the basis of an exclusion of liability clause in its contract with the plaintiff.

knowing there is a contract between the plaintiff and a third party, induces the third party, without justification, to break the contract, with the intention of procuring the breach of contract.[114] Expressed in this way, this principle has the potential virtually to eliminate the separation between corporate and management liability for breaches of contract, though the measure of damages would be different. However, an important exception to this general rule was described in *Said* v. *Butt*:

> . . . if a servant acting bona fide within the scope of his authority procures or causes the breach of a contract between his employer and a third person, he does not thereby become liable to an action of tort at the suit of the person whose contract has thereby been broken.[115]

In *McFadden* v. *481782 Ontario Ltd.*,[116] it was held that the effect of this exception was to excuse directors and officers if they were acting "under the compulsion of a duty to the corporation." In that case, two directors authorized payments to themselves as shareholders that put the corporation in a position where it could not fulfil its contractual obligations to an employee. The employee successfully sued the directors on the basis that they induced the corporation to breach its contract with him. The court held that the directors could not fall within the *Said* v. *Butt* exception since they were acting with a view to their own interests and not those of the corporation, and so could not be said to be acting under the compulsion of a duty to the corporation. Several cases have held directors and officers of a corporation liable for inducing the breach of a contract to which the corporation was a party.[117]

This "compulsion of duty" defence, however, has been held not to be applicable in the context of other torts, including deceit and negligent misstatement. In *Toronto Dominion Bank* v. *Leigh Instruments Ltd. (Trustee of)*,[118] the court refused to strike out a statement of claim against certain directors and officers of a corporation alleging that they had fraudulently given false information to the bank to encourage it to grant the corporation more credit. The court said that it is no excuse

---

114　*Quinn* v. *Leathem*, [1901] A.C. 495 at 510 (H.L.).

115　[1920] 3 K.B. 497 at 506.

116　(1984), 47 O.R. 134 (H.C.J.).

117　*Aiken* v. *Regency Homes Inc.*, [1991] O.J. No. 1201 (C.A.) (QL), and *Einhorn* v. *Westmount Investments Ltd.* (1969), 6 D.L.R. (3d) 71 (Sask Q.B.), aff'd (1970), 11 D.L.R. (3d) 509 (Sask. C.A.). In *Lehndorff Canadian Pension Properties Ltd.* v. *Davis & Co.* (1987), 10 B.C.L.R. (2d) 342 (S.C.), an unsuccessful attempt was made to hold officers of the corporation liable for conspiring to induce a breach of contract. The extent to which the corporation is willing or obliged to indemnify the director or officer will have an impact on the effect of imposing liability. See chapter 8.

118　(1991), 4 B.L.R. (2d) 220 (Ont. Div. Ct.).

that the employee was obeying orders of the employer or that the act was expressly authorized or ratified by the corporation. With regard to the cases on inducing breach of contract, including *Said* v. *Butt,* the court simply said it was not dealing with such a case.[119]

J. APPLICATION OF THE *CHARTER OF RIGHTS AND FREEDOMS* TO CORPORATIONS

As discussed above, incorporation brings into existence a new legal person whose rights and obligations may be thought of as analogous to those of a human person. Does a corporate person have rights under the *Charter?* Though it is too early to answer in a definitive way, several cases have considered this question in different contexts, and it is possible to sketch the outlines of this aspect of a corporation's separate legal personality.

The *Charter* defines the classes of person who benefit from *Charter* rights in different ways. The defining language used in relation to some rights excludes corporations. The right to vote (s. 3), mobility rights (s. 6), and minority language rights (s. 23) are conferred only on "[e]very citizen." Since corporations cannot obtain Canadian citizenship, they cannot benefit from these rights. "Every individual" is entitled to equality rights under section 15. Although it might seem obvious that a corporation is not an individual, several arguments have been made to the contrary and there has not yet been a definitive judicial statement on this issue.[120]

Other language used in the *Charter* is broad enough to include corporations. The rights granted on being charged with an offence (s. 11) on certain mobility rights under section 6(2) are granted to "[e]very person" and may extend to corporations, since corporations have the capacity, rights, powers, and privileges of a natural person under most corporate legislation (e.g., *CBCA,* s. 15(1)). Some of the provisions in section 11 may sensibly apply to corporations, such as the right to be tried within a reasonable time (s. 11(b)) and to be presumed innocent until proven guilty (s. 11(d)).[121] In *Parkdale Hotel Ltd.* v. *Canada*

---

119 *Ibid.* at 252.
120 See G.D. Chipeur, "Section 15 of the Charter Protects People and Corporations — Equally" (1986), 11 Can. Bus. L. J. 304.
121 In *R.* v. *741290 Ontario Inc.* (1991), 2 O.R. (3d) 336 (Prov. Div.), it was held that a corporation has a right to be tried within a reasonable time in accordance with section 11(b), but the presumption of prejudice associated with a delay is weaker for a corporation than for a natural person. In a pre-*Charter* case, *R.* v. *N.M. Paterson & Sons Ltd.,* [1980] 2 S.C.R. 679, it was held that the right against self-incrimination, now protected under section 11(c) of the *Charter,* did not prevent a manager of a corporation from being compelled to testify at a trial of the corporation.

(A.G.),[122] however, the court held that a person did not include a corporation for the purpose of enjoying the mobility right under section 6(2), on the basis that the purpose of the provision was not the protection of corporations. Such a purposive approach to interpretation has been applied generally in relation to the *Charter*.

"Everyone" defines those who have the protection of the most important provisions of the *Charter*: the fundamental freedoms of expression, conscience, religion, peaceful assembly and association guaranteed under s. 2; the right to life, liberty, and security of person under section 7; the rights against arbitrary search and seizure under section 8; and the legal rights under sections 10 and 12. "Everyone" does not inherently exclude corporations, and the extension of any specific protection to corporations will depend on whether the substance of the protection is one that a corporation may enjoy.

Although it has been held that a corporation cannot enjoy freedom of religion,[123] corporations do enjoy freedom of expression, at least to some extent, even though such expression may be of an entirely commercial nature, such as advertising.[124] There has been no case law on the applicability of the other fundamental freedoms to corporations.

In the *Irwin Toy*[125] case it was held that because a corporation cannot be imprisoned or lose its life, it cannot enjoy life, liberty, or security of the person guaranteed under section 7. This decision was confirmed by the Supreme Court of Canada in *R. v. Wholesale Travel Group Inc.*[126] Corporations are entitled to protection against unreasonable search and seizure under section 8.[127] It is not clear if the rights arising under sections 9 and 10 on being detained or arrested can sensibly be applied to corporations.

As with the protection of individuals under the *Charter*, the protection available to corporations is subject to the balancing requirement contained in section 1: the provision infringed in the *Charter* right must not be a "reasonable . . . [limit] prescribed by law as can be demonstrably

---

122   [1986] 2 F.C. 514 (T.D.).

123   *R. v. Big M Drug Mart Ltd.*, [1985] 1 S.C.R. 295. [*Big M*].

124   *Irwin Toy Ltd. v. Quebec (A.G.)*, [1989] 1 S.C.R. 927 [*Irwin Toy*]; *RJR-MacDonald Inc. v. Canada (A.G.)*, [1995] 3 S.C.R. 199 [*RJR*].

125   *Irwin Toy*, ibid.

126   [1991] 3 S.C.R. 154 [*Wholesale Travel*]. But see *Southam Inc. v. Canada (Combines Investigation Branch, Director of Investigation & Research)* (1982), 42 A.R. 109 (Q.B.), aff'd on other grounds (*sub nom. Canada (Director of Investigation & Research, Combines Investigation Branch) v. Southam Inc.*) [1984] 2 S.C.R. 145 [*Southam*] which suggests that a corporation should be granted status, but denied protection intended for human persons.

127   *Southam*, ibid.

justified in a free and democratic society." Several judicial statements have suggested that the balancing required by section 1 should be different if the person whose rights have been infringed is a corporation. In *Reference Re S. 94(2) of the Motor Vehicle Act (British Columbia)*,[128] Mr. Justice Lamer suggested, in *obiter*, that an exception under section 1 could more easily be justified in such a case:

> Even if it be decided that s. 7 does extend to corporations, I think the balancing under s. 1 of the public interest against the financial interests of a corporation would give very different results from that of balancing the public interest and the liberty or security of the person of a human being.

He repeated this view in *Wholesale Travel*. This relative hostility to corporations claiming *Charter* rights was recently expressed by the dissenting justices in *RJR-MacDonald Inc. v. Canada (A.G.)*, in which the federal government's ban on tobacco advertising and promotions was upheld. Mr. Justice LaForest, in this respect writing for L'Heureux-Dubé, Gonthier, and Cory, confirmed the position taken by the court in *Rocket v. Royal College of Dental Surgeons*[129] that, though no "special tests" apply to commercial expression, a sensitive, case-oriented approach should be taken to the determination of its constitutionality. The court must consider the expression in its factual and social context. Because of the harm engendered by tobacco and the profit motive underlying its promotion, cigarette advertising was described as being "as far from the "core" of freedom of expression values as prostitution, hate mongering, or pornography"[130] and thus entitled to a very low degree of protection under section 1. Mr. Justice Iacobucci, joined in this respect by Chief Justice Lamer, did not find that the legislation could be justified under section 1, but they agreed that expression, solely for the purpose of financial gain from selling a product with known deleterious effects on public health, was deserving of narrow protection.[131] Even Madame Justice McLachlin, with Justices Sopinka and Major, acknowledged that restrictions on commercial speech may be easier to justify than other infringements, though she determined that "motivation to profit is irrelevant to the determination of whether the government has established that the law is reasonable or justified as an infringement of freedom of expression."[132]

---

128   [1985] 2 S.C.R. 486 at 518.
129   [1990] 2 S.C.R. 232 at 246.
130   *RJR*, above note 124 at 282–83.
131   *Ibid.*, at 354.
132   *Ibid.*, at 348.

Finally, a line of cases has held that even where particular *Charter* provisions have no application to corporations, a corporation may argue that the provision is unconstitutional because it would violate the rights of an individual. Where a corporation has been charged with a penal offence and an individual charged with the same offence could successfully argue that the provision creating the offence violated her rights under the *Charter* in some way, the provision will be struck down as it applies to the corporation on the basis that no one may be convicted under an unconstitutional law.[133] This defence will not be available to a corporation if the provision is expressed to apply only to corporations.[134]

K. CHAPTER SUMMARY

This chapter builds on the introduction to the corporation begun in chapter 1 in several ways. It provides additional background information on the history of Canadian corporate law, the constitutional responsibilities of the federal and provincial governments, and the incorporation process. In addition, it develops the discussion in chapter 1 of the context in which corporate law operates through an examination of the economic function of corporate law, the application of the *Charter* to corporations, and the relationship between corporate and securities law. Finally, this chapter describes the legal nature of the corporation and the circumstances in which the courts will disregard it.

Canadian corporate law developed from both English and American antecedents. The current federal corporate law, the *CBCA*, was enacted in 1975 and has formed the model that subsequent corporate law reform in most, but not all, provinces has followed. The *CBCA* model is the focus of this book.

Both the federal and provincial governments have constitutional authority to create corporations, the primary difference being that provincial corporations have the capacity but not the right to carry on business outside their province of incorporation, whereas federal corporations have both the capacity and the right in Canada. Federal and provincial jurisdictions both have a limited power to regulate corporations not incorporated in other jurisdictions, so long as such regulation is otherwise within their legislative competence.

---

133   *Big M*, above note 123 at 313–14, applied in *R. v. Metro News Ltd.* (1987), 56 O.R. (2d) 321 (C.A.) and *Wholesale Travel*, above note 126.
134   *Wholesale Travel, ibid.*

Corporate law in all Canadian jurisdictions is designed to encourage investment in business. It does so by increasing the returns to shareholder investors and decreasing the risk associated with those returns. Corporate law accomplishes the former largely by reducing the transaction costs associated with setting up and operating a corporation. It does the latter primarily by limiting the loss exposure of shareholders to the amount of their investment and by imposing mandatory rules designed to protect shareholders. Corporate law contains various sorts of protection for non-shareholder stakeholders as well, but this is very much a secondary role.

Unlike corporate law, the purpose of securities laws is to regulate the market in which securities are traded for the purpose of ensuring that such markets operate fairly. Securities laws have come to overlap with corporate law substantially as the reach of securities laws has extended into corporate decision making, including the holding of shareholder meetings, in the interests of protecting investors on an ongoing basis. Nevertheless, there are significant distinctions between corporate and securities laws in terms of their respective scope of application, enforcement, and substantive provisions.

Under corporate law the corporation has a separate legal existence, a status that has various important implications. It means that a shareholder may contract with the corporation, including being an employee or a creditor. More important, it means that shareholders have limited liability. There are, however, various statutory exceptions to limited liability. Also, the courts have determined that they have the power to disregard the separate existence of the corporation, although it is far from clear in what circumstances such a power may be exercised. In some cases, courts have permitted the separate legal existence of the corporation to be disregarded simply because they have concluded that it would not be fair to refuse to do so. In others, they have concluded that the corporation is not truly carrying on business on its own behalf but on behalf of its shareholder as an agent.

The courts have also used tort law in some circumstances to impose liability personally on directors and officers of corporations. This is not necessarily technically inconsistent with the separate existence of the corporation, since it may be viewed as simply imposing tort liability on the person who has committed the tort. Nevertheless, since in most corporations carrying on a small business the directors and officers are the same people as the shareholders, the effect of imposing liability on them may reduce the value of separate legal existence. Unfortunately, the principles on which tort liability may be imposed are not clear.

With regarding to the *Charter*, the courts have permitted corporations to claim *Charter* rights where the language of the *Charter* may be interpreted to extend to corporations and there is some sensible way in which the substance of the rights may be exercised by a corporation. The Supreme Court of Canada, however, has suggested that the courts should be less vigilant in protecting rights of corporations as compared with those of individuals.

FURTHER READINGS

ALBOINI, V.P., *Securities Law and Practice*, 11 vols., (Toronto: Carswell, 1984) (looseleaf)

BERLE, A.A., & G.C. MEANS, *The Modern Corporation and Private Property*, rev. ed. (New York: Harcourt, Brace & World, 1968)

BOURGEOIS, D.J. *The Law of Charitable and Non-Profit Organizations*, 2d ed. (Toronto: Butterworths, 1995)

BUCKLEY, F.H., M. GILLEN, & R. YALDEN, *Corporations: Principles and Policies*, 3d ed. (Toronto: Emond Montgomery, 1995)

CARY, W.L., & M.A. EISENBERG, *Cases and Materials on Corporations*, 6th ed. (Mineola, N.Y.: Foundation Press, 1994)

CHAPMAN, B., "Trust, Economic Rationality, and the Corporate Fiduciary Obligation" (1993) 43 U.T.L.J. 547

"Corporate Law in the 80s" [1982] Spec. Lect. L.S.U.C.

DANIELS, R.J., & B. LANGILLE, eds., "Special Issue on the Corporate Stakeholder Debate: The Classical Theory and Its Critics" (1993) 43 U.T.L.J. 297–796

DANIELS, R.J., & J.G. MACINTOSH, "Toward a Distinctive Canadian Corporate Law Regime" (1991) 29 Osgoode Hall L.J. 863

DAVIES, WARD, & BECK, *Canadian Corporate Law Precedents* (Toronto: Carswell, 1989)

DICKERSON, R.V.W., J.L. HOWARD, & L. GETZ, *Proposals for a New Business Corporations Law for Canada*, 2 vols. (Ottawa: Information Canada, 1971)

EASTERBROOK, F.H., & D.R. FISCHEL, *The Economic Structure of Corporate Law* (Boston: Harvard University Press, 1991)

GILLEN, M.R., *Securities Regulation in Canada* (Toronto: Carswell, 1992)

GOWER, L.C.B., *Principles of Modern Company Law*, 5th ed. (London: Stevens, 1993)

HALPERN, P., M.J. TREBILCOCK, & S. TURNBULL, "An Economic Analysis of Limited Liability in Corporation Law" (1980) 30 U.T.L.J. 117

ISH, D., *The Law of Canadian Co-operatives* (Toronto: Carswell, 1981)

LABRIE, F.E., & E.E. PALMER, "The Pre-Confederation History of Corporations in Canada" in J.S. Ziegel, ed., *Studies in Canadian Company Law*, vol. 1 (Toronto: Butterworths, 1967) 33

ONTARIO, *Interim Report of the Select Committee on Company Law* (Toronto: Queen's Printer, 1967)

PETERSON, D.H., *Shareholder Remedies in Canada* (Toronto: Butterworths, 1989) (looseleaf)

POSNER, R.A., & K.E. SCOTT, eds., *Economics of Corporation Law and Securities Regulation* (Boston: Little, Brown & Co., 1980)

RISK, R.C.B., "The Nineteenth Century Foundations of Business Corporations in Ontario" (1973) 23 U.T.L.J. 270

ROMANO, R., *The Genius of American Corporate Law* (New York: AEI Press, 1993)

ROMANO, R., ed., *Foundations of Corporate Law* (Oxford: Oxford University Press, 1993)

SARGENT, N.C., "Corporate Groups and the Corporate Veil in Canada: A Penetrating Look at Parent-Subsidiary Relations in the Modern Corporate Enterprise" (1988) 17 Man. L.J. 156

SARNA, L., ed., *Corporate Structure, Finance and Operations: Essays on the Law and Business Practice*, 7 vols. (Toronto: Carswell, 1986)

TOLLEFSON, C., "Corporate Constitutional Rights and the Supreme Court of Canada" (1993) 19 Queen's L.J. 309

WAINBERG, J.M., *Company Meetings Including Rules of Order*, 3d ed. (Don Mills: CCH Canadian Ltd., 1982)

WAINBERG, J.M., & M.I. WAINBERG, *Duties and Responsibilities of Directors in Canada*, 6th ed. (Don Mills: CCH Canadian Ltd., 1987)

WALDRON, M.A., "The Process of Law Reform: the New B.C. Companies Act" (1976) 10 U.B.C. L. Rev. 179

WEGENAST, F.W., *The Law of Canadian Companies* (Toronto: Burroughs, 1931)

ZIEGEL, J.S., *et al.*, *Cases and Materials on Partnerships and Canadian Business Corporations*, 3d ed. (Toronto: Carswell, 1994)

CHAPTER 4

INCORPORATION: CONSIDERATIONS AND PROCESS

A. INTRODUCTION

The process of incorporation was briefly described in chapter 3. In this chapter we will examine the process in more detail. We will look at both the legal requirements and some of the practical aspects of incorporation, as well as some of the considerations related to which jurisdiction an incorporator should choose.

B. THE PROCESS OF INCORPORATION AND ORGANIZATION

1) Incorporation

Under most Canadian corporate statutes, a corporation may be incorporated by one or more corporations or individuals, or a combination of both. Although there are no qualifications that must be met by corporate incorporators, under the *CBCA* individual incorporators cannot be any of the following:

- less that eighteen years of age;
- of unsound mind as found by a court in Canada or elsewhere; or
- bankrupt (*CBCA*, s. 5).

The incorporators must file certain prescribed material with the Corporations Directorate of the Department of Industry if incorporation under the *CBCA* is sought, or, if incorporation under the laws of a province is chosen, with the branch of the provincial government having responsibility for incorporations.[1] Under the *CBCA* it is necessary to file the following:

- articles of incorporation (s. 6, Form 1);
- notice of registered office (s. 19(2), Form 3);
- notice of directors (s. 106, Form 6);
- a name search report on the proposed name of the corporation; and
- the fee of $500.

a) Articles

As noted in chapter 3, the articles are by far the most important of these documents filed on incorporation because they set out the fundamental characteristics of the corporation: its name, the place within Canada where its registered office is to be situated, the class and number of shares authorized to be issued, the number of directors, any restrictions on transferring shares, and any restrictions on the business the corporation may carry on. Each of these items deserves some discussion.

i) Names

The problems often associated with corporate names are both legally complex and practically troublesome. On a practical level, it is difficult to find a name that is not already in use; once a name is chosen and begins to have value associated with it, its use by someone else will be subject to attack. Legally, name regulation is a tangle of provincial and federal jurisdictions. The *CBCA* and the provincial corporate statutes have provisions regulating the use of names by corporations incorporated under them. In addition, the federal *Trade-marks Act*[2] grants rights in names based on their use in association with goods and services. Each province regulates the use of names by corporations, wherever they are incorporated, if they are carrying on business in the province, and the provincial common law protects certain interests in names through the tort of passing-off.

Why are names protected? Apart from any personal attachment to a corporate name, a name may have substantial value associated with it. It may be recognized by consumers or business customers as indicative of prestige, product quality, or service. This sort of value is commonly referred to as goodwill. One policy behind name regulation is the protec-

---

1   See section C, "Jurisdiction of Incorporation," below, for a discussion of consideration relevant to choosing under which jurisdiction to incorporate.

2   R.S.C. 1985, c. T-13[*TA*].

tion of the legitimately created goodwill of a particular business against appropriation by others. There is also a general public interest in the regulation of names. The courts have identified that "the danger to be guarded against is that the person seeing or hearing one name will think it to be the same as another which he has seen or heard before."[3] In other words, name regulation seeks to prevent confusion in the marketplace.

The following subsections outline briefly the legal framework for corporate names.

a. Corporate Law Rules Regarding Names

The *CBCA*, like other corporate statutes in Canada, regulates the use of names of corporations to ensure that they are neither confusingly similar with other names used by businesses nor deceptively misdescriptive. The starting point is section 12(1)(a), which provides that a *CBCA* corporation may not be incorporated with or carry on business using a name that is "prescribed, prohibited or deceptively misdescriptive." If a name is contrary to this provision, the Director who administers the *CBCA* may refuse to incorporate a corporation that proposes to use it or, if the name is already being used by a corporation, order that the name be changed (*CBCA*, s. 12(2)).[4] Under the *OBCA*, a hearing must be held before any name change is ordered (*OBCA*, s. 12(1)).

The *CBCA Regulations* set out both absolute and qualified prohibitions for the purposes of section 12. Names that may never be used are those which are obscene (*CBCA*, s. 18) or those which contain phrases like "United Nations" and "Air Canada" (*CBCA*, s. 16). Sections 17 and 21 prohibit the use of certain names without consent. For example, one cannot use a name which suggests that a business is sponsored by or affiliated with the government of Canada, a university, a professional association, or a person's family name without consent.

Of greater practical significance are the provisions that deal with names which are not distinctive enough or are confusing. Section 19 sets out the criteria by which the inherent distinctiveness of a name must be judged. A name is not distinctive and cannot be used if it is

- too general, such that it could apply to any products or services anywhere (e.g., Industries Inc.);

---

3   *John Palmer Co. v. Palmer-McLellan Shoepack Co.* (1917), 45 N.B.R. 8 at 56 (C.A.).
4   As noted above, it is necessary for each corporation to have a legal element in its name, such as "Inc." or "Limited." The Director may exempt a corporation continued under the *Canada Business Corporations Act*, R.S.C. 1985, c. C-44 [*CBCA*] from the requirement to have a legal element in its name (s. 10(2)). It is not clear why the Director would do so.

- only descriptive, in any language, of the quality, function, or other characteristic of the goods or services in which the corporation deals or intends to deal (e.g., Apples Inc.);
- primarily or only the name or surname used alone of an individual who is living or has died within thirty years preceding the request for the name (e.g., Pierre Trudeau Inc.); and
- primarily or only a geographic name used alone (e.g., Japan Inc.).

An exception to these prohibitions permits the use of names which are not inherently distinctive but which, through use, have acquired a secondary meaning (e.g., General Motors Inc.). In other words, if a name has been used in Canada for so long that it has obtained a level of recognition which distinguishes it from its competitors, it is not prohibited. Usually, in order to ensure that a name is found to be distinctive, it must combine a distinctive element with a descriptive element. Distinctive elements may be a coined word (e.g., "Xerox" in Xerox Corporation), an arbitrarily chosen real word (e.g., "Dome" in Dome Mines Ltd.), a family or geographic name, or some other word. A descriptive element describes the business in which the corporation is engaged (e.g., "Mines" in Dome Mines Ltd.).

It is the whole name that must be distinctive (*CBCA Regulations*, s. 14). So, if the distinctive element is a highly original coined word, like Xerox, no descriptive element may be required. If the distinctive element is weaker, a descriptive element will be necessary.

This question of distinctiveness is not simply a technical legal issue. It is very important to business. There are already many similar and general names in the marketplace. A highly distinctive name is most likely to be noticed and remembered and is, therefore, very valuable.

In addition to inherent distinctiveness, the *CBCA Regulations* address confusion with other names and trade-marks. Other names include all names under which a business is carried on, whether it is being carried on through a corporation, partnership, or individual (collectively referred to as "trade-names"). A corporate name is confusing with a trade-name or trade-mark if its use would likely lead to the inference that the business carried on under the corporate name and the business carried on under the trade-name or trade-mark are one business (*CBCA Regulations*, ss. 12 & 13). Section 20 of the *Regulations* sets out a list of circumstances to be considered in assessing whether a corporate name is confusing with a trade-mark or trade-name:

- the inherent distinctiveness of the whole or any element of the corporate name and the trade-mark or trade-name, and the extent to which either has become known;

- the length of time the corporate name and the trade-mark or trade-name have been in use;
- the nature of the goods or services associated with the corporate name and with the trade-mark or trade-name, including the likelihood of any competition between the corporation using or proposing to use the name and other businesses using the trade-mark or trade-name;
- the nature of the trade with which the corporate name and the trade-mark or trade-name is associated, including the nature of the products or services and the means by which they are offered or distributed;
- the degree of resemblance between the corporate name and the trade-mark or trade-name in appearance or sound, or in the ideas suggested by them; and
- the territorial area in Canada in which the corporate name or the trade-name is likely to be used.[5]

In *I. Browns Packaging Inc.* v. *Canada (Consumer and Corporate Affairs)*,[6] the court considered an appeal from a decision by the Director that I. Browns Packaging Inc. was not confusing with Brown's Bottle (Canada) Limited. I. Browns Packaging Inc. was incorporated by Irwin Browns, a former shareholder in Browns Bottle (Canada) Limited. The court found that I. Browns Packaging Inc. designed packaging products for a small number of industrial customers, whereas Browns Bottle (Canada) Limited acted as a distributor for various packaging products. Although these businesses were not found to be identical, the court determined that there was some overlap, in the sense that the two businesses bought from some of the same suppliers and sold to some of the same customers. They might find themselves in competition in the future, although, since the market was a specialized one with few purchasers, there was little likelihood of confusion — and no actual confusion was established. The court also noted that the descriptive elements of the names, "Packaging" and "Bottle," were different. This difference, along with the use of the initial "I," rendered the names distinguishable. The court also noted that, at common law, a person has a right to use his own name and that the assessment of confusion should take this

---

5   This provision was interpreted in *Unitel International Inc.* v. *Unitel Communications Inc.*, (1992), 101 Sask. R. 48 (Q.B.). This case was an appeal of a decision of the Director under the *CBCA*, above note 4, s. 246(b), refusing to grant Unitel International Inc.'s application for an order requiring Unitel Communications Inc. to change its name. Based on a review of the application of the factors set out above, the court refused to overturn the Director's decision. The court indicated that great deference should be shown to the Director's decisions regarding names.

6   (1982), 24 B.L.R. 44 (Que. S.C.).

right into account. The court concluded that the Director's decision should not be changed.

Sections 22 and 25 through 28 of the *CBCA Regulations* contain further rules about the possible confusion of names. These provisions deal with a variety of particular circumstances, including what a corporation must do to use a name that is confusing with the name of another corporation but where that corporation has not carried on business for two years (s. 26), or where a corporation previously carried on the business of the present corporation (ss. 27, 28(2)). In general, the required procedure is to get the corporation with the name that is confusing with the desired name to consent to the use of the name and to undertake to dissolve or to change its name.

Names are also prohibited if they are "deceptively misdescriptive." Section 23 of the *CBCA Regulations* defines what is meant by this term. A corporate name is deceptively misdescriptive if it misdescribes, in any language,

- the business, goods, or services with which it is proposed to be used;
- the conditions under which the goods or services will be produced or supplied, or the persons to be employed in the production or supply of those goods or services; or
- the place of origin of those goods or services.

Subject to the rules described above, the *CBCA* specifically provides that the articles may set out the corporate name in an English form, a French form, an English and a French form, or a combined English and French form. A corporation may also have a form of its name in a third language for use outside Canada. A corporation may use and be legally designated by any of these forms (*CBCA*, ss. 10(3) & (4)).

b. Provincial Registration and Licensing Rules Regarding Names
Each province regulates names used to carry on business within its borders. For example, in chapter 1 we saw that most sole proprietorships and partnerships carrying on business in Ontario must register their names under the Ontario *Business Names Act* (*OBNA*). Corporations carrying on business in Ontario using a name other than their full corporate name must also register. Failure to do so means that the defaulting party cannot maintain an action in the courts of Ontario in connection with an obligation of the business. With the consent of the court, however, an action may be permitted to proceed if the failure to register was inadvertent and there is no evidence that the public has been deceived or misled and, at the time of the application to court, the name has been registered (*OBNA*, s. 7). Failure to register is also an offence under section 10, but enforcement is rare.

Section 6 of the Ontario *Business Names Act* provides an incentive to private enforcement of the Act. A person who has registered a name may claim compensation of up to $500 for damages suffered against a person who registers a name that is the same as or deceptively similar to such name. If the claim is successful, the court must order the Registrar appointed under the Act to cancel the offending registration. Claims for compensation under the *Business Names Act* are legally independent of any question of confusion under corporate statutes, trade-mark infringement, or common law passing-off, though liability under these various heads will often overlap in practice.

As discussed below, all provinces have statutes imposing certain requirements on corporations incorporated outside the province. Corporations incorporated in other provinces or outside Canada must obtain permission in the form of a licence to carry on business.[7] These licences are routinely granted, except where the name of the extraprovincial corporation is confusing with the name of a business already being carried on in the province. Federally incorporated corporations have a right to carry on business in any province; it has been held that a province has no jurisdiction to refuse to permit a federal corporation to use its corporate name, since use of its name relates to the status of the corporation.[8]

In the same case, the Manitoba Court of Appeal had to consider to what extent a province is competent to regulate a federal corporation's use of names other than its corporate name and any trade-mark it owns. It held that the provincial power to regulate the use of a business name depends on whether the corporation conducts business interprovincially or wholly within the province. Only in the latter case may the province regulate the use of the name.[9] The power granted to the Registrar under the Act to order the change of a name could not apply to a federal corporation carrying on an interprovincial business.[10] The court held, however, that the provisions of the Manitoba *Business Names Registration Act* equivalent to section 2 of the Ontario Act, which require

---

7   See section C, "Jurisdiction of Incorporation" below.

8   *Reference Re Constitution Act, 1867, ss. 91 & 92* (1991), 80 D.L.R. (4th) 431 (Man. C.A.). See section C(1)(c), "Jurisdiction to Regulate," in chapter 3.

9   The court acknowledged that, in practice, this will be a very difficult test to apply, since it was conceivable that a corporation may be carrying on business in more than one province and still not be carrying on an interprovincial business (*ibid.* at 445).

10   *Ibid.* at 449. Provincial laws dealing with passing-off, discussed later in this section, would still apply.

registration of a business name used by a corporation, were within the constitutional competence of the province regardless of the nature of the corporation's business. They were validly enacted to permit the public in Manitoba to find out who is responsible for a business being carried on under a name other than the legal name of the person carrying on the business, a matter of civil rights within the province. The registration requirement was held not to impede the ability of interprovincial businesses to carry on their businesses.

The Manitoba Court of Appeal also held that a province has no jurisdiction to restrict the use of a trade-mark by a corporation on the basis that it is similar to a business name in use in the province. A province is not prevented, however, from restricting the use of the trade-mark in a business name used by a corporation other than its corporate name in the manner described above. Any challenge to the use of the trade-mark itself would have to be under federal law, not provincial name registration legislation.

c. *Trade-marks Act* Rules Regarding Names

A trade-mark is a word, phrase, or symbol used in association with goods or services. Use of the mark in association with goods or services gives the owner certain rights to the exclusive use of the mark in association with them, including a right to claim damages against anyone who infringes the mark. Registration of trade-marks is not required, but is provided for under the *Trade-marks Act*[11] and gives the registrant certain benefits, such as a presumption that the trade-mark is valid. Under section 20 of the *Trade-marks Act* a trade-mark is infringed by the use of a confusing trade-mark or trade-name.[12] Confusion is defined in section 6 of the Act in essentially the same terms as in section 20 of the *CBCA Regulations*.

A trade-name is simply a name used by a business. It may be a corporate name or another name used by the business. A trade-name is not a trade-mark unless it is used also to identify the goods or services of the business. It may be simple enough to distinguish a trade-mark from a trade-name where a business produces goods and the goods are sold with a mark attached to them which is different from the corporate name (e.g., Honda uses the trade-mark "Accord" on some of its cars), but in other cases it will be hard to tell what is the trade-mark and what is the trade-name. For example, many businesses use a trade-mark as part of their corporate name (e.g., Coca Cola uses the trade-mark "Coca-Cola" on its cola products as well as in its corporate name).

---

11   *TA*, above note 2.

12   Registration of a trade-mark that is confusing with a registered trade-mark is prohibited under section 12.

The relationship between rights under the *Trade-marks Act* and corporate legislation dealing with names is complex, and a full discussion is beyond the scope of this book. Nevertheless, a few points should be made.

First, a corporate name or other trade-name is not necessarily a trade-mark, and use of a mark in a corporate name will be only one factor the court will consider in deciding whether a trade-mark is valid.

Second, there are no cases that address the extent to which confusion for the purposes of trade-mark infringement and for the purposes of the corporate statutes are the same. So, for example, it is not clear whether a finding that corporate names are confusing means that trade-marks contained in those names are confusing, or *vice versa*. Indeed, use of a trade-mark in a name, in some circumstances, may not be an infringing use of the mark. To be specific, it may be possible, in some circumstances, for a corporation to obtain an order under the relevant corporate law directing someone to change its corporate name because its use is confusing, but not be able to obtain damages for the use of the name as a trade-mark under the *Trade-marks Act*.

Third, the remedies are very different. A successful trade-mark infringement action may entitle the plaintiff to damages and an injunction directing the defendant to cease using the trade-mark and to deliver up any goods bearing the mark. A successful complaint under the corporate statutes results in a direction to the corporation to change its name.

Fourth, the Federal Court has jurisdiction over trade-mark matters, whereas corporate names disputes under the *CBCA* must be resolved, first, before the Director appointed under the *CBCA* and, then, on appeal, in provincial superior courts.[13]

d. Passing-Off

A person carrying on business under a name has a right to seek an injunction to prevent someone else from selling products in a manner that is likely to deceive purchasers of the products into thinking they are purchasing the first person's products, thereby depriving her of profit.[14] Damages may also be claimed. Passing-off actions may now also be brought under section 7(b) of the *Trade-marks Act*.

In *Consumers Distributing Co. v. Seiko Time Canada Ltd*,[15] the Supreme Court of Canada indicated that the passing-off action is

---

13   *Brick's Fine Furniture Ltd. v. Brick Warehouse Corp.* (1989), 25 C.P.R. (3d) 89 (Man. C.A.), and *Brick Warehouse Corp. v. Brick's Fine Furniture Ltd.* (1992), 42 C.P.R. (3d) 158 (Fed. T.D.). The appeal right is provided for in the *CBCA*, above note 4, s. 246.

14   *Fastening House Ltd. v. Fastway Supply House Ltd.* (1974), 3 O.R. (2d) 385 (H.C.J.).

15   [1984] 1 S.C.R. 583.

founded on the tort of deceit. The Court also held that there is no requirement to find an intent to deceive, but there is a requirement that "confusion in the minds of the public be a likely consequence" of the sale by the defendant. The Supreme Court quoted with approval from *Erven Warnink BV v. J. Townend & Sons (Hull) Ltd.*,[16] where the House of Lords held that to establish an action for passing-off, the plaintiff must show that a trader made a misrepresentation in the course of trade to prospective customers which was calculated to injure the business or goodwill of another trader, in the sense that such injury is a reasonably foreseeable consequence of the misrepresentation. Also, the representation must cause actual damage to a business or the goodwill of the plaintiff, or be likely to do so.

Claims for damages for passing-off are legally independent of any question of confusion under corporate statutes, trade-mark infringement, or liability under business names legislation. There are several important limitations on a passing-off action which do not apply to trade-mark infringement. Most importantly, to establish passing-off, the plaintiff must prove that it has a reputation associated with the mark and some likelihood that the public will be deceived. Registration of a trade-mark is not a requirement for a passing-off action. Registration of a trade-mark does, however, require a court to recognize the plaintiff's right to use the mark regardless of the extent to which it has been used for the purposes of trade-mark infringement actions.

e. Names and the Incorporation Process
As part of the incorporation process, a name search from a commercial name search house, including an opinion that the name may be used, must be obtained and submitted with the other documents required for incorporation. The name search is done to ensure that the name chosen for incorporation is not confusing with names already in use. Most provincial jurisdictions take no responsibility for names chosen. The incorporator takes the risk that he may be required to change the corporation's name if it is deceptively similar to a trade-name, trade-mark, or corporate name already in use (*CBCA*, s. 12), or be sued for trade-mark infringement or the common law tort of passing-off. Most provincial jurisdictions no longer even review the required name search. The obligation to get one is imposed simply to ensure that the incorporator has done the search. By contrast, the federal Corporations Directorate of Industry Canada carefully reviews name searches and will

---

16 [1979] A.C. 731 at 742 (H.L.).

not permit an incorporation to go ahead if it has concerns about the name. Sometimes this concern can result in extended discussions between the incorporator (or more likely her lawyer) and the Corporations Directorate and can cause frustrating delays in the incorporation process. Accordingly, where an incorporation must take place on a certain date, it is advisable to "pre-clear" the name by taking advantage of the possibility of reserving the name for up to ninety days in advance of incorporation (*CBCA*, s. 11). By doing so, if the Corporations Directorate has any concerns about the name, there is an opportunity to address them in advance of the proposed incorporation date.

The name search, which takes the form of a computer printout, may be obtained from various commercial search firms for a fee. The search is conducted in a database owned by the Corporations Directorate of Industry Canada and is called NUANS (Newly Upgraded Automated Name Search System). The NUANS database includes corporate names, trademarks, and business names in use across Canada. It is necessary to request a search which is "biased," meaning weighted, in favour of the jurisdiction chosen for incorporation. The NUANS database contains an enormous number of names, and the bias request is to ensure that the search picks up those names that are being used in the jurisdiction in which incorporation is sought. In addition to the required NUANS search, it is advisable to search local telephone and trade directories for similar names to ensure that the name chosen is not confusing with other names and trade-marks.

A name search is not required if the incorporators are content simply to have a number assigned as the name by the corporate regulator (e.g., 123456 Ontario Inc.). This may be attractive if the corporation will be carrying on no business in which public recognition would be an asset, such as simply holding a portfolio of investments, or where a suitable name cannot be found.[17] A corporation with a number name may use another name so long as it complies with the provincial registration requirements described above.

ii) Registered Office

Under the *CBCA*, it is necessary to identify the place in Canada — meaning, generally, the municipality — where the registered office is to

---

17   Where a corporation is incorporated with a number name, the directors may amend the articles to adopt another name without the approval of shareholders, a requirement for any other amendment (*CBCA*, above note 4, s. 173(3)). Number names are not permitted under the laws of Prince Edward Island, Nova Scotia, British Columbia, or the Northwest Territories. Amendment of articles is discussed in chapter 10.

be situated. The street address of the registered office is set out in the Notice of Registered Office (Form 19). The "registered office" concept was introduced with the *CBCA*. It need not be the head office, but only a place within the jurisdiction at which the records of the corporation are kept (*CBCA*, s. 20(1)) and which may serve as the address for correspondence with the Director and for service of documents (*CBCA*, s. 254). The place specified for the registered office may only be changed by amending the articles (*CBCA*, s. 173(1)(b)). A change in the address within the place specified in the articles may be made with the approval of the directors. Where the directors approve such a change, a Notice of Change of Registered Office must be filed with the Director (s. 19(3), Form 19).

The registered office of a provincial corporation must be located inside the incorporating province (*OBCA*, s. 5(1) & *NBBCA*, s. 4(1)).[18] The place in which the registered office is located may be changed by special resolution of the shareholders (*OBCA*, s. 14(3)).

iii) Class and Number of Shares

The articles define the classes of shares the corporation is authorized to issue. To do so, they must set out the name by which each class of shares is to be identified (e.g., "common shares") as well as the "rights, privileges, restrictions and conditions" of each class, such as whether they vote, may receive dividends, or share in the distribution of the assets of the corporation on its dissolution after creditors are paid. We will discuss some of the many possibilities for creating shares with different characteristics and some of the rules regarding share provisions in chapter 6.

In many small corporations there is only one class of shares, typically identified as common shares, which vote and are entitled to receive dividends declared by the board of directors and which receive the remaining property of the corporation on dissolution. Corporations may have other classes of shares with different characteristics. In general, the bundle of characteristics belonging to each class of shares will determine their price and their attractiveness to investors with different sorts of preferences. For example, investors who want to receive a fixed annual return, but do not want to participate in the management of the corporation, would be interested in a class of shares that offers a fixed annual dividend, paid before any dividend on any other class, even if the class had no voting right. Such shares are commonly referred to as "preferred shares."

---

18   In British Columbia (*Company Act*, R.S.B.C. 1979, c. 59, ss. 39 & 40), and the Yukon (*Business Corporations Act*, R.S.Y. 1986, c. 15, s. 22), the place of the registered office may also be changed by directors' resolution.

It is also necessary to specify the number of shares the corporation may issue. Shares are issued by the directors, but they can issue shares only up to any maximum amount provided for in the articles. Additional shares may be issued only by amending the articles to raise or to remove the limit. This amendment requires shareholder approval by special resolution. It is common practice to state that corporations may issue an unlimited number of shares of each class, but in some circumstances limits may be desired. If, for example, shareholders want to avoid having additional shares issued by the directors to dilute their proportionate interest in the corporation, they may want the maximum number of shares authorized to be issued set at the total number of shares to be held by them. If no limit is specified, the corporation may issue an unlimited number of shares.

iv) Number of Directors

Under the *CBCA*, it is necessary in the articles to specify the number of directors or a minimum and a maximum number of directors.[19] The choice of the appropriate number of directors will depend on a variety of factors specific to each corporation, including the scale of the corporation's business, the desire of shareholders to be members of or to be represented on the board, and the desirability of involving people with no relation to the corporation as directors on the board — perhaps because they have some needed expertise or experience. In addition, corporate statutes contain certain requirements: under the *CBCA*, corporations that have distributed their shares to the public[20] must have three directors, at least two of whom are not officers or employees of the corporation or affiliated corporations;[21] all other corporations need to have only one director (*CBCA*, s. 102(2)). The number of directors or the minimum and maximum number of directors may be changed only by amendment of the articles.[22]

---

19 Where cumulative voting is provided for in the articles, a fixed number of directors must be specified (*CBCA*, above note 4, s. 107(a)).

20 The *CBCA*, *ibid.*, defines "distributing corporation" as a corporation that has issued a prospectus or sold shares for which a prospectus would be now required, but does not refer to shares being listed on a stock exchange or any requirement that shares be outstanding (s. 2(7) & (8)). The *CBCA* permits a corporation to apply to the Director to be deemed not to be distributing its securities to the public. See "Considerations Relating to the Scale of the Corporation" in this section.

21 There is no requirement for outside directors in the corporate statutes of Prince Edward Island, Quebec, or British Columbia.

22 Under the New Brunswick *Business Corporations Act*, S.N.B. 1981, c. B-9.1, the number of directors is specified in the by-laws (s. 60(2)).

v) Restrictions on Issuing, Transferring, or Owning Shares
In the absence of a restriction in the articles on the transfer of shares, shares, unlike partnership interests, are presumed to be freely transferable. It is commonplace, however, for corporations with few shareholders to have some kind of transfer restriction in the articles. In such corporations, each shareholder has a strong interest in having some control over who the other shareholders are. Shareholders in such corporations typically work in the business and will not want their fellow shareholders selling out, nor will they want to have another person involved as a shareholder without their consent. Against these considerations, each shareholder is likely to want as much flexibility as possible to sell his own shares. In a corporation with few shareholders, this flexibility is especially important because it is often difficult for a shareholder in such a corporation to find a buyer. There is no ready marketplace into which the shares of such a corporation may be sold. As a result, when drafting share transfer restrictions, shareholders typically try to strike some form of balance between their interest in controlling who the other shareholders are and their interest in having the fewest restrictions on their right to sell their own shares. As will be discussed in chapter 6, this conflict often leads to the creation of complex mechanisms in shareholder agreements, such as provisions giving shareholders a right to buy the shares of any shareholder who wants to sell her shares before they may be sold to a third party (called a "right of first refusal"). In the articles, the usual restriction is simply a short provision requiring the directors or some specified majority of shareholders to consent to the transfer. People to whom shares are transferred are not subject to any restriction unless they are actually aware of the restriction, or it is conspicuously noted on the face of the share certificates they receive (*CBCA*, s. 48(3)).

Another reason to have a restriction on transfer in a corporation's articles is to avoid the obligations imposed on public corporations under securities legislation. The Ontario *Securities Act*[23] provides a broad exemption from most of the obligations of the Act for shares of a "private company," defined as a corporation that has the following provisions in its articles:

- a restriction on the transfer of its shares;
- a limit on the number of shareholders to not more than 50; and
- a prohibition on any invitation to the public to subscribe for its securities (s. 1(1)).

---

23   R.S.O. 1990, c. S.5 [*OSA*].

Consequently, provisions expressing these limitations should be included in the articles of all corporations other than those contemplating an offer of their shares to the public.[24]

Restrictions may be imposed on the issuance of shares as well. The *CBCA* model corporate statutes permit the inclusion in the articles of a right for each existing shareholder of a corporation to purchase shares issued in proportion to his holdings of shares prior to issuance to anyone else (*CBCA*, s. 28). Such a right is referred to as a "pre-emptive right." Variations on the form of pre-emptive right are permitted under some of the provincial statutes (e.g., *OBCA*, s. 26) but, in practice, most pre-emptive rights are set up like the *CBCA* provision. Pre-emptive rights are also commonly found in shareholder agreements.

Another kind of restriction on transfer or issuance defines the class of acceptable shareholders. For example, a corporation may want to prohibit transfers outside the existing group of shareholders. The most common restriction, however, is to prohibit transfers to non-Canadians, perhaps to ensure that the corporation continues to qualify under a government program requiring Canadian ownership. A corporation's articles may provide for restrictions on ownership of shares for similar purposes. Restrictions for ensuring a minimum level of Canadian ownership and for certain other purposes are expressly contemplated in the *CBCA* and in the provincial statutes modelled after it (*CBCA*, ss. 49(9) & 174, *OBCA*, s. 42). Where such restrictions have been included in the articles, the corporate statutes provide a procedure for the corporation to force the sale of any shares owned in a manner contrary to the restrictions (*CBCA*, ss. 46–47; *OBCA*, s. 45).

vi) *Restrictions on the Business the Corporation May Carry On*
As discussed in chapter 3, under earlier corporate statutes a corporation had to specify its "objects" in the corporate constitution. This obligation inevitably led to problems caused by corporations engaging in activities that were not contemplated in their objects. Such activities were considered *ultra vires* the corporation, and any obligations to third parties which were entered into by the corporation in connection with these activities were of no effect.

Under the *CBCA* model statutes, it is not necessary for the corporation to describe the activities in which it will engage. The corporation

---

24   It should be noted that the inclusion of these provisions in the articles does not mean that the sale of shares of the corporation will never be subject to the Ontario *Securities Act*. To qualify for the exemption, such shares must not be offered to the public (*OSA*, *ibid.*, ss. 73(1)(a) & 35(2)(10)).

has all the capacity and, subject to certain limitations in the corporate statute, the rights, powers, and privileges of a natural person (*CBCA*, s. 15). In order to avoid the risk of *ultra vires* activities, it is common practice not to include in the articles any restrictions on the business the corporation may carry on.

In any event, the rule that *ultra vires* obligations were unenforceable against the corporation has been largely mitigated under the *CBCA*. If a restriction is included in the articles, the *CBCA* provides that the corporation is forbidden to act in a manner contrary to the restriction (*CBCA*, s. 16(2)). Nevertheless, if the corporation does something contrary to the restriction, the act is not invalid by reason only that it is contrary to the articles (*CBCA*, s. 16(3)). As a result, no third party should be prejudiced because the corporation entered into an obligation with the third party which was contrary to its articles.[25]

This provision does not mean, however, that the restrictions in the articles are of no effect. Shareholders may seek relief from any contravention of such a provision if its effect on the shareholders is "oppressive, unfairly prejudicial to or unfairly disregards [their] interests" (*CBCA*, s. 241). Also, both shareholders and creditors may apply to a court for an order restraining the corporation, or anyone acting on its behalf, from acting in a manner contrary to the articles or directing compliance with the articles (*CBCA*, s. 247). It remains to be seen if a court would make such an order where the effect would be to deprive a third party of the benefit of a contract it had with the corporation.

vii) Other Provisions

A variety of other provisions are sometimes put in the articles. The *CBCA* contemplates that the articles may deal with the following types of matters: requirements for super majorities of directors or shareholders to approve certain decisions (s. 5(4)), limitations on the right to purchase shares (ss. 30 & 31), liens on the shares of shareholders who are indebted to the corporation (s. 40(1)), the quorum for directors' meetings (s. 126(3)), and a requirement for an executive committee of the board of directors (s. 127). In addition, any provision permitted by the *CBCA* to be included in a by-law may be included in the articles (s. 6(2)). The content of by-laws will be discussed below, but, in general, what may be included in a by-law is virtually unrestricted (*CBCA*, s. 103(1)). The main difference between including a rule in the articles and in the by-laws is that the articles can be amended only by a special resolution of shareholders requiring a two-thirds majority

---

25 See chapter 5, "Liability of Corporations in Contract," regarding a qualification to this protection.

of shareholders voting. In contrast, by-laws require approval by a simple majority only.[26] Many lawyers suggest that the content of the articles should be minimized in order to simplify the process of incorporation and to avoid the need to amend the articles later if changes are desired.

Finally, if a corporation will be doing business in Quebec, it is the practice of some lawyers to include in the articles the borrowing powers and the powers to mortgage property contemplated by the *Special Corporate Powers Act* of Quebec.[27] The Act permits a corporation to mortgage property in Quebec only when authorized by its constitution. Without the special provision, there is a risk that a corporation might be found not to have the powers dealt with in the Act.

b) Other Documents Required to Be Filed on Incorporation

The Notice of Directors simply lists the directors and their addresses, and indicates whether they are resident Canadians. The *CBCA* requires that a majority of the directors be resident Canadians (s. 105(3)).[28] The Notice of Registered Office simply indicates the street address at which the registered office is located. The only reason for separate documents containing this information is to permit updated notices to be filed each time the information on directors or the address of the registered office changes (*CBCA*, ss. 19 & 113), without amending the articles. Under the *OBCA*, the address of the registered office and the identity, address, and Canadian residency status of the directors are contained in the articles (*OBCA Regulation*, s. 46, Form 1). There is, however, no need to amend the articles when the directors change. It is sufficient to file an information document called a Notice of Change under the *Corporations Information Act*.[29] Under the *OBCA*, it is necessary for each director named in the articles to file a consent to act as a director (*OBCA*, s. 5(2); *OBCA Regulation*, s. 46(2), Form 2).[30]

All jurisdictions charge a fee on incorporation. The fee for incorporation under the *CBCA* is $500 (*CBCA Regulations*, Schedule II, s. 2(a)),

---

26   A special resolution is a resolution signed by all shareholders or passed at a meeting of shareholders by a majority of not less than two-thirds of the votes cast by shareholders present and voting at the meeting (*CBCA*, above note 4, s. 2). Amendment of articles and by-laws is discussed in chapter 10.

27   R.S.Q. 1977, c. P-16, ss. 27 & 34.

28   "Resident Canadian" is defined in the *CBCA*, above note 4, s. 2, and *CBCA Regulations*, SOR/79-316, s. 11. Other qualifications for directors are described in chapter 7.

29   R.S.O. 1990, c. C.39, s. 4 [*CIA*].

30   The *Ontario Business Corporations Act*, R.S.O. 1990, c. B.16 [*OBCA*], was amended recently to add a requirement for directors named in the articles (or elected or appointed in any other manner) to consent in writing within ten days, or their election or appointment would not be effective (S.O. 1994, c. 27, s. 71, amending *OBCA*, s. 119(9)).

while the fee under most provincial statutes is somewhat less. Under the *OBCA* it is $315 (*OBCA Regulation*, Schedule 1, s. 1).[31]

c) Completion of Incorporation

Once these documents are properly filed along with the fee, the Director appointed to administer the *CBCA* issues a certificate (Form 2) certifying that the corporation, the articles of which are attached, was incorporated on the date of the certificate (*CBCA*, ss. 8 & 9). The corporation comes into existence on the date of the certificate (*CBCA*, s. 9). The directors named in the Notice of Directors hold office until the first meeting of shareholders (*CBCA*, s. 106(2)). The provisions in the articles may be changed only by articles of amendment filed with the Director after approval by a special resolution of shareholders. This process is discussed in chapter 10.

The actual process of filing the requisite documents with the fee and receiving a certificate of incorporation is expeditious and may be engaged in by anyone. Lawyers routinely incorporate corporations for their clients but now there are also a variety of commercial services offering to do incorporations more quickly and cheaply. Individuals may also obtain incorporation kits to permit do-it-yourself incorporations.[32] As will be discussed below incorporation is only the first step in organizing a business so consideration must be given to the desirability of professional advice in connection with incorporations.

d) Post-Incorporation Organization

On incorporation, the corporation may commence carrying on a business. It may be a new business, or an existing business may be transferred to it. Unlike a partnership, there is no need for a corporation to carry on business; its existence derives exclusively from the issuance of the certificate under the statute.[33] Several more steps are required, however, before the corporation is fully organized.

---

31 Name searches must also be filed with the articles, as discussed above under "Names and the Incorporation Process."

32 Several incorporation kits are available, including the "Business Incorporators Handbook" published by the Ontario Ministry of Consumer and Commercial Relations. The main purpose of this kit is to assist incorporators in choosing an effective corporate name. Software designed to enable computer users to incorporate quickly and easily has also become available commercially.

33 *Campbell v. Taxicabs Verrals Ltd.* (1912), 27 O.L.R. 141 (H.C.J.). Section 212 of the *CBCA*, above note 4, provides that the Director appointed to administer the Act may dissolve a corporation that has not commenced business within three years of incorporation or has not carried on business for three consecutive years. This discretion is rarely exercised. See chapter 10.

First, the directors should have a meeting and pass a resolution to issue shares to the shareholders. Under the *CBCA* this issuance is essential since, until the shares are issued, the only persons who may act for the corporation are the directors named in the Notice of Directors. Should anything happen to them, the corporation would be unable to act. Under the *OBCA*, in instances where there are no directors, any person who manages or supervises the management of the business and the affairs of the corporation is deemed to be a director (*OBCA*, s. 115(4)). There is no requirement for any minimum amount to be paid into the corporation for shares. Some foreign jurisdictions impose minimum capitalization requirements to discourage frivolous incorporation.[34]

Also at the first meeting, the directors will typically adopt arrangements for carrying on the formal legal business of the corporation, including the following:

- requirements for directors;
- procedure for meetings of directors (e.g., how notice of meetings is given, what constitutes a quorum);
- remuneration and indemnification of directors;
- designation and specification of duties of officers;
- procedure for meetings of shareholders;
- procedure for payment of dividends;
- financial year of the corporation; and
- designation of those persons who may sign documents on behalf of the corporation.

These arrangements are typically set out in a by-law. The *CBCA* provides that certain elements of its default rules may be changed only by a by-law (e.g., the location, notice of, and quorum for directors' meetings (s. 114), location of shareholder meetings (s. 132), quorum (s. 139), and voting procedures (s. 141)). All other matters may be dealt with in a resolution passed by the directors. It is common practice, however, to deal with all these matters in a general by-law. A general by-law is also useful as a handbook on corporate procedures, and it sometimes recites rules provided for in the *CBCA* in the interests of providing a complete compendium of applicable rules.

To take effect, a by-law must be passed by the directors, but it continues in effect only if it is passed by the shareholders at their next meeting following the approval of the by-law by the directors (s. 103, *CBCA*). Because making, amending, and repealing by-laws ultimately requires shareholder

---

34   Minimum capitalization requirements are discussed in chapter 3 (section G(2)(a) and in chapter 6.

approval, including these arrangements in a by-law serves to entrench them more than dealing with them by resolution of the directors.[35]

Typically at the first meeting, directors will pass resolutions dealing with other organizational matters as well, such as appointing officers and an auditor and making banking arrangements, including authorizing the opening of a bank account for the corporation and designating certain people to sign cheques on behalf of the corporation. Banks have standard form resolutions that they require to be passed. A corporate seal for the corporation may be approved in such an organizational meeting, though a seal is no longer required (*CBCA*, s. 23; *OBCA*, s. 13). It is also usual to designate a form of share certificate. As will be discussed in chapter 6, there is no need for a corporation to issue share certificates, though shareholders have a right to receive one on request (*CBCA*, s. 49(1)).

Once the shares are issued, it is necessary to have a shareholders' meeting at which any by-laws approved by the directors are voted on (*CBCA*, s. 104(1)). By-laws must be approved by a simple majority of shareholder votes represented at the meeting. For small corporations with few shareholders, this meeting typically takes place immediately after the directors' meeting.

A final step in organization, which often occurs in corporations with few shareholders, is the entry into an agreement by the shareholders. Shareholders may wish to customize the way in which the corporation is governed by agreeing to alter the rights and obligations provided for in the *CBCA*. For example, all shareholders may agree to vote their shares for certain of them as directors. Shareholder agreements also often deal with the circumstances in which shares may be transferred. Shareholder agreements are discussed in chapter 6.

As mentioned in chapter 3, in order to determine the rules that govern a corporation, along with its shareholders, directors, and officers, it is necessary to take into account not just the governing corporate statute and the case law but also the elements of the corporate constitution identified above: the articles of incorporation, the by-laws, directors' resolutions, shareholders' resolutions, and any shareholders' agreement. These documents are agreed to by the directors or shareholders, or both, and represent, in that sense, private arrangements between them. They are private arrangements which are bounded by various mandatory provisions of the corporate statutes and which are, to a greater or lesser extent, enforceable through statutory mechanisms that will be

---

35   See chapter 10 for the process of making, amending, or repealing by-laws.

described in chapter 9. As indicated, these arrangements may derogate from or respond to the provisions of the governing corporate statute.

All these documents, along with a register showing who owns the securities of the corporation, must be maintained by the corporation at its registered office or at any other place in Canada designated by the directors (*CBCA*, s. 20(2)). Shareholders and creditors must be given access to them, except for minutes of meetings and resolutions of directors (*CBCA*, s. 21). Access includes a limited right to make copies. These documents are usually bound in hard copy form in something called a "minute book," though the *CBCA* permits them to be retained in "any system of mechanical or electronic data processing or any other information storage device that is capable of reproducing any required information in intelligible written form within a reasonable time" (s. 22(1)). Articles and any other document filed with the Director, such as the Notice of Directors and the Notice of Registered Office, are filed in a publicly accessible record maintained by the Corporations Directorate of Industry Canada.

e) Considerations Relating to the Scale of the Corporation

Corporations are used by businesses ranging from small businesses involving a single person as shareholder, director, and employee to huge multinational business with thousands of shareholders and employees. The terms "public corporation" and "private corporation," or "widely held corporation" and "closely held corporation," are sometimes used to distinguish corporations having a large number of shareholders from those having only a few. Although the vast majority of corporations fall into this second category, those that fall into the first are nevertheless extremely important owing to their enormous role in the economy.

To be effective, corporate law rules must be responsive to the often very different requirements of business enterprises of different scales. Certain procedures and other provisions of corporate law may be appropriate for one form and not for another. Consider, for example, the fundamental issue of how management will be made accountable to shareholders. Many public corporations have a large number of shareholders, most of whom have a relatively small stake in the corporation relative to its total value. Such corporations are managed by professional managers, with little direct participation from shareholders, and require rules of governance which impose formal mechanisms to ensure that management is held accountable to shareholders. For a small corporation with few shareholders, all of whom are involved in the business actively, the same formal measures will not only be unnecessary but will create a burden. The question of appropriate rules becomes even more complex when one takes into account some of the common characteristics of public corporations in Canada: the presence of a majority shareholder, with the power to determine the outcome of most shareholder votes, and of large institutional shareholders, such as pension funds and insurance companies, who have the financial incentive and the skills and expertise necessary to participate effectively as shareholders.

Both the federal and the provincial Acts address this problem of differences in scale in a modest way by imposing different requirements on certain defined types of corporations. The *OBCA* distinguishes between "offering" and "non-offering" corporations. Essentially, offering corporations are those that have offered their shares to the public. Non-offering corporations are all the rest.

Figure 4.1   Definition of Offering Corporation under the *OBCA*

An "offering corporation" is defined as "a corporation that is offering its securities to the public . . ." (s. 1(1)(27)).

Offering securities to the public means that the corporation has

(a) filed a prospectus or statement of material facts with respect to any of its securities and some of the securities remain outstanding; or
(b) has securities listed on the Toronto Stock Exchange.

Non-offering corporations are all corporations not caught by this definition.

A corporation may obtain an order from the Ontario Securities Commission (OSC) to be deemed not to be an offering corporation if the corporation

(a) has fewer than fifteen security holders and
(b) the OSC determines such an order would not be prejudicial to the public interest.

Certain provisions of the *OBCA* apply only to offering corporations, such as management's obligation to facilitate the exercise of shareholders' right to vote by sending all shareholders information about the corporation and what is on the agenda for shareholders' meetings, as well as a form allowing them to send in their vote without attending in person (s. 111) or requiring them to file financial statements (s. 160). The form is called a "form of proxy" and the sending of information is called "mandatory proxy solicitation."[36] Other provisions of the *OBCA* apply

---

36   Proxies and proxy solicitation are discussed in chapter 7.

differently. For example, the minimum number of directors of an offering corporation is three, while for a non-offering corporation it is one (s. 115(3)); offering corporations must have their financial statements audited, while the shareholders of non-offering corporations may dispense with the requirement to have an audit if they unanimously agree.

The *CBCA* takes a similar but slightly different approach. It defines distributing securities to the public in essentially the same way as the *OBCA* defines offering securities to the public, although the federal Act does not refer to shares being listed on any stock exchange (ss. 2(7) & (8)). Like the *OBCA,* the *CBCA* permits a corporation to apply to the Director to be deemed not to be distributing its securities to the public when there are few shareholders. The Director may grant such an order provided it does not prejudice any security holder.

Under the *CBCA*, if a corporation has distributed securities to the public and they remain outstanding and held by more than one person, it becomes subject to a more onerous set of obligations. All such distributing corporations must have three directors, while others need only one (s. 102(3)), they must appoint an auditor[37] and an audit committee (ss. 162 & 171), and they must file financial statements (ss. 155, 160, 162–63 & 171(8)). In addition, all such corporations must comply with insider trading obligations (s. 127). Insider trading is governed by securities laws in most provinces and is discussed in chapter 11.

The *CBCA* also makes some further distinctions among corporations to determine the applicability of particular provisions. The most important is that all corporations with more than fifteen shareholders, whether distributing corporations or not, must comply with mandatory proxy solicitation requirements (s. 149(2)) and with takeover bid rules, if someone makes a bid to acquire the shares of the corporation (s. 194).[38] Takeover bids are regulated under provincial securities laws and are discussed in chapter 11.

The chief advantage of the *OBCA* and *CBCA* schemes is that it is easy to know whether a particular corporation is public or private; the criteria are specific. This specificity is also their main disadvantage. Because they rely on rigid, technical criteria to distinguish corporations of dif-

---

37   All corporations governed by the *CBCA*, above note 4, must appoint an auditor, but the shareholders of corporations that are not distributing corporations, or where the securities distributed to the public are no longer outstanding or are held by one person only, may agree not to appoint an auditor (s. 163).

38   The trust indenture provisions in Part VIII of the *CBCA* apply only if the debt obligations issued under the indenture were issued as part of a distribution to the public (*CBCA, ibid.,* s. 88(2)).

ferent scales, rather than functional ones, these definitions tend to be both under and overinclusive. For this reason, and because the circumstances in which different rules apply are fairly limited, the schemes in Canadian corporate statutes do not approximate distinct, comprehensive codes for small and large corporations.[39]

C. JURISDICTION OF INCORPORATION

1) Introduction

In section B, we discussed the process of incorporation under the *CBCA*. In this section we discuss the factors that someone who wanted to incorporate would consider in choosing whether to incorporate under the federal statute or one of the provincial statutes. It is, of course, possible that incorporation in a jurisdiction outside Canada may be considered preferable in particular circumstances. Foreign incorporation will be discussed here only with respect to the requirements for such corporations to carry on business in Canada.

2) Factors Affecting Choice of Jurisdiction

a) Disclosure Obligations
Each jurisdiction under which a corporation may incorporate imposes certain obligations to disclose information regarding the corporation and the people involved in it. Disclosure may be a concern for competitive, personal, or other reasons. In Canada, disclosure does not play a significant role in the selection of an incorporation jurisdiction because information filings are similar in all jurisdictions of incorporation and, in most cases, will not be considered onerous. The federal and Ontario disclosure requirements are set out in figure 4.2 below.

Regardless of the jurisdiction of incorporation, a corporation must also make provincial filings in every province where it begins to carry on business. For example, upon commencing business in Ontario, a corporation must file an initial notice under the *Corporations Information Act* (ss. 2(1) & (4)) which requires disclosure of information similar to that required for corporations incorporated in Ontario. In addition to the

---

39   As noted under "Articles" above, the provisions of the *OSA*, above note 23, define a private company for the purposes of the obligations under that statute.

Figure 4.2 Examples of Disclosure Obligations Imposed by Jurisdiction of Incorporation in Addition to Disclosure Required in Articles

---

CBCA

Filing: Annual return, s. 263, Form 22; Notice of Change of Directors, s. 113, Form 6; Notice of Change of Registered Office, s. 19, Form 3

- Financial year end
- Main types of business
- Changes in directors, registered office
- Date of last annual meeting
- Whether distributes securities to the public
- Whether assets exceed $5 million or whether revenues exceed $10 million
- Whether there are more than 15 shareholders
- Name, address, occupation, date of election or appointment, and Canadian residency status of new director
- Name of anyone ceasing to be a director or officer and date of departure

OBCA

Filing: Initial return, annual return, and notices of change under *Corporations Information Act* (ss. 3(1), 3.1 & 4)

- Name and residence address of the officers of the corporation
- Name, address, date of election or appointment, and Canadian residency status of new directors
- Name of anyone ceasing to be a director or officer and date of departure
- Activities Classification Code applicable to the corporation (Regulation made under the *Corporations Information Act* (R.R.O. 1990, Reg. 182, s. 1(a)).

---

information listed in figure 4.2, the extraprovincial corporation must disclose the following:

- name of the jurisdiction in which the corporation was incorporated, continued, or amalgamated, whichever is the most recent;
- address of the corporation's head or registered office;
- date on which the corporation commenced or ceased activities in Ontario;
- name and office address of the corporation's chief officer or manager in Ontario and the date the person assumed or ceased to hold this position; and
- address of the corporation's principal office in Ontario.[40]

---

40   Regulation made under the *CIA*, above note 29 (R.R.O. 1990, Reg. 182, s. 2).

Failure to make required filings and filing untrue or misleading information are offences under the *CBCA* and under provincial law (*CBCA*, ss. 250 & 251, Ontario *Corporations Information Act*, ss. 13 & 14). Under some provincial statutes, the failure to file also deprives a corporation of the right to sue in the province in connection with the business being carried on by the corporation except with leave of the court (e.g., Ontario *Corporations Information Act*, s. 18). Whenever any information in an initial filing changes a new filing is required (e.g., Ontario *Corporations Information Act*, s. 4).

b) Where the Corporation Will Carry on Business

As discussed above,[41] *CBCA* incorporation gives a corporation the right to carry on business in all provinces, whereas provincial incorporation gives the right to carry on business only in the province of incorporation. Provincial incorporation means that a corporation may carry on business in another province if it obtains a licence under provincial extraprovincial licensing legislation in place in each province. As noted above, although the granting of an extraprovincial licence is discretionary, it is rarely refused unless there is a problem with the corporation's name. Under the Ontario *Extra-Provincial Corporations Act*[42] (*OEPCA*), corporations incorporated under the laws of other provinces are exempt from the requirement to obtain a licence. Certain other provinces have reciprocal arrangements under which a corporation incorporated under the laws of one need not obtain a licence to carry on business in the other. All corporations incorporated in foreign jurisdictions must obtain a licence.

Where a corporation is required to obtain an extraprovincial licence, it must submit an application that includes a name-search report, a certificate setting out that the corporation is a valid and subsisting corporation under the laws of its governing jurisdiction, an appointment of an agent for service in the province in which it wants to do business, and the required fee. In Ontario the fee is $315. An agent for service is a person in Ontario who is authorized to accept service of documents on behalf of the corporation in connection with any lawsuit in which the corporation is involved. This requirement is intended to ensure that persons dealing with the corporation in Ontario are able to commence civil proceedings to pursue any claim against the corporation.

---

41 See chapter 3.
42 R.S.O. 1990, c. E.27.

The obligation to obtain an extraprovincial licence arises when a corporation begins to carry on business in a province. What constitutes "carrying on business" varies from province to province. In Ontario a corporation carries on business if it has a place of business in Ontario, holds an interest in real property, or otherwise engages in business in the province.[43] A corporation is deemed not to carry on business if it is only taking orders or buying or selling goods or services through travelling representatives, advertisements, or the mail (*OEPCA*, s. 1(1)). Some provinces have even broader definitions of carrying on business (e.g., *ABCA*, s. 264, which includes soliciting business in the province).

Failure to obtain a licence when one is required to do so under a provincial extraprovincial licensing statute is an offence. Liability extends to "any person who contravenes this act," and includes the corporation and any person who carries on its business in the province as well as directors and officers who authorized, permitted, or acquiesced in the offence (e.g., *OEPCA*, s. 20). An unlicensed extraprovincial corporation cannot sue before any provincial tribunal in respect of any contract made by it (e.g., *OEPCA*, s. 21). In some provinces, like Ontario, an unlicensed extraprovincial corporation may not own land (*OEPCA*, s. 22). Licences may also be cancelled by the provincial official responsible for administering the extraprovincial licensing regime.

c) Liability for Provincial Tax

The tax liability of a corporation is not significantly affected by its jurisdiction of incorporation. Provincial income tax is based on income earned in the province regardless of its jurisdiction of incorporation. As a result, tax is not usually a significant consideration in choosing a jurisdiction in which to incorporate.

d) Provisions of Corporate Law

In Canada, there has never been competition among incorporation jurisdictions for incorporation business as there has been in the United States. Both provincial and federal governments have worked towards more uniform laws across the country, and, indeed, uniformity has been one of the express objectives of the *CBCA* (s. 4). As a result, the differences in the corporate law regimes federally and in the provinces and territories are not so significant as to permit major relative advantages and disadvantages to be easily identified. Since the *CBCA* was introduced in 1975, almost

---

43 This provision was recently interpreted in *Success International Inc.* v. *Environmental Export International of Canada Inc.* (1995), 23 O.R. (3d) 137 (Gen. Div.).

identical statutes have been introduced in Ontario, Alberta, Saskatchewan, Manitoba, and New Brunswick. Corporate legislation in Newfoundland is based on the *CBCA* model, though it is not identical to the federal statute. Quebec has its own scheme, but, in many respects, it is similar in effect to the *CBCA*. The British Columbia and Nova Scotia legislation still follow a registration model based on the English *Companies Act*, although both provinces have adapted the model in significant ways. Nova Scotia recently passed a Part III to its corporate statute which gives *CBCA*-like remedies to shareholders. Prince Edward Island is the only jurisdiction to retain a letters patent statute. See chapter 3 for a discussion of the differences between these three models of incorporation and their consequences.

Some differences in substantive law may be overcome through private arrangements. For example, under section 126(2) of the *OBCA*, a majority of directors' meetings must be held in Canada, unless the articles or by-laws provide otherwise. There is no equivalent restriction in the *CBCA*. This difference may be mitigated, however, by simply including an exception in the by-laws or articles as provided in the *OBCA*. Alternatively, the directors could take decisions by all of them signing a written resolution rather than having a meeting (*OBCA*, s. 129(1)).[44]

As a consequence of the similarity in corporate law regimes, the practice of most lawyers is to incorporate under provincial law in the province where business is to be carried on and to incorporate federally if it is contemplated that business will be conducted in more than one province. Differences in fees charged by the different jurisdictions will also have a significant effect, given the lack of other bases of differentiation. Currently, at $500, the *CBCA* is the most expensive.

Corporate law in foreign jurisdictions may be significantly different, and there may be substantial benefits to certain stakeholders to incorporation under the laws of particular jurisdictions.

e) Prestige

If a business is to be carried on outside Canada, it may be preferable to incorporate under the *CBCA*. Foreign persons doing business with the corporation may be unfamiliar with the provincial or territorial jurisdictions.

3) Continuance

After a decision is made regarding the jurisdiction for incorporation, it is possible under the corporate laws of most jurisdictions to migrate

---

44   This process of acting by signed resolution is discussed in chapter 7.

from one to another (e.g., *CBCA,* ss. 187–88; *OBCA,* ss. 180–81). In Canada this migration is called continuance. The procedure for continuance will be discussed in chapter 10 below.

D. PRE-INCORPORATION CONTRACTS

A final difficult area related to incorporation is the effect of contracts entered into on behalf of a corporation before the date of its incorporation. Sometimes a person, typically referred to as an agent or promoter, will purport to enter into a contract with a third party on behalf of a corporation that has not yet come into existence. This pre-incorporation contract may occur, for example, when there has not been time to set up the corporation. In these circumstances, several difficult issues arise:

- Is the agent liable to perform the contract personally?
- Is the corporation liable if it adopts the contract after it comes into existence?
- If the corporation becomes liable, does the agent cease to be liable?

At common law it was clear that the corporation was not liable for contracts purported to be entered into on its behalf before its coming into existence and could not be made so by any act of adoption or acceptance afterwards. For the corporation to be liable, there had to be a new contract between the corporation and the third party.[45] Such a contract would involve a post-incorporation exchange of promises between the corporation and the third party.

The circumstances in which the agent would be personally liable were much less clear. Liability of the agent depended on the intention of the parties as determined by the courts based on all the circumstances. Although it was possible for the parties to state clearly whether the agent was to be liable, they seldom did so. In many cases the intention of the parties was divined from very refined interpretations of the language the parties used in the contract. For example, some cases held that the agent was not liable if the contract was expressed as made "by" the corporation, but was liable if the contract was made "for" the corporation. Nevertheless, some general statements may be made regarding the situation at common law.

If the parties both knew that the corporation was not in existence, a presumption arose that the parties intended that the agent would be

---

45   *Kelner v. Baxter* (1866), L.R. 2 C.P. 174.

personally liable. This was the case in *Kelner* v. *Baxter*.[46] In that case the conclusion was confirmed by a provision in the contract requiring immediate delivery. The court reasoned that the parties must have intended that someone was to be liable for payment for the goods delivered. It was not reasonable to think that the supplier had agreed that payment was to be contingent on the incorporation of a corporation.

If the parties both thought the corporation was in existence, no such presumption arose and the parties' intention had to be determined from all the circumstances. In *Black* v. *Smallwood*,[47] Black entered into a contract with Smallwood purporting to act on behalf of Western Suburbs Holdings Pty. Ltd., both believing the corporation was incorporated. Smallwood signed the contract as director of the corporation. In fact, the corporation had not been incorporated. When Black sued Smallwood alleging that Smallwood was personally liable, the court held that he was not. Since the parties both believed the corporation was in existence, the court determined that they had not intended Smallwood to be personally liable.

Where the agent knew no corporation was in existence but the third party believed she was dealing with an existing corporation through the agent, one might think that no contract could arise because there would be no consensus between the parties. Some courts have reached this conclusion.[48] Nevertheless, often the courts have held the agent liable in contract in these circumstances. If the contract cannot be enforced against the agent, the third party may be able to claim damages where she can show a misrepresentation by the agent which induced her to enter the contract to her detriment.[49]

The common law rules were unsatisfactory for several reasons. In many cases, third parties were denied relief based on highly artificial conclusions regarding the parties' intention. More important, the inability of the corporation to adopt contracts made for its benefit was often manifestly inconsistent with what the parties, in fact, intended. As a result, statutory reform has been attempted in most jurisdictions.

---

46   *Ibid.*
47   [1966] A.L.R. 744 (Austl. H.C.).
48   For example, *Wickberg* v. *Shatsky* (1969), 4 D.L.R. (3d) 540 (B.C.S.C.) [*Wickberg*].
49   One other possible claim the third party could make in these circumstances would be breach of warranty of authority (see *A.E. Lepage Ltd.* v. *Kamex Developments Ltd.*, [1979] 2 S.C.R. 155, discussed in chapter 2; *Wickberg, ibid.* and *General Motors Acceptance Corp.* v. *Weisman* (1979), 23 O.R. (2d) 479 (Co. Ct)). A practical problem which often arises with such a claim is that the damages suffered by the plaintiff are not the result of the breach of warranty, because the corporation either never came into existence, as in *Wickberg*, or is insolvent.

Section 14 of the *CBCA* and section 21 of the *OBCA* attempt to reform the law to make the individual agent liable in most circumstances and to permit the corporation to adopt contracts made on its behalf before it came into existence. The elements of both schemes are as follows:

- A person who enters into a contract with a third party by or on behalf of a corporation before it comes into existence is personally bound to perform the contract and is entitled to its benefits.
- If a corporation comes into existence and adopts the contract
  - the corporation is bound by and is entitled to the benefits of the contract, and
  - the agent is no longer bound by or entitled to the benefits of the contract.
- The third party may apply to a court for an order fixing both the corporation and the agent with liability (joint, joint and several, or apportioned) regardless of whether the corporation has adopted the contract or not.
- The third party and the agent may agree in the contract that the agent is not bound by the contract in any event.

The statutory reforms have tried to eliminate the problems of the common law. Now agents bear the risk of all liabilities prior to adoption of a contract, unless the agent's liability is expressly excluded by the agent and the third party, in which case the risk of non-adoption is transferred to the third party. This arrangement reflects the view that the agent is usually in a position to ensure that the corporation is incorporated and adopts the contract, and so can manage the risk of non-adoption more effectively than the third party. There are, however, several problems with the statutory scheme.

First, the *CBCA* and the corporate laws of Alberta, Manitoba, and Saskatchewan apply only to written contracts, so the old common law rules still apply to oral contracts made by or on behalf of a corporation. By contrast, the *OBCA*, *NBBCA*, and *QCA* do not distinguish between oral and written contracts, while the corporate laws of British Columbia, Nova Scotia, and Prince Edward Island do not address pre-incorporation contracts at all. These differences may lead to anomalous results, depending on the jurisdiction in which the agent chooses to incorporate. For example, if an agent enters into an oral pre-incorporation contract and then incorporates an Ontario corporation for the purpose of fulfilling the contract, the corporation can adopt the oral contract made by him and he is relieved from liability. If he incorporates a federal corporation, it cannot adopt the contract and his liability is determined at common law.

Second, if a corporation is never incorporated, it is unclear what rules should apply. It may be argued that the provisions of a corporate statute, such as *CBCA*, s. 14, come into play only when there has been an incorporation under that statute, since they refer to contracts made "before [the corporation] comes into existence" and moreover, the scope of corporate law in each jurisdiction is limited to corporations incorporated in the jurisdiction (see chapter 3). There is also uncertainty regarding what law is applicable to determine the respective liability of the agent and the corporation. Jacob Ziegel has suggested that any provincial court in which this question arises should decide what law applies based on the conflicts of laws rules of that province. Others, like Maureen Maloney, have suggested that the applicable law should be determined by the intention of the promoter.[50]

Third, the language used in the corporate statutes is problematic. Section 14(1) of the *CBCA* says that the agent is liable if she "enters into a written contract in the name of or on behalf of a corporation before it comes into existence. . . ." A close reading of this provision suggests that it is necessary to determine that a *contract* exists in order for the section to have any application. But if it is necessary to find an effective contract, then the provision simply restates the common law and does not improve it. Similarly, section 14(2) permitting the corporation to adopt a contract made for its benefit applies only if there is a contract, suggesting that adoption is permitted only where the agent is bound personally at common law. Such an interpretation has been suggested by some commentators and was adopted in *Westcom Radio Group Ltd.* v. *MacIsaac*.[51] Such an interpretation seems clearly contrary to overall intention of the provision and has been strongly criticized.[52] The federal government has circulated a proposal to amend the *CBCA* to eliminate this problem.[53]

Finally, the courts have been reluctant to grant relief under the provision permitting a court to hold the agent wholly or partly liable after the contract has been adopted by a corporation. The provision was

---

50   J.S. Ziegel, "Promoter's Liability and Preincorporation Contracts: *Westcom Radio Group Ltd.* v. *MacIsaac*" (1990) 16 Can. Bus. L.J. 341 at 346–47; M.A. Maloney, "Pre-Incorporation Transactions: A Statutory Solution?" (1985) 10 Can. Bus. L.J. 409 at 432–35.

51   (1989), 70 O.R. (2d) 591 (Div. Ct.). The *Westcom Radio* decision was applied in *Vacation Brokers Inc.* v. *Joseph*, [1993] O.J. No. 3036 (Co. Ct.) (QL).

52   For example, Ziegel, above note 50.

53   Industry Canada, *Proposals for Technical Amendments* (*Canada Business Corporations Act* Discussion Paper) (Ottawa: Industry Canada, 1995) at 14–15.

intended to provide a remedy in circumstances where the agent had arranged to have the contract adopted by a corporation with insufficient assets to satisfy the obligations under the contract. In *Bank of Nova Scotia* v. *Williams*[54] the court refused to exercise its discretion, since the third party entering the contract was not misled as to who he was really contracting with and who would be responsible for performing the obligations under the contract.

E. CHAPTER SUMMARY

In this chapter we discussed the process of incorporation in some detail. We reviewed the documents required to be filed, identifying the information that must be included and briefly analysing the legal and practical issues to be addressed in completing the incorporation documents. We concentrated on the articles and the decisions that must be made by incorporators about the corporate name, the classes and number of shares to be created, the number of directors, the registered office, restrictions on issuing, transferring, and owning shares, and restrictions on the business that the corporation may carry on. The corporate name is often one of the most difficult and frustrating decisions faced by incorporators for practical and legal reasons. It is difficult to find a distinctive name that is not already in use, and names are governed by a tangle of provincial and federal legislation.

We also discussed the steps that must be taken after incorporation to flesh out the characteristics of the corporation through by-laws and directors' and shareholders' resolutions. In incorporating and organizing a corporation, one must bear in mind that there are some differences in the rules which apply and the provisions which need to be included in the articles of incorporation, depending on whether the corporation distributes its shares to the public or not.

One important choice faced by incorporators is what jurisdiction they should choose for incorporation. In this regard we noted that there are few differences between the Canadian jurisdictions in the terms of requirements for public disclosure, liability for provincial tax, or the provisions of corporate law. In any event, whatever jurisdiction is chosen, it is possible subsequently to change to another jurisdiction through the continuance process.

---

54   (1976), 12 O.R. (2d) 709 (H.C.J.).

Finally, we discussed the special situation that arises when an agent purports to enter into a contract with a corporation to be incorporated. In most Canadian jurisdictions, such contracts are now enforceable against the agent unless a corporation is incorporated and adopts the contract, in which case the corporation alone is liable. The provisions regulating pre-incorporation contracts have some defects that have undermined their effectiveness in some circumstances.

FURTHER READINGS

BLACK, B., & R. KRAAKMAN, "A Self-enforcing Model of Corporate Law" (1996) 109 Harv. L. Rev. 1911

CANADIAN CORPORATE LAW REPORTER (Toronto: Butterworths) (looseleaf)

DANIELS, R.J., & J.G. MACINTOSH, "Toward a Distinctive Canadian Corporate Law Regime" (1991) 29 Osgoode Hall L.J. 863

EASSON, A.J., & D.A. SOBERMAN, "Pre-Incorporation Contracts: Common Law Confusion and Statutory Complexity" (1992) 17 Queen's L.J. 414

KINGSTON, R.A., & W. GROVER, Canada Corporations Manual (Toronto: Carswell, 1996) (looseleaf)

KOKONIS, J.D., "The Scheme of the Canadian Trade-marks Act" in G.F. Henderson, ed., Trade-Marks Law of Canada (Toronto: Carswell, 1993) 75

LAW SOCIETY OF UPPER CANADA, Bar Admission Course Reference Materials: Business Law (Toronto: Law Society of Upper Canada, 1995) c. 5

WADLOW, C., The Law of Passing-Off (London: Sweet & Maxwell, 1990)

CHAPTER 5

THE CORPORATION
IN ACTION

A. INTRODUCTION

As discussed in chapter 3, it is often helpful to think of corporations as having legal characteristics similar to those of natural persons. The comparison may only be taken so far, of course, and in this chapter we look at one of the most important differences between corporate and natural persons: the necessity for corporate persons to act through human agents. In particular, we will look at how corporations can be said to enter into contracts and to commit crimes and torts. The rules governing corporate liability are fundamentally important to all the stakeholders in the corporation because they determine the legal consequences of the corporation's behaviour in the marketplace and, as a result, influence the behaviour itself.

The theories of liability developed by the courts over the years have varied depending on whether the liability sought to be imposed was, on the one hand, contractual or, on the other hand, criminal or tortious. In imposing contractual liability, the courts focused on whether the individual whose actions are alleged to give rise to corporate liability was an *agent* of the corporation for that purpose and so capable of binding the corporation. By contrast, to impose liability on a corporation for a crime or a tort, the courts have asked whether the person could be considered to be the same as the corporation for the purpose of the activity alleged to constitute the crime or the tort. The significance of these distinctions should become clearer in the following sections.

B. LIABILITY OF CORPORATIONS FOR CRIMES

1) Introduction

Because corporations have "no soul to be damned; no body to be kicked,"[1] but fundamentally comprise a locus of claims by the various stakeholders as discussed in chapter 1, the reasons for and consequences of imposing criminal liability on corporations are somewhat different from those associated with imposing such liability on natural persons. It seems unlikely, for example, that conviction for a criminal offence would have the same deterrent effect on a soulless corporation as it would have on an individual. Also, the remedies used to sanction criminal behaviour are problematic when a corporation is the offender. Imprisonment is not practical and, if a fine is imposed on a corporation, its shareholders and others with financial claims against the corporation, including employees, will suffer. At the same time, despite the conceptual challenges associated with corporate criminality, the prospect of this most pervasive form of business organization, which wields such enormous economic power, being immune to criminal sanction is impossible to imagine. These issues are explored in more detail in chapter 12.

For a time the courts held that corporations were immune from criminal liability. More recently, the courts have developed rules on the basis of which corporations may be convicted of absolute and strict liability offences as well as offences for which the accused must have a certain state of mind, or *mens rea*.

2) Absolute Liability Offences

The simplest types of offences to deal with are absolute liability offences. These offences require only that the accused engaged in certain prescribed behaviour. No state of mind or *mens rea* needs to be shown, and no defence is available once the behaviour has been proven. Corporate liability for such an offence arises when a person who engages in the behaviour does so on behalf of the corporation. All acts of employees in the course of their employment will be caught.

Absolute liability offences punishable by imprisonment have been held to be unconstitutional as violating section 7 of the *Charter* — the right to life, liberty, and security of the person — with respect to

---

1   Lord Thurlow, quoted by Glanville Williams, in *Criminal Law: The General Part*, 2d ed. (London: Stevens, 1961) at 856.

individual accused.[2] No case has held that such offences infringe the rights of a corporate accused. Indeed, since a corporation may not be imprisoned, it is hard to imagine how a corporation could have a section 7 right in the circumstances. As noted in chapter 3, however, a corporation may challenge the constitutionality of an offence if it would violate section 7 of the *Charter* were an individual to be charged.[3]

3) Strict Liability Offences

As in the previous category of offence, liability for a strict liability offence arises on the commission of some prescribed act. As with absolute liability offences, it is fairly straightforward to determine if a person was acting on behalf of a corporation in committing the act.

Liability is subject to a defence that the accused acted reasonably in the circumstances, often referred to as a "due diligence defence." In other words, the fault required to be shown is negligence. The burden is on the accused to show that it was not negligent. The person who must exercise due diligence on behalf of the corporation is someone who can be considered to be the directing mind and will of the corporation in such a way that she may be considered to be the corporation itself.[4] This will be the person or persons who have responsibility to manage the business of the corporation in the area in which the offence occurred. As we will see, this concept, "directing mind and will" of the corporation, is also used to determine whether the corporation is liable for a *mens rea* offence, and it will be discussed in more detail in the next section.

4) Offences Requiring *Mens Rea*

Most criminal offences require that the accused have a degree of knowledge or intention, referred to as *mens rea*, before there can be a conviction. Early common law cases held that a corporation could not be convicted of an offence requiring *mens rea*. Now liability may be found on the basis of the "identification theory." Under this theory, criminal liability may attach if the person having the necessary mental state and committing the crime has the identity of the corporation; in other words, he or she *is* the corporation for the purposes of the behaviour constituting the offence. Typically the natural person will be criminally responsible

2   *R. v. Nguyen (sub nom. R. v. Hess)*, [1990] 2 S.C.R. 906.
3   *R. v. Wholesale Travel Group Inc.*, [1991] 3 S.C.R. 154 at 180–81.
4   *R. v. Sault Ste. Marie (City)*, [1978] 2 S.C.R. 1299 [*Sault Ste. Marie*].

himself as well.[5] While simple to state, this theory is fraught with various complexities in practice.

The general test for whether the identity of the corporation and the individual coincide is as follows: Is the human actor who committed the crime a vital organ or a directing mind of the corporation? Any person who has governing executive control over an area of the corporation's business or affairs is considered to be the corporation in relation to that area. One consequence of this conception of directing mind is that, in a given corporation, there may be many directing minds; there is no need for the directing mind to have general decision-making power for all aspects of the corporation's business. Not just the president or the board of directors may be the directing mind; each person responsible for a discrete aspect of the corporation's business, whether defined functionally, geographically, or otherwise, may incur criminal liability for the corporation. So, for example, in R. v. *Waterloo Mercury Sales Ltd.*,[6] liability was imposed on a corporation operating a car dealership as a result of the used car sales manager fraudulently causing odometers on used cars to be turned back. The used car sales manager was found to be the directing mind of the corporation for the purposes of the criminal activity. In essence, the test is whether an employee has been delegated, expressly or by implication, the authority to design and supervise the implementation of corporate policy, as opposed to only the authority to carry out such policy.[7]

Actions by employees giving rise to corporate liability are not limited to those in the course of their employment — that is, in accordance with the terms of their contracts of employment. The corporation is responsible for any act by a directing mind in the general area of her responsibility, even if not specifically authorized. As a result, the existence of a corporate rule or policy prohibiting the action is no defence to corporate liability. In *Waterloo Mercury Sales*, the dealership had a policy against turning back odometers, but the court held that this did not absolve the dealership from responsibility. Similarly, although a person must have actual power to make decisions in the relevant area for her mind to constitute the corporate mind, it is not necessary to find that the responsibility over a particular area was created in accordance with the express provisions of the corporate constitution or was formally

---

5   Because the natural person is the corporation for the purposes of committing the offence, it is not possible for him, at the same time, to conspire with the corporation to commit the offence.

6   (1974), 49 D.L.R. (3d) 131 (Alta. Dist. Ct.).

7   "Rhone" (The) v. "Peter A.B. Widner" (The), [1993] 1 S.C.R. 497.

authorized in any other way. The courts have imposed liability on corporations where, by virtue of the practice of the corporation, the person with the guilty mind exercised corporate authority in the area in which the offence was committed.

The result of holding corporations liable for acts by people in the area of their responsibility is that the corporation bears the risk associated with unauthorized activity; no simple statement of policy that crimes should not be committed will save the corporation. It is not clear whether there is anything a corporation may do to avoid liability. In the United Kingdom it has been held that a corporation will be able to avoid liability for an offence involving the actions of a manager if it takes sufficient care to train employees and has in place an adequate system for selecting managers as well as a system for supervising and controlling them.[8] Although the *Tesco* case has been cited in a number of Canadian cases, it has been interpreted as holding that, as a result of such a system of supervision and control, a manager could not be considered to be a directing mind and will of the corporation.[9] Canadian courts have criticized *Tesco* on the basis that it set too high a standard for finding that a person is the directing mind and will of the corporation.[10]

One difficult question in connection with corporate criminality is whether there can be corporate liability where the person alleged to be the directing mind of the corporation was acting in his own interests and against the corporation's. This issue was considered in the leading case on corporate criminal liability, *R. v. Canadian Dredge and Dock Ltd.*[11] In that case, several corporations were charged with fraud consisting of their agreeing in advance on who would submit the lowest bid to do dredging work at an inflated price. The lowest bidder would make payoffs to the others and subcontract some of the work to them. This fraud was negotiated by senior officers of each of the corporations. Sometimes an officer would keep for himself a portion of the payoff that was supposed to go to his corporation. The corporations argued that the identification theory could not operate when the alleged directing mind is perpetrating a fraud on the corporation in this way.

The court accepted that where a person ceases completely to act in the interests of the corporation and acts "totally in fraud of the corporation," appropriating to herself all the benefits that should have gone to the corporation, the identification theory should not operate. On the

---

8   *Tesco Supermarkets Ltd. v. Nattrass*, [1972] A.C. 153 (H.L.).

9   *Sault Ste. Marie*, above note 4.

10   *R. v. Canadian Dredge & Dock Co.*, [1985] 1 S.C.R. 622.

11   *Ibid.*

facts of this case, however, the requirements of this very narrow exclusion were not met. The directing minds were not engaged in a scheme to deprive their corporations of all benefits associated with the dredging contracts and so the corporations were liable.

C. LIABILITY OF CORPORATIONS IN TORT

1) Introduction

A corporation may be liable in tort both directly, in the sense that the corporation itself is found to be committing the tort, and vicariously.

2) Vicarious Liability

The corporation may be vicariously liable where a tort has been committed by someone acting on behalf of the corporation. In such a case, the natural person is personally liable for the tort, but the corporation is also vicariously liable. For vicarious liability to attach, two criteria must be met:

- There must be a relationship of master and servant between the person and the corporation. In other words, the person must have the legal status of an employee, not an independent contractor.
- The person committing the tort must have been acting in the course of her employment, and not on a frolic of her own.

Vicarious liability of corporations is very broad and relatively easy to establish once an employee has been identified as the person committing the tort. Vicarious liability will catch most situations where direct liability could have been found because a person who is a "directing mind" will usually also be an employee. Perhaps because of the broad reach of vicarious liability in most cases of alleged corporate liability, the law on the circumstances in which direct corporate liability for torts arises is not very clear or well developed.[12]

Finally in this context, it is necessary to remember that a director or an officer of a corporation is not an employee simply by being a director or an officer. In many cases, especially in smaller corporations, the directors and officers will also be in employment relationships with the corporation, but these are distinct legal relationships.

---

12   B. Welling, *Corporate Law in Canada: The Governing Principles*, 2d ed. (Toronto: Butterworths, 1991) at 152–73.

3) Direct Liability

The corporation may be directly liable for a tort if the person committing the tort is not merely an employee but can be considered the directing mind and will of the corporation in such a way that the acts done are the acts of the corporation itself. Direct liability has been imposed on essentially the same basis as described above for the imposition of criminal liability.

For example, direct liability was imposed on a corporation where the boilers of a ship owned by the corporation proved defective and the cargo was lost. The English House of Lords held that the person who was negligent in not knowing about the defective boilers was the responsible manager of the ship. Since this person was the directing mind and will of the corporation for the purposes of taking care of the ship, the corporation was held liable to the owner of the cargo for its loss.[13]

D. LIABILITY OF CORPORATIONS IN CONTRACT

1) Introduction

A corporation can act only through natural persons to conclude contracts and otherwise enter into transactions. This section explains when a corporation is liable to perform contracts as a result of commitments made by persons purporting to act on its behalf. As previously discussed, a person acting on behalf of someone else is referred to as an agent, and the law dealing with the ability of such person to bind the corporation is a branch of the law of agency. With respect to corporations, the law of agency is particularly hard to apply because of the size and complexity of many corporate organizations. There may be many people within a given corporation whom one could consider to be an agent in connection with particular types of corporate obligations. Agents will include, but are not limited to, officers and directors. Depending on the circumstances, sales people, purchasing clerks, and others may all be considered agents of the corporation for particular purposes. Moreover, the way agents get their authority to act on behalf of the corporate principal is not always easy to pinpoint. In many corporate organizations, the sources and lines of authority are not clearly drawn.

---

13   *Lennard's Carrying Co. Ltd. v. Asiatic Petroleum Co. Ltd.*, [1915] A.C. 705 (H.L.).

The law of agency must seek to balance the interests of the principal, for our purposes the corporation, with the interests of third parties seeking to enter into binding contracts with the corporation. The principal will not want to be bound by any actions of an agent purporting to act on its behalf which it has not authorized. On the other hand, a third party will want to be able to rely on an agent having the authority to bind the principal with whom it seeks to contract without spending more than a minimal amount of time and money investigating whether the principal has conferred such authority on the agent. Investigation to determine with certainty that authority exists is a transaction cost, and business transactions will be promoted if such transaction costs can be minimized. If, in a particular area of business, the third party reasonably has relied on commonly accepted indicators of authority, such as a letter of introduction from the president on the corporation's letterhead indicating a person's title, in entering into a contract with the corporation, that reliance should be respected and the contract enforced. Any rule about the authority of agents must take into account that it may be impossible for the third party to determine if actual authority has been given because authority may be conferred in a document to which the third party has no access, such as the agent's contract with the principal.

In large transactions, the parties will do a significant amount of investigation to satisfy themselves that the person executing the agreements making up the transaction has authority to do so. These investigations will be supplemented by documentation, such as certificates as to who the officers of a corporation are, certified copies of board resolutions authorizing certain people to enter into the transaction, and legal opinions regarding authority. The vast majority of transactions between third parties and corporations, however, are entered into without the third party enquiring, to any significant extent, into the authority of the person it is dealing with to bind the corporation. The size of the transaction simply does not justify incurring the costs associated with attaining the degree of legal certainty typical of large transactions. Fortunately, most transactions proceed without issues of authority arising. The issue of authority comes up most often in circumstances in which the corporation has refused to perform its obligations, on the basis that the agent had no authority to bind the corporation, and the third party sues the corporation. It is in these situations that the rules described in the remainder of this chapter are most relevant. The sections that follow set out the common law rules regarding the liability of corporations in contract, followed by a review of the efforts at statutory reform.

2) Common Law Rules

In the extreme case where an agent has no connection of any kind with the principal, the law is clear that the principal is not liable. The agent who falsely represents that he has authority may be liable for breach of warranty of authority or fraudulent misrepresentation, but the corporate principal is not. Where the agent has some connection with the principal, some ability to act on the principal's behalf, the general rule is that an agent cannot bind a corporation unless she has some kind of authority from the corporation to do so. At common law, the following types of authority were recognized:

- *Actual authority* In some manner, the agent was actually authorized by the corporation to enter into the obligation sought to be enforced against the corporation.
- *Apparent authority* Also called "ostensible authority," this authority was created by a representation by someone on behalf of the corporation to a third party that the person the third party was dealing with had authority to bind the corporation. It was the authority of the agent as it appeared to the third party.

These two types of authority will often coincide in practice. For example, the office manager of a consulting business being carried on through a corporation may have actual authority to enter into a contract on behalf of the corporation for the purchase of photocopier paper because this power is given to the office manager in her contract of employment with the corporation. The office manager may also have apparent authority created by a letter from the president of the corporation to the paper supplier saying so. Nevertheless, one may exist without the other, and there are conceptual distinctions that must be kept in mind.

Actual authority is a legal relationship between the corporation and the agent which may arise as a result of powers being conferred on the agent by statute, the articles, the by-laws, a resolution of the board of directors, the terms of an employment contract, or some other permitted delegation within the organization of the business carried on by the corporation. Where the authority is conferred on a position or office, such as president, a person will have that authority so long as he has been properly appointed to that position or office. A third party dealing with an agent may be completely ignorant of the existence of the person's actual authority, but any agreement entered into by that person within her actual authority with the third party is binding on the corporation.

A careful third party will want to know that the person she is dealing with has authority to contract on behalf of the corporation. In many cases, however, it will be difficult for third parties to satisfy themselves that actual authority is present because they will not have access to the internal corporate records or other private documents that create the authority. Only powers conferred in the articles and the statute are matters of public record.

As a result of the difficulty in establishing actual authority, third parties must often rely on apparent authority. Apparent authority is a legal relationship between the corporation and the third party created by a representation on behalf of the corporation that the agent has authority to contract with the third party. The representation may be express, as in the example above, or implied from the conduct of the corporation, including acquiescence to a person acting with certain authority. Perhaps the most common situation in which apparent authority arises is where a corporation appoints some person to hold a certain position. The courts have held that putting someone in a particular position constitutes a representation that the person has the authority usual for such a position. This kind of apparent authority is referred to as "usual authority." What is usual is determined by reference to the authority of agents in similar positions in similar corporations. This will be a question of fact in each case. Agents with titles like vice-president, treasurer, and secretary may have widely varying degrees of authority in different industries and even within industries. Also, cases in which usual authority has been considered must be applied with caution because of the tendency for the responsibilities associated with particular positions in corporations to change over time.

In order for a third party to rely on apparent authority, the representation creating it must be made by someone with actual authority, to make such a representation. Actual authority may consist in general authority to manage the business and affairs of the corporation, such as is held by the board of directors (*CBCA*, s. 102), or authority over the specific area of business within which the obligation arises. If a person has authority to manage a particular area of a business, that person will have authority to represent that another person has authority to enter into obligations in that area. A person who has authority to manage will not have authority to make a representation that someone else has authority, however, if there is a relevant restriction on his ability to delegate responsibility.[14]

The final requirement which must be satisfied before a third party may rely on apparent authority is that the representation must have

---

14   Section 115(3) of the *Canada Business Corporations Act*, R.S.C. 1985, c. C-44 [*CBCA*], sets out a list of powers that the board of directors may not delegate. These powers are discussed in chapter 6. In general, these restrictions are not relevant to relations between the corporation and third parties, but rather to internal corporate matters such as declaring dividends.

induced the third party to have entered into the contract with the corporation. As a practical matter, this requirement is seldom hard to prove.

The leading case on these principles of corporate agency is *Freeman & Lockyer* v. *Buckhurst Park Properties (Mangal) Ltd.*[15] In that case the defendant corporation had been formed by Kapoor and Hoon to purchase, develop, and resell a large estate. Kapoor and Hoon and a nominee of each of them made up the board of directors. The articles of the corporation permitted the appointment of a managing director, but this was never done. To the knowledge of the board, however, Kapoor acted in that capacity. Kapoor hired a firm of architects in connection with the development of the property for sale. The architects did their work, but were not paid and they sued the corporation for their fee. The Court of Appeal held that, by permitting Kapoor to act as managing director, the board had represented that he had authority to enter into contracts of a kind that a managing director would, in the normal course, be authorized to enter into, including the contract with the architects. Since the articles of association conferred full management powers on the board, it had actual authority to make this representation. The Court of Appeal found that the architects had relied on Kapoor's being authorized to contract on behalf of the corporation when they entered the agreement. As a result, the corporation was held liable to pay the architects' fee.

At common law, a claim by a third party could not succeed if she knew of some restriction on the authority of the agent. This rule was fairly onerous because of another special rule applying to corporations. All persons dealing with a corporation were deemed to have knowledge of any restriction on the authority of an agent which was contained in any publicly filed document. So, for example, if the articles of a corporation stated that all leases must be signed by the president and the secretary, a third party could not enforce a lease signed by the president alone, even though a president would normally have the usual authority to enter into a lease on behalf of the corporation.[16]

---

15 [1964] 2 Q.B. 480 (C.A.).

16 Under the common law constructive notice rule, a third party dealing with the corporation was deemed to know of any restriction on the business the corporation may engage in which is contained in the articles or other public document. Any contract entered into outside the permitted business would be *ultra vires* and unenforceable. The third party could not rely on apparent authority. As noted in chapter 4, it is no longer necessary to include a statement of the permitted business of the corporation in the articles and, although it is possible to state restrictions on a corporation's business, this is not often done in practice. More important, even if restrictions are present they have no effect on the enforceability of a claim by a third party (see chapter 4).

In order to balance this rule of "constructive notice," the courts developed a qualification that is referred to as the "indoor management rule" or the "rule in *Turquand*'s case."[17] Under this rule, a person dealing with a corporation has no obligation to ensure that a corporation has gone through any procedures required by its articles, by-laws, resolutions, contracts, or policies to authorize a transaction or to give authority to a person purporting to act on behalf of the corporation. Compliance with such procedures is a matter of internal or "indoor" management with which outsiders do not have to concern themselves. For example, if a corporation's articles require a resolution of the board authorizing the president to borrow money, a third party lender can assume that such a resolution has been passed. This rule does not relieve the third party from having to establish actual or apparent authority in order to successfully enforce its claim against the corporation. So, in the example, if the necessary board resolution had not been passed, the lender would have to be able to establish that the president had apparent authority to borrow money on behalf of the corporation in order to enforce its claim for repayment of the loan. What the rule does do is limit the effect of the constructive notice rule by making clear that it is only actual restrictions on authority of agents in public documents which will defeat a third party's claim. If a provision in a public document grants authority only on certain conditions or if certain procedures are followed, the third party does not need to enquire whether the conditions have been satisfied or the procedures complied with.

3) Statutory Reform

a) Introduction
When the *CBCA* was enacted in 1975 it abolished constructive notice and codified and supplemented the other common law rules described above. Similar statutory reforms have been undertaken in New Brunswick (*NBBCA*, s. 15), Newfoundland (*NCA*, s. 33), Nova Scotia (*NSCA*, s. 31), Ontario (*OBCA*, s. 18), Manitoba (*MBCA*, s. 17), Saskatchewan (*SBCA*, s. 17), and Alberta (*ABCA*, s. 17). In British Columbia, constructive notice has been abolished (*BCCA*, s. 26).

b) Constructive Notice Abolished
Section 17 of the *CBCA* provides that no person is deemed to have knowledge of any document relating to the corporation "by reason

---

17   *Royal British Bank v. Turquand* (1856), 6 E.&B. 327, 119 E.R. 886 (Ex. Ct.).

only" that the document has been filed with the Director and so is a matter of public record. The use of "by reason only" suggests that the drafters intended to leave open the possibility that knowledge may be deemed in some circumstances. As will be discussed below, this possibility is further addressed in section 18 of the *CBCA*.

c) Common Law Rules Codified and Expanded

Section 18 codifies the basic rules regarding apparent authority and enhances the ability of third parties to enforce contractual claims against corporations. The structure of section 18 is to deny corporations the ability to rely on certain kinds of defects in the authority of a person purporting to act on behalf of a corporation in entering into a contract with a third party where a claim is made by the third party to enforce the contract:

A corporation or a guarantor of an obligation of the corporation may not assert against a person dealing with the corporation or with any person who has acquired rights from the corporation that

(*a*) the articles, by-laws and any unanimous shareholder agreement have not been complied with,

(*b*) the persons named in the most recent notice sent to the Director under section 106 [notice of directors] or 113 [notice of change of directors] are not the directors of the corporation,

(*c*) the place named in the most recent notice sent to the Director under section 19 [notice of registered office and notice of change of registered office] is not the registered office of the corporation,

(*d*) a person held out by a corporation as a director, an officer or an agent of the corporation has not been duly appointed or has no authority to exercise the powers and perform the duties that are customary in the business of the corporation or usual for such director, officer or agent,

(*e*) a document issued by any director, officer or agent of a corporation with actual or usual authority to issue the document is not valid or not genuine, or

(*f*) financial assistance referred to in section 44 [to insiders of the corporation] or a sale, lease or exchange of property referred to in subsection 189(3) [of "all or substantially all the property of a corporation other than in the ordinary course of business"] was not authorized,

except where the person has or ought to have by virtue of his position with or relationship to the corporation knowledge to the contrary.

The basic common law rules are set out in section 18(d). If a corporation makes a representation to a third party by holding someone out as a director, officer, or agent, the corporation cannot deny that the person is duly appointed or that she has the authority customary or usual for such a director, officer, or agent. Though the section does not expressly require that the holding out be by someone with actual authority to do so on behalf of the corporation, no case has interpreted the provision as ousting the pre-existing common law rule and there would seem to be nothing in the language which would suggest a legislative intention to make such a change.

The balance of section 18 deals with specific situations in which the corporation cannot rely on defects in actual authority to defeat claims by third parties that the corporation is bound by a contract entered into by an agent. The main purpose of these provisions is to ensure that corporations cannot escape their obligations to third parties because of internal corporate restrictions on authority or their failure to follow their own procedures.

Under section 18(a), any provision in a corporation's articles, by-laws, and unanimous shareholder agreement that restricts the authority of any person to bind the corporation, or requires some procedure to be followed before a transaction may be entered into, has no effect on a third party. Similarly, under section 18(b), if a person appears as a director in the most recently filed notice of directors or notice of change of directors, the corporation cannot deny that such person is a director and, under section 18(c), a third party may rely on the registered office being that identified in the most recently filed notice of registered office. The effect of section 18(b) is that even if a person is no longer a director, he will have the usual authority of a director as long as his name appears on the public file. Section 18(c) is intended to ensure that a third party can rely on the address on the public file for the purposes of communicating with the corporation, including ultimately initiating legal proceedings to enforce its claim.

All these provisions are based on the same policy as the common law indoor management rule: third parties should not have to worry about whether internal corporate housekeeping is in order. The corporation is responsible for ensuring that its agents respect internal restrictions and procedures and that the public file is kept up to date. As noted in chapter 4, under the *CBCA* there is no need to state a corporation's objects, though it is possible to include in the corporation's articles restrictions on the business the corporation is permitted to carry on. Section 18(a) makes clear that no such restriction impairs the ability of a third party to enforce a contract inconsistent with the restriction. Section 16(3), mentioned above, provides expressly for this enforcement.

Section 18(f) protects third parties against claims by corporations that two specific kinds of transactions were entered into by the corporation in a manner contrary to the *CBCA*. Under section 44, certain financial assistance, including assistance to any shareholder, director, officer, or employee and assistance to purchase a share, is prohibited if the corporation is insolvent or would become so after the assistance.[18] The effect of section 18(f) is to make clear that if any assistance is given contrary to this restriction, the transaction will nevertheless be enforceable by the person receiving the assistance. A sale, lease, or exchange of "all or substantially all the property of a corporation other than in the ordinary course of business" as referred to in section 189(3) must be authorized by a special resolution of shareholders. In accordance with section 18(f), the failure to obtain this shareholder approval has no effect on the ability of the person or persons who acquired the property to enforce their claim to it.

Finally, section 18(e) addresses the situation in which, in accordance with the organizational structure of a corporation, the person who signs a document is not the same person as the one who is authorized to issue the document — that is, to deliver a signed copy to the other party. Such a division of responsibility is common in organizations that must deal in large numbers of originally signed documents. For example, property management businesses may permit only the president to sign leases on behalf of the corporation. The signed lease is issued to the tenant by someone else, like the leasing manager or, perhaps, the superintendent of the building. The effect of section 18(e) is that a third party, like the tenant, can rely on a document issued to her by a person who has actual or usual authority to issue it. The corporation cannot later say that it was not signed by the proper person — in the example, the president.

Another common situation in which the authority to sign and the authority to issue are separated is the issuance of share certificates. Most share certificates are only valid if they are signed by the president and the secretary of the corporation. It is usual in most corporations to

---

18   Section 44 of the *CBCA*, above note 14, also prohibits financial assistance if the realizable value of the corporation's assets would be less than the aggregate of the corporation's liabilities and stated capital of all classes. In essence, stated capital is the historical total of all amounts paid to the corporation in return for shares. The concept of "stated capital" and the meaning of this standard are discussed in chapter 6.

authorize someone else, often a third-party transfer agent, to deliver share certificates to the shareholder. Under section 18(e), as long as a shareholder receives his share certificate from a person with the actual or usual authority to issue share certificates, the corporation cannot claim that the share certificate is not valid.

Section 18(e) is a commonsense solution to a real-world problem. It also was necessary to reverse an old common law rule that a share certificate that had been fraudulently issued by the person responsible for issuing certificates was invalid. In *Ruben* v. *Great Fingall Consolidated*,[19] the secretary of a corporation who was responsible for issuing share certificates arranged to borrow money from a bank on the security of 5000 shares of the corporation he claimed to own. He issued a share certificate for 5000 shares in the name of the bank, delivered it to the bank, and received the loan. The secretary did not own the shares. He had forged the signatures of two directors of the corporation and affixed the corporate seal. The court held that the forgery rendered the issuance of the certificate a nullity; it was not simply a matter of internal management with no effect on third parties. The court also held that the secretary's authority was only to issue the share certificates, not to create them, so the secretary could not be said to have apparent authority to create the certificate. Under section 18(e), the bank would have been able to rely on the certificate.

All the provisions of section 18 are subject to the significant qualification that the third party dealing with the corporation cannot seek to rely on them if she knew of a defect in the authority of the person she was dealing with, or ought to have known of the defect by virtue of her "position with or relationship to the corporation." This qualification essentially codifies the common law position.[20] It is likely often to apply to financial assistance given to officers and directors contrary to section 44 and to other arrangements with directors, officers, and shareholders who may be deemed to know of any defect in authority.

Finally, it is important to note that the *CBCA* and most other Canadian corporate statutes contain a provision to the effect that an act of a director or officer is valid notwithstanding any irregularity in his election or appointment or any defect in his qualifications (*CBCA*, s. 116; *OBCA*, s. 128; *BCCA*, s. 148; *ABCA*, s. 111(1)). Thus, a corporation cannot rely on such irregularities or defects to dispute the existence of actual authority. It has been held that the section does not apply where

---

19   [1906] A.C. 439 (H.L.).
20   *Morris* v. *Kanssen*, [1946] A.C. 459 at 475 (H.L.).

there was no appointment at all as opposed to an irregular one. In *Morris* v. *Kanssen* a director who continued to act after his term expired, where the "office has been from the outset usurped without the colour of authority,"[21] was found not to have been appointed rather than irregularly appointed. Where a director's or officer's action is not saved under this provision, however, the director or officer may still be found to have apparent authority, applying the principles discussed above.

E. CHAPTER SUMMARY

In this chapter we discussed how the corporation acts through its human agents. In particular, we looked at the circumstances in which a corporation is liable in contract and when it is responsible for crimes and torts.

For absolute and strict liability offences, as well as most forms of negligence where no particular mental state on the part of the wrong-doer need be shown, it is sufficient if the actions of a person were on behalf of the corporation. Even where some state of mind is an element of a tort, there is often no need to meet this requirement because, so long as the tort is committed by an employee acting within the scope of her employment, the corporation, as employer, will be vicariously liable. Since there is no vicarious liability in criminal law, the courts have developed a standard for attaching criminal responsibility for the acts of human agents: the agent who committed the criminal act must have acted in his capacity as the directing mind and will of the corporation in doing so, meaning that it is necessary to be able to identify the person who committed the crime as being the corporation for the purposes of the illegal act. In general, this identification requires that the wrongdoer have authority to make management decisions in relation to the area of the corporation's business in which the crime was committed. It is no defence to corporate liability to assert that the corporation sought to prevent the agent from engaging in the criminal activity.

At common law, for a third party to be able to enforce a contract against a corporation, it was necessary to show that the person who acted on behalf of the corporation had actual or apparent authority to bind the corporation to the contract. To establish the latter, there must be some representation on behalf of the corporation that the agent had the requisite authority. The representation must be made by someone

---

21   *Ibid.* at 471.

with actual authority to do so. The most common type of representation is putting an agent in an office or position that would usually have the authority to bind the corporation to the type of contract sought to be enforced.

The *CBCA* and the statutes modelled after it have codified these common law rules. They have also, by abolishing the constructive notice rule and providing that a corporation will not be able to rely on its failure to act in accordance with the corporate legislation or its own internal procedures to escape liability in most circumstances, decreased the risk that a third party will be unable to claim successfully against a corporation.

FURTHER READINGS

COFFEE, J.C., " 'No Soul to Damn: No Body to Kick': An Unscandalized Inquiry into the Problem of Corporate Punishment" (1981) 79 Mich. L. Rev. 386

HANNA, D., "Corporate Criminal Liability" (1989) 31 Crim. L.Q. 452

HANSMANN, H., & R. KRAAKMAN, "A Procedural Focus on Unlimited Shareholder Liability" (1992) 106 Harvard L. Rev. 446

HANSMANN, H., & R. KRAAKMAN, "Toward Unlimited Shareholder Liability for Corporate Torts" (1991) 100 Yale L.J. 1879

LEEBRON, D.W., "Limited Liability, Tort Victims and Creditors" (1991) 91 Colum. L. Rev. 1565

PEARCE, F., & L. SNIDER, eds., *Corporate Crime: Contemporary Debates* (Toronto: University of Toronto Press, 1995)

RUBY, C., & K. JULL, "The Charter and Regulatory Offences: A Wholesale Revision" (1992) 14 C.R. (4th) 226

WELLS, C., *Corporations and Criminal Responsibility* (Oxford: Oxford University Press, 1993)

CHAPTER 6

SHARES

A. INTRODUCTION

A share is a bundle of rights against a corporation. Although a share is personal property, the claim it represents in the corporation is not a property right in the corporation's assets,[1] nor is it a proportionate ownership interest in the corporation itself.[2] The particular rights, privileges, restrictions, and conditions of each class of shares (referred to here collectively as "characteristics") are set out in the articles of the corporation, as discussed in chapter 4. Subject to a few statutory and common law limitations, the characteristics that may be given to shares are restricted only by the imagination of the person drafting the articles. The characteristics of a share determine the risks associated with the holder's investment, the degree of control she has over the corporation, and her right to share in its profits. In this chapter we will set out the statutory scheme relating to shares, as well as the most important common law rules. Some of the more common practices in drafting share provisions will also be described.

The basic rights associated with shares are as follows:

- to vote at any meeting of shareholders;
- to receive dividends declared by the board of directors; and

---

1 *Macaura v. Northern Assurance Co.*, [1925] A.C. 619 (H.L.).
2 *Bradbury v. English Sewing Cotton Co. Ltd.*, [1923] A.C. 744 (H.L.).

- on dissolution of the corporation, to receive the property of the corporation remaining after creditors and any other persons with claims against the corporation are paid.

Where a corporation has only one class of shares, the rights of the holders of shares of that class are equal in all respects and must include each of these three basic rights (*CBCA*, s. 24(3)). If the articles provide for more than one class of shares, then each of the basic rights must be possessed by at least one class of shares, although all the rights are not required to be attached to a single class (*CBCA*, s. 24(4)). If a corporation had three classes of shares, Class A, Class B, and Class C, for example, each of the basic rights would have to be possessed by at least one of these classes. A single class, say Class A, might have all three rights and the other two none, or the rights might be distributed across the classes in some other way. If the articles are silent on the right to vote, then each share has one vote (*CBCA*, s. 140(1)). Where a corporation has multiple classes of shares, all such shares are presumed to have equal rights, regardless of class, except to the extent specifically provided in the articles.

Each owner of a share is entitled to a share certificate and, if a corporation is authorized to issue more than one class of shares, or more than one series of shares of a class as discussed below, the characteristics of the class or series must appear on the certificate or a notice must appear stating that there are particular characteristics and that copies of the text of such characteristics may be obtained from the corporation (*CBCA*, ss. 49(1) & (13)). Unless a shareholder requests one, there is no need for a corporation to issue a share certificate and, in order to minimize paper work, many smaller corporations do not bother. In any event, a record of ownership of shares, called a securities register, must be maintained as part of the corporate records at the registered office of the corporation or any other place in Canada designated by the directors (*CBCA*, ss. 20 & 50). An entry in a securities register or a share certificate issued by a corporation is proof, in the absence of evidence to the contrary, that the person in whose name the share is registered is the owner of the shares described in the register or in the certificate (*CBCA*, s. 257(3)).

B. COMMON CHARACTERISTICS OF SHARES

1) Classes

The *CBCA* refers only to "shares" (*CBCA*, s. 25). There are no legal restrictions on what shares can be called or, with some qualifications, what characteristics they can be given in the articles. In practice it is usual to designate one class of shares as "common shares" and give these shares the three basic rights. Usually, no dividend may be paid on common shares until all other claims, including the dividend entitlements of all other classes of shares, are paid. In addition, no payment to common shareholders on dissolution may occur before all other claimants, again including the holders of all other classes of shares, have been paid what is owed to them. The claims of others typically are limited to a fixed amount, but the common shares represent residual claims: they are entitled to whatever is left after everyone else is paid. Because of the residual nature of the claims of common shares, their value will vary with the success of the business. If the business generates a substantial surplus over what is needed to pay other claim holders, the value of the common shares will be large. If income is insufficient to pay the other claimholders, the common shares may be worthless. Because common shares rank behind all others with claims against the corporation, they are considered the riskiest form of investment.

In small corporations, common shares may be the only class of shares, but multiple classes with a wide variety of characteristics are frequently found. Some public corporations have voting and "non-voting" or "subordinate voting" common shares. Non-voting common shares have the same characteristics as common shares except that they do not vote. Similarly, subordinate voting shares are the same as common shares except that they have fewer votes than the common shares. In practice, this difference is often accomplished by giving the regular common shares multiple votes, say ten, and the subordinate voting common shares only one vote. Usually, in such cases, most of the shares issued to the public are non-voting or subordinated voting common shares, while most of the voting shares are retained by a small group of shareholders, often the original shareholders in the corporation. In this way the corporation can raise capital by issuing shares without the original shareholders having to give up much control. Non-voting and subordinate voting shares have been very popular with investors.

Many corporations also have one or more classes of "preferred" or "preference" shares which do not vote but which have a preference related to receiving some fixed dividend and on dissolution. A preference as to dividends means that dividends are paid on these shares first, before dividends are paid on common shares (or any other class over which the preferred shares have a priority as expressed in the share conditions set out in the articles). A preference on dissolution usually means that all the money paid into the corporation in return for the issuance of the preference shares must be paid back to the preferred shareholders before the remaining assets can be distributed to the holders of the common shares (or any other class of shares over which the preferred shares have priority).

Preferred shares will be attractive to an investor who does not want to have any say in how the business is managed but is interested in a fixed return. In promising a fixed return, preferred shares resemble debt, but there are some important differences between an investment in a corporation in the form of debt, such as a loan bearing interest, and one in the form of the purchase of preferred shares. An investment in preferred shares is riskier because, as will be discussed below, the directors may decide that it is in the corporation's best interests not to pay dividends, in which case a preferred shareholder will have no recourse in most circumstances. By contrast, if management decided not to pay interest on a debt, the creditor could then sue to recover the amount owed or even put the corporation into bankruptcy. Also, on dissolution, preferred shareholders get their investment back only after all loans and other prior claims have been paid. Because of the increased risks associated with an investment in preferred shares, investors typically require higher rates of return on preferred shares than they would require on debt.

2) Dividends

The profits of a corporation belong to it and not to its shareholders. Profits may be distributed to shareholders by way of dividend declared to be payable by the corporation's board of directors. Once declared, the dividend becomes a debt of the corporation owed to all shareholders entitled to share in the dividend.[3] Under the *CBCA*, dividends are paid to a person who is registered as a shareholder at a certain date referred to as a record date. If no record date is fixed by the directors, the record date is the close of business of the day on which the directors pass the resolution declaring the dividend (*CBCA*, s. 134).

Each share has an equal right to receive any dividend declared by the corporation unless there are specific provisions in the articles granting different dividend entitlements to different classes of shares. The kinds of arrangements that may be made regarding dividends are infinitely variable, but there are two invariable rules:

- The declaration of dividends is a matter within the discretion of the directors. This rule has two corollaries:
  - the power to declare dividends cannot be delegated by the board of directors (*CBCA*, s. 115(3)(d)), although, like any other power

---

3   *Re Severn & Wye and Severn Bridge Railway Co.*, [1896] 1 Ch. 559.

of the directors, it can be assumed by shareholders in a unanimous shareholders' agreement; and

- no provision of the articles or any shareholders' agreement can compel the directors to declare and pay dividends.[4]

- Dividends cannot be paid if there are reasonable grounds for believing that the corporation cannot meet either of the following financial tests:
  - the corporation is, or would after the payment be, unable to pay its liabilities as they become due (referred to as the "solvency test"); or
  - the realizable value of the corporation's assets would, after the payment, be less than the aggregate of its liabilities and stated capital of all classes (referred to as the "capital impairment test")(CBCA, s. 42).

The meaning of stated capital is discussed in section C, "Issuing and Paying for Shares," but essentially it consists of the historical total of all money or other assets paid into the corporation in return for shares. If dividends are paid in contravention of these requirements, the directors who consented to the declaration of the dividend are personally liable to pay the amount of the dividend back to the corporation (CBCA, s. 118(2)(c)). This obligation is discussed further in chapter 8.

Directors may be compelled to declare dividends if the failure to pay would be oppressive to shareholders (CBCA, s. 241) or would breach the directors' fiduciary duty, though such circumstances are likely to be rare. The failure to pay dividends was held to be oppressive in Ferguson v. Imax Systems Corp.[5] when it occurred as part of a concerted effort by management to prevent one shareholder from receiving any benefit from the corporation. The shareholder was the estranged wife of the major shareholder. The other shareholders were not hurt by the failure to pay dividends because they or their spouses were compensated as employees.

Because the directors always have the discretion not to pay dividends, one of the most important characteristics of dividends is whether they are "cumulative" or not. If a dividend entitlement is cumulative and the dividend is not paid when it is supposed to be, the entitlement continues until it is paid. Cumulative dividend provisions in corporate articles typically state that no dividends may be paid on other classes of shares until all cumulative dividends have been paid or that the amount of any unpaid cumulative dividends are added to the amount that the shareholder is entitled to be paid by the corporation if the share is repurchased or redeemed, or on dissolution. Redeeming and repurchasing shares are discussed in section D, "Redemption and Repurchase of

---

4   Burland v. Earle, [1902] A.C. 83 (P.C.).

5   (1983), 43 O.R. (2d) 128 (C.A.).

Shares." If a dividend is not cumulative and is not paid when it is supposed to be, the shareholder has no claim ever to receive it.

If a share is entitled to a dividend in priority to dividends on shares of another class and the entitlement is not described as non-cumulative, it is presumed to be cumulative.[6] It is not clear if a simple reference to a fixed dividend without a preference gives rise to this presumption. This discussion demonstrates the importance of being as clear and explicit as possible in drafting share provisions.

Whether a class of shares participates in dividends in excess of those expressly provided for in the articles will depend on the interpretation of the specific language used to describe the dividend entitlements of that class. Where a fixed dividend is specified for a particular class of shares, the courts have held that holders of shares of that class are not entitled to participate equally with the holders of shares of other classes in any other dividend declared.[7]

3) Rights on Dissolution

As noted, the *CBCA* requires that at least one class of shares be entitled to receive the remaining property of the corporation on dissolution and that this is a right usually associated with common shares. As a result of the principle of equality of shares, where there are multiple classes of shares, each share is entitled to participate on an equal basis in any remaining property of the corporation in the absence of any limitations on such entitlements which are expressly provided for in the articles.[8] Frequently, preferred shares are given the right to receive their "capital" back before any payment to the common shareholders, but do not otherwise participate on dissolution. The share provisions must define what capital means for this purpose. The preference may attach to the amount paid for the shares, plus all unpaid cumulative dividends. If shares of the class were issued for different prices, the preference may attach to the average amount paid for the shares or, for each share, the portion of the stated capital for the class determined by dividing the stated capital for the class by the total number of issued shares of the class.

---

6   *Ferguson & Forester Ltd. v. Buchanan*, [1920] Sess. Cas. 154 (Scot).
7   *Re Porto Rico Power Co.*, [1946] S.C.R. 178.
8   *Ibid.*

4) Voting

a) Introduction

Voting is probably the most important shareholder right, though there may be practical impediments to exercising that right, particularly in large corporations, as discussed in chapter 7. As noted, all shares carry the right to one vote unless the articles provide otherwise. It is possible to provide that votes attach only in certain circumstances, such as the failure to pay dividends, or only on certain issues, or even that voting rights are different on different issues. *Bushell* v. *Faith*[9] is an example of the last situation. The share provisions in that case gave shares one vote on all matters except the election of directors. On that issue, each share had three votes. The court refused to strike down the share provisions. Because of the principle of equality of shares, however, all shares within a class must have the same voting rights. In *Jacobsen* v. *United Canso Oil & Gas Ltd.*,[10] a by-law that purported to restrict each shareholder's votes to 1000, regardless of the number of shares held, was struck down on this basis.[11]

Shareholders can agree to vote their shares in a particular way, and this is commonly done in shareholders' agreements (see chapter 7). Otherwise, in general, shareholders can vote their shares however they like, subject to the limits imposed by the oppression remedy (*CBCA*, s. 241) discussed in chapter 9.

Since it is possible and, indeed, now commonplace for a corporation to have classes of shares that do not vote, there is a possibility that holders of shares that do vote may exercise their power to the detriment of the holders of those that do not. Also, for significant changes to the corporation which will fundamentally alter the nature of shareholders' investments by affecting the returns to shareholders or the risks associated with those returns, even shareholders who do not otherwise have the right to vote may feel that they should have some say. It is open to shareholders to try to negotiate for protection in these circumstances, perhaps by requiring that a voting right, which arises only in these special circumstances, be included in the share provisions. The policy of the *CBCA* and the statutes based on it, however, is to provide voting

---

9   [1970] A.C. 1099 (H.L.).

10   (1980), 11 B.L.R. 313 (Alta. Q.B.).

11   At the time of this decision the corporation was governed by the *Canada Business Corporations Act*, R.S.C. 1985, c. C-44 [*CBCA*]. It was subsequently continued under the *NSCA* and a court stated, in *obiter*, that such a provision might not be prohibited under that statute (*Jacobsen* v. *United Canso Oil & Gas Ltd.* (1980), 40 N.S.R. (2d) 692 (S.C.T.D.)). As discussed below, the *CBCA* does permit holders of shares of one class to be treated differently if they hold different *series* of the class.

rights as mandatory protection for all shareholders in such circumstances, whether voting rights are provided for in the articles or not.

b) Special Vote
All shares vote on certain fundamental changes, even if they do not otherwise have the right to vote. These fundamental changes include the following:

- an amalgamation of the corporation with another corporation (*CBCA,* s. 183(3));
- the sale, lease, or exchange of all or substantially all the assets of the corporation, other than in the ordinary course of business (*CBCA,* s. 189(6));
- the continuance of a corporation incorporated under the *CBCA* under some other corporate law, with the result that it is governed by that law (*CBCA,* s. 188(4)); and
- the liquidation or dissolution of the corporation (*CBCA,* s. 211(3)).

c) Class Vote
All shares of a class are entitled to vote separately as a class on certain fundamental changes, even if they are not otherwise entitled to vote, if shares of that class will be affected in ways that are different from the ways that shares of other classes will be affected. These changes include an amalgamation (*CBCA,* s. 183(4)); a sale, lease, or exchange of all or substantially all the assets of the corporation, other than in the ordinary course of business (*CBCA,* s. 189(7)); and certain amendments to articles (*CBCA,* s. 176) if the amalgamation, sale, lease, or exchange or amendment affects a class differently.

Since these changes must all be approved by a special resolution,[12] the necessary two-thirds majority of shares must be obtained from all shares entitled to vote and from each class entitled to vote separately as a class. The *CBCA* also provides that any shareholder who disagrees with the outcome of any such vote may opt out of the corporation by requiring the corporation to buy his shares at their fair value (*CBCA,* s. 190). This remedy, referred as the "dissent and appraisal remedy," is discussed in chapter 9.[13]

---

12 Recall that a special resolution must be approved by two-thirds of the shares voted in person or by proxy.

13 Under the *Ontario Business Corporations Act*, R.S.O. 1990, c. B.16 [*OBCA*], transactions that have the effect of terminating a shareholder's interest in an offering corporation (referred to as "going-private transactions") must be approved by a majority of the shareholders whose interest is being terminated (s. 190). The Ontario Securities Commission has issued policy statements requiring a similar approval by a "majority of the minority" for certain transactions (Policies 1.3 & 9.1). The Director under the *CBCA*, above note 11, has issued a policy statement indicating that so long as these steps are followed, she will not challenge such a transaction as oppressive (Ottawa: Industry Canada, 1994). Going-private transactions are discussed in chapter 10.

5) No Par Value

All shares used to have a nominal or "par" value, which was expressed in the articles. This value was to represent the intended issue price of the shares. In practice, however, the issue price of a share was sometimes "at par," but just as often it was not. Shares were often issued at prices above the par value (i.e., at a premium to par). The par value served no useful purpose because it did not disclose anything about the actual price at which a share was issued. In some cases, dividend entitlements and redemption entitlements were calculated by reference to par.

Par value has now been abolished under the *CBCA* and under corporate statutes in provinces other than Quebec (*QCA*, s. 123.39), Nova Scotia (*NSCA*, s. 10), New Brunswick (*NBBCA*, s. 22(1)), British Columbia (*BCCA*, s. 42), and Prince Edward Island (*PEICA*, s. 6). Section 24 of the *CBCA* provides that all shares issued under the *CBCA* are without nominal or par value. If a corporation incorporated under a regime that permits par value has shares with par value, and the corporation is continued under the *CBCA*, the shares are deemed to be without par value once the continuance occurs. Par value may be referred to in the articles of older corporations.

6) Series of Shares

Because of the rule that rights of holders of shares of a class are equal in all respects, a corporation must have more than one class of shares if it wants to give different rights to different shareholders. The only circumstance in which shares within a class may be given different rights is when shares in that class are issuable in "series." Section 27 of the *CBCA* provides that the articles may authorize the issue of any class of shares in one or more series and authorize the directors to fix the following characteristics attaching to the shares of each series:

- number of shares in the series;
- designation of the series (i.e., a name such as "series F"); and
- other characteristics in the series (i.e., the "rights, privileges, restrictions, and conditions").

In order to be able to issue shares in series, the articles must expressly permit it. Then a directors' resolution must be passed setting the characteristics of the series. The directors must send articles of amendment to the Director appointed under the *CBCA* setting out the number, designation, and characteristics of the shares in the series before any such shares may be issued (*CBCA*, s. 27(4)).

Why would a corporation want to be able to issue shares in series? Generally, issuing shares in series is only of interest to public corporations. It permits such corporations to create shares with particular characteristics faster and more cheaply than if the corporation had to amend its articles in the usual way to create a new class of shares by calling a meeting of shareholders to approve articles of amendment. Speed is usually important, so that a corporation can give the shares the exact characteristics that will make them attractive in the marketplace at a particular time, such as a certain dividend rate. An opportunity to issue shares at a low dividend rate may be lost if the corporation has to call a meeting of shareholders to amend articles to create a new class of shares; by the time the shareholder meeting had been held, the dividend rate in the market may have changed. Another saving is the cost of shareholder meetings. Public corporation shareholder meetings are expensive because they involve legal fees in connection with the preparation of materials to be sent to shareholders, the cost of mailing to large numbers of shareholders, renting rooms, and so on.

The only restriction on the use of series is that all shares of the same class must have the same priority in relation to receiving dividends and return of capital, even if they are in different series (*CBCA*, s. 27(3)). In other words, shares of one series cannot have a right to receive dividends or to receive what has been paid into the corporation on issuance of the shares if such payment gives them priority over the same rights of shares of the class in other series. If any cumulative dividends or amounts payable on return of capital to a series are not paid in full, the shares of all series of the same class participate rateably in respect of accumulated dividends and return of capital (*CBCA*, s. 27(2)).

7) Pre-emptive Rights

Both the *CBCA* and *OBCA* specifically provide that the articles or a unanimous shareholder agreement may contain a "pre-emptive right" (*CBCA*, s. 28; *OBCA*, s. 26). If the articles contain such a right, unless shares are offered first to the existing shareholders, the corporation cannot issue shares. Once the existing shareholders have had a chance to buy the shares, any unsold shares may be offered for sale to others. Under the *CBCA*, it is contemplated that the pre-emptive right would permit shareholders to purchase shares only in proportion to their existing holdings. So, if a shareholder holds 10 percent of the currently issued shares, she would be entitled to purchase 10 percent of any new issue. Under the *OBCA*, there is no such restriction, and a corporation may set up the right however it likes in its articles. Most pre-emptive rights schemes work like the *CBCA* scheme in practice, however. In British Columbia, a pre-emptive right is mandatory for non-reporting corporations (*BCCA*, s. 41).[14]

A pre-emptive right may be attractive to shareholders for three reasons:

Avoiding dilution: A pre-emptive right allows existing shareholders to avoid the dilution of their proportionate interest in the corporation. For example, if a shareholder holds 10 out of 100 issued common shares, he has 10 percent of the shares and the same percentage of votes; if the corporation issues another 100 shares to someone else, however, his interest is diluted to 5 percent. With a pre-emptive right, he would be entitled to buy 10 percent of the new issue to keep his overall interest at 10 percent.

Constraining inappropriate issuance of shares: A pre-emptive right impairs the ability of directors to issue shares for improper purposes. For example, if an offer is made to acquire all the shares of a corporation (a "takeover bid"), the directors might be tempted to try to prevent the bid from being successful out of fear that they might lose their jobs. One way they could do so would be to issue more shares to make the bid more expensive or, if the shares were issued to a person who will not sell to the takeover bidder (called a "White Knight"), more difficult to complete.[15] A pre-emptive right will limit the ability of the directors to issue shares in this way. The issuance becomes more time consuming, since the directors must comply with the pre-emptive right provision; such provisions usually specify some time period within which existing shareholders may decide whether they want to purchase shares. The pre-emptive right also prevents the issuance of shares only to the White Knight.

Preventing issuance of shares at under value: The issuance of shares for less than they are worth would water down the price of all shares. Issuing shares at under value would likely be a breach of fiduciary duty in any event, but the pre-emptive right is a more direct way of ensuring that it does not happen and, if it does, that existing shareholders benefit.

---

14   A non-reporting company is similar to a non-offering corporation under the *OBCA*, above note 13, and a non-distributing corporation under the *CBCA*, above note 11 (see British Columbia *Company Act*, R.S.B.C. 1979, c. 59, s. 1(1)).

15   Issuances of shares for the purpose of affecting control has been held to be a breach of fiduciary duty (*Bonisteel* v. *Collis Leather Co.* (1919), 45 O.L.R. 195 (Ont. H.C.J.)). More recent cases have permitted the issuance of shares to affect control if the directors acted honestly and in good faith and in the reasonable belief that they were acting in the best interests of the corporation (*Teck Corp.* v. *Millar* (1972), 33 D.L.R. (3d) 288 (B.C.S.C.); *Olson* v. *Phoenix Industrial Supply Ltd.* (1984), 9 D.L.R. (4th) 451 (Man. C.A.)). See chapter 8.

An important limitation on the effectiveness of the pre-emptive right for any of these purposes is that it can only be exercised by those with the ability to pay. The courts have recognized that requiring shareholders to buy additional shares or face dilution of their proportionate interest will sometimes be unfair to shareholders who cannot afford to participate, contrary to section 241 of the *CBCA*, the oppression remedy.[16]

C. ISSUING AND PAYING FOR SHARES

1) Introduction

As discussed in chapter 3, no minimum investment in shares of the corporation is required as a condition of incorporation. Also, there is no requirement to set a maximum number of shares of a class that may be issued, though the articles may provide for one. If there is a maximum, shares can only be issued up to that maximum number. In order to issue additional shares, the articles would have to be amended to increase or remove the maximum number. The number of shares of a class authorized to be issued is called the "authorized capital."

The directors have the power to issue shares, and this power cannot be delegated to anyone else (*CBCA*, s. 115(3)(c)). The shareholders may, however, assume this power by means of a unanimous shareholders' agreement (USA). Under a USA, shareholders can assume any or all the powers of the directors. The use of USAs is discussed in chapter 7.

Subject to the articles, by-laws, and any USA, shares can be issued to any person for whatever consideration the directors determine (*CBCA*, s. 25). Shares may be issued for money, property, or past services. If consideration is other than money, directors are obliged to be sure that whatever is received is not less in value than the "fair equivalent of the money that the corporation would have received if the share had been issued for money." Pursuant to section 118(1) of the *CBCA*, if the directors fail to get the "fair equivalent," they are personally liable, jointly and severally, to make up the shortfall, unless they could not reasonably have known that the value of the property was not sufficient (*CBCA*, s. 118(6)) or they relied on a professional opinion regarding the value of the property (*CBCA*, s. 123(4)).

---

16 For example, *Re Sabex International Ltée.* (1979), 6 B.L.R. 65 (Que. S.C.); *Mazzotta v. Twin Gold Mines Ltd.* (1987), 37 B.L.R. 218 (Ont. H.C.J.).

Consideration for the issuance of shares must be paid in full, whatever it is, at the time the shares are issued under the corporate laws of all Canadian jurisdictions except Quebec (*QCA*, s. 66), Prince Edward Island (*PEICA*, s. 41), and Nova Scotia (*NSCA*, s. 48). It used to be that shares could be issued on the basis that payment of some part of the subscription price would be paid later. Such shares were referred to as "not fully paid." Under the *CBCA*, only "fully paid" shares can be issued (*CBCA*, s. 25(2)).[17] Consistent with this requirement for full payment, section 25(5) provides that a promissory note or a promise to pay is not property for which shares may be issued.[18]

It used to be, as well, that shareholders could be asked by the directors to pay into the corporation more money from time to time as the corporation needed it. Such shares were called "assessable." Now all shares are "non-assessable" (*CBCA*, s. 25(2)).

2) Stated Capital Account

A corporation must maintain a separate account for each class and series of shares it issues, recording the "stated capital" for each class or series (*CBCA*, s. 26(1)). Stated capital for a class or series is simply a historical total of the amount paid into the corporation in return for the issuance of shares of that class or series.[19] It is aggregated for each class or series of shares, rather than recorded on an individual share basis. The stated capital per share is simply the total for the class divided by the number of shares, even if shares of a class are issued for different prices at different times. The example of the calculation of stated capital at the end of section D shows how stated capital calculations are made.

Stated capital is not cash; it is simply a bookkeeping record. Once money, property, or past services are contributed to the corporation, it may be spent or otherwise used in the corporation's business. Stated capital remains the same whether the money, property, or past services are wasted or used to increase the value of the corporation's assets.

---

17   It should be noted, however, that, if the corporation lends the shareholder the money to purchase the shares, the effect is the same as if the shares were not fully paid.

18   Most Canadian corporate statutes permit the corporation to pay a commission to a person in return for her agreement to purchase shares or to procure someone else to purchase shares (e.g., *CBCA*, above note 11, s. 41).

19   For certain transactions among related parties, including amalgamations, statutory arrangements, and continuance under the laws of another jurisdiction, the full amount of consideration received for the issuance of shares may not be added to the stated capital account (*CBCA*, above note 11, ss. 26(3) & (7)). These transactions are discussed in chapter 10.

Stated capital must be adjusted whenever shares are issued, including the payment of a dividend in the form of a share, or reacquired by the corporation. See the discussion in section D, "Redemption and Repurchase of Shares." Stated capital is also relevant for calculating whether the capital impairment test has been satisfied. As discussed above, the capital impairment test is required to be met before certain actions, such as declaring dividends, are permitted. See the discussion in section B under "Dividends."

It is also possible to adjust stated capital with the approval of the shareholders by special resolution, subject to certain limits (*CBCA*, s. 38). This might be done where the stated capital exceeds the realizable value of the corporation's assets and the capital impairment test referred to above cannot be satisfied, or where the corporation wants to distribute capital to its shareholders. Except where the reduction is to match a shortfall in realizable assets, a corporation cannot reduce its stated capital if there are reasonable grounds for believing that

- the corporation is, or after the reduction would be, unable to pay its liabilities as they become due; or
- the realizable value of the corporation's assets would thereby be less than the aggregate of its liabilities.

The procedure for making adjustments to the stated capital account is discussed in chapter 10.

D. REDEMPTION AND REPURCHASE OF SHARES

1) Introduction

In general, a corporation may not hold shares in itself or in a corporation that controls it (referred to in this section as a "parent corporation") (*CBCA*, s. 30). There are two exceptions to this rule: the corporation may hold its own shares as security or as a trustee. A corporation may acquire its own shares by purchase or redemption, subject to certain limitations.

2) Holding Shares as Security or as a Trustee

A corporation may hold shares in itself or its parent corporation as trustee, or as security for a transaction in the ordinary course of business (*CBCA*, s. 31). To illustrate the second case, consider the following example. I own shares of Canadian Imperial Bank of Commerce (CIBC). I pledge my shares to the CIBC as security for a car loan. If I fail to repay the loan, the CIBC can dispose of the shares and use the proceeds to pay itself back, giving any excess to me. The CIBC holds shares of itself as security for its loan to me, a transaction in the ordinary course of its business.

Under the *OBCA*, if a corporation does hold shares as security or as a trustee, it cannot vote them unless the corporation is holding as a trustee and then only in accordance with written instructions from the beneficiary (*OBCA*, ss. 33 & 153). There is no such restriction in the *CBCA*.

3) Purchase or Redemption of Shares

a) Purchase
A corporation can buy its own shares on any terms negotiated by the parties so long as doing so would not breach the financial tests in the *CBCA*, sections 34 & 35. For most purposes, these are the same financial tests as for solvency and impairment of capital, which must be satisfied for the payment of dividends (*CBCA*, s. 34). If, however, the purchase is to settle or compromise a debt asserted by or against the corporation, to eliminate fractional shares, or to fulfil the terms of a contract between it and a director, officer, or employee, the capital impairment test is relaxed to the extent that the realizable assets of the corporation after the payment need only exceed its liabilities plus the amount required to be paid on a liquidation or on a redemption of all the shares held by holders who have the right to be paid prior to the holders of shares to be purchased or acquired (*CBCA*, s. 35(1) & (3)). A corporation may purchase shares, even if the financial tests are not satisfied (*CBCA*, s. 35(2)), to satisfy the claim of a shareholder who has dissented from some action approved by the shareholders and who is entitled, as a result, to have his shares purchased under section 190 of the *CBCA*, or where the court has found oppression under section 241, to comply with a court order to purchase shares.

If a corporation does buy its own shares, it must either cancel them or, if its articles provide for a limited number of shares of that class, restore them to the status of authorized but unissued (*CBCA*, s. 39(6)).

b) Redemption
A corporation may redeem its own shares, which simply means buying them in accordance with an express term permitting the purchase in the corporation's articles. Such a term defines the circumstances in which redemption is permitted and specifies the price. Usually the price is the issue price plus all unpaid cumulative dividends.

Redemption may be at the option of the corporation, in which case the shares are referred to as "redeemable" or "callable"; at the option of the shareholder, in which case they are referred to as "retractible" or "putable"; or at the happening of a specified event, such as the expiry of a time period or the failure to pay dividends for a certain number of years.

4) Adjustments to Stated Capital

Whenever a corporation repurchases, redeems, or otherwise acquires its shares, it must deduct from its stated capital account the stated capital per share before the transaction, multiplied by the number of shares acquired (*CBCA*, ss. 37 & 39). Figure 6.1 is an example of the way stated capital is adjusted for a repurchase and a stock dividend.

Figure 6.1   Example of Changes to Stated Capital Account

Corporate Action	Date	Price	Stated Capital Adjustment
Issues			
50 shares	1 January 1996	$5 per share	Add 5(50) = 250
50 shares	1 July 1996	$10 per share	Add 10(50) = 500
Stock dividend			
(1/10 of a share for each share held) 10 shares	1 September 1996	$15 per share*	Add 15(10) = 150
Repurchase			
10 shares	31 December 1996	$20 per share	Subtract 20(10) = 200

At 31 December 1996

Issued shares = [50 + 50 + 10] − 10 = 100
Stated capital = [250 + 500 + 150] − 200 = $700
Stated capital per share = 700/100 = $7.00

* When a stock dividend is declared, the declared amount of the dividend stated as an amount of money must be added to the stated capital account maintained for the shares of the class issued in payment of the dividend (*CBCA*, s. 43(2)).

E. CHAPTER SUMMARY

In this chapter we described the nature of shares as a bundle of rights against the corporation, the characteristics of which are largely determined by provisions in the corporation's articles. The shares of a corporation may be divided into one or more classes with different characteristics, though the rights of holders of shares of each class are equal in all respects. The right to vote, to receive dividends, and to receive the remaining property of the corporation on dissolution must belong to at least one class of shares, but no class is required to have any particular right. Shares of a single class may be given some different characteristics if the articles of the corporation permit the corporation to issue shares in series. Where they do, the directors may create and set the characteristics of each series from time to time.

In practice, most corporations have common shares, which have all the basic rights. Often a corporation will also have preferred shares, which are entitled to receive fixed dividends and the return of the capital invested on issuance before any such payment to the holders of the common shares.

There is almost no limit on the characteristics that may be given to shares, including dividend rights, voting rights, and pre-emptive rights. The *CBCA* does prohibit the payment of dividends if the corporation is or would be rendered insolvent or its ability to repay its capital would be reduced. Also, the *CBCA* requires that shareholders get a right to vote on certain fundamental changes to the corporation, even if they do not otherwise have a right to vote. In addition to this mandatory special voting right, the shareholders of a particular class have a right to vote separately as a class if fundamental changes affect them differently from other classes.

The directors may issue shares for money, property, or past services that are equivalent to what the shares would have been issued for had they been issued for money. Whatever is paid must be paid in full at the time the shares are issued. The historical total of the amount paid to a corporation in return for shares of each class is recorded in the stated account.

Although a corporation may not hold its own shares, except in limited circumstances, it can acquire them in a negotiated purchase or in accordance with a redemption process set out in the corporation's articles, so long as doing so would not make the corporation insolvent or impair its ability to repay its capital. Whenever a corporation acquires its own shares it must adjust its stated capital account accordingly.

FURTHER READINGS

BRYDEN, R.M., "The Law of Dividends" in J.S. Ziegel, ed., *Studies in Canadian Company Law*, vol. 1 (Toronto: Butterworths, 1967) 270

KRISHNA, V., & J. A. VANDUZER, "Corporate Share Capital Structures and Income Splitting: *McClurg v. Canada*" (1993) 21 Can. Bus. L.J. 335

WELLING, B., *Corporate Law in Canada: The Governing Principles*, 2d ed. (Toronto: Butterworths, 1991) c. 8

CHAPTER 7

MANAGEMENT
AND CONTROL OF
THE CORPORATION

A. INTRODUCTION: SHAREHOLDERS, DIRECTORS, AND OFFICERS

In this chapter we will discuss how powers are allocated among directors, officers, and shareholders. As will be seen, the *CBCA* and most other modern corporate statutes in Canada provide for a clear division of powers. In many situations, however, the powers given to shareholders do not provide them with the practical ability to control management in the ways contemplated in the corporate legislation. Similarly, boards of directors often do not play the pivotal role in managing the corporation contemplated by the legislation. By contrast, in many large corporations the officers dominate decision making in a manner not addressed in the legislation in any significant way.

We will set out first the basic allocation of powers under Canadian corporate statutes and then discuss some of the problems with the operation of the statutory scheme in practice. The remainder of the chapter consists of a more detailed and technical discussion of how directors and shareholders exercise power under the *CBCA*.

B. MANAGEMENT AND CONTROL UNDER THE *CBCA*

The traditional breakdown of power to manage and control the corporation is as follows:

- directors are responsible for managing the business and the affairs of the corporation;
- officers exercise the power to manage delegated to them by the directors, and serve at the pleasure of the board; and
- shareholders are the residual claimants to the assets of the corporation, but their only power is to vote for the election of directors and to vote on proposals made to them.[1]

Under this breakdown, shareholders are essentially passive; they have no power to initiate action, to control management, or to act in relation to the ordinary business of the corporation except as specifically provided in the articles or by-laws.

In general, the *CBCA* adopts this traditional breakdown (*CBCA*, ss. 102, 115, & 121) but enhances the shareholder's traditional passive role in several ways. Approval by shareholders is required before certain significant changes can occur to the corporation. The *CBCA* also gives shareholders a limited scope for actively initiating corporate action. To facilitate both kinds of shareholder action, the *CBCA* gives shareholders certain rights of access to information. Finally, the *CBCA* improves shareholders' ability to seek relief from the behaviour of management.

The situations in which the *CBCA* specifically provides for shareholder approval include, in particular, approval of the following fundamental changes to the corporation:

- amendment of articles (*CBCA*, s. 173);
- initiation, amendment, and repeal of by-laws (*CBCA*, s. 103);
- sale, lease, or exchange of "all or substantially all the property of a corporation" other than in the ordinary course of business (*CBCA*, s. 189(3));
- amalgamation with another corporation (*CBCA*, s. 183); and
- dissolution of the corporation (*CBCA*, s. 211).[2]

The *CBCA* also provides for an active role for shareholders in two ways:

- proposals: shareholders can have matters put on the agenda for discussion at shareholders' meetings, including making, amending, or repealing by-laws (*CBCA*, ss. 137 & 103(5));
- unanimous shareholders' agreements: shareholders can assume all powers of the board of directors, completely altering the allocation of

---

1   *Automatic Self-Cleansing Filter Syndicate* v. *Cunninghame*, [1906] 2 Ch. 34 (C.A.) (shareholders cannot, by ordinary resolution, vary the mandate of the directors; amendment of the articles required); *Kelly* v. *Electrical Construction Co.* (1907), 16 O.L.R. 232 (H.C.J.) (shareholders cannot initiate the creation of a by-law).

2   All these corporate changes are discussed in chapter 10.

powers as between directors and shareholders, if they unanimously agree (*CBCA*, s. 106). Such an agreement may then allocate the assumed powers among the shareholders.

Both proposals and unanimous shareholders' agreements are discussed later in this chapter in detail.

The *CBCA* gives shareholders rights of access to information about the corporation, including information about past meetings of shareholders and financial records (*CBCA*, ss. 20, 21, 143, 160, & 243; Part XIX & Part XI). These shareholder rights are discussed later in this chapter.

The *CBCA* provides remedies for abuse of directors' power to manage such as the following:

• a right to apply to have the corporation's existence terminated (*CBCA*, s. 214);

• a right to bring an action on behalf of the corporation, in some circumstances, for breach by management of duties owed to the corporation (a "derivative action," *CBCA*, s. 239);

• a right to seek relief from "oppression" of the interests of shareholders or others by management (*CBCA*, s. 241);

• a right to seek an order directing management to comply with or to restrain management from breaching the *CBCA*, the articles, by-laws, or any unanimous shareholder agreement (s. 247); and

• a right to seek rectification of corporate records (ss. 243 & 257).[3]

Notwithstanding these adjustments, under the scheme of the *CBCA*, directors manage the corporation; shareholder power consists primarily of retaining ultimate control by virtue of shareholders' ability to determine the composition of the board of directors and to vote on matters put to them. If a majority of shareholders are unhappy with the board of directors' management, they can replace the board at the next annual meeting, or can requisition a special meeting for this purpose (*CBCA*, s. 143 (requisition); s. 109 (removal by ordinary resolution)).

C. OBSERVATIONS ON MANAGEMENT AND CONTROL OF THE CORPORATION IN THEORY AND PRACTICE

In order to understand how the allocation of power and responsibility under the *CBCA* works, it is necessary to consider the various practical

---

3   All these remedies are discussed in chapter 9.

contexts to which it applies. These vary from the corporation with a single shareholder who is also the sole director and officer to the large public corporation with thousands of shareholders spread out around the world and a few directors who work as managers in the corporation. How the corporate law rules for corporate management and control operate will vary significantly, depending on a corporation's position between these two extremes.

Consider first the corporation where one person is the sole shareholder, director, and officer. In these circumstances, the allocation of rights and responsibilities contemplated in the *CBCA* are formalistic and, for most practical purposes, irrelevant. As the sole participant in the corporation, this person has no incentive to favour her interests as a director or officer over her interests as a shareholder and no one, other than herself, to bear the consequences if she does so. If, for example, she pays herself an excessive salary in her capacity as an officer, she will suffer a corresponding diminution in the value of her interest as a shareholder. Equally, if she takes no salary or other compensation for her work for the corporation, she benefits to the same extent in terms of the increase in the value of her interest in the corporation.

This unity of interest breaks down as soon as our sole shareholder permits someone else to invest in shares of the corporation. Assume she sells 50 percent of her shares to her father, who will not be active in the business. Now, if she pays herself an excessive salary, she receives 100 percent of the benefit of doing so, but her interest as a shareholder is diminished by only 50 percent — that is, to the extent of her remaining percentage interest in the corporation. The potential for opportunistic behaviour of this kind to result in her personal enrichment gives our formerly sole shareholder an incentive to engage in it. This raises a concern for our new investor, her father. He is exposed to the risk of his daughter's opportunistic behaviour and will be interested in putting in place some mechanism to prevent it. Corporate law provides a variety of such mechanisms in the form of the shareholder approval requirements and shareholder remedies referred to above. The costs to shareholders associated with losses due to opportunistic behaviour by corporate managers or agents, and any expenditures by shareholders for the purpose of preventing these losses, are referred to as agency costs. They are the costs associated with an agent (i.e., someone other than the shareholder) managing the corporation in which the shareholder has his investment.

As the number of shareholders in a corporation increases and this separation between management and share ownership widens, the incentive for managers to engage in opportunistic behaviour also rises. If managers are shareholders at all, the size of their interest, typically, is very small relative to the aggregate of all shareholder interests, so the proportion of benefit to them associated with acting in ways that further the corporation's interests, rather than their own, is correspondingly small. At the same time, the ability of shareholders to ensure that directors are accountable to act in the corporation's interests, through the legal mechanisms described above, is reduced. In practice, at least in relation to larger corporations, the principal legal mechanisms referred to above — shareholder voting rights, information rights, and shareholder remedies — may be ineffective for a variety of reasons.

Notwithstanding the access to information rights described above, shareholders will often lack sufficient information to understand and evaluate management's performance. In addition, most shareholders will have a small financial stake relative to the cost of obtaining adequate information, especially considering that effective evaluation will often require paying for professional advice. As a result, shareholders will be discouraged from trying to acquire such information. Individual shareholders may also hope and expect that others will do the information gathering and analysis. Since the benefits associated with an investment in information gathering will accrue to all shareholders regardless of their individual contribution, it may seem to make sense to let others spend their money on doing it.

Even if shareholders were able to gather sufficient information and to analyse it, mobilizing the large number of geographically and otherwise disparate shareholders that would be needed to defeat a management proposal or to elect a new board of directors will be difficult and costly. Again, the relatively small financial stake of individual shareholders discourages collective activity.

Also under the *CBCA*, the directors control the proxy solicitation process (*CBCA*, ss. 137(4), 149, & 150). This process will be described in some detail later in this chapter. For now it is sufficient to point out that, for the most part, the directors determine what goes on the agenda for meetings and how it is described. In this context, some commentators have noted that the increasingly active participation in the securities markets of institutional investors with large financial interests in individual firms, and the resources and contacts to facilitate coordinated behaviour, may result in more effective monitoring of opportunistic behaviour by management. Whether and how corporate law should respond to this relatively recent development is an important issue for future legislative reform.[4]

---

4   R.J. Daniels & E.J. Waitzer, "Challenges to the Citadel: A Brief Overview of Recent Trends in Canadian Corporate Governance" (1994) 23 Can. Bus. L.J. 23; J. G. MacIntosh, "The Role of Institutional and Retail Investors in Canadian Capital Markets" (1993) 31 Osgoode Hall L.J. 371. See chapter 12.

Shareholder litigation to seek the enhanced remedies provided in the *CBCA* and other modern corporate statutes also faces certain challenges. Most important, litigation is an expensive, time consuming, and uncertain exercise. Also, despite the improvements made recently in some jurisdictions, such as Ontario, in facilitating class actions by shareholders, the impediments to shareholders acting collectively to exercise their voting rights effectively apply equally to shareholder litigation.

Another problem with the existing legal accountability mechanisms in the *CBCA* is that they focus on the board of directors as the locus of management power and do not speak much of officers at all. Reading the *CBCA* and the older case law, one may get the impression that the board is engaged in high-level management activities such as setting business objectives and policy, choosing the senior management personnel, and closely supervising their activities. In fact, the board plays this role in very few corporations. This focus on directors is out of step with reality.

In small closely held corporations where all the shareholders are actively involved in the business, the formal separation of powers described in section B has little significance for how such a corporation operates. Although the shareholders must still elect a board and the board will still choose the officers, the effective decision makers will be the shareholder managers by whatever means they agree on. Even if the board has a few directors from outside the shareholder group, in most cases they will act merely as advisers. As will be discussed below, the possibility of using a unanimous shareholder agreement to transfer directors' powers to shareholders was introduced in the *CBCA* as a way of permitting these kinds of corporations to adopt a legal structure that more closely reflects their practice of direct management by shareholders.

In large public corporations as well, the board of directors seldom exercises the role traditionally ascribed to it, but for different reasons. As noted above, in such corporations there are various impediments to the effective exercise of shareholder power over directors. Typically, however, this limitation does not result in the board becoming the locus of management power. Boards tend to be dominated by the full-time professional managers of the corporation. There are a variety of reasons for this result. It is management who is actively involved in the affairs of the corporation and has the necessary knowledge, experience, and expertise regarding its operations to deal with the complex issues that arise on a daily basis. Members of the board who are not part of the management team, on the other hand, are usually busy professionals or business people who do not have the time to engage in the continuous analysis that would be required to set policy and objectives and to make major decisions regarding the business. Even if they sought to do so, they would be largely dependent on the information and analysis provided by management and so would rarely be in a position to challenge management.

Research has shown that outside directors tend to defer to management because of what Mace has called a "culture of deference."[5] Outside directors are picked by management and may receive substantial compensation from the corporation. Sometimes an outside director of one corporation is also the chief executive of another and may have picked the chief executive of the first corporation to be on her board. As a result, each has a reciprocal interest in not challenging each other's authority around the boardroom table. Similarly, it is common for professionals such as lawyers, accountants, and investment dealers to be represented on the boards of corporations that are their clients. For these directors, challenging management may put substantial fee revenue at risk. These reservations should not be taken as suggesting that outside directors are incapable of meeting their obligations to the corporation, nor is it suggested that substantial delegation to management is not permitted by the *CBCA*. As discussed below, such delegation is expressly permitted. Nevertheless, it does suggest that there are factors militating against boards of directors playing the kind of direct management role that the *CBCA* seems to contemplate, and that corporate law rules based on such an assumption may not serve their purpose.[6]

Finally, an examination of corporate law rules, at least as they apply to public corporations with many shareholders, discloses only one set of accountability mechanisms. Where shares are traded in a marketplace, the dynamic of the marketplace itself will impose a certain discipline on management. Although it is beyond the scope of this book to describe the vast empirical and theoretical literature which has developed on this subject, it is important to point out some of the basic insights that a consideration of market forces yields.

In markets for corporate shares and other securities, prices are set, as in other markets, as a result of supply and demand, the buying and selling activity of people trading in the market. Empirical evidence has demonstrated that prices in markets for securities tend to reflect accurately all

---

5   M.L. Mace, *Directors: Myth and Reality* (Boston: Harvard University Graduate School of Business Administration, Division of Research, 1971) at 184–206.

6   The effectiveness of boards of public corporations in Canada was recently criticized in the *Report of the Toronto Stock Exchange Committee on Corporate Governance in Canada: Where Were the Directors?* (Toronto: Toronto Stock Exchange, 1994). For an example of outside directors playing an effective role, see *Brant Investments* v. *KeepRite Inc.* (1991), 3 O.R. (3d) 289 (C.A.).

publicly available information.[7] This characteristic, called market efficiency, means that all public information about agency costs should be factored into the price. Expressed another way, a shareholder need not worry about the risk of management engaging in opportunistic behaviour because the price of the shares was already reduced to reflect that risk at the time she bought it. Prospective investors can get a sense of what the market thinks agency costs for a particular firm are by comparing changes in the price of the firm's shares to those of its industry competitors.

Unfortunately, there are still risks associated with opportunistic behaviour by management. For example, not all risks of such behaviour are foreseeable and so may not be factored into share price. Also, studies of stock markets suggest that prices do not reflect non-public or insider information known only to officers and directors of the corporation.[8] Agency cost risks known only to insiders will not be factored into share price. Nevertheless, to the extent that agency costs are factored into share price, the corporate law mechanisms designed to monitor and control agency costs become less important.

The operation of securities markets can also enhance shareholders' ability to take advantage of these corporate law mechanisms. Once a person has acquired shares, a drop in the price may reflect some new information or a change in circumstances that increases agency costs. In such a case, the shareholder may either sell, in which case he bears the full amount of this increase in agency costs, or he may try to exercise his vote to try to discipline management in some way. In choosing this second option, he would be faced with the problems described above in terms of collecting and analysing information and mobilizing his fellow shareholders. While neither of these options permit the shareholder to avoid agency costs, the general point is that prices in securities markets, in effect, provide information about agency costs and so facilitate the effective exercise of shareholder voting.

What is sometimes called the market for corporate control also reduces agency costs. A corporation that is being managed in the interests of enriching its management represents an opportunity; by gaining control of the corporation by acquiring sufficient shares, a person could enhance the value of the firm by improving management. Such a change in control is accomplished by what is known as a takeover bid: a bidder offers to buy some or all of the shares held by existing shareholders,

---

7   This evidence is reviewed in R.J. Daniels & J.G. MacIntosh, "Toward a Distinctive Canadian Corporate Law Regime" (1991) 29 Osgoode Hall L.J. 863 at 872–74.

8   J.N. Gordon & L.A. Kornhauser, "Efficient Markets, Costly Information and Securities Research" (1985) 60 N.Y.U. L. Rev. 761.

typically at a price in excess of the current market price, for the purpose of acquiring enough shares to replace the board of directors and have a new board put new management in place. The threat of such a hostile takeover bid, which, if successful, will result in the board and the officers losing their positions, should discourage management from engaging in the behaviour that created the opportunity for the bidder in the first place. Some commentators have suggested that the discipline provided by the market for corporate control is so important that management's ability to defend against a hostile takeover bid should be severely limited.[9] This point is discussed in more detail in chapters 8 and 11.

The existence of these market mechanisms to address agency problems has led some corporate law scholars to assert that legal rules can only be justified to the extent that the market can be shown not to operate effectively and that this inefficiency leaves a narrow sphere of operation for corporate law.[10] Others have suggested that the capital and corporate control markets do not work efficiently, so a substantial role must be played by mandatory corporate law rules.[11] Still others argue that it is not appropriate to use the market as the exclusive model for thinking about what corporate law rules should be.[12]

In discussing the ways in which shareholders and directors exercise power under the existing corporate law regimes in Canada in the remainder of this chapter, it is important to keep in mind the issues raised in the foregoing discussion.

D. SHAREHOLDERS AND HOW THEY EXERCISE POWER

1) Shareholders' Meetings and Resolutions

To exercise their power to vote, shareholders must act collectively. Most commonly this is done by having a meeting at which a vote takes place. This section sets out the *CBCA* rules regarding shareholders' meetings.

---

9   F.H. Easterbrook & D.R. Fischel, "The Proper Rule of a Target's Management in Responding to a Tender Offer" (1982) 94 Harv. L. Rev. 1161.

10   For example, F.H. Easterbrook & D.R. Fischel, "Corporate Control Transactions" (1982) 91 Yale L.J. 698 at 700–3.

11   For example, V. Brudney, "Corporate Governance, Agency Costs, and the Rhetoric of Contract" (1985) 85 Colum. L. Rev. 1403 at 1410–11.

12   For example, B. Chapman, "Trust, Economic Rationality, and the Corporate Fiduciary Obligation" (1993) 43 U.T.L.J. 547.

a) Types of Meetings

Annual meetings must be held at least every fifteen months (*CBCA*, s. 133). Annual meetings are identified and defined by the happening of three items of business:

- the election of directors;
- the receipt of financial statements and the auditor's report on the statements; and
- the appointment of an auditor (unless dispensed with by unanimous agreement of shareholders in certain circumstances) (*CBCA*, s. 133(5)).

Meetings to conduct any business other than these three items are called "special meetings" (*CBCA*, s. 135(5)). These may be called any time (*CBCA*, s. 133(b)). To the extent any such special business is carried on at an annual meeting it is called an "annual and special meeting."

b) Calling Meetings

The directors are responsible for calling annual and special meetings of shareholders, but shareholders holding not less than 5 percent of shares that carry the right to vote at the meeting may require the directors to call a meeting (*CBCA*, s. 143). This kind of shareholder action is called a requisition. If the directors fail to call a meeting within twenty-one days of any such requisition by a shareholder, he or she may call a meeting and the corporation must reimburse the shareholder for the expenses of doing so. Also, any director or shareholder entitled to vote may apply to a court to have a meeting called if it is impracticable to call a meeting in the ways mentioned above, or to have a meeting conducted as prescribed in the by-laws or the *CBCA* (s. 144).

c) Place of Meetings

Shareholders' meetings must be at the place specified in the by-laws. In default of such specification, meeting must be in a Canadian location specified by the directors, or, with unanimous shareholder consent, at a place outside Canada (*CBCA*, s. 132).

d) Notice of Meetings

The *CBCA* provides minimum and maximum notice periods for meetings. The maximum is fifty days and the minimum is twenty-one days (*CBCA*, s. 135). Both statutes permit notice to be waived, and attendance by a shareholder is deemed to be a waiver of notice unless the shareholder attends for the purpose of claiming that the meeting is improperly called (*CBCA*, s. 136). Notice must go to

- each shareholder entitled to vote;
- each director; and
- the auditor of the corporation.

Under section 135 of the *CBCA*, shareholders who are entitled to notice are those who appear in the shareholders' register on a certain date called the "record date." The record date is most significant for public corporations, whose shares change hands on a daily basis. The directors may fix a record date by resolution which is no more than fifty days or less than twenty-one days before the meeting (*CBCA*, s. 134). If, as is common, the directors do not do so, the *CBCA* provides that the record date is at the close of business on the day immediately preceding the day on which notice is given (s. 134(3)(a)). Even if a shareholder is not entitled to notice under this scheme, perhaps because he acquired his shares after the record date, he is not deprived of the right to attend and vote at the meeting (*CBCA*, s. 138(3)).

Where the meeting is a special meeting, the notice must state the nature of the special business and the text of any special resolution to be put to the meeting for a vote (*CBCA*, s. 135(6)).

e) Proxies and Proxy Solicitation

Any person not able to be personally present at a meeting may appoint a person, who need not be a shareholder, to represent her at the meeting and vote her shares. The appointment, called a "proxy," must be in writing and signed by the shareholder. A proxy may be revoked at any time before the meeting with respect to which it was given. The person appointed to exercise the shareholder's vote (also referred to as a "proxy" or "proxy holder") has all the powers of a shareholder at the meeting, but the authority of the proxy is limited to that conferred by the proxy. In other words, the proxy holder must vote in accordance with any direction given by the shareholder. Failure to do so is an offence (*CBCA*, s. 152(4)). Voting by proxy is exclusively a statutory right. It was not permitted at common law.

For all corporations with more than fifteen shareholders incorporated under the *CBCA*, management must send certain information, in a document called a "management proxy circular," and a form of proxy to shareholders (*CBCA*, ss. 148, 149, & 150). As the number of shareholders of a corporation increases, the proxy solicitation process is an increasingly important way of directly facilitating the exercise by shareholders of their voting rights through the proxy and of enhancing shareholder participation by providing both general information and specific information regarding management proposals.

Under the *CBCA*, management is required to send annual financial statements to shareholders in connection with annual meetings (*CBCA*, s. 155). Provincial securities laws require similar material to be sent to shareholders. Most public corporations include the financial statements in a glossy annual report that also contains material such as statements from management and descriptions of the corporation's operations.

The contents of the management proxy circular are prescribed by regulation (*CBCA Regulations*, ss. 35–36) and include the following categories of information:

- a description of shareholders' rights to appoint a proxy and how this appointment must by done;
- transactions with insiders of the corporation (e.g., affiliated corporations, significant shareholders, directors, and officers);
- disclosure of shareholders holding more than 5 percent of the issued shares of the corporation;
- details about the directors who are proposed for election; and
- details about any special business to be dealt with at the meeting.

Shareholders who disagree with management proposals may also solicit the votes of their fellow shareholders. Dissident shareholders are entitled to obtain a list of shareholders, the shares they hold, and their addresses from the corporation and to contact other shareholders for the purpose of influencing their voting (*CBCA*, s. 21(3) & (9)). If a shareholder does solicit proxies, however, she must send out a "dissident's proxy circular" in the form prescribed by the regulations (*CBCA*, s. 150(b), *CBCA Regulations*, ss. 38–41). Dissident proxy circulars are relatively rare in the Canadian marketplace. They sometimes occur in connection with hostile takeover bids. When they do occur, they are often accompanied by advertising campaigns conducted by management and dissidents in the financial press.

The rules about proxies and proxy solicitation may be enforced in the same way as other shareholder rights. A shareholder may seek a court order directing the directors to comply with the rules (*CBCA*, s. 247). In addition, section 154 of the *CBCA* specifically provides that a shareholder may apply to a court to restrain the distribution of a proxy circular that contains "an untrue statement of a material fact or omits to state a material fact . . . [that is] . . . necessary to make a statement contained therein not misleading in the light of the circumstances in which it was made." The court can also order that the implementation of any resolution that was passed at a meeting held after the distribution of such a circular be restrained, or it can make any other order it sees fit.

f) Shareholder Proposals

Normally, the agenda for shareholder meetings is set by the directors. This is especially true in large corporations where shareholders are remote from management. The *CBCA* provides a limited right for shareholders to add items to the agenda (*CBCA*, s. 137), including the amendment of by-laws and articles (*CBCA*, ss. 103(5) & 175(1)). Any shareholder entitled to vote may submit to the corporation notice — called a proposal — of any matter he or she proposes to discuss. If the corporation is required to send out a management proxy circular (*CBCA*, s. 150), the proposal must be included, along with a supporting statement of up to 200 words from the proposing shareholder. Essentially the proposal mechanism is intended to facilitate communication among shareholders at the expense of the corporation.

There are certain limits on the content of a proposal, designed, in part, to prevent frivolous use of this process. The proposal may include nominations for the election of directors only if the proposal is signed by the holders of not less than 5 percent of the shares entitled to vote. The corporation does not have to circulate a proposal in five circumstances:

- the proposal is not received at least ninety days before the anniversary date of the last annual meeting;
- it clearly appears that the proposal is primarily for the purpose of
  - enforcing a personal claim or redressing a personal grievance against the corporation, the directors, officers, or security holders; or
  - promoting general economic, political, racial, religious, social, or similar causes;
- the proposing shareholder made a proposal within the last two years, then failed to show up, in person or by proxy, to speak to it at the meeting;
- substantially the same proposal was submitted to a meeting of shareholders and defeated; or
- the right to make a proposal is being abused to secure publicity.

The limits on what may be subject to a proposal apply equally to what may be the subject of a shareholder requisitioned meeting.

Several cases have considered the scope of these limits on the use of proposals. In *Varity Corp.* v. *Jesuit Fathers of Upper Canada*,[13] a shareholder sought to have a corporation circulate a proposal to have the corporation divest its investments in South Africa. It was held that the primary purpose of the proposal, based on the language used and the

---

13   (1987), 59 O.R. (2d) 459 (H.C.J.), aff'd (1987), 60 O.R. (2d) 640 (C.A.).

supporting statement, was the abolition of apartheid in South Africa; since the proposal was primarily for the purpose of promoting a political or social cause, the corporation was not obliged to distribute it. The court acknowledged that there was also a more specific purpose relating to the business of the corporation — the divestment of its interests in South Africa — but held that this objective did not prevent the exception from operating. Similarly, in *Re Greenpeace Foundation of Canada & Inco Ltd.,*[14] a proposal to institute pollution control measures to limit sulphur dioxide emissions was held to be for the purpose of advancing an environmental cause and so fell within the exception. In the same case, the court ruled that the corporation could also refuse to circulate the proposal because a resolution to impose restrictions on emissions, although at a different level, had been defeated at a previous meeting.

Perhaps because of the relatively broad construction given to these limitations, the proposal mechanism has been used rarely. A recent study of 480 public corporations in Canada found only one proposal submitted in 1990, and none in 1991 or 1992.[15]

g) Conduct of Meetings

Meetings are conducted by the same rules regarding quorum and procedure as apply to Parliament, except where the *CBCA* or the by-laws provide otherwise. A discussion right is expressly provided for in section 137(1)(b), which provides that a shareholder is entitled to discuss any matter with respect to which she could have submitted a proposal at an annual meeting. The corresponding provision in the *OBCA* gives a discussion right at both special and annual meetings (s. 99(1)(b)).

In addition to this statutory right, shareholders have a right to speak to the matters on the agenda, and the chair cannot arbitrarily terminate the meeting to prevent shareholders from discussing an agenda item and voting on it.[16] The right to discuss may be terminated by the chair if she determines, in good faith, that it is being abused, such as where a shareholder seeks to obstruct the meeting.[17]

---

14 (23 February 1984), (Ont. H.C.J.) [unreported] [summarized at (1984), 24 A.C.W.S. (2d) 349], aff'd (21 March 1984), (Ont. C.A.) [unreported] [summarized at (1984), 25 A.C.W.S. (2d) 322].

15 C. McCall & R. Wilson, "Shareholder Proposals: Why Not in Canada?" (1993) 5 Corp. Governance. Rev.

16 *National Dwellings Society v. Sykes,* [1894] 3 Ch. 159 (Ch.); *Bomac Batten Ltd. v. Pozhke* (1983), 43 O.R. (2d) 344 (H.C.J.); *Canadian Express Ltd. v. Blair* (1989), 46 B.L.R. 92 (Ont. H.C.J.) [*Blair*]. The chair is obliged to act in a quasi-judicial fashion.

17 *Wall v. London and Northern Assets Corp.,* [1898] 2 Ch. 469 (C.A.).

h) Quorum

A majority of shares entitled to vote, represented in person or by proxy at the meeting, constitute a quorum unless the by-laws provide otherwise (*CBCA*, s. 139). Most by-laws also provide that a certain number of shareholders, often only two, must be present in person or by proxy.

i) Voting

Unless the articles provide otherwise, each share gets one vote and matters are decided by a majority of votes cast on any resolution at the meeting. Special resolutions, required for amendments to articles and certain other fundamental changes, must be passed by two-thirds of the votes cast at the meeting (*CBCA*, ss. 140, 173, 183, & 189). Unless the by-laws provide otherwise, voting is by a show of hands, but any shareholder may require that a ballot be taken — meaning that each vote is recorded on a ballot, which is collected and counted.

2) Access to Information

a) Introduction

The *CBCA* requires a corporation to provide shareholders with access to certain information to enhance their ability to monitor management and to exercise their rights as shareholders. A corporation must maintain certain records and allow access to them by shareholders as well as certain other people, such as directors, officers, and creditors.

b) Specific Requirements

The articles, by-laws, and any unanimous shareholder agreement, minutes of meetings of shareholders, all notices of directors and notices of registered office, and a share register showing the owners of all shares must be maintained by the corporation (*CBCA*, s. 20(1)). All these documents may be examined and copied by shareholders and creditors, and their legal representatives, during business hours (*CBCA*, s. 21). If the corporation is a distributing corporation, the copies are free; otherwise a reasonable charge may be imposed. Every shareholder, however, is entitled free of charge to one copy of the articles, by-laws, and any unanimous shareholder agreement (*CBCA*, s. 21(9)).

Any list of shareholders that has been obtained cannot be used except in an effort to influence the voting of shareholders, to acquire shares of the corporation, or for any other purpose relating to the affairs of the corporation. All other inspection rights may be used for any other purpose, including competition with the corporation.[18] There is no right

---

18   *Johnston v. West Fraser Timber Co.* (1980), 22 B.C.L.R. 337 (S.C.).

to inspect the minutes of directors' meetings. Other access to information rights includes the right to requisition meetings and to ask questions (*CBCA*, s. 143) and the right to have inspectors and auditors appointed (*CBCA*, Part XIX). The inspection right is discussed in chapter 9 on "Shareholder Remedies."

A corporation is also required to make certain limited disclosures to the public which shareholders may take advantage of. These disclosures were discussed in chapter 4. Under the *CBCA* the following items must be filed:

- articles (including all amendments);
- notices of directors and change of directors;
- notices of registered office and change of registered office;
- insider trading filings (Part XI);
- annual information returns (*CBCA*, s. 263; Form 22); and
- annual financial statements for distributing corporations (*CBCA*, s. 160).

In Ontario, additional publicly available information filings are required under the Ontario *Corporations Information Act*[19] and, for public corporations, under the Ontario *Securities Act*.[20]

3) Signed Resolutions and Single Shareholder Meetings

In general, any action taken by shareholders must be given effect by a resolution passed at a meeting. Under the *CBCA*, if a class or series of shares has but a single shareholder, he alone can constitute a meeting, notwithstanding the etymological impossibility (*CBCA*, s. 139(4)). The *CBCA* also provides an alternative to meetings. If a single shareholder or each shareholder, if there is more than one, signs a written resolution, it will be effective just as if it had been passed at a meeting (*CBCA*, s. 142). Proceeding in this way eliminates the need for shareholders to actually get together to meet, and the need to worry about notices and other formalities associated with meetings. It is a commonplace expedient in small corporations especially if the shareholders are not in the same location. Such a signed resolution becomes effective once the last shareholder has signed it.

---

19   R.S.O. 1990, c. C.39.
20   R.S.O. 1990, c. S.5.

E. DIRECTORS AND HOW THEY EXERCISE POWER

1) Qualifications

A person is not qualified to be a director if she is

- less than 18;
- of unsound mind so found;
- an undischarged bankrupt; or
- not an individual (*CBCA*, s. 105).

With regard to the last qualification, it is important to note that even though a corporation cannot be a director, a corporation may be an incorporator (*CBCA*, s. 5)).

There is no statutory requirement for directors to hold shares in the corporation, though the articles may provide for such a requirement (*CBCA*, s. 105(2)). A majority of directors must be resident Canadians (*CBCA*, s. 105(3)). "[R]esident Canadian" is defined in section 1(1) to include Canadian citizens ordinarily resident in Canada, and a permanent resident within the meaning of the *Immigration Act*[21] who is ordinarily resident in Canada.[22]

A director ceases to hold office on becoming disqualified (*CBCA*, s. 108(1)(c)), but any act of a director after she becomes disqualified is valid, notwithstanding the defect in her qualification (*CBCA*, s. 116).

2) Election and Appointment of Directors

a) General

The election and appointment of directors under the *CBCA* and statutes modelled after it follow certain technical rules. The first directors of a corporation are those listed in the notice of directors filed with the articles. They become directors at the time the certificate of incorporation is issued and incorporation occurs (*CBCA*, s. 106(2)). These directors hold office until the first meeting of shareholders, which must be held not more than eighteen months after incorporation (*CBCA*, s. 133). At that

---

21   R.S.C. 1985, c. I-2.

22   An exception is provided for persons who have been permanent residents more than one year after they became entitled to apply for Canadian citizenship. *Canada Business Corporations Act Regulations*, SOR/79-316, s. 11, lists other categories of "resident Canadians."

meeting, and at each subsequent annual meeting at which an election is required, shareholders must, by simple majority, elect directors. The term of directors cannot extend for longer than the date of the third annual meeting following their election. In most cases, directors must be elected annually. If no term is specified on their election, the directors stay in office only until the annual meeting following their election (*CBCA*, s. 106(3)). If, however, the shareholders fail to elect directors when they are supposed to, for whatever reason, the incumbents stay in until their replacements are elected, so there is no problem with the authority of the board of directors to act in the interim (*CBCA*, s. 106(6)).

b) Filling Vacancies on the Board

A vacancy on the board may occur for a variety of reasons: a director may resign, be removed by shareholders, or become disqualified. If there is no quorum remaining in place or a vacancy has occurred because somehow the shareholders failed to elect the required number of directors at the shareholders' meeting, the remaining directors must call a shareholders' meeting to fill the vacancy (*CBCA*, s. 111(2)). If a quorum remains in place, the remaining directors may fill the vacancy by appointing a new director for the unexpired term of the director whose departure created the vacancy (*CBCA*, s. 111(1)). The articles may provide that all vacancies must be filled by shareholders (*CBCA*, s. 111(4)).

Significant changes, including the wholesale replacement of the board, may be effected without getting shareholder approval, if one can obtain the cooperation of both the departing and the incoming directors and follow a process of sequential resignations and appointments. For example, assume that it is desired to change all the members of a board of five directors and that the required quorum is four directors. One director may resign and the remaining four appoint her successor. Then a second director resigns, and the remaining four, including the newly appointed director, fill the vacancy. In this way, the whole board may be replaced without a shareholder vote. This might be desirable if several directors wanted to resign and the board wanted to continue to operate until the next annual meeting, avoiding the expense of calling a special meeting just to elect new directors.

3) Number of Directors

Apart from one restriction, the choice of the number of directors is a matter for the shareholders to decide. Under the *CBCA* and other statutes modelled after it, if the corporation has made a distribution of its shares to the public and those shares remain outstanding and are held by more than one person, the corporation must have three directors, at least two of whom are not officers or employees of the corporation (*CBCA* s. 102(2)).

The number of directors or a maximum and minimum number of directors must be specified in the articles of the corporation (*CBCA*, s. 6(1)(e)). The corporation may change the number or the minimum and maximum number of directors by articles of amendment. The process of amending articles is described in chapter 10. In general, amendments require the approval of shareholders by special resolution.

4) Directors' Meetings

Like shareholders, directors exercise their power collectively, primarily at meetings. Modern corporate statutes set out a code for directors' meetings (e.g., *CBCA*, s. 114).

a) Place
Unless the articles or by-laws specify a particular place, meetings may be held at whatever place the directors decide. There is no statutory requirement under the *CBCA* (s. 114(1)).

b) Notice
Notice of meetings must be as specified in the corporation's by-laws under the *CBCA*. There is no default provision (s. 114). Under the *OBCA*, in default of any provision in the by-laws, ten days notice must be given (*OBCA*, s. 126(9)). Notice may be waived and is deemed waived by attendance at a meeting, except if a director attends the meeting for the purpose of objecting to the meeting on the basis that it is not lawfully called (*CBCA*, s. 114(6)).

c) Conducting Meetings
At directors' meetings, as at shareholders' meetings, certain procedures must be followed. Some minimum number of directors, called a quorum, must be present, or no business may be carried on. A quorum may be set out in the articles or the by-laws. In default of such provision, a quorum consists of a majority of directors, if the articles specify a fixed number of directors, or a majority of the minimum number of directors permitted by the articles (*CBCA*, s. 114(2)).[23] Regardless of what quorum

---

23   Under the Ontario *Business Corporations Act*, R.S.O. 1990, c. B.16 [*OBCA*], there is less flexibility. Quorum cannot be less than two-fifths of the number of directors or the minimum total number of directors (s. 126(3)).

is, the directors may not carry on business unless a majority of the directors present are resident Canadians (*CBCA*, s. 114(3)). This requirement may be satisfied, however, if, after a meeting, a majority of resident Canadians approves any business transacted at the meeting.

Directors may participate in meetings by telephone if all consent and if all can hear each other (*CBCA*, s. 114(9)). It is common to obtain a general form of consent to telephone meetings from a person when he or she becomes a director.

When business is transacted at a meeting, it must be approved by the majority directors' votes, which is specified in the articles or by-laws. There is no statutory default in the *CBCA*.

Directors can transact whatever business they like, except that, at the first meeting following incorporation, the agenda is specified in section 114. This agenda is discussed in chapter 4. Also, directors must call an annual meeting at least every fifteen months, and directors must approve financial statements annually.

d) Dissent by a Director

If a director is present at a meeting, including presence by telephone, he is deemed to consent to any resolution passed at the meeting unless he expresses his dissent in one of the following ways:

- requests that the dissent be recorded, and it is, recorded in minutes;
- sends a written dissent to the secretary of the meeting before it is adjourned; or
- sends a dissent by registered mail or delivers it to the office of the corporation immediately after the meeting is adjourned.

If a director votes for a resolution, she cannot dissent after the meeting. If a director is not present, she is deemed to consent if she does not, within seven days of becoming aware of a resolution, cause a dissent to be recorded in the minutes or send a written dissent to the corporation.

The purpose of these rules is to determine what position was taken by a director at a meeting in order to see if he was fulfilling his duty of care and fiduciary duty discussed in chapter 8. Deemed consent simplifies evidentiary matters and encourages the involvement of directors in decisions of the board.

e) Signed Resolutions and Single Director Meetings

Where a corporation has only one director, that director may constitute a meeting. As an alternative to holding meetings, directors may act by resolution signed by all directors (*CBCA*, s. 117). As when shareholders act by signed resolution, this alternative eliminates the need to deal with the requirements for notice of meetings as well as the need to have all the directors present at one place and time. The resolution becomes effective when it is signed by the last director.

F. OFFICERS

1) General

There is nothing in Canadian corporate legislation which addresses what officers a corporation should have or what they are to do. Most corporations have officers called "president" and "secretary." Other common officers include "vice-president" and "treasurer," though a variety of other offices are also in use.

Directors have power to designate officers, like president and secretary, and to specify the duties of those officers, including delegating to them the power to manage the business and affairs of corporation. Usually this delegation is done in a by-law passed at the time the corporation is organized just after incorporation. The directors may subsequently delegate further matters to the officers they appoint. Limitations on the directors' ability to delegate are discussed below. After setting up the offices in this way, the directors may appoint people, the officers, to fill them (CBCA, s. 121).

Canadian corporate legislation has few requirements for officers. Directors can be officers, but need not be. Any person may hold two or more offices. No qualifications are required for officers except that they must be of "full capacity" (CBCA, s. 121(a)). This phrase is not defined in the Act, but presumably means, at least, that officers must not be of unsound mind. If the board decides to appoint a managing director, he must be a resident Canadian (CBCA, s. 115(1)). No act of an officer is invalid by reason only of a defect in her appointment or qualification (CBCA, s. 116).

Because officers are typically given power to manage the business and affairs of the corporation, they are subject to the same duty of care and fiduciary duty as directors (CBCA, s. 122). These duties are discussed in detail in chapter 8.

The legal relationship created by appointing a person as an officer is distinct from any employment relationship that the person may have with the corporation, though, in practice, many or all of the duties associated with the employment contract may be coextensive with the duties of the office. The principal situation in which conflict between these relationships arises is termination of the person's involvement with the corporation. An officer can always be removed by the corporation. It is common for corporations to provide in their by-laws that officers hold office at the pleasure of the board of directors, so their appointment may be terminated at any time by a decision of the directors. An officer's employment contract, by contrast, may be terminated only for cause or on reasonable notice.[24] The termination of a person as an officer will usually be a breach of his employment agreement in the absence of cause or notice, even where the right to remove officers from their offices has been stipulated in the articles or by-laws.[25]

2) Delegation

a) Delegation within the Corporation

At common law, directors had no power to delegate to others the management of the corporation. The power to delegate was necessary, however, for the development of large-scale organizations. Now sections 115 and 121 of the *CBCA* create a statutory code for delegation within the corporation. Directors can delegate their powers "to manage the business and affairs of the corporation," or any other of their powers, to a managing director (who must be a resident Canadian), to a committee of directors (a majority of whom must be resident Canadians), or to one or more officers.

The language in section 121(a) permitting delegation to officers is the same as that giving directors their general authority to manage the corporation in section 102(1). Both refer to the power "to manage the business and affairs of the corporation." Directors, then, can delegate all their power to officers, though such delegation is subject to an important limitation: they cannot delegate powers listed in section 115(3). These powers relate mostly to decisions regarding shares, including the power to issue shares, to declare dividends on shares, and to purchase or redeem shares.

b) Delegation outside the Corporation

To what extent may power to manage be delegated to third parties outside the corporation? It may seem odd, at first glance, that a board of directors would be delegating power to a person outside the corporation, but, in fact, such delegation is very common. For example, many corporations grant power to manage their affairs in relation to some specific area of their business to a management company that has special expertise in the area. Where the returns to the corporation can be

---

24   Provincial employment standards legislation may impose additional obligations, such as severance pay (e.g., Ontario *Employment Standards Act*, R.S.O. 1990, c. E.14).

25   *Southern Foundries (1926) Ltd.* v. *Shirlaw*, [1940] A.C. 701 (H.L.).

improved by such delegation, management should not be precluded from adopting such a strategy.

External delegation is not dealt with in the *CBCA* or in other corporate statutes, but there is little doubt that it is now permitted. The main rule is that the board of directors may not delegate completely its control over the day-to-day management of the corporation's business, but must retain the power to supervise the delegate in the performance of its duties. *Kennerson* v. *Burbank Amusement Co.*[26] is an example of a board exceeding this limit. In that case the board delegated all control over the only asset it was responsible for managing — a theatre. It attempted to transfer control over "bookings, personnel, admission prices, salaries, contracts, expenses" and fiscal policies to Kennerson, subject only to an obligation to report to the board periodically. The court determined that the contract in that case conferred on Kennerson the practical control and management of the corporation subject only to a duty to report and account, and permitted no possibility of control being exercised by the board. It was held not enforceable.[27] The court stated that the power of the directors to manage was "completely sterilized." The length of delegation is also relevant to determining whether the board has retained sufficient control.[28]

What is permissible is a question of degree. It is important to note that in choosing a delegate and supervising the delegate, the directors are bound by their duty of care and their fiduciary duty.[29]

G. REMUNERATION AND INDEMNIFICATION OF DIRECTORS AND OFFICERS

1) Remuneration

Unless some arrangement is made in a corporation's articles, by-laws, or a unanimous shareholder agreement, the directors may set their own remuneration as well as that of all officers and employees (*CBCA*, s. 125). Deciding on their own remuneration involves a conflict between directors' personal interests and the interests of the corporation they have a fiduciary duty to put first (*CBCA*, s. 122). This conflict is expressly

---

26   260 P. 2d 823 (Cal. C.A. 1953).
27   The court relied on *Long Park v. Trenton–New Brunswick Theatres Co.*, 77 N.E.2d 633 (N.Y. C.A. 1948).
28   *Sherman & Ellis v. Indiana Mutual Casualty Co.*, 41 F.2d. 588 (7th Cir. 1930).
29   *R. v. Bata Industries Ltd.* (1992), 9 O.R. (3d) 329 (Prov. Div.) [*Bata*].

addressed in the *CBCA* and other modern corporate statutes by a provision permitting directors to vote on the terms of their compensation (*CBCA*, s. 120(5)(b)).

The issues associated with this kind of conflict depend on the scale of the corporation. For closely held corporations where managers, directors, and shareholders are the same individuals, the potential for disagreements among classes of stakeholders — that is, between managers, directors, and shareholders in their respective capacities — is nonexistent. Nevertheless, there inevitably will be disagreements among the individuals involved about the amounts of compensation paid to each as well as, for example, the form of compensation. Because each individual will have differing needs for money from the corporation and will be in a different tax position, each will have her own preferences whether money is paid out as salary or as dividends, or is retained in the corporation to increase the value of her share investment. Revenue Canada will have a corresponding interest in these decisions. Decisions about compensation in the closely held corporation will be made on whatever basis has been agreed among the parties. Where this results in the interests of one or more of the shareholders being prejudiced, a shareholder's only remedy is likely to be to sue for relief from oppression (*CBCA*, s. 241). In many oppression cases the court has found excessive compensation to be oppressive.[30]

As the scale of the corporation increases and the identity of managers, directors, and shareholders diverges, different sorts of problems arise with the setting of compensation. As discussed above, in these circumstances directors and officers have an incentive to engage in opportunistic behaviour, including giving themselves excessive levels of compensation. The costs associated with the payment of excessive compensation and shareholder monitoring of compensation are specific examples of the agency costs discussed above.

2) Indemnification

As will be discussed in chapter 8, directors and officers are subject to a wide range of potential liability in connection with fulfilling their responsibilities. Exposure to these liabilities creates a strong disincentive to becoming a director or an officer of a corporation. The disincentive is strongest for prospective directors since, in Canada, they are

---

30   See, for example, *Stech v. Davies*, (1987), 80 A.R. 298 (Q.B.). For a successful oppression application by a creditor based on excessive compensation, see *Prime Computer of Canada v. Jeffrey* (1991), 6 O.R. (3d) 733 (Gen. Div.).

likely to receive little financial compensation for being a member of a corporation's board.

For this reason, a practice developed for corporations to indemnify directors and officers against liabilities they incurred. A scheme for indemnification is now set out in the CBCA (s. 124). The scheme seeks a balance: to permit indemnification in sufficiently broad circumstances to encourage responsible people to become directors or officers and to deny indemnification in circumstances where directors are engaged in improper conduct. It has three parts. The corporation must indemnify directors and officers in certain circumstances, may indemnify in additional circumstances, and may obtain insurance for the benefit of directors and officers in a still broader range of circumstances. Most commentators have argued that the scheme is not exclusive of the circumstances in which indemnification may be granted,[31] though the issue has never been litigated.

A corporation must indemnify a director or an officer against any costs or expenses reasonably incurred by him in connection with the defence of any civil, criminal, or administrative action to which he was made a party because he was a director of the corporation, if the director or officer (1) was substantially successful on the merits of his defence, (2) complied with his fiduciary duty to act honestly and in good faith with a view to the best interests of the corporation, and (3) had reasonable grounds for believing his conduct was lawful. Even where a director or officer does not meet criterion (1) because he was not substantially successful on the merits, a corporation still has a discretion to indemnify the director or officer for the same costs and expenses plus any amount not directly relating to the defence, including any amount paid to settle an action or settle a judgment, so long as the other two criteria are met.

The Supreme Court of Canada recently addressed the availability of an indemnity in Consolidated Enfield Corp. v. Blair.[32] Blair was the President and a director of Consolidated Enfield Corporation (Enfield). At the annual meeting of Enfield, a slate of nominees proposed by management, and including Blair, stood for election. Canadian Express Ltd., a major shareholder, nominated a candidate for director to replace Blair. On the basis of the votes cast by Canadian Express and its supporters, the Canadian Express candidate would have been elected. Before the

---

31   For example, J.I.S. Nicholl, "Directors' and Officers' Liability Insurance," in L. Sarna, ed., Corporate Structure, Finance and Operations, vol. 4 (Toronto: Carswell, 1986).

32   [1995] 4 S.C.R. 5, aff'g (1993), 15 O.R. (3d) 783 (C.A.), rev'g [1992] O.J. No. 2291 (Gen. Div.) (QL).

meeting, however, Blair had been advised by legal counsel that Canadian Express could use its proxies to vote only for the management slate. After the votes on the election of directors were cast, Blair was advised by legal counsel for the corporation that he, as chair, had to make a ruling about the results of the vote, notwithstanding that his own election was at stake, and that the votes cast by Canadian Express and its supporters against Blair were invalid. He took that advice and ruled that the management slate was elected. In subsequent legal proceedings, a court ruled that the votes cast in favour of the Canadian Express nominee were valid and so Blair had not been re-elected.[33]

Blair sought an order that he be indemnified by Enfield for his legal costs in connection with these proceedings. The trial court held that he could not be indemnified because he had not fulfilled his fiduciary duty in connection with the vote. Ultimately, the Supreme Court of Canada granted an indemnification order. Significantly, the court held that the corporation had the obligation to establish that Blair had not acted in good faith with a view to the best interests of the corporation to avoid an obligation to indemnify. The court also stated that while reliance on legal advice is not a guarantee that indemnification will be available, where that reliance is reasonable and in good faith, the court will conclude that the director acted in compliance with his fiduciary duty. Here, where Blair was confronted with a novel and difficult legal question, it was reasonable to seek legal advice and to rely on it. Finally, the court held that indemnification in these circumstances was consistent with the broad policy goals underlying the indemnification provisions. Indemnification should balance limiting the availability of indemnification to encourage responsible behaviour with permitting sufficient flexibility in allowing indemnification to attract strong candidates as officers and directors.

Under the *CBCA*, insurance may be obtained by the corporation for the benefit of a director or officer against any liability incurred by her in her capacity as a director or officer, unless she did not fulfil her fiduciary duty (*CBCA*, 124(3)).

The availability of indemnities and insurance has become an increasingly complex issue as governments, seeking to improve compliance with environmental and other regulatory schemes, have turned to imposing personal liability on directors and officers. On the one hand, with the range and seriousness of potential liability increasing, indemnities and insurance become more and more important as a way of ensuring that competent people are willing to become officers and

---

33   *Blair*, above note 16, Holland J.

directors. On the other hand, indemnification and insurance will tend to reduce the effectiveness of the legislative scheme. The intended effect of imposing liability on directors and officers is to discourage businesses from acting illegally. If directors and officers are insulated from this liability, the intended effect will not occur. An interesting example of this problem arose recently in *R. v. Bata Industries Ltd.*[34] Several officers were convicted for offences under the *Ontario Water Resources Act*[35] consisting of "failing to take all reasonable care to prevent . . . [the corporation] from causing or permitting an unlawful discharge [of wastes]." The judge ordered that the accused pay fines and that the corporation, Bata Industries, not indemnify them. The judge indicated that if the corporation could indemnify officers against the consequences of their wrongdoing, the intended effect of the legislative scheme in imposing liability — discouraging illegal behaviour by businesses — would be undermined. On appeal, the court determined that the trial judge had no authority to make such an order because the statutory scheme expressly permitted indemnification in the circumstances of the case.[36]

H. SHAREHOLDERS' AGREEMENTS

1) Introduction

Where a corporation has few shareholders, they will often want to customize their relationship to create an arrangement which is different from that contemplated in the relevant corporate legislation in several ways, including changing shareholder voting entitlements, imposing share transfer requirements, and providing for a dispute settlement mechanism. Under the *CBCA* and statutes modelled after it, the shareholders may even assume the powers of the directors.

2) Voting and Management

Shareholders may want to exercise their power to vote on a basis different from the votes determined according to share ownership. To do so, shareholders may, by contract, agree on how they will vote their shares.

---

34   (1995), 101 C.C.C. (3d) 86 (Ont. C.A.), as varied by (1993), rev'g *Bata*, above note 29, 14 O.R. (3d) 354 (Gen. Div.).

35   R.S.O. 1990, c. O.40.

36   In Industry Canada, *Directors' Liability (Canada Business Corporations Act Discussion Paper)* (Ottawa: Industry Canada, 1995), several amendments were proposed to the indemnification provisions at 26–43.

Imagine that three individuals, Sherry, Amman, and Yves, decide to set up a corporation to carry on a business of distributing computer software. Yves will contribute the $500,000 needed to set up the business and will be the sales manager. Amman, who recently completed his MBA but has little money, will be responsible for the financial side of the business. Sherry will contribute some software she has developed and will be in charge of supporting the software sold. Because of his large financial contribution, Yves gets 60 percent of the shares, while Amman and Sherry get 20 percent each. This division would entitle Yves to determine who will be on the board. He need not include Sherry or Amman. But what if Yves, Sherry, and Amman consider themselves to be in a relationship in which each should have an equal say and each wants to be on the board?

This problem could be addressed in a shareholder agreement in a variety of ways. All three could agree that they will vote their shares to elect all three as directors.[37] They could further agree on who the officers should be. Amman, Sherry, and Yves may also agree that all decisions, or certain listed decisions, must be approved by shareholders unanimously.

The potential scope for shareholders to agree on decision-making structures is subject to one important limitation. Shareholders may not by contract require directors to vote in a certain way. Directors have duties, the fiduciary and the duty of care which will be discussed in chapter 8, and their decision-making discretion cannot be restricted so as to prevent them from fulfilling these duties.[38] This rule applies, even though directors and shareholders are the same persons. In short, shareholders can bind how they vote their shares, but not how they exercise their discretion as directors.

One way to deal with this problem is to have the shareholders agree that certain matters will be decided only by the shareholders, not the directors. As discussed below, this distinction is expressly contemplated in the *CBCA* and in statutes modelled after it where the parties to the shareholders' agreement include all shareholders. Unfortunately, it is not clear that such an agreement, called a "unanimous shareholder agreement," is an effective solution to this problem.

---

37 Section 146(1) of the *Canada Business Corporations Act*, R.S.C. 1985, c. C–44 and s. 108(1) of the *OBCA*, above note 23, expressly permit shareholders to contract how they will vote their shares.

38 *Ringuet v. Bergeron*, [1960] S.C.R. 672; *820099 Ontario Inc. v. Harold E. Ballard Ltd.* (1991), 3 B.L.R. (2d) 113 (Ont. Gen. Div.), aff'd (1991), 3 B.L.R. (2d) 113 (Ont. Div. Ct.).

3) Share Transfer

In small corporations, share transfer is problematic for several reasons. Shares of closely held corporations are hard to sell because, typically, the business is tied up with the individuals who are the shareholders. Unless the individuals who are running the business, perhaps even including the person who wants to sell, are agreeable to continuing to run the business, it may have little value. In the example above, it may be that the business could not continue without all three shareholders being involved in the business. Although there is no legal impediment to a person selling his shares and continuing to be an employee or even a director and officer, in most real-world situations shareholders in closely held corporations seek to sell their shares only when they have decided to cease being active in the business. It is easy to see the motivation: once a person ceases to be active in the business, the agency costs to her are increased; she loses her ability to monitor her fellow shareholder managers informally. By contrast, the value of shares in a large publicly traded corporation is independent of who holds them. Most shareholders are not active in the business, so there will be no change in the business on the sale of their shares.

Another problem with finding a buyer for an interest in a closely held corporation is that such interests are inherently hard to value. There is no market like the Toronto Stock Exchange to establish prices. Also, where there is a dominant controlling shareholder, the value of a minority interest may have to be discounted.

Share transfers are also difficult for non-financial reasons. Shareholders who are not selling their shares will want some say in who will be able to purchase the shares that are for sale. They will want to be able to control who becomes a shareholder, and will want some restrictions on share transfer. At the same time, each shareholder has an interest in having a minimum of restrictions on his ability to sell his own shares, especially given the impediments to selling them described above.

To address these issues, it is common to set up some mechanism in a shareholders' agreement to restrict share transfers. In addition to the approval by directors or shareholders usually provided for in the articles, as discussed in chapter 4, a variety of other mechanisms are used. Typically, transfers are prohibited except as provided in the agreement. Perhaps the most common circumstance in which transfers are permitted is upon compliance with a "right of first refusal." In its simplest form a right of first refusal is a requirement for a shareholder who wants to sell her shares to offer them first to the other shareholders at some price set by the shareholder. The other shareholders then have a limited time to purchase her shares at that price, usually in proportion to their existing share interests. If they do not purchase the shares, the shareholder may offer them for sale to third parties at the same price for a limited time. The requirement to sell to third parties at the same price that she offered the shares to the other shareholders discourages the shareholder from stipulating an unreasonably high price for her shares.

Transfers may be permitted in certain circumstances, without triggering transfer mechanisms such as the right of first refusal. These exceptions include transfers to financial institutions as security for loans, and transfers to family members and to corporations controlled by the shareholder.

Shareholders' agreements also often provide that a shareholder must transfer his shares, either to the other shareholders or to the corporation, in some situations. For example, agreements commonly provide that on the death of a shareholder, his estate must transfer his shares to the other shareholders. This is done so the remaining shareholders do not end up with the heirs of the deceased shareholder as shareholders. Shareholders' agreements with mandatory transfers on death often require the corporation or the shareholders to maintain some form of life insurance, the proceeds of which will be used to fund the purchase commitment. Other common situations in which transfers are mandatory include a shareholder retiring from active participation in the corporation's business, ceasing to be able to perform her duties in the business, and breaching the shareholders' agreement. In order to make these mandatory transfer provisions effective it is necessary to have a value assigned to the corporation's shares, or to provide for a method to determine value, such as a formula based on annual income or valuation by the corporation's accountant.

Pre-emptive rights, which were discussed in chapter 4, also may be included in shareholders' agreements. Under a pre-emptive right a corporation cannot issue shares without offering them first to the existing shareholders. One reason to have such a right in a shareholders' agreement rather than the articles is that the articles are a matter of public record.

4) Dispute Settlement

A shareholders' agreement may govern the parties' relationships for a long time. Inevitably, as circumstances change, disputes among shareholders will arise. Some form of dispute settlement mechanism, such as arbitration, is often included in shareholders' agreements to avoid the necessity of going to court to resolve such disputes. A full discussion of alternative dispute settlement is far beyond the scope of this book, but in general the parties must agree on what disputes will be subject to dispute settlement and what the process for the dispute settlement will be. If alternative dispute settlement is to be used by the shareholders, it is essential that it be agreed to at the time the shareholders' agreement is entered. Once a dispute has arisen, the likelihood of agreeing on a dispute settlement process is substantially reduced.[39]

5) Unanimous Shareholders' Agreements

When the *CBCA* was enacted in 1975, it sought to address the needs of closely held corporations by permitting all the shareholders of a corporation to agree to alter the allocation of power between directors and shareholders provided in the statute. In particular, decision-making power could be transferred from the directors to the shareholders (s. 146). This transfer permits great flexibility for the corporate organization to be shaped to reflect the bargaining among shareholders. Although such flexibility seems a laudable objective, the provisions dealing with unanimous shareholders' agreements leave many issues unresolved in terms of how they are to work in practice.

Unanimous shareholders' agreements under the *CBCA* may restrict "in whole or in part, the powers of the directors to manage the business and affairs of the corporation." A shareholder who is party to such an agreement has "all the rights, powers and duties of a director" to the extent of the restriction and "the directors are thereby relieved of their duties and liabilities . . . to the same extent." This statutory language does not state that the liabilities from which the directors are relieved are transferred to the shareholders. This problem had been remedied in the *OBCA* and in proposed amendments to the federal Act. Even under the Ontario scheme, however, the effectiveness of the transfer of liability is far from clear. For example, it is unclear whether the *OBCA* is capable of removing liabilities imposed on directors under legislation validly enacted in other jurisdictions. What is the constitutional basis for an Ontario government to enact a law that purports to remove the liability imposed on directors under a validly enacted federal law? A second and more serious problem is that it is not clear that the *CBCA* effectively corrects the problem associated with the inability of shareholders to fetter the discretion of directors. Because the "duties" of the directors are transferred to the shareholders it may be that the shareholders are similarly

---

39   See *Seel v. Seel*, [1995] 7 W.W.R. 214 (B.C.S.C.), in which it was held that the arbitration provision should be enforced where there was a dispute over share valuation and the original valuation was not done in accordance with the agreement.

fettered, at least when exercising powers which would have been exercised by the directors in the absence of the shareholders' agreement.

There are a variety of other unresolved issues regarding how a corporation subject to a unanimous shareholder agreement is to function.[40] Does it need a board of directors? How are shareholders' to vote in exercising their acquired powers as directors: one vote per shareholder, or according to their share interests? Although shareholders can address the issues in their agreement, these uncertainties are bound to result in practitioners avoiding the unanimous shareholder agreement.[41]

6) Enforcing Shareholders' Agreements

In addition to any right a shareholder may have to go to court to enforce a shareholders' agreement as a contract, the *CBCA* and statutes modelled after it provide a range of other remedial options, including an application for relief from oppression under section 241 of the *CBCA*. Breach of any shareholder agreement may be held to constitute oppression. In one case even the actions of a shareholder which were technically consistent with the provisions of the shareholder agreement but for the purpose of improperly excluding the other shareholder from the corporation were found to be oppressive.[42] Notwithstanding the apparent unfairness, it is not obvious that the court should have intervened in an agreement freely made between the parties. Nevertheless, this approach has been followed in other cases.[43]

Additional statutory rights benefit unanimous shareholders' agreements. Under section 247 a shareholder may make a summary application to have the provisions of any unanimous shareholders' agreement enforced. Failure to comply with the terms of a unanimous shareholders' agreement may be grounds for dissolution of the corporation, and the *CBCA* expressly provides that a court may dissolve a corporation if some specified event has occurred which, under a unanimous shareholders' agreement, entitles a complaining shareholder to demand dissolution (*CBCA*, s. 214).

---

40 These issues were recently addressed in some detail in M. Disney, "The Shareholder Agreement: Some Basic Issues (Part 2)" (1995) 14 Nat'l Banking L. Rev. 51 at 54–62.

41 Many of these issues were discussed and options for reform suggested in Industry Canada, *Unanimous Shareholder Agreements* (*Canada Business Corporations Act* Discussion Paper) (Ottawa: Industry Canada, 1996).

42 *Deluce Holdings Inc. v. Air Canada* (1992), 12 O.R. (3d) 131 (Gen. Div.).

43 For example, *Re Bury and Bell Gouinlock Ltd.* (1984), 48 O.R. (2d) 57 (H.C.J.), aff'd (1985), 49 O.R. (2d) 91 (Div. Ct.) (exercise of right under agreement found oppressive).

A unanimous shareholders' agreement is enforceable against a person acquiring shares from an existing shareholder if the transferee is aware of it. If, however, there is a conspicuous reference to the agreement on the share certificate, any transferee is bound by the agreement even if she was not aware of it (*CBCA*, ss. 49(8) & 146(4)). In order to take advantage of this scheme, many shareholders' agreements provide that a notice of the agreement will be endorsed on all share certificates. One of the unresolved issues associated with unanimous shareholders' agreements is what happens when there is no notice and shares are transferred. Now that the agreement is no longer unanimous, does it lose all effect?

Shareholder agreements that are not unanimous shareholders' agreements do not benefit from this statutory enforceability. Such an agreement is binding on a transferee, or a person issued shares by the corporation, only if the transferee signs it. For this reason, it is common in shareholder agreements to provide that the shareholders agree that all transfers and share issuances are conditional upon the new shareholder signing the agreement.

I. CHAPTER SUMMARY

In this chapter we discussed how powers are allocated among shareholders, directors, and officers. We began by noting the very clear division of responsibilities and powers contained in the *CBCA*. Then we discussed, in general terms, how this division is unrealized in the context of the operation of public corporations, both in terms of the practical ability of shareholders to take advantage of the control mechanisms provided in the Act and the degree of control that directors really have over the management of the business and affairs of the corporation. We also discussed the ways in which the division of powers is often of little relevance for closely held corporations.

With this context, we discussed the rules governing how shareholders exercise power through voting at meetings. We surveyed the various technical requirements for calling and holding meetings, including the use of proxies, someone the shareholder appoints to vote on his behalf, and management's responsibility to solicit proxies, by sending out a form of proxy as well as a variety of other information in a "management proxy circular." This document contains both general information regarding the corporation and specific information on matters to be voted on. We also discussed shareholder proposals, the mechanism by which shareholders can get matters put on the agenda for discussion at meetings. Finally, other access to information rights, which facilitate effective shareholder participation in the corporation, were identified.

Next we discussed directors and how they exercise power, beginning with the rules governing how people become directors and continuing with a survey of the technical rules governing the calling and holding of meetings. We noted that, to facilitate the use of corporations for all but the smallest businesses, directors must delegate some of their powers to officers and, in some cases, to persons outside the corporate hierarchy. The CBCA requires that some powers remain with the directors, but most may be delegated so long as the board remains able to exercise control over the delegate.

An important aspect of the law governing directors and officers is to what extent they may be indemnified for liabilities incurred in connection with fulfilling their responsibilities. With the expanding range of circumstances in which directors and officers may have personal liability, it will be difficult to attract competent people to assume these roles if they have to bear all the costs associated with such liability. On the other hand, if indemnification is too extensive, directors and officers will have no incentive to avoid conduct that is contrary to the interests of the corporation and to regulatory laws that impose personal liability. Under the CBCA, the primary way in which this balance is addressed is to require, as a condition of qualifying for indemnification, that a director or officer must have discharged her fiduciary duty to act in the best interests of the corporation. In R. v. Bata Industries, the CBCA scheme for indemnification was upheld, even though the corporation was proposing to indemnify officers who were found guilty of offences under provincial environmental laws.

Finally, we discussed shareholder agreements. Such agreements serve two primary purposes: to create specific arrangements regarding the exercise of shareholders' powers which is different from what the governing corporate law would otherwise provide; and to create rules to govern share transfers. Where shareholder agreements are unanimous, they may further customize the structure of the corporation by transferring some or all of the directors' powers and responsibilities to the shareholders. Such unanimous shareholders' agreements are specifically sanctioned by the CBCA and statutes modelled after it, and benefit from certain enhanced enforcement rights in these statutes.

FURTHER READINGS

BOWAL, P., "Expensive Day at the Office: Can Corporations Indemnify Their Agents Who Suffer Personal Liability for Regulatory Offenses?" (1995) 45 U.T.L.J. 247

CLARK, R., *Corporate Law* (Boston: Little Brown & Co., 1986)

CRÊTE, R., *The Proxy System in Canadian Corporations: A Critical Analysis* (Montreal: Wilson & Lafleur, 1986)

DANIELS, R.J., & S.M. HUTTON, "The Capricious Cushion: The Implications of the Directors' and Officers' Liability Insurance Crisis on Canadian Corporate Governance" (1993) 22 Can. Bus. L.J. 182

DANIELS, R.J., & E.J. WAITZER, "Challenges to the Citadel: A Brief Overview of Recent Trends in Canadian Corporate Governance" (1994) 23 Can. Bus. L.J. 23

DISNEY, M., "The Shareholder Agreement: Some Basic Issues (Parts 1, 2, & 3)" (1995) 14 Nat'l Banking L. Rev. 47, 51, & 67

EASTERBROOK, F.H., & D.R. FISCHEL, "Corporate Control Transactions" (1982) 91 Yale L.J. 698

EASTERBROOK, F.H., & D.R. FISCHEL, *The Economic Structure of Corporate Law* (Boston: Harvard University Press, 1991)

HAY, R.J., & L.A. SMITH, "The Unanimous Shareholder Agreement: A New Device for Shareholder Control" (1985) 10 Can. Bus. L.J. 440

INDUSTRY CANADA, Unanimous Shareholder Agreements (*Canada Business Corporations Act* Discussion Paper) (Ottawa: Industry Canada, 1996)

JENSEN, M.C., & W.H. MECKLING, "Theory of the Firm: Managerial Behavior, Agency Costs and Ownership Structure" (1976) 3 J. Fin. Econ. 305

MCCALL, C., & R. WILSON, "Shareholder Proposals: Why Not in Canada?" (1993) 5 Corp. Governance. Rev.

MACINTOSH, J.G., "The Role of Institutional and Retail Investors in Canadian Capital Markets" (1993) 31 Osgoode Hall L.J. 371

NATHAN, H.R., & M.E. VOORE, *Corporate Meetings: Law and Practice* (Toronto: Carswell, 1995)

NICHOLL, J.I.S., "Directors' and Officers' Liability Insurance" in L. Sarna, ed., *Corporate Structure, Finance, and Operations*, vol. 4, (Toronto: Carswell, 1986)

WAINBERG, J.G., *Company Meetings Including Rules of Order*, 3d ed. (Don Mills: CCH Canadian Ltd., 1982)

DUTIES OF DIRECTORS AND OFFICERS

A. INTRODUCTION

In previous chapters we discussed the problem of the agency costs faced by shareholders as a result of the incentives for directors and officers to act in their own interests rather than those of the corporation. In this chapter we will examine some of the ways the law addresses this problem in the form of duties imposed on directors and officers. Directors and officers are subject to a fiduciary duty to act "honestly and in good faith with a view to the best interests of the corporation," as well as a duty of care to "exercise the care, diligence and skill that a reasonably prudent person would exercise in comparable circumstances." These duties were developed by the common law courts and are now enshrined in statute in most Canadian jurisdictions (e.g., *CBCA*, s. 122(1)).

The duties are owed to the corporation rather than to the shareholders directly. Because shareholders are not the direct beneficiaries of these duties, the common law courts developed rules that made it difficult for shareholders to take action when these duties were not complied with. Many of these problems have been resolved under the *CBCA* and statutes modelled after it which greatly enhance access to shareholder remedies by, for example, expanding the circumstances in which shareholders can initiate actions for a breach of duty owed to the corporation if the directors refuse to do so. Also, the so-called oppression remedy creates not only a process for obtaining a remedy but a new substantive basis for shareholders to obtain one as well. As a result, the oppression provisions create a new standard of behaviour for directors and officers which both complements and overlaps with the fiduciary duty and the duty of care. This standard will be discussed in detail in chapter 9, as will a variety of remedial options available under the *CBCA* and other corporate statutes.

In addition to these obligations under corporate law, directors and officers face continually expanding sources of liability under a wide range of regulatory statutes that seek to promote enforcement of corporate obligations by imposing personal liability on directors, officers, and employees involved in the failure of the corporation to meet its obligations. In the last section of this chapter, we briefly discuss these statutory liabilities.

B. FIDUCIARY DUTY

1) Introduction

The fiduciary duty is a general standard of behaviour imposed on directors and officers in relation to their dealings with and on behalf of the corporation. The *CBCA* provides the following pithy formulation of the duty:

> Every director and officer of a corporation in exercising his powers and discharging his duties shall . . . act honestly and in good faith with a view to the best interests of the corporation . . . (s. 122(1)(a)).

Even though countless cases have addressed the fiduciary duty, its content and even its rationale remain elusive. As noted, some commentators from the law and economics school seek to justify and give content to the fiduciary duty based on the agency cost analysis referred to in chapter 7. They argue that the duty is necessary to counteract the incentive for directors and officers to benefit themselves personally at the expense of the corporation. The wide range of self-interested activity in which fiduciaries may engage renders it infeasible for shareholders to negotiate to be protected against such behaviour at the time of their investment. It would be simply too costly and too time consuming to specify fully all the types of behaviour that fiduciaries are prohibited from engaging in. Because the negotiating costs preclude a fully bargained agreement, the imposition of a general statutory standard is justified. Based on this analysis, a court trying to determine what the fiduciary duty requires in any particular case must ask what the shareholders would have agreed to if they had been permitted to bargain costlessly.[1] Another theory to explain the fiduciary duty is that it promotes the basic values of responsibility

---

1   For example, F.H. Easterbrook & D.R. Fischel, "Corporate Control Transactions" (1982) 81 Yale L.J. 689.

and integrity which are common to all members of society. A third is that the duty is imposed because directors and officers have the power to expose the corporation to risk of loss. Despite these efforts and others, there is no generally accepted theory that assists in deciding what the obligation requires in any particular case.

Nevertheless, the *CBCA* formulation does provide some guidance. The duty to act "honestly" seems straightforward enough: directors and officers are prohibited from acting fraudulently in relation to the corporation. They must not intend to deprive the corporation for their personal gain of some asset or benefit to which it is entitled. Beyond honesty, directors and officers must try to do what is best for the corporation. As noted, the duty is owed to the corporation, not to the shareholders or to any other stakeholder or group of stakeholders. Thus, in each case, the content of the duty will be defined by reference to the interests of the corporation in the circumstances. Unfortunately, while it is fairly simple to determine the interests of particular stakeholders, it is often difficult, in the abstract, to think of what the interests of the corporation are, particularly if we think of the corporation as essentially the focus of stakeholder claims as discussed in chapter 1. Also, the nature of stakeholder claims on the limited resources of the corporation is that, inevitably, they will be in conflict. To take a simple example, the interests of employees in high wages may conflict with shareholders' and creditors' interests in high profits. To what extent do the "best interests" of the corporation require it to accommodate the divergent interests of these groups, and on what basis should such accommodation be effected? The courts have tended to disregard the interests of other stakeholders and to treat the interests of the corporation as coextensive with the interests of shareholders.[2] This approach led to the development of a rule that shareholders could agree to absolve a fiduciary of her breach of duty. The process of absolution by shareholders, called ratification, has now been abolished by statute, though shareholder approval may be taken into account for certain purposes that will be discussed at the end of this section.

What the fiduciary duty requires in relation to the interests of the corporation is similar to the obligation of a trustee to a beneficiary, at least to the extent that it requires directors and officers not to put their personal interests ahead of the interests of the corporation. What this involves in practice can be discussed most meaningfully in the context of particular fact situations. We will deal with the following typical situations in some detail:

---

2   Recent challenges to this view are discussed in chapter 12.

- conflicts of interest where the director or officer is involved in some transaction with the corporation in his personal capacity;
- taking advantage of opportunities personally which it was her duty to try to obtain for the corporation; and
- competing with the corporation.

A specific example of the conflict of interest described in the first situation arises when directors set their own compensation, as we discussed in chapter 7. Certain other situations in which conflicts of interest arise, including hostile takeovers, are discussed at the end of this section and in chapter 11.

In almost all cases in which a breach of fiduciary duty occurs, the fiduciary has made some profit or received some advantage at the expense of the corporation. The principal remedy granted by the courts where a breach of fiduciary duty has occurred is to require the fiduciary to account for his profits to the corporation. The rationale behind this kind of relief is easy to see: if a fiduciary cannot profit from a breach of his fiduciary duty, he has no incentive to commit a breach.

2) Transacting with the Corporation

The conflict of interest arising when a director or officer contracts with the corporation may be illustrated by the following simple example. Someone seeks to sell goods to the corporation of which she is a director. As the seller, she has an incentive to negotiate the highest possible price for her goods. The corporation's interest is precisely the opposite: it wants to get the goods for the lowest possible price. If, as a director, she is charged with negotiating the contract on behalf of the corporation, the conflict is acute. Even if she is not directly involved in the negotiations on behalf of the corporation as a director, she is in a position to influence the corporation's decision making either directly, as a member of the board if the contract must be approved by the board, or indirectly, by virtue of her relationship with the corporation and its personnel. At the same time, her duty binds her to do whatever is in her power to get the best price for the corporation.

Because of the inevitable conflict in such situations, the court developed a rule that these kinds of transactions were voidable — that is, they could be set aside — at the option of the corporation. There was no enquiry as to whether the transaction was a good or a bad deal for the corporation. This rigid standard was described in *Aberdeen Railway Co. v. Blaikie Bros.*,[3] a case involving the purchase of some chairs from a partnership in which a director was a partner:

---

3   (1854), [1843–1860] All E.R. Rep. 249 (H.L.) [*Aberdeen*].

> ... it is a rule of universal application that no one having such duties to discharge shall be allowed to enter into engagements in which he has or can have a personal interest conflicting or which possibly may conflict with the interests of those whom he is bound to protect. So strictly is this principle adhered to that no question is allowed to be raised as to the fairness or unfairness of a contract so entered into.

Under this strict rule it did not matter if the fiduciary's interest was direct and beneficial, such as where she was dealing with the corporation herself, or indirect and as a trustee. An example of the latter case is *Transvaal Lands Co.* v. *New Belgium (Transvaal) Land and Development Co.*[4] In that case, a director of one corporation held certain shares in a second corporation as a trustee for the benefit of his wife under his father-in-law's will. In a transaction in which the director took no active part, all the shares held by the second corporation were sold to the first corporation. The court held that the lack of a conflict between his personal interest and his duty as director did not matter. As a trustee, the director was obliged to do his best to ensure that the second corporation got the highest price for the shares to be sold, just as he would if he were managing his own assets. In light of the conflict, the contract was voidable.

Part of the rationale for this strict rule is that the courts are reluctant to take responsibility for making difficult judgments about when a conflict is permissible. They did not want to have to assess when a personal interest in a transaction was significant enough to affect someone's judgment and behaviour. Such an assessment would depend significantly on the fiduciary himself and the situation in which he found himself. It would be hard for a court, many months later and removed from the situation, to make such an assessment. Also, the courts wanted to establish a clear rule which did not require the person in the conflict of interest to make the decision about whether it was a conflict of sufficient seriousness that she should refrain from entering the transaction or that she should take some other step to exclude herself from the transaction. Even transactions in which the director's or officer's interest "possibly may conflict" with her duty were prohibited.

The *CBCA* and most other Canadian statutes have modified this rigid rule to permit certain transactions between a director or officer and her corporation which are beneficial to the corporation, provided certain procedural safeguards are observed. This change was motivated by the recognition that in some cases the best price or, perhaps, the only source of supply may be a person related in some way to a director or

---

4   [1914] 2 Ch. 488 (C.A.) [*Transvaal*].

officer. This situation will frequently occur in the case of transactions between affiliated corporations and transactions with closely held corporations. The scheme set out in section 120 of the *CBCA* (*OBCA*, s. 132) applies where a director or officer of a corporation

- is a party to a material contract[5] or proposed material contract with the corporation, or
- is a director or officer, or has a material interest in any person who is a party to a material contract or proposed material contract with the corporation.

No definition of material contact is found in the *CBCA*, and no cases have considered it. It would appear that contracts which are not material, or in connection with which the director or officer does not have a material interest, cannot benefit from the scheme, though in such circumstances the technical breach of fiduciary duty may have no practical consequence. If a contract is not material, neither the corporation nor an interested director or officer will have much to gain or lose. For example, a director holding a few hundred shares in Bell Canada Enterprises Ltd., Canada's largest corporation, is not likely to be affected in performing his duty in connection with negotiating a telephone contract for the corporation. The materiality threshold may be intended simply to eliminate the need to comply with the requirements of the scheme for such trivial conflicts. In this regard, one way of defining the materiality threshold for directors' or officers' interests is to ask whether the interest is such that it possibly may affect his ability to perform his duty.

If these threshold requirements are met, section 120 sets out three further requirements that must be met to render the contract enforceable against the corporation: the director or officer must give adequate notice of her interest; the director or officer must not vote on the approval of the contract by the board of directors; and the contract must be fair and reasonable to the corporation. Each of these requirements will be considered in turn.

An interested director or officer must give written notice to the corporation of the nature and extent of his interest or request to have this information entered in the minutes of a director's meeting (*CBCA*, s. 120(1)). The Act sets out specific requirements regarding when notice

---

5   The provision in the Ontario *Business Corporations Act*, R.S.O. 1990, c. B.16 [*OBCA*], equivalent to section 120 is section 132. It uses "contract or transaction" instead of "contract." The *Canada Business Corporations Act Regulations* provide some guidelines about the meaning of material for the purpose of what must be disclosed in a management proxy circular (SOR/79-316, s. 35(w)).

must be given in section 120(2) and (3). There is no precise formula for how much detail must be provided in the notice. It will depend on the nature of the contract proposed and the context in which it arises. Nevertheless, in general, it must be sufficiently detailed to disclose the costs incurred and the possible profits to be received by the director or officer.[6] In other words, as the statute suggests, it is not sufficient merely to mention that a fiduciary has an interest; it is necessary to state what the interest is and how far it goes.[7] In some cases, such as where a director of a corporation is also the director of a corporation that is a customer of the corporation, disclosure would have to be made repeatedly. To address this kind of situation, the *CBCA* permits a general notice to be made to the effect that a director or officer is interested in all contracts with a particular corporation (*CBCA*, s. 120(6)). There is no express requirement to disclose the nature and extent of one's interest in such a general notice, though it would be consistent with the scheme of section 120 to read such a requirement into the provision.

A contract in which a director or officer has an interest must be approved by the directors or shareholders to be enforceable (*CBCA*, s. 120(7)). Subject to certain limited exceptions, in addition to giving notice a director is prohibited from voting on any contract in which she has an interest (*CBCA*, s. 120(5)). Such a director or officer may, however, be present at a meeting of directors called to approve the contract and may be counted in the quorum. As noted in chapter 7, the exceptions include contracts relating to remuneration of the director and her indemnification, as well as contracts with affiliates (*CBCA*, s. 120(5)).

If, in addition to the proper notice and approval requirements being met, the contract is fair and reasonable to the corporation, it is neither void nor voidable.[8] The *CBCA* is silent as to whether the common law remedy of an accounting for profits is also excluded. The drafters of the *CBCA*, the Dickerson Committee, intended that there would be no

---

6   *Wedge v. McNeill* (1981), 33 Nfld. & P.E.I.R. 272 (P.E.I.S.C.), rev'd on other grounds (1982), 39 Nfld. & P.E.I.R. 205 (P.E.I.C.A.).

7   In *Neptune (Vehicle Washing Equipment) Ltd. v. Fitzgerald*, [1995] 3 All E.R. 811 (Ch.), a decision under the *English Companies Act*, (U.K.), 1985, c. 6, which contains a provision similar to section 120 of the *Canada Business Corporations Act*, R.S.C. 1985, c. C-44 [*CBCA*], it was held that a sole director must declare his interest at a meeting with himself. Though he need not say anything out loud, his interest must be entered in the minutes.

8   A contract that is *void* cannot be enforced by either party. As noted, if a contract is *voidable* at the instance of one party, the contract is enforceable or not enforceable at the option of that party.

accounting for profits,[9] but this intention is not reflected in the legislation. By contrast, the equivalent provision in the *OBCA* expressly excludes this remedy.[10] Accordingly, there is some uncertainty as to whether an accounting may still be claimed.

If any of these requirements have not been satisfied, the conflict of interest results in a breach of fiduciary duty and the contract is voidable at the option of the corporation. As will be discussed in chapter 9, in some circumstances with the permission of the court a shareholder may initiate a derivative action on behalf of the corporation to seek relief for breach of fiduciary duty (*CBCA*, s. 239). If the reason that the requirements of section 120 are not met is that the director or officer failed to disclose his interest, the *CBCA* provides an additional more direct and expeditious way for shareholders to seek relief. A shareholder may apply directly to a court to set aside the contract (*CBCA*, s. 120(7)). The equivalent provision in the *OBCA* permits such an application whenever any of the requirements are not satisfied, and expressly permits the court to make an order directing an accounting for profits as well (*OBCA*, s. 132(9)).

The *OBCA* also provides an alternative scheme to save contracts where the requirements set out above have not been complied with. The contract may still be rendered enforceable if three requirements are met:

- the transaction was reasonable and fair to the corporation at the time it was approved;
- the contract was approved by a special resolution of the shareholders at a meeting called for that purpose; and
- the nature and extent of the director's or officer's interest is disclosed in reasonable detail in the notice of the meeting (*OBCA*, s. 132(8)).

Also under the *OBCA*, a director or officer of a corporation is not accountable for any profits realized only because she was a director or officer of a corporation contracting with the first corporation (*OBCA*, s. 132(8)).

It is important to note that compliance with the scheme set out in section 120 is the only way to avoid the consequences of a fiduciary

---

9   R.W.V. Dickerson, J.L. Howard, & L. Getz, *Proposals for a New Business Corporations Law for Canada* (Ottawa: Information Canada, 1971).

10   *OBCA*, above note 5, section 132(7). At common law there was some uncertainty whether a corporation could accept a contract and claim an accounting. *Cook v. Deeks*, [1916] 1 A.C. 554 (P.C.) [*Cook*] suggests that an accounting is not available in these circumstances. Professor Welling, however, suggests that it is. B. Welling, *Corporate Law in Canada: The Governing Principles*, 2d ed. (Toronto: Butterworths, 1991) at 453–54.

breach under the *CBCA*. It used to be that corporations could insert in their constitution or by-laws their own mechanisms to render such contracts enforceable, such as a provision that rendered contracts enforceable if approved by shareholders;[11] this option is not available under the *CBCA* and the statutes modelled after it. The fiduciary duty, notwithstanding its common law roots, is now a statutory duty, as indicated above. The *CBCA* model statutes provide that "no provision in a contract, the articles, the by-laws or a resolution relieves a director or officer from the duty to act in accordance with this Act or the regulations or relieves him from liability for a breach thereof" (*CBCA*, s. 122(3); *OBCA*, s. 134(3)).

3) Taking Corporate Opportunities

A second situation in which a conflict between the personal interests of a fiduciary and her duty to the corporation arises when the fiduciary considers investing or otherwise taking advantage of some project or opportunity in which the corporation may be said to have an interest. This situation arises frequently, since one of the principal tasks of management is to make choices about what projects the corporation should invest in, whether it be the acquisition of an asset, establishing a business, or entering a lucrative contract. If fiduciaries were permitted to invest personally in projects to the exclusion of the corporation, there is a risk that fiduciaries, in pursuit of their self-interest, would appropriate to themselves valuable investment opportunities that they should have sought for the corporation. The fiduciary duty applies to prohibit fiduciaries from allowing their personal interest to conflict with their duty to the corporation in this way.

A variety of difficult issues arise in determining what the fiduciary duty requires in relation to the appropriation of corporate opportunities. How does one determine if the opportunity belongs to the corporation, so that the fiduciary should be prohibited from taking it? Can it be said to belong to the corporation if the corporation, for some reason, could not have exploited the opportunity in any case, or had expressly rejected the opportunity? Is every opportunity in the area of the corporation's business a corporate opportunity? Does it make any difference if the fiduciary found out about the opportunity by virtue of his position as a director or officer? To what extent can a fiduciary take an opportunity after he has resigned as a director and officer? In the following

---

11   For example, *Transvaal*, above note 4.

section we will seek to respond to these questions, though, as will become clear, it is very difficult and ultimately unhelpful to try to establish brightline distinctions in this area of the law.

Where a corporation is actively negotiating for an opportunity and has a reasonable prospect of getting it, there is no question that the corporation has an interest in the opportunity and a fiduciary is prohibited from exploiting it in her personal capacity. In *Cook* v. *Deeks*,[12] three directors of a corporation were negotiating with a railway for a construction contract, as they had done on previous occasions. During the negotiations they decided to obtain the contract for themselves, not the corporation. They informed the railway of their plan and the contract was made between the directors and the railway. The court held that the directors had breached their fiduciary duty to the corporation because they had actively promoted their own interests at the expense of the corporation and used their positions with the corporation to do so. As a result, they were liable to pay any profits they had obtained over to the corporation.

Where there is some impediment to the corporation obtaining an opportunity, the courts have held that it nevertheless belongs to the corporation, with the result that the fiduciaries cannot exploit it themselves. An interesting example of this kind of situation occurred in *Regal (Hastings) Ltd.* v. *Gulliver*.[13] The corporation, Regal (Hastings) Ltd. (Regal), owned one cinema and was seeking to obtain a lease of two others through a wholly owned subsidiary corporation. The landlord of the two cinemas refused to agree to the lease unless either the directors guaranteed the lease obligations personally or the amount invested in shares of the subsidiary was at least £5000. The directors were reluctant to provide the guarantees, and Regal had only £2000 to invest in shares of the subsidiary. At a meeting of the directors it was agreed that they would resolve the problem by personally investing the remaining £3000 in shares of the subsidiary. The shares were issued to the directors at a price of £1 per share. At the same meeting, the directors voted to approve the sale of Regal's interest in the three theatres to a purchaser. Ultimately this sale was accomplished by selling all the shares of Regal and the shares of the subsidiary held by the directors. The directors received £3.16 for their shares, giving them a profit of £2.16 per share. The new shareholders of Regal elected a new board. The new board caused Regal to sue the former directors, alleging that they had

---

12   *Cook*, above note 10.
13   [1942] 1 All E.R. 378 (H.L.).

breached their fiduciary duty and demanding that they hand over the profits they had made.

The court granted judgment for Regal. The court held that the directors had used their positions as directors to make a personal profit, which the board was obliged to try to obtain for the corporation. The court stated that there was no requirement to find that the directors had not acted in what they thought was the best interests of the corporation, nor was it relevant whether the corporation could have otherwise obtained the leases. There does not have to be an actual conflict of interest. This reasoning reflects the policy referred to above in *Aberdeen Railway* v. *Blaikie*[14] in support of the high standard for fiduciaries: fiduciary duty rules should be designed to remove any possible incentive for fiduciaries to put their interests first. Fiduciaries must not be permitted to decide whether to adopt a corporate strategy which benefits them personally over alternatives which do not. In addition to the obvious risk that directors might be tempted to characterize the opportunity as one the corporation could not obtain in any other way, permitting the directors to make this call would pose a problem for judicial oversight. Courts generally do not like to second guess directors on issues such as whether there was any viable business alternative to the strategy benefiting the directors. They recognize that they do not have business expertise and that their conclusion on such questions necessarily would be speculative. On the facts of Regal it seems likely that some alternative could have been found which would not have involved the enrichment of the directors. Perhaps Regal could have borrowed the money on the strength of the offer to purchase the three cinemas. In any event the rule is clear: the directors' fiduciary duty precluded them from profiting from any strategy they adopted. Given this basis for the rule, the fact that the new shareholders of Regal received an unexpected windfall was found to be irrelevant.[15]

In *Regal (Hastings)* v. *Gulliver*, the House of Lords articulated various tests for determining if the directors had breached their duty. In essence, the Lords said the directors had breached their duties if they received a profit through the acquisition and resale of their shares only by reason of the fact that they were directors and in the course of acting as directors. What does this mean as applied to the facts in this case?

---

14   Above note 3.

15   Now under the *CBCA* and similar statutes, former shareholders can seek relief under the oppression remedy (*CBCA*, above note 7, s. 241) (*OBCA*, above note 5, s. 238 (a)). If the same situation occurred today, the former shareholders of Regal could have claimed that their interests were oppressed or unfairly disregarded.

First, it means that the opportunity arose only because they were directors; otherwise, they would not have known of the opportunity,[16] nor would they have been able to obtain the shares in the subsidiary. Second, they acted as a board in conceiving and implementing the financing arrangement from which they benefited. Only the board could have issued the shares to provide the necessary financing.

The scope of the test in *Regal (Hastings)* v. *Gulliver* was narrowed in *Peso Silver Mines Ltd.* v. *Cropper.*[17] The board of directors of a mining corporation named Peso Silver Mines Ltd. (Peso) considered and, after receiving professional advice, rejected an opportunity to acquire certain mining claims because of constrained finances and other business reasons. Cropper was a member of the board and an officer of the corporation. A few months after Peso had rejected the opportunity, Cropper, along with others, formed a corporation that acquired them. Ultimately Peso sued Cropper, alleging breach of fiduciary duty and claiming that Cropper's interest in the claims be turned over to it. The court rejected the claim on two bases. First, Peso ceased to have an interest in the claims when the board decided not to buy them. Second, the court rejected the notion that merely because Cropper acquired knowledge of the opportunity by virtue of being a director and officer of Peso, he was thereafter prohibited from taking advantage of the opportunity personally. He must have had access to the opportunity only because of his position and, even then, the only thing he could not do was to take personal advantage of the opportunity through some action in his capacity as a director. Since here the claims were acquired independently of his position as a director, there could be no breach of his fiduciary duty.

This case has been criticized as making an express rejection of an opportunity a complete defence to a claim that a fiduciary breached his duty to the corporation. This simple expedient creates a risk that fiduciaries seeking to acquire an opportunity will simply contrive to have it rejected by the board.[18] The facile nature of this rule can be seen by noting how it led to opposite results on fundamentally similar facts in *Peso Silver Mines* v. *Cropper* and *Regal (Hastings)* v. *Gulliver*. In both cases,

---

16   In *Phipps* v. *Boardman*, [1965] Ch. 992 (C.A.), aff'd (*sub nom. Boardman* v. *Phipps*) (1966), [1967] 2 A.C. 46 (H.L.), the court held that knowledge gained by a trustee while acting as a trustee cannot be used by the trustee to gain personal profit.

17   (1965), 56 D.L.R. (2d) 117 (B.C.C.A.), aff'd [1966] S.C.R. 673.

18   This risk was cited by the court in *Irving Trust Co.* v. *Deutsch*, 73 F.2d 121 (2d Cir. 1934), in holding directors liable for breach of their fiduciary duty where they had acquired an opportunity after the board had decided that the corporation could not obtain sufficient financing to obtain the opportunity for itself.

the directors decided they could not proceed as planned because of the financial constraints on the corporation. Arguably the only difference was that in *Regal (Hastings)* v. *Gulliver* this decision was implicit in the directors' decision to implement an alternative strategy, while in *Peso Silver Mines* v. *Cropper* the board expressly rejected the opportunity.

Also, by requiring the fiduciary to have access to an opportunity and to have exploited the opportunity in the course of acting in his capacity as a fiduciary, the court in *Peso Silver Mines* v. *Cropper* severely constrained the classes of cases in which a breach of fiduciary duty could be found. This constraint was shattered in the decision of the Supreme Court of Canada in *Canadian Aero Service Ltd.* v. *O'Malley.*[19]

Canadian Aero Service Ltd. (Canaero) was in the business of mapping and geographic exploration. O'Malley, the president, and Zarzicki, the executive vice-president, were assigned to Guyana for the purpose of procuring a contract for mapping the country. After working on this project for some time, they resigned from Canaero and incorporated Terra Surveys (Terra) to perform work similar to what they were doing for Canaero. Subsequently, the government of Guyana asked for bids to map the country, and Terra's proposal to map Guyana was accepted in competition with Canaero's. Canaero sued O'Malley and Zarzicki, alleging that they had breached their fiduciary duty to the corporation by taking the benefit of a corporate opportunity belonging to Canaero.

The Supreme Court of Canada ultimately held that O'Malley and Zarzicki did breach their duty. In reaching its conclusion, the court determined that the test from *Regal (Hastings)* v. *Gulliver* was too restrictive to be used as a general test. In the view of the Supreme Court, the court in *Regal (Hastings)* v. *Gulliver* characterized a breach of fiduciary duty as occurring where the fiduciary received "profits by reason only of being directors and in course of the execution of their office" simply because that reflected the facts in that case. It was not intended to define exhaustively the circumstances in which a fiduciary duty could be breached. Note that the court had to free itself from the limits imposed in *Regal (Hastings)* v. *Gulliver* because in *Canadian Aero Service Ltd.* v. *O'Malley*, the Regal test clearly was not met: O'Malley and Zarzicki were not acting as fiduciaries when Terra acquired the project; they did not obtain the project in the course of exercising powers; and the project Terra acquired was somewhat different from the one they had been working on while with Canaero so, arguably, it was not even the same opportunity. Saying that the categories of breach of fiduciary duty are

---

19   (1973), [1974] S.C.R. 592.

never closed, the court developed an open-ended analysis based on a weighing of various factors that the court stated could not be listed exhaustively. In relation to an opportunity, the purpose of this analysis is to determine the answers to two questions:

- Does the opportunity belong to the corporation, considering how closely it is connected to the corporation?
- What is the relationship of the fiduciaries to the opportunity?

On the first question, the court cited several factors as tending to show that the contract to map Guyana was a corporate opportunity of Canaero's. It was a specific opportunity which the corporation had been actively pursuing through the efforts of O'Malley and Zarzicki, rather than one which was simply in the same business area as the corporation's business. Though the ultimate contract was different in some respects from the one that O'Malley and Zarzicki had been working on while they were at Canaero, it was substantially the same opportunity. It was also a mature opportunity, in the sense that O'Malley and Zarzicki had done extensive work in preparing for it while they were with Canaero. The court noted that a factor which was not present, but which would have made the corporation's interest even stronger, would have been the awarding of the contract without a public bidding process but simply on the basis of the relationship that O'Malley and Zarzicki had developed while they were working for Canaero.

Regarding the relationship of the fiduciaries to the opportunity, the court cited several factors as suggesting that they were directly involved in the opportunity they appropriated. They did preparatory work relating to the opportunity and negotiated for it on behalf of the corporation. They learned all about the opportunity through their positions. They quit to take advantage of it. The court also cited the fact that O'Malley and Zarzicki were high-ranking officers in the corporation as imposing a higher duty on them. Based on the strength of the corporation's interest in the opportunity and the close relationship of the fiduciaries to the opportunity while they were acting in their fiduciary capacities, the court concluded that O'Malley and Zarzicki had breached their fiduciary duty to Canaero.

In summary, a breach of fiduciary duty arises when a fiduciary takes something belonging to the corporation, putting her personal interests ahead of her duty to act in the best interests of the corporation. The policy of the common law is that such behaviour should be discouraged by requiring that any financial benefit from engaging in the behaviour be turned over to the corporation. With respect to the appropriation of corporate opportunities, the courts will not enquire into whether the corporation would have obtained the opportunity or whether the appropriation caused some loss to the corporation. If these exceptions are acknowledged, it is like saying to the fiduciaries, "You decide if the corporation could have obtained the opportunity or would be hurt if you took it." It would put the person with the conflict of interest in the position of having to decide when it is permissible to take the opportunity, an inherently untenable situation. Moreover, courts do not want to second guess fiduciaries' business judgment about these matters. Consequently, they set up a rigid rule to ensure that corporations can seek relief every time an opportunity is appropriated. The problem then is how do you know when an opportunity belongs to the corporation and cannot be appropriated by a fiduciary?

While in cases like *Cook* v. *Deeks* it will be obvious that a breach has occurred, in many others it will not. Whether a breach will be found depends on many factors relating to the nature or strength of the corporation's interest and the relationship to the opportunity of the person alleged to have breached his duty. What factors will be relevant will depend on the facts of each case. Some relevant factors are set out in figure 8.1.

Figure 8.1   Factors Relevant to Determining Whether Appropriation of Opportunity is a Breach of Fiduciary Duty

---

Nature or Strength of the Corporation's Interest

Maturity: Had the corporation done anything to develop the opportunity? How close was the corporation to acquiring the opportunity?

Specificity: Was the opportunity identified by the corporation? How precisely? Was it only in the same general business area as the corporation's business? How closely did the opportunity appropriated resemble the opportunity the corporation was working on?

Significance of opportunity: Would the opportunity represent a major component of the corporation's business if acquired? Was it a unique opportunity or merely one of many?

Public or private opportunity: Was the opportunity publicly advertised or otherwise widely known? Was it one to which the fiduciaries had access only by virtue of their positions? Was it offered to the corporation?

Rejection: Had the opportunity been rejected in good faith by the corporation before the fiduciary acquired it?

Relationship of the Fiduciary to the Opportunity

Position of fiduciary: The higher up the fiduciary is in the organization of the corporation, the higher the level of duty.

Relationship between the fiduciary and the opportunity: Was the opportunity in an area of the fiduciary's responsibility? Did the fiduciary negotiate for the opportunity on behalf of the corporation?

Knowledge as a fiduciary: How much knowledge did the fiduciary acquire about the opportunity through her position?

Involvement in competing business: Did the fiduciary acquire the opportunity through an existing business which was similar to or even competed with the business of the corporation and in which the fiduciary was involved?

Use of position: To what extent did the fiduciary accomplish the appropriation of the opportunity through his position?

Time after termination: If the fiduciary took the opportunity after she terminated her relationship with the corporation, how long was it after termination? What were the circumstances of her termination? Was she fired or did she leave voluntarily? Did she leave for the purpose of pursuing the opportunity she had been on working on for the corporation?

The more factors in favour of a corporate interest and a close relationship between it and the fiduciary, the more likely it is that a court will find that there has been a breach of duty. In cases where the fiduciary has terminated her relationship with the corporation, as in *Canadian Aero Service* v. *O'Malley*, the fiduciary duty derives not from the statute but from the common law, since the statutory duty applies only while a person is a director or officer. In such cases the court will seek to balance the interests of the corporation against the interests of the fiduciary to terminate her connection with the corporation and to carry on business for her own account.

Various reasons may be cited in favour of this loose situation-based standard in appropriation of corporate opportunity cases. As an opportunity becomes more remote from the corporation, ultimately extending to any profitable business in which the corporation may engage, the likelihood of loss to the corporation is diminished. In these circumstances, the argument that it is inequitable to the corporation to permit the fiduciary to appropriate the opportunity becomes weak. Similarly, the agency cost argument based on the potential cost to the corporation and shareholders of opportunistic behaviour by the fiduciary weakens. Two other factors may be cited in favour of a situation-based standard. It may be that different standards should be applied depending on whether the fiduciary is a person who is a full-time employee with the firm or an outside director receiving, perhaps, no compensation for her time. Also, the scale of the corporation, a factor not expressly cited by in *Canadian Aero Service* v. *O'Malley,* should be taken into account. As discussed in chapter 7, the ability of shareholders in closely held corporations to choose their fiduciaries and to monitor them is much greater than that of shareholders in public corporations, so, arguably, a stricter standard should be applied in the latter case.[20]

4) Competition by Directors and Officers

In general, as indicated above, it is not a breach of fiduciary duty to terminate one's relationship with a corporation and go into competition with it; otherwise, the fiduciary duty might become an unreasonable restraint of trade, something the common law has tried to avoid. What a fiduciary cannot do is to compete with the corporation while she remains in her capacity as a fiduciary. The conflict between the personal interests of the fiduciary and her duty to act in the best interests of the corporation is obvious in such situations and the courts, traditionally, have provided relief whenever any competition has been found.[21] Any competing fiduciary will be forced to pay over all her profits from the competing business to the corporation.

In addition, a fiduciary cannot use her fiduciary position and the opportunities afforded to her in that position to develop a competing business, then quit to begin competing.[22] In such cases, as we saw in *Canadian Aero Service* v. *O'Malley,* the courts will impose fiduciary obligations extending beyond the termination by the fiduciary.

Consistent with the strict approach of the common law, competition includes not only competition by the fiduciary in his personal capacity but also competition by a corporation in which the fiduciary has an interest. One difficult area in this regard, which has been the subject of several cases, is persons with multiple directorships. Some old English cases have held that being a director of two corporations, even if they are competitors, did not constitute a breach of fiduciary duty. The only restriction on a director in these circumstances was that she was prohibited from disclosing confidential information about one

---

20 V. Brudney & R. C. Clark, "A New Look at Corporate Opportunities" (1981) 94 Harv. L. Rev. 997.
21 In *Re Thomson,* [1930] 1 Ch. 203, the court granted relief against an executor who entered into competition with a business owned by the estate for which he was responsible.
22 *Bendix Home Systems Ltd.* v. *Clayton,* [1977] 5 W.W.R. 10 (B.C.S.C.).

corporation to the other.[23] This relaxed approach is inconsistent with the strict approach expressed in such cases as *Aberdeen Railway* v. *Blaikie* and probably does not accurately state the law in Canada. Recently it has been held that there is no absolute rule regarding multiple directorships. In each case, the question of breach of fiduciary duty will depend on the facts. The relevant question will be whether the fiduciary could act in the best interests of both corporations?[24] Where corporations are in active competition, it will be hard to avoid the conclusion that a director of both is not in a conflict of interest in breach of his fiduciary duty. For example, it is hard to imagine that a person could be a member of the boards of Ford Motors Inc. and General Motors Inc. simultaneously and always be able to act in the best interests of both. On the other hand, it may be possible to be on the board of two corporations that carry on identical businesses, but in geographically distinct markets, without facing a conflict of interest.

Before leaving this section we should briefly discuss what is meant by competition. In order to assess whether one business is in competition with another it is necessary to determine the nature of the first business and then ask what effect will, or could, the second business have on the first? In particular, if the second business seeks to sell the same product to the same customers, competition will be found.

5) Other Breaches of Fiduciary Duty

What has been described above are the most common situations in which a breach of fiduciary duty may occur. These categories are not immutable. Situations will arise in which more than one of them will be implicated. More important, as Mr. Justice Laskin said in *Canadian Aero Service* v. *O'Malley*, the categories of breach of fiduciary duty are not closed. There are an unlimited number of possible situations in which, if the fiduciary refers back to the broad statutory formulation in section 122(1)(a) of the *CBCA* and the principles developed in the case law, he may find himself in a situation where his personal interest and his duty conflict.

In chapter 7, for example, we discussed the problem of directors deciding on their own compensation, a conflict that has been expressly sanctioned by statute (*CBCA*, s. 120(5)). Another situation that often occurs is where a director of a corporation with a majority shareholder must make a decision in circumstances where the interests of the

---

23 *London and Mashonaland Exploration Co. Ltd.* v. *New Mashonaland Exploration Co. Ltd.*, [1891] W.N. 165 (Ch.).

24 *Abbey Glen Property Corp.* v. *Stumborg* (1978), 9 A.R. 234 (C.A.).

majority shareholder and those of the minority shareholders conflict. For example, the majority shareholder may want the corporation to enter into a transaction with it which is highly favourable to the majority shareholder but not good for the corporation or, as a result, the minority shareholders.[25] Because the majority shareholder has the statutory right to replace the director, it will be tempting for a director to act in the way desired by the majority shareholder rather than in the interests of the corporation as a whole. If a director were to do so, she would be in breach of her fiduciary duty.[26]

Even if a director is elected to represent a particular constituency, it does not permit him to favour this constituency. In all his actions, such a director, like all directors, must act in the best interests of the corporation, even though this may disappoint the constituency that elected him. Under the *ABCA*, a director who is elected or appointed by the holders of a class or series of shares, or by employees or creditors, may give "special, but not exclusive, consideration to the interests of those who elected or appointed him" (*ABCA*, s. 117(4)). In a recent discussion paper, the Corporations Directorate of Industry Canada raised the question whether a similar provision should be added to the *CBCA*.[27]

Finally, the most written about situation in which issues of fiduciary obligation arise is the hostile takeover bid. When a bidder offers to purchase a controlling interest in a corporation, often one of the reasons is that the bidder believes the value of the corporation can be increased by some changes in management, typically including the replacement of existing directors and senior managers. In such circumstances, the self-interest of directors and senior managers may lead them to try to defeat the takeover bid. Often, this will be contrary to the interests of shareholders. The bidder will often offer a substantial premium over the market price, so shareholders who sell will receive a better price than they could otherwise get. Those who do not sell will reap the benefit of the

---

25   In this example, the majority shareholder will also suffer from any disadvantage or loss to the corporation in its capacity as a shareholder. The majority shareholder would enter the transaction only if the benefits it receives in its personal capacity through the transaction more than compensate it.

26   See, for example, *Teck Corp. v. Millar* (1972), 33 D.L.R. (3d) 288 (B.C.S.C.). An example of another situation in which the fiduciary duty was held to be relevant is *Tongue v. Vencap Equities Alberta Ltd.*, (1994), 148 A.R. 321 (Q.B.). In that case, it was held that the fiduciary duty of directors buying shares from minority shareholders required them to disclose information regarding resale possibilities known at time of purchase.

27   Industry Canada, Directors' Liability (*Canada Business Corporations Act* Discussion Paper) (Ottawa: Industry Canada, 1995) at 22 [*Directors' Liability*].

improvements made by the bidder and the resulting increase in value of their shares. To the extent that directors and management may act to defeat the bid, not only will the shareholders lose the immediate benefits of the bid but incentives to engage in value-enhancing takeover bids generally will be reduced, because hostile takeover bids will be made more expensive. In this way, the general disciplinary effect of the market for corporate control described in chapter 7 will be impaired. If no defensive measures are available, the only way directors and management could prevent a takeover bid would be to manage the corporation so effectively that no bidder could improve value by making the bid. Following this argument, the courts should apply the fiduciary duty to prevent all defensive measures. Such a position is supported by the traditional common law policy that a fiduciary should not be permitted to be involved in situations where her personal interest possibly may conflict with her duty. To permit management to defend against takeover bids puts them in the kind of conflict of interest the common law has sought to avoid. The problem with prohibiting management from engaging in defensive tactics is that there may be takeover transactions which are not in the best interests of the corporation, its shareholders, and other stakeholders. The simplest example is a bid for a price that the directors and officers correctly believe is less than the actual value of the corporation.[28] The challenge then is to fashion the duty in a way that reconciles the objective of avoiding conflicts of interest with permitting directors and officers to act in the best interests of the corporation. This subject is pursued in more detail in chapter 11.

6) Reliance on Management and Others

In discharging their responsibility to manage in the best interests of the corporation, the directors in all but the smallest corporations must rely to some extent on management and other professionals. Under the *CBCA* and the statutes modelled after it, a limited defence to an alleged breach of fiduciary duty is available to directors who rely on others. Section 123(4) of the *CBCA* provides that a director is not liable for a breach of fiduciary duty if he relies, in good faith, on

---

28   For this to be the case, there would have to be some inefficiency in the way in which the market priced the shares of the corporation. The most likely situation in which this might occur is where the directors possess inside information that suggests a higher value.

- financial statements of the corporation represented to him by an officer or the auditor of the corporation to present fairly the financial position of the corporation; or
- a report of a lawyer, accountant, engineer, appraiser, or other person whose profession lends credibility to a statement made by her.[29]

This defence is limited by the specific circumstances in which reliance is permitted. It does not permit the directors to avoid liability by demonstrating that they acted reasonably in the circumstances. Except in relation to these specific circumstances, the strict fiduciary obligation continues to apply.[30]

7) Shareholder Ratification of Breach of Fiduciary Duty

Before the enactment of the *CBCA*, it was possible in most jurisdictions for shareholders to absolve fiduciaries of the consequences of a breach of fiduciary duty by voting to approve or ratify it. The only circumstances in which a breach could not be ratified were where the transaction was oppressive to the interests of the minority or was obtained by some improper means.[31] The first exception was narrowly applied. It should not be confused with the much broader concept of oppression from which shareholders may seek relief under the *CBCA* and other Canadian statutes. To fit within the common law oppression exception, one usually had to show that there had been some give-away of corporate assets to the fiduciary, such as a sale of corporate assets at less than market value. Such an appropriation of a corporate asset, as in *Cook* v. *Deeks*,[32] could not be ratified. The second exception was limited to circumstances in which the appropriate majority specified in a corporation's by-laws was not obtained or the notice of the meeting at which the ratification vote took place was improper.[33]

---

29   This defence is also available in connection with improper share issuances contrary to section 118, directors' liability for unpaid wages under section 119, and breach of the duty of care in section 122(1)(b) (*CBCA*, above note 7).

30   In Industry Canada's recent discussion paper, *Directors' Liability*, above note 27, it was recommended that a general "due diligence" defence be added to the *CBCA* so that a director would be excused as long as she had acted reasonably in the circumstances.

31   The rules on shareholder ratification were first set out in *Foss* v. *Harbottle* (1843), 2 Hare 461, 67 E.R. 189 (Ch).

32   Above note 10.

33   *Bamford* v. *Bamford*, (1969), [1970] Ch. 212 (C.A.).

The rationale for permitting shareholder ratification was that it was needed to balance the strict application of the common law rules as expressed in *Aberdeen Railway* v. *Blaikie*. If, in any given case, the shareholders decided that a transaction involving a breach of duty was good for them, they could approve it. Conceptually this rationale is suspect, since fiduciary duties flow to the corporation, not the shareholders. The rule was also problematic in application because there was no prohibition against majority shareholders voting their shares to ratify breaches of fiduciary duty in which they were involved personally.[34] This shortcoming, combined with the narrow interpretation given to oppression of the interests of the minority, gave wide scope for abuse of the ratification process.

For this reason, the *CBCA* greatly reduced the effect of shareholder approval of fiduciary breaches. Except in accordance with the scheme for rendering self-dealing contracts enforceable under section 120 of the *CBCA* and comparable provincial schemes, a shareholder resolution approving a breach of fiduciary duty has no effect on whether a breach has occurred or on the fiduciary's liability for the breach (*CBCA*, s. 122(3)). The only legal effect of such a resolution is that it must be considered by the court in deciding whether to grant a shareholder the right to bring a derivative action on behalf of the corporation for breach of fiduciary duty (*CBCA*, s. 242(1)), and in the context of any action for oppression under section 241 of the *CBCA*. Practically speaking, management may take some comfort from a shareholder resolution approving of their fiduciary breach, but it does not mean that shareholders are precluded from complaining about the breach at a later date. The effect of shareholder approval will be discussed further in chapter 9.

C. DUTY OF CARE

1) Introduction

Section 122(1)(b) of the *CBCA* imposes a duty of care on directors and officers in the following terms:

---

34   *North-West Transportation Co. Ltd. and Beatty* v. *Beatty* (1887), 12 App. Cas. 589 (P.C.).

> Every director and officer of a corporation in exercising his powers
> and discharging his duties shall . . . exercise the care, diligence and
> skill that a reasonably prudent person would exercise in comparable
> circumstances.[35]

Although the content of this duty, like the fiduciary duty, is highly
dependent on the facts, as evidenced by the reference to "comparable
circumstances," it is essentially an objective standard. As such, it represents a significant departure from the common law, which required
directors to exercise only the care that could be reasonably expected for
a person of their knowledge and experience.[36] The honest and diligent,
but incompetent, director had nothing to fear. Under the statutory
formulation, as will be discussed below, there is now a minimum
threshold of competence.

2) The Standard of Care

The standard of care is impossible to define exhaustively. Nevertheless,
the case law provides some useful guidance to the application of the
broadly worded statutory standard. Before examining some of the cases,
however, it is useful to refer to several additional relevant provisions of
the *CBCA*.

First, traditionally the courts viewed the directors' responsibilities
as intermittent in nature, to be performed at periodic board meetings.
Although a director should go to meetings, she was not bound to. As
will be discussed below, the general standard of care in the *CBCA*
demands a higher level of involvement, but, in addition, the Act contains a specific incentive to attend meetings and treat decisions respon-
sibly. Under section 123 a director is deemed to consent to all resolutions passed at a meeting at which she was present unless she records
her dissent. If the director misses a meeting, she is deemed to have consented to any resolutions passed unless, within seven days of finding out
about what was done, she takes certain steps to record her dissent. The
effect of this provision, which was discussed in chapter 7, is that a director cannot escape responsibility by not attending meetings.

---

35   Other provinces, other than Nova Scotia and Prince Edward Island, also impose a
     duty of care: for example, British Columbia *Company Act*, R.S.B.C. 1979, c. 59,
     s. 142(1)(b); Quebec Companies Act, R.S.Q. 1977, c. C-38, s. 123.83; *OBCA*,
     above note 5, s. 134(1)(b).
36   *Re City Equitable Fire Insurance Co. Ltd.* (1924), [1925] Ch. 407 (C.A.)[*City
     Equitable*].

Second, inevitably, especially in large corporations, officers must rely on the advice of experts, including accountants, lawyers, investment dealers, and engineers. This is even more true for directors. Before the enactment of the *CBCA*, directors and officers were entitled to trust employees and others to act honestly in performing their obligations and could rely on what they were told. Reliance on others is now subject to an express statutory standard. As discussed above in relation to fiduciary duties, a director is not liable if she in good faith relies on financial statements and reports of lawyers and other professionals (*CBCA*, s. 123(4)).[37]

Third, it used to be commonplace for corporations to set their own standard of care at a level even lower than that imposed by the common law.[38] This practice is now precluded by statute. No provision in a contract, the articles, the by-laws, or a resolution relieves a director or officer from the statutory duty of care or from liability for breaching it (*CBCA*, s. 122(3)). Also, the duty cannot be delegated; in a small corporation, for example, the fact that one director is assigned responsibility for a certain area does not relieve the other directors from their duty of care in relation to that area. If one director, who was a chartered accountant, was responsible for dealing with the financial side of a corporation's business, the other directors would still be required to comply with a standard of care in relation to these matters. If one of these other directors became aware of a problem with the payment of debts, for example, he would be required to do everything reasonably possible to ensure that the corporation put in place procedures to prevent a recurrence. This might include requesting a board meeting to discuss the problem, inquiring into the problem, designing a solution, and monitoring to ensure that the solution is put into effect.[39]

Apart from these statutory provisions, the substance of the duty of care must be gleaned from the case law. As noted, in contrast to the common law standard, the statutory formulation of the duty imposes a minimum standard of competence. Directors must have at least a rudimentary understanding of the business. If a person who is a director does not have this minimal level of understanding, she should acquire it or resign.[40] This requirement is a significant departure from the com-

---

37   A more detailed discussion is set out above in section B(6), "Reliance on Management and Others."

38   For example, *City Equitable*, above note 36. The by-laws of the corporation provided that the directors were liable only for their "wilful neglect or default."

39   *Fraser v. MN.R.* (1987), 87 D.T.C. 250 (T.C.C.).

40   *Selangor United Rubber Estates Ltd. v. Cradock, (A Bankrupt) (No. 3)*, [1968] 2 All E.R. 1073 (Ch.).

mon law and one that is often not appreciated in practice. It is still common for boards to have some number of passive "dummy" directors who take no interest in the affairs of the corporation and merely act as someone else's nominee. The statute is clear that being a nominee does not relieve a director from observing the standard of care.

The reference in the statutory formulation to a person "in comparable circumstances" does, however, suggest that the duty, to a certain extent, has a kind of subjective element. If a person has significant knowledge or experience, it will result in a higher standard of care being required.[41] Also, the standard of care will vary, depending on a person's position in relation to whatever is the activity alleged to constitute breach of duty. For example, serving on board committees will constitute different comparable circumstances. All public corporations must have an audit committee charged with reviewing the financial statements and the financial reporting process. Serving on the audit committee gives directors a greater opportunity to obtain knowledge about and to examine the affairs of the corporation than is available to directors who are not members. As a result, more would be expected of them in terms of overseeing the financial reporting process and warning other directors about problems.[42]

In addition to some level of competence, some level of monitoring of the corporation is required by the duty of care. A director must keep himself informed about the business and affairs of the corporation. This requirement does not mean a detailed inspection of the day-to-day activities of the corporation, but general monitoring of the corporation's policies and affairs. It does include attending board meetings regularly.

Specifically with respect to the financial affairs of a corporation, it is not necessary for directors to audit the financial records of the corporation; the corporation pays its auditor to do that. What is required is that directors maintain some general familiarity with the financial status of the corporation through regular review of its financial statements. The nature and scope of the review will depend on the corporation and the business. As noted above, directors may rely on statements represented fairly to reflect the financial situation of the corporation; but if the financial statements show some problem, directors will have a duty to enquire about the problem and, in some cases, take further action.

---

41   *Re Standard Trustco Ltd.* (1992), 6 B.L.R. (2d) 241 (Ont.S.C.) [*Standard*]. This case has been criticized as raising the standard for directors too much. J.G. MacIntosh, "Standard Trustco Case Signals Expansion of the 'Public Interest' Powers of Securities Regulators" (1993) 1 Corp. Financing 38.

42   *Standard, ibid.*

In *Francis v. United Jersey Bank,*[43] for example, a director was found to have breached her duty of care where she paid no attention to a problem appearing clearly on the face of the corporation's balance sheet. The financial statements disclosed ballooning loans to her sons which ultimately led to the insolvency of the corporation. The court held that she had a duty to review the financial statements and that, if she had done so, she would have seen the loans. On becoming aware of the loans, she would have had a duty to enquire about them and, if they were improper, as they were, to demand that the impropriety be addressed. The court went on to state that if no action was taken at that point by the wrongdoers, the director may have a duty to resign.

In *Francis v. United Jersey Bank,* the court also indicated that there are situations in which it is not enough simply to object and, if no adequate response is made, to resign. In some cases the director's duty will require her to take some further positive action, such as attempting to initiate legal action on the corporation's behalf to remedy some wrongdoing. This will be an unusual situation, perhaps like that in *Francis v. United Jersey Bank,* in which there is some activity that is both clearly identifiable and clearly wrongful. In such a situation, the action of a single director quite plausibly may stop the injury being caused to the corporation. Where the problem confronting the director is harder to pin down or remedy, such as general managerial incompetence, such extreme action likely would not be demanded of a director. Not only would it not be an appropriate response, but it would be unlikely to remedy the problem. To express this aspect of the duty more generally, what will be expected of a director will be determined, in part, by what strategy would have a reasonable likelihood of success. Another useful way of expressing it is to say that the breach of duty must be a contributing cause of the injury to the corporation. In some cases, directors may have to seek advice of independent legal counsel to understand the nature of their obligations in particular situations.

Where the breach of the duty of care alleged relates to business decisions rather than failing to detect and address wrongdoing, the courts have been reluctant to second guess management. This reluctance has a variety of sources. The most commonly cited is the courts' lack of business expertise. As well, courts often say that they do not want to set the standard of care so high as to inhibit business people from doing their jobs or, as a result of the increased risk of personal liability, discourage

---

43   432 A.2d 814 (N.J.S.C. 1981). This case considered a statutory duty of care expressed in terms similar to section 122(1)(b) of the *CBCA,* above note 7.

people from becoming directors at all. In the United States this reluctance has received recognition in what is referred to as the "business judgment rule." Under this rule, decisions will be presumed not to be a breach of duty in the absence of fraud, illegality, or conflict of interest on the part of the decision maker.[44] Some courts have also required that the process for making the decision must have been reasonable in the circumstances. For example, the decision maker must have made reasonable efforts to ensure that she had the information and advice necessary to make the decision.[45] In Canada, the courts have not formally adopted a business judgment rule standard, though the approach taken by the Canadian courts is not easily distinguished from that in the United States.

Finally, it should be noted that, unlike breaches of the fiduciary duty, the corporation can indemnify the breaching officer or director for breaches of the duty of care.

D. OTHER DUTIES IMPOSED ON DIRECTORS AND OFFICERS

Directors and officers are subject to a wide range of additional duties under corporate statutes and an increasing array of regulatory laws. Indeed, the burden of these statutory duties is so great that numerous commentators have argued that they are substantially interfering with the governance of corporations. They argue that the risks of liability discourage people from becoming directors and encourage them to resign in situations where the risks are increased, such as impending insolvency. Unfortunately, it is in those situations in which the risk is greatest that the need for good, experienced directors is greatest. Perhaps even more important, it is argued that the increased risks have two other pervasive negative effects. They represent strong disincentives for directors to agree that the corporation should embark on activities presenting increased liability risks, no matter how much doing so may be beneficial to its business. They also encourage directors to become overinvolved in the day-to-day operations of the business in order to try to manage their risk.[46]

---

44   *Shlensky v. Wrigley*, 237 N.E.2d 776 (Ill. App. 1968).

45   *Smith v. Van Gorkom*, 488 A.2d 858 (Del. S.C. 1985).

46   R.J. Daniels, "Must Boards Go Overboard? An Economic Analysis of the Effects of Burgeoning Statutory Liability on the Role of Directors in Corporate Governance" (1994) 24 Can. Bus. L.J. 229.

A discussion of the many regulatory statutes imposing personal liability on directors and officers is far beyond the scope of this book. In the remainder of the chapter we will discuss the subset of duties imposed in corporate legislation.

Directors are liable to employees for up to six months unpaid wages if the corporation is either bankrupt or in liquidation proceedings, or the corporation has been successfully sued for the debt and the judgment has been unpaid for six months (*CBCA*, s. 119). A director's responsibility ceases two years after he ceases to be a director (*CBCA*, s. 119(3); six months under the *OBCA*). If a director pays, he becomes entitled to enforce the rights of the employee to the extent of the payment and is entitled to contribution from the other directors (*CBCA*, ss. 119(5) & (6)). The Supreme Court of Canada held recently that liability does not extend to an unsatisfied judgment for wrongful dismissal or other severance or termination payments.[47] In light of the overlap between this provision and provincial labour standards and other legislation, Industry Canada recently raised the question whether this provision should be repealed.[48]

Directors are also personally liable under section 118 of the *CBCA* in various circumstances. They are liable if they vote for or consent to a resolution authorizing the following:

- a purchase or redemption or other acquisition of shares contrary to sections 34, 35, or 36;
- paying a dividend contrary to section 42; or
- paying financial assistance to directors, officers, shareholders, and other insiders of the corporation contrary to section 44 (*CBCA*, ss. 118(2)(a), (c) & (d)).

Essentially, in each case the payment is prohibited where either the solvency or capital impairment tests would be breached. As we saw in chapter 6, these tests require that the corporation must be able to pay its liabilities as they become due, and the realizable value of its assets must not be less than its liabilities plus its stated capital for all classes of shares.

Directors are also liable for paying an unreasonable commission on the issuance of shares contrary to section 41, paying an indemnity where doing so is not permitted under section 124, or making a payment that

---

47   *Barrette* v. *Crabtree Estate*, [1993] 1 S.C.R. 1027. Liability for wrongful dismissal was found by the Saskatchewan Court of Appeal based on the different wording of Saskatchewan's *The Business Corporations Act*, R.S.S. 1978, c. B-10, (*Meyers* v. *Walters Cycle Co.* (1990), 85 Sask. R. 222 (C.A.)).

48   *Directors' Liability*, above note 27 at 10.

results in oppression under section 241 (*CBCA*, ss. 118(2) (b), (e) & (f)). In each case, the directors are responsible for repaying the corporation any amounts paid out. Each director who has satisfied a judgment under any of these provisions is entitled to contribution from the other directors who were liable and has a right to seek a court order compelling the recipient to pay any money received to the director.

Directors are liable under the *CBCA* if they vote for or consent to a resolution authorizing the issuance of shares in return for property that is less than the fair equivalent of money the corporation could have received if the shares were issued for money. Where directors are liable, they must compensate the corporation to the extent of the shortfall (*CBCA*, s. 118(1)). Each director is entitled to contribution from the others. Directors are excused, however, if they did not know and could not reasonably have known that the share was issued in return for inadequate consideration (*CBCA*, s. 118(6)). This might occur, for example, if the directors relied on an expert valuation that turned out to be wrong.

This sort of excuse, sometimes referred to as a "due diligence defence," is also available under many of the statutes imposing liability on directors. In general, the due diligence defence requires directors to do what is reasonable in the circumstances to prevent the offence from occurring. The circumstances relevant to determining what is reasonable are similar to those relevant to determining the scope of the duty of care. In its recent discussion paper on directors' liabilities, Industry Canada recommended adding a general due diligence defence to the *CBCA* which could be invoked against any statutory liability.[49]

E. CHAPTER SUMMARY

In this chapter we considered the range of duties to which directors and officers are subject under Canadian corporate law. We mentioned the discrete liabilities imposed on directors for certain discrete activities, such as paying dividends or issuing shares, in ways contrary to corporate law. Most of the chapter, however, was devoted to the general standards of behaviour created by the fiduciary duty and the duty of care now expressly provided for in most corporate statutes.

The fiduciary duty strictly prohibits directors and officers from allowing their personal interests to interfere with their duty to act in the best interests of the corporation. Acting in the best interests of the

---

49   Above note 27 at 25. See chapter 12.

corporation also means not favouring the interests of one group of shareholders over another. Aside from these very general principles, it is not possible to articulate what the fiduciary duty requires; it will depend on the circumstances of each case. We looked at three kinds of situations in which the issue of fiduciary duty arises: fiduciaries having an interest in a contract with the corporation, fiduciaries appropriating an opportunity alleged to belong to the corporation, and competition with the corporation by fiduciaries. It is important to remember that the circumstances in which a breach of fiduciary duty may occur are not limited to these situations.

A contract in which a fiduciary has an interest is voidable but, because of a special provision in the corporate statutes, if the fiduciary discloses her interest, the contract is approved by the directors or shareholders, and it is fair and reasonable to the corporation, the contract will be enforceable. Where a fiduciary takes an opportunity belonging to the corporation, she will be required to account to the corporation for any profit she makes as a result. One difficult issue in this area is to determine when an opportunity belongs to the corporation and when a fiduciary is precluded from taking advantage of it. If the corporation's interest in the opportunity is strong and the relationship of the fiduciary to it is close, the fiduciary cannot take it. Determining whether this is the case will depend heavily on the facts of each case. In almost all cases, competition by a fiduciary with the corporation will be a breach of fiduciary duty and the fiduciary will have to account for any profits earned by such competition.

The duty of care under modern corporate statutes is objectively determined, though its specific content will depend on the facts of each case, including the position occupied by the director or officer. In general, the duty requires a minimum standard of competence and requires directors to attend meetings regularly. As an incentive to attending meetings, directors are deemed to consent to decisions taken at meetings unless they record their dissent. In addition, the duty requires that directors stay generally informed about the business and affairs of the corporation and monitor what is going on. If directors are put on notice that there is a problem, the duty of care requires them to take steps to address it.

Finally, as noted in the introduction to this chapter, the oppression remedy contained in most Canadian corporate statutes establishes a new substantive standard of behaviour for directors and officers which complements and overlaps with the duties described in this chapter. This standard is described in detail in chapter 9.

FURTHER READINGS

BECK, S.M., "The Quickening of Fiduciary Obligation: Canadian Aero Services v. O'Malley" (1975) 53 Can. Bar. Rev. 771

BRAITHWAITE, W.J., "Unjust Enrichment and Directors' Duties: Abbey Glen Property Corp. v. Stumborg" (1979) 3 Can. Bus. L.J. 210

BRUDNEY, V., Corporate Governance, Agency Costs, and the Rhetoric of Contract" (1985) 85 Colum. L. Rev. 1403

BRUDNEY, V., & R.C. CLARK, "A New Look at Corporate Opportunities" (1981) 94 Harv. L. Rev. 997

DANIELS, R.J., "Must Boards Go Overboard? An Economic Analysis of the Effects of Burgeoning Statutory Liability on the Role of Directors in Corporate Governance" (1994) 24 Can. Bus. L.J. 229

DeMOTT, D.A., "Beyond Metaphor: An Analysis of Fiduciary Obligation" [1988] Duke L.J. 879

EASTERBROOK, F.H., & D.R. FISCHEL, "Corporate Control Transactions" (1982) 81 Yale L J. 689

EISENBERG, M.A., "Self-Interested Transactions in Corporate Law" (1988) 13 Journal of Corp. L. 997

FINN, P.D., Fiduciary Obligations (Sydney: Law Book Co., 1977)

FLANNIGAN, R., "The Fiduciary Obligation" (1989) 9 Oxford. J. Legal Stud. 285

GLASBEEK, H.J., "More Direct Director Responsibility: Much Ado About . . . What?" (1995) 25 Can. Bus. L.J. 416

INDUSTRY CANADA, Directors' Liability (Canada Business Corporations Act Discussion Paper) (Ottawa: Industry Canada, 1995)

JOHNSEN, K.C., "Golden Parachutes and the Business Judgement Rule: Toward a Proper Standard of Review" (1985) 94 Yale L.J. 909

KLINCK, D., "Things of Confidence: Loyalty, Secrecy and Fiduciary Obligation" (1990) 54 Sask. L. Rev. 73

MACINTOSH, J.G., "Standard Trustco Case Signals Expansion of the 'Public Interest' Powers of Securities Regulators" (1993) 1 Corp. Financing 38

MACINTOSH, J.G., J. HOLMES, & S. THOMPSON, "The Puzzle of Shareholder Fiduciary Duties" (1991) 19 Can. Bus. L.J. 86

OSLER, HOSKIN, & HARCOURT, *Directors' Duties in Canada: A Guide to the Responsibilities of Corporate Directors in Canada*, 2d ed. (Toronto: Osler, Hoskin, & Harcourt, 1995)

Report of the Toronto Stock Exchange Committee on Corporate Governance in Canada: Where Were the Directors? (Toronto: Toronto Stock Exchange, 1994)

WAINBERG, J.M., & M.I. WAINBERG, *Duties and Responsibilities of Directors in Canada*, 6th ed. (Don Mills: CCH Canadians Ltd., 1987)

WEINRIB, E.J., "The Fiduciary Obligation" (1975) 25 U.T.L.J. 1

CHAPTER 9

SHAREHOLDER REMEDIES

A. INTRODUCTION

Shareholder remedies are the means of ensuring that the interests of shareholders are protected and that the rights to which they are entitled under statute, at common law, or under the corporation's articles, by-laws, directors' and shareholders' resolutions, and any unanimous shareholder agreements may be exercised. The initial focus of this chapter is procedural. We are concerned with the procedures available to shareholders to assert claims, rather than the substantive bases for those claims, which, in large part, are the subject of the previous chapters of this book. When we turn to deal with the oppression remedy, however, we are discussing both a substantive basis of protection as well as a procedure for making a claim. The oppression remedy, which we have referred to extensively throughout the book, represents an emerging standard of behaviour that not only complements the duties imposed on management described in chapter 8 but, increasingly, is coming to rival the fiduciary duty as the operative measure against which all management activities must be judged.

The three main bases on which a shareholder may assert a claim for relief are the personal action, the derivative action, and the oppression action. Before the enactment of the *CBCA* there was no oppression remedy available in most Canadian jurisdictions,[1] and the personal action

---

1   The oppression remedy was first introduced in Canada in the British Columbia *Companies Act*, R.S.B.C. 1960, c. 67, in 1960. It was interpreted narrowly until it was amended to add, among other things, "unfair prejudice" as a ground for relief in 1973 (S.B.C. 1973, c. 18).

and the derivative action were subject to certain limitations. One of the major objectives of the *CBCA* was to provide greater access to more effective remedies for minority shareholders.[2]

The personal action is an ordinary civil suit initiated by a shareholder to seek relief for some injury caused directly to her rights as a shareholder, such as the failure to receive notice of a meeting to which she was entitled. The remedy obtained as a result of such a suit is personal to the shareholder. The major limitation on the personal action is that the most important legal constraints on directors and officers, the fiduciary duty and the duty of care, are obligations owed to the corporation, rather than directly to the shareholder. As a result, breaches of these duties cannot be the basis of a personal action by a shareholder.

In some circumstances, a shareholder may commence what is referred to as a "derivative action" on behalf of the corporation for breach of these duties, or any other obligation to the corporation where the corporation is not taking action to pursue its own rights. This is not an uncommon situation since, in many cases, the same people who have allegedly breached their duties, the directors and senior officers, are the people who must decide whether to cause the corporation to sue. In such a case, the directors may well have a different view of whether their conduct constitutes a breach of duty. As will be discussed below, before the enactment of the *CBCA*, the circumstances in which shareholders could initiate such a derivative action were very narrow. Most breaches could be ratified by the shareholders and, as long as ratification was possible, the courts would refuse to hear a complaint by a minority shareholder that there had been a breach.

It is impossible to draw a clear and satisfactory distinction between an injury to the shareholder and an injury to the corporation. As the holder of the residual claim to the assets of the corporation, the shareholders' interests will be substantially affected by any injury to the corporation, as will the interests of many other stakeholders. The coincidence of shareholder and corporate interests is most obvious where the shareholder holds all the shares of the corporation,[3] but it will occur in virtually every case. Nevertheless, in terms of the procedure to be followed, it was essential to characterize a claim clearly and successfully as personal rather than merely incidental to an injury to the corporation if

---

2   R.V.W. Dickerson, J.L. Howard, & L. Getz, *Proposals for a New Business Corporations Law for Canada*, vol. 1 (Ottawa: Information Canada, 1971) at 158–63.

3   The effect of a loss of corporate assets on a sole shareholder was recognized by the Supreme Court of Canada in *Kosmopoulos v. Constitution Insurance Co. of Canada*, [1987] 1 S.C.R. 2, discussed in chapter 3.

a shareholder was to be able to proceed without being forced to seek relief by a derivative action. This was often difficult to do, since most actions injurious to shareholders could be characterized as a breach of fiduciary duty. Even the example of a breach of a personal right given above may be characterized as a breach of the directors' fiduciary duty. Is it not always contrary to the corporation's best interests to send out an inadequate notice of a meeting? Historically, the courts gave broad scope to what was considered a breach of directors' duties to the corporation. This limited the ability of shareholders to use the personal action.

In short, both the derivative action and the personal action were beset by significant limitations restricting access to relief for shareholders. As noted, one of the primary purposes of the drafters of the *CBCA* was to enhance the ability of shareholders to obtain relief. This purpose was accomplished by improving access to derivative actions and by introducing the oppression remedy. Under the *CBCA* and the statutes modelled after it, the shareholders may commence a derivative action for any injury to the corporation with leave of a court (*CBCA*, s. 239). Ratification by shareholders is no longer a bar. With the enactment of the oppression remedy, the need to be able to characterize a claim as personal as a condition of initiating an action on a shareholder's behalf was eliminated. Relief from oppression seems to be available whether or not the claim is essentially personal or derivative, so long as the prescribed standard of behaviour has been violated.

Following a discussion of these general remedies, we will discuss briefly the various other types of remedies found in the *CBCA* and statutes modelled after it, including the following:

- orders directing compliance with the Act, a corporation's articles, or a unanimous shareholder agreement, or orders to restrain a breach (*CBCA*, s. 247);
- orders requiring the rectification of corporate records (*CBCA*, s. 243);
- orders to investigate the affairs of the corporation (*CBCA*, ss. 229–37);
- the right of a shareholder to dissent from certain proposed fundamental changes to the corporation and to be bought out by the corporation (*CBCA*, s. 190); and
- termination of the corporation's existence (*CBCA*, s. 214).

B. PERSONAL ACTION

Owning a share carries with it certain rights that are clearly personal to the holder of the shares, such as the right to vote, the right to timely and informative notice of meetings, and the right to inspect the books and records of the corporation. These rights may derive from the governing corporate statute, the articles and by-laws of the corporation, the common law, or a shareholders' agreement. A significant limitation on this remedy, however, is that there are few duties other than these which are owed directly to shareholders. More important, as indicated above, the courts have traditionally been reluctant to grant a wide scope to the personal action because of the view that most cases of misconduct by directors and officers are properly characterized as a breach of the fiduciary duty owed by directors and officers to the corporation. As noted, only the corporation can sue for such a breach. Indeed, even the examples cited could be characterized as breaches of the director's fiduciary duty; failing to accord shareholders the right to vote, adequate notice of meetings, and access to information could hardly be said to be in the interests of the corporation.

Eventually, however, the courts began to allow personal actions in a wider range of circumstances. Personal actions were permitted so long as breach of a personal right was alleged. It was irrelevant if the same breach might constitute a breach of fiduciary duty as well. The general test developed by the courts to ascertain whether misconduct was a breach of an obligation to shareholders or to the corporation was to ask if the injury to the shareholders was merely incidental to the injury to the corporation.[4] So long as the injury did not occur only because the corporation was injured, then the claim will be permitted to proceed. An example of such an injury, which is only incidental to an injury to the corporation, would be the diminution in the value of a shareholder's shares caused by the appropriation of a corporate asset by the directors.

C. DERIVATIVE ACTION

The general rule that only a corporation may sue for an injury to it was developed in an old case called *Foss* v. *Harbottle*.[5] That case developed the rule based on a notion that since the shareholders could approve or ratify breaches of duty to the corporation, it would be an inappropriate interference with majority rule for courts to permit actions by minority

---

4   *Goldex Mines Ltd.* v. *Revill* (1974), 7 O.R. (2d) 216 (C.A.) (sending out misleading information circular and misleading annual report described as breach of personal right; pleading struck down because inextricably linked with claims for injuries to the corporation).

5   (1843), 2 Hare 467, 67 E.R. 189 (Ch.).

shareholders where the action had been or could be ratified by the majority. There were only four situations in which a minority shareholder could sue for an injury to the corporation:

- Fraud on the minority: This situation was sometimes referred to as oppression of the minority, but common law oppression included a much narrower range of activities than oppression under the *CBCA* and other modern corporate statutes. Essentially it was limited to situations in which the management of the corporation was giving corporate assets away, typically to the majority shareholder. In such cases, the courts recognized that permitting majority rule would work hardship on the minority shareholder.
- *Ultra Vires* Acts: In situations where the act complained of was outside the limited powers of the corporation or was illegal, the majority was not permitted to ratify it and minority shareholders could sue on behalf of the corporation.
- Defect in majority approval: In situations where the relevant corporate legislation or the articles of the corporation required approval by a specified majority, and approval at the special level was not obtained, shareholders could sue on behalf of the corporation.
- Personal right: In situations where the personal rights of a shareholder were infringed, he could sue for relief. Such a suit is not an action on behalf of the corporation at all, but rather a situation to which the bar on derivative actions does not apply, so it is not really an exception to the general rule.[6]

Under the *CBCA* and other modern corporate statutes in Canada, the curative effect of ratification has been abolished (*CBCA*, s. 122(3)). These restrictive conditions developed following *Foss* v. *Harbottle* have been replaced by a scheme allowing shareholders to proceed with derivative actions with court approval. Under the scheme, approval will be given if three conditions are met:

- the shareholder gives reasonable notice to the directors of the corporation of her intention to apply for leave to bring an action if the directors do not;
- the shareholder is acting in good faith; and
- the action proposed to be initiated by the shareholder appears to be in the interests of the corporation.

---

6   *Edwards* v. *Halliwell*, [1950] 2 All E.R. 1064 (C.A.).

The requirement for notice does not mean that a shareholder must specify all the legal bases on which a claim might be made or the facts or evidence on which the shareholder relies. It is sufficient if the shareholder gives some general information disclosing the nature of the claim.[7] For example, a notice that refers to a sale of specific corporate assets at under value without specifying the legal basis of the claim is sufficient.[8]

An application for leave will be considered to meet the "good faith" requirement so long as no bad faith is shown. If the application is shown to be frivolous or vexatious, it will not be granted. In this regard it has been held that a shareholder bringing an oppression action for an injury to him, based on the same facts as the derivative action, is not vexatious.[9] Where an applicant is motivated by a potential tactical advantage to be gained against directors in another proceeding, instead of the potential gain by the corporation, the applicant will be found not to be acting in good faith.[10]

The requirement that the action "appear to be in the interests of the corporation" represents a very low threshold of merit. This is justified, in part, because minority shareholders are not often in a position to obtain evidence to establish their case. It has been held to be less onerous than establishing a *prima facie* case (i.e., one which, in the absence of contradicting evidence, would be sufficient for the eventual lawsuit for breach of duty to be successful). Leave should be denied only if it appears that the action is bound to be unsuccessful.[11] Claims that a corporate asset has been sold at under value,[12] that the directors were subject to a conflict of interest in relation to a particular transaction they approved,[13] or that a mortgage should be found to be held in trust for the corporation[14] have all been held to be claims that appear to be in the interests of the corporation.

Several other aspects of the scheme governing derivative actions deserve mention. First and most important, the *CBCA* expressly provides that evidence of shareholder approval, or the possibility of future shareholder approval, is not determinative of whether a derivative

---

7   *Marc-Jay Investments Inc. v. Levy* (1974), 5 O.R. (2d) 235 (H.C.J.) [*Marc-Jay*]; *Bellman v. Western Approaches Ltd.* (1981), 33 B.C.L.R. 45 (C.A.) [*Bellman*].

8   *Re Northwest Forest Products Ltd.*, [1975] 4 W.W.R. 724 (B.C.S.C.); *Bellman, ibid.* (failure to specifically refer to non-compliance with takeover bid rules not fatal).

9   *Bellman, ibid.*

10   *Vedova v. Garden House Inn Ltd.* (1985), 29 B.L.R. 236 (Ont. H.C.J.).

11   *Marc-Jay*, above note 7.

12   *Ibid.*; *Bellman*, above note 7.

13   *Bellman, ibid.*

14   *Walter E. Heller Financial Corp. v. Powell River Town Centre Ltd.* (1983), 49 B.C.L.R. 145 (S.C.).

action may proceed (*CBCA*, s. 242(1)), thus eliminating the rule in *Foss v. Harbottle*.[15] Shareholder approval may still be taken into account by a court, however, in deciding if leave to commence a derivative action should be given.

Second, once an application is made, it cannot be stayed, discontinued, or settled without approval of the court (*CBCA*, s. 242(2)). This rule was introduced to prevent corporations from settling so-called "strike suits" where a shareholder brings a frivolous suit to extort a financial settlement out of the corporation. The inability of a corporation to settle without court approval should discourage such suits. It also may prevent corporations from buying off a shareholder who has obtained the leave of the court to commence an apparently meritorious action for the benefit of the corporation. The approach taken by the court will be to ask if the potential rewards of successful litigation, with its attendant risks and costs, are outweighed by the benefits of the proposed settlement.[16]

Third, contrary to the usual rules of civil procedure, a shareholder making an application for leave to commence a derivative action cannot be required to give security for the corporation's costs. Security for costs is often ordered against plaintiffs in ordinary civil suits on the basis of an application by the defendants. Under such an order, the plaintiff must post money or other security to cover any eventual award of costs by the court in favour of the defendant. Such an award would usually be made if the defendant successfully defends against the plaintiff's claim. The availability of orders to provide security for costs is intended to discourage frivolous law suits. The exemption in the case of derivative actions is intended to assist an impecunious shareholder to take actions in the corporation's interest (*CBCA*, s. 242(3)). Since there is an opportunity for judicial scrutiny at the hearing on the leave application, security for costs is not necessary to prevent frivolous suits.

Finally, a court may award an impecunious shareholder interim costs to assist her to pay counsel to proceed with an action, though she may be required to repay them if she is unsuccessful (*CBCA*, s. 242(4)). There is some judicial authority to suggest that such costs in derivative actions will be routinely awarded.[17]

---

15 *Farnham v. Fingold*, [1973] 2 O.R. 132 (C.A.); *Pappas v. Acan Windows Inc.* (1991), 90 Nfld. & P.E.I.R. 126 (Nfld. S.C.T.D.) [*Pappas*].

16 *Sparling v. Southam Inc.* (1988), 66 O.R. (2d) 225 (H.C.J.) [*Sparling*].

17 *Wilson v. Conley* (1990), 1 B.L.R. (2d) 220 (Ont. Gen. Div.) [*Wilson*].

Although the people most likely to bring an application for leave to commence a derivative action are shareholders, the *CBCA* permits a much wider class of persons to do so. The *CBCA* permits applications for leave to be brought by a "complainant," which is defined to mean

- a current or former registered or beneficial holder of securities of the corporation or any affiliated corporation;
- a director or officer of the corporation or any of its affiliates;
- the Director appointed under the *CBCA*; and
- any other person whom a court determines is a proper person to make an application.

Notwithstanding the very broad scope of the class of persons who, potentially, can bring a derivative action, it has been used primarily by current shareholders. None of the other identified kinds of complainants have made an application. In several cases a creditor has sought a court order recognizing it as a complainant, but none have been successful.[18] A complainant also defines the class of persons who may seek relief from oppression. Unlike derivative action cases, there have been many oppression cases in which non-shareholder complainants, including the Director and creditors, have sought and obtained relief. Those who may seek relief from oppression are discussed in more detail in the next section.

D. OPPRESSION REMEDY

1) Introduction

Shortly after the oppression remedy was introduced as part of the new *Canada Business Corporations Act*[19] (*CBCA*), in 1975 Stanley Beck described it in the following terms: ". . . beyond question, the broadest, most comprehensive and most open-ended shareholder remedy in the common law world . . . unprecedented in its scope."[20] Since the enactment of the *CBCA*, the accumulated judicial decisions addressing the oppression remedy have demonstrated the accuracy of Beck's appraisal.

---

18   *Re Daon Development Corp.* (1984), 54 B.C.L.R. 235 (S.C.); *First Edmonton Place Ltd. v. 315888 Alberta Ltd.* (1989), 71 Alta. L.R. (2d) 61 (C.A.).

19   Now R.S.C. 1985, c. C-44, s. 241 [*CBCA*].

20   S.M. Beck, "Minority Shareholders' Rights in the 1980's" [1982] Spec. Lect. L.S.U.C. 311 at 312; recently cited in *Deluce Holdings Inc. v. Air Canada* (1992), 12 O.R. (3d) 131 at 150 (Gen. Div.) [*Deluce*]. See to similar effect B. Welling, *Corporate Law in Canada: The Governing Principles,* 2d ed. (Butterworths: Toronto, 1991) at 563-64.

The oppression remedy has fundamentally changed not only what conduct by a corporation, its affiliates, and their respective directors gives rise to a claim for relief but also who may claim relief and what remedies may be sought. Traditional remedies such as the shareholder's derivative action for injuries to the corporation have been significantly displaced by the flexible and procedurally simple oppression action.

2) The Statutory Scheme

The key provisions of the *CBCA* governing the oppression remedy are sections 238, 241, and 242.[21] As noted above, section 238 defines "complainant," the class of persons entitled to apply for relief from oppression, and section 242 deals with interim costs. Section 241, which sets out the substantive standard, is set out in figure 9.1. For the sake of

Figure 9.1 Definition of Oppression in *CBCA*, s. 241

---

241. (1) A complainant may apply to a court for an order under this section.
(2) If, on an application under subsection (1), the court is satisfied that in respect of a corporation or any of its affiliates
   (a) any act or omission of the corporation or any of its affiliates effects a result,
   (b) the business or affairs of the corporation or any of its affiliates are or have been carried on or conducted in a manner, or
   (c) the powers of the directors of the corporation or any of its affiliates are or have been exercised in a manner
that is oppressive or unfairly prejudicial to or that unfairly disregards the interests of any security holder, creditor, director or officer, the court may make an order to rectify the matters complained of.

---

21 The following Canadian corporate statutes provide for an oppression remedy on substantially these terms:
   Alberta *Business Corporations Act*, S.A. 1981, c. B-15, s. 234 [*ABCA*]; British Columbia *Company Act*, R.S.B.C. 1979, c. 59, s. 224 [*BCCA*]; Manitoba, *The Corporations Act*, R.S.M. 1987, c. C225, s. 234 [*MBCA*]; New Brunswick *Business Corporations Act*, S.N.B. 1981, c. B-9.1, s. 166 [*NBBCA*]; Newfoundland *Corporations Act*, R.S.N. 1990, c. C-36, s. 371 [*NCA*]; Nova Scotia *Companies Act*, R.S.N.S. 1989, c. 81 s. 133(4)(k) [*NSCA*]; Ontario *Business Corporations Act*, R.S.O, 1990, s. 248 [*OBCA*]; Saskatchewan, *The Business Corporations Act*, R.S.S. 1978, c. B-10, s. 234 [*SBCA*].
   There are some differences in wording. For example, unlike the *CBCA*, the *OBCA* specifically refers to threatened behaviour.

convenience, "oppression" will be used as a short-hand expression for the behaviour giving rise to remedy under section 241, unless expressly indicated otherwise.

3) Interim Costs

Section 242(4) of the *CBCA* provides that, in any application for relief from oppression,

> the court may at any time order the corporation or its subsidiary to pay to the complainant interim costs, including legal fees and disbursements, but the complainant may be held accountable for such interim costs on final disposition of the application or action.

There have been only two reported cases in which motions for interim costs have been considered in oppression cases, and both were decided under the similar provisions of the *OBCA* (s. 249).

In the first, *Wilson v. Conley*,[22] the applicant was a minority shareholder of the respondent corporation. She claimed to have been oppressed by the respondent shareholders as a result of excessive travel and similar expenses charged to the corporation by the respondents, excessive remuneration being paid to the respondents, and a complete discontinuance of the past practice of paying regular dividends despite a substantial increase in profits. Rosenberg J. set out the following as the considerations applicable to the motion:

- that the applicant is in financial difficulty;
- that the financial difficulty arises out of the alleged oppressive actions of the respondents; and
- that the applicant has made out a strong *prima facie* case.

Based on the material before him, consisting only of the application and the applicant's affidavit, which demonstrated the oppressive acts referred to above, Rosenberg J. concluded that these requirements had been met. He directed the corporation to pay $20,000 in interim costs, even though the principal relief sought by the applicant was that the other shareholders buy her out and no relief was claimed against the corporation other than an order to cease making payments to the shareholder respondents.[23]

---

22   Above note 17.
23   *Ibid.* Rosenberg J. also stated that he would have had some concern about ordering costs against the corporation except that there is "not the usual danger that such advance will not be repaid if later my order is found to be inappropriate," because the applicant's shares appeared to be worth "many hundreds of thousands of dollars" (at 223).

The interim costs provision was also considered in *Alles* v. *Maurice*.[24] In that case, the applicant was also a minority shareholder and complained of similar acts of oppression: certain other shareholders charging excessive bonuses and expenses to the corporation. R.A. Blair J. considered the three requirements referred to in *Wilson* v. *Conley*. Regarding the first requirement, he found that the applicant was in financial difficulty, having depleted her savings to pay legal fees in connection with pursuing her claim and being unable to pay significant outstanding fees. Regarding the second, he expressed the view that, if Rosenberg J. had meant that the applicant's financial situation must, in all cases, be caused directly by the alleged oppressive conduct, he disagreed. In his view it would be sufficient if the financial difficulties resulted from the "great drain on her resources"[25] due to her pursuit of the lawsuit: "There is nothing in the language of the statute or in its purpose which, to my mind, requires that the applicant demonstrate a cause and effect relationship between the conduct of the respondents and the need for funding."[26] Regarding the third requirement, R.A. Blair J. was of the view similarly that showing a strong *prima facie* case, the test for an interlocutory injunction, was unduly onerous for the exercise of the discretion to award interim costs. Rather, he stated, the applicant need only establish that there is a case of sufficient merit to warrant pursuit.[27] He was satisfied that this requirement was met on the facts before him. R.A. Blair J. ordered interim costs in the amount of $55,000 to be paid to the applicant by the corporation.

4) Who May Claim Relief from Oppression: The Complainant

a) Introduction

Oppression is not just a "shareholder remedy." Recent cases have exploited the broad statutory language contained in the *CBCA* and the statutes modelled after it which defines the classes of persons who may claim relief from oppression to include creditors, employees, and even the corporation itself. These cases are still relatively few in number and mostly at a trial level, but they are potentially significant. Extending protection to creditors and others by giving them access to the oppression

---

24 (1992), 5 B.L.R. (2d) 146 (Ont. Gen. Div.).
25 *Ibid.* at 151.
26 *Ibid.*
27 *Ibid.* at 152.

remedy was not contemplated by the Dickerson Committee, which was responsible for drafting the new federal legislation,[28] and, moreover, it challenges traditional corporate law notions about whom corporate managers are responsible to. These cases may represent an important enhancement in the position of creditors and other non-shareholder stakeholders seeking relief from corporate conduct.

Unfortunately, most of these recent cases provide little in the way of guidance about the circumstances in which creditors and others will be permitted to claim relief from oppression. Nor is there any effort to reconcile these decisions with traditional corporate theory or the intention of the drafters of the *CBCA*.

The *CBCA* definition of complainant is set out above.[29] Each of the categories of complainant will be examined in turn.

b) Statutory Complainants

i) Security Holder, Section 238(a)

The first statutory category of complainant is defined as "a registered holder or beneficial owner, and a former registered holder or beneficial owner, of a security of a corporation or any of its affiliates." Some of these terms used in definition are themselves defined in section 1(1) of the *CBCA*. "[B]eneficial ownership" is defined broadly to include "ownership through any trustee, legal representative, agent or any other intermediary." "[S]ecurity" means "a share of any class or series of shares or a debt obligation of a corporation and includes a certificate evidencing such a share or debt obligation." "[D]ebt obligation," in turn, is defined to mean "a bond, debenture, note or other evidence of indebtedness or guarantee of a corporation, whether secured or unsecured."

---

28 Dickerson, above note 2 at 158–63. The same observation was made recently by J.S. Ziegel, "Creditors as Corporate Stakeholders: The Quiet Revolution — An Anglo Canadian Perspective" (1993) 43 U.T.L.J. 511 at 527.

29 See above note 18 and accompanying text. Provincial statutes based on the *CBCA* model contain identical provisions defining "complainant: *ABCA*, above note 21, s. 231; *MBCA*, above note 21, s. 231; *NCA*, above note 21, s. 368; *OBCA*, above note 21, s. 245; *SBCA*, above note 21, s. 231. Section 7(5) of the Third Schedule to the *NSCA*, above note 21, defines "complainant" in the same terms. Section 163 of the *NBBCA*, above note 21, also contains essentially the same definition of "complainant" except that "creditor" is expressly included. Section 224 of the *BCCA*, above note 21, permits "members" to apply for relief. Section 225(8) defines members for the purpose of section 224 to include "a beneficial owner of a share" and "any other person who, in the discretion of the court, is a proper person to make an application."

In drafting the *CBCA*, the Dickerson Committee did not set about to revolutionize corporate law by permitting creditors and others to seek relief from corporate behaviour. Their concern was to protect minority shareholders, and the broad language used in section 241(2) to describe the specific interests protected — those of "any security holder, creditor, director or officer" — was intended only to ensure that shareholders' interests were protected in whatever capacity they arose, implicitly acknowledging the complex multifaceted relationships that shareholders may have with the corporation, particularly where it is closely held.[30] As Jacob Ziegel has pointed out, "[i]t is obvious that the language of s. 241(2) does not remotely reflect this limited intention."[31] Nevertheless, many cases have expressed the view that the primary category of persons who should be entitled to seek relief from oppression are minority shareholders.[32] Most oppression cases have been commenced by minority shareholders and in these courts have acknowledged, either expressly or implicitly, that minority shareholders have status as complainants under section 238(a) as security holders. The courts also have given effect to the express reference to "affiliates" in section 238(a), holding in *Moriarity* v. *Slater*[33] that a minority shareholder of an affiliate of the corporation in respect of which oppression is alleged may be a complainant. The courts also have confirmed that former shareholders are complainants within the meaning of section 238(a).[34] It has been held also that a person continues to have status as a complainant under section 238(a) even after the person has invoked her appraisal rights

---

30   Dickerson, above note 2 at 163; Ziegel, above note 28 at 527.

31   Ziegel, *ibid.*

32   See, for example, *Jacobs Farms Ltd.* v. *Jacobs*, [1992] O.J. No. 813 (Gen. Div.) (QL); *Royal Trust Corp. of Canada* v. *Hordo* (1993), 10 B.L.R. (2d) 86 (Ont. Gen. Div.) [*Hordo*].

33   (1989), 67 O.R. (2d) 758 (H.C.J.). In that case, a shareholder of a New York corporation, which wholly owned the Ontario corporation in respect of which the oppression was alleged, was permitted to commence an oppression action. The court expressed the view that notwithstanding its holding regarding complainant status, it was not "crystal clear" that the shareholder was a "security holder" for the purposes of the substantive standard of protection against oppression. See also *PMSM Investments Ltd.* v. *Bureau* (1995), 25 O.R. (3d) 586 (Gen. Div.) [*PMSM*], discussed under section D(5)(b)(v), "What Interests Are Protected?" An affiliate of a corporation is a corporation that is controlled by, controls, or is under common control with the first corporation (*CBCA*, above note 19, s. 2(2)).

34   *Ontario (Securities Commission)* v. *McLaughlin* (1987), 11 O.S.C.B. 442 (H.C.J.) [*McLaughlin*]. See also *Michalak* v. *Biotech Electronics Ltd.*, (1986), 35 B.L.R. 1 (S.C.) [*Michalak*], where, although complainant status was acknowledged, relief was denied on the basis that the interests of the applicants were not being currently oppressed at the time of the application (at 9–11).

under section 190 of the *CBCA,* with the result that, by virtue of the operation of section 190(11) of the *CBCA,* the person loses all rights as a shareholder other than the right to be paid fair value for her shares.[35]

One recent case addressed whether applicants claiming a right to become security holders were complainants. *Csak* v. *Aumon*[36] held that applicants with a contractual claim to be issued shares, a claim that was being denied by the controlling shareholder of the corporation, were beneficial owners of securities of the corporation for the purposes of section 238(a). In *Csak,* the court noted that the *CBCA* was remedial legislation and contemplates a "large and . . . sweeping jurisdiction"[37] such that, in the absence of some reason inherent in the legislation or policy, the meaning of "beneficial owner" should be interpreted broadly. The court also cited the definition of "security" in the *CBCA* as indicating that ownership of a security means more than being the holder of a certificate, and the remedial provisions of the *CBCA* which contemplate, on a finding of oppression, "an order directing an issue . . . of securities . . . " (s. 241(3)(d)).[38]

Significantly, the court added that it is not a bar to complainant status that the applicant's claim to be a beneficial owner of shares is disputed. In the court's view:

> Parliament did not intend the absence of legal title to prevent the applicants here from bringing an application under ss. 238 and 241 until some other court had passed upon the validity of their claim to beneficial ownership. Their status is to be dealt with within the CBCA application and not as a condition precedent.[39]

The court also said that any issues of fact regarding the claim to be issued shares could be dealt with through a trial of an issue, and that requiring a party to establish its status in a separate proceeding before coming to court to seek relief from oppression would "multiply litigation to no good purpose."[40]

A further related point was raised in *Csak.* It was alleged that even if a person with contractual claim to be issued a share was entitled to complainant status as a "beneficial owner" of a security under section

---

35   *Brant Investments Ltd.* v. *KeepRite Inc.* (1987), 60 O.R. (2d) 737, (H.C.J.), additional reasons at (1987), 61 O.R. (2d) 469 (H.C.J.), aff'd (1991), 3 O.R. (3d) 289 (C.A.) [*Brant*].

36   (1990), 69 D.L.R. (4th) 567 (Ont. H.C.J.) [*Csak*]. The court distinguished an earlier case, *Bernstein* v. *335861 (Alta.) Ltd.* (1986), 73 A.R. 188 (Q.B.).

37   *Csak, ibid.* at 571.

38   *Ibid.* at 572.

39   *Ibid.*

40   *Ibid.* at 573.

238(a), such a person did not have an interest protected under section 241(2), since that section refers only to "security holder," not beneficial owner. Lane J. rejected this argument, holding, in effect, that if a person was entitled to complainant status under section 238(a), the person's interests were deserving of protection under section 241(2).

Even though the primary purpose of the oppression remedy envisioned by the drafters of the *CBCA* may have been the protection of minority shareholders, there is nothing in the section which expressly precludes a majority shareholder from commencing an oppression action as a complainant. Indeed, the availability of an oppression claim to a majority shareholder would appear to be consistent with the broad spectrum of situations where relief may be claimed. It seems quite possible that a majority shareholder could be oppressed by the acts of a corporation's directors.[41] The only question is whether, on the facts, the shareholder was oppressed.[42]

It is apparent in the statutory definition of "security" that holders of debt obligations are also entitled to bring oppression actions, though no such actions have been brought successfully. At least one commentator has suggested that the reference to "registered holders" in section 238(a) suggests a legislative intention to limit claims by debt holders to those holding registered obligations or obligations that are susceptible of registration (such as some bonds and debentures), to the exclusion of other kinds of debts (such as trade debts), which are not registrable.[43] Given the expansive definition of debt obligation in the *CBCA*, it is not obvious that this is the correct interpretation.

Nevertheless, in the only reported decision to date to address directly the circumstances in which a debt holder may be a complainant for the purposes of section 238(a), it was held that only holders of registrable obligations have status. In *First Edmonton Place*, the court

---

41 See, for example, *Hui v. Yamato Steak House Inc.*, [1988] O.J. No. 9 (Gen. Div.) (QL) [*Hui*], where the oppression alleged by the 90 percent shareholder was the directors' attempt to issue shares for the purpose of diluting the majority shareholder's interest to 10 percent.

42 The availability of the oppression remedy to non-minority shareholders has been recognized in many cases: *Gandalman Investments Inc. v. Fogle* (1985), 52 O.R. (2d) 614 (H.C.J.) (50% shareholder); *Tesari Holdings Ltd. v. Pizza Pizza Ltd.* (14 August 1987), (Ont. H.C.J.) [unreported] [summarized at 5 A.C.W.S. (3d) 430] [*Tesari*] (majority shareholder); *Cairney v. Golden Key Holdings Ltd.* (1987), 40 B.L.R. 263 (B.C.S.C.) (45% shareholder with effective control); *Hui, ibid.* (90% shareholder); *Jabaco Inc. v. Real Corporate Group Ltd.*, [1989] O.J. No. 68 (Gen. Div.) (QL) (60% of equity and 50% voting power); *Trnkoczy v. Shooting Chrony Inc.* (1991), 1 B.L.R. (2d) 202 (Ont. Gen. Div.) [*Trnkoczy*] (50% shareholder); *M. v. H.* (1993), 15 O.R. (3d) 721 (Gen. Div.) (50% shareholder).

43 Welling, above note 20 at 521–23.

determined that an unpaid lessor was not a "security holder."[44] Some debt holders have been successful, however, in getting courts to exercise their discretion under section 238(d) to permit them to make an application as a complainant (see "Discretionary Complainants" below).[45]

ii) Directors and Officers and the Director, Section 238 (b) and (c)
There are few cases in which each of the other types of complainants expressly referred to in section 238 have sought relief from oppression. Several cases have addressed whether a claim by an officer or director that he was wrongfully dismissed may be the subject of an oppression proceeding. In these cases the courts have expressed their reluctance to consider wrongful dismissal claims.[46] In *Naneff*[47] the applicant was an employee, director, officer, and shareholder of a corporation carrying on a family business. His family tried to exclude him from participating in the corporation in all his capacities, not for any legitimate reason connected with the business of the corporation, but because the family disapproved of his personal life. The trial court had held that although "[in] normal circumstances, the wrongful dismissal of an employee would not of itself provide the basis or standing to make an 'oppression remedy' claim,"[48] in this case the dismissal was part of an "overall pattern of oppression"[49] such that the oppression of the applicant's interests as an employee were inextricably intertwined with the oppression of his interests in other capacities. This analysis was rejected by the Ontario Court of Appeal, which held that a court could only protect the interests of a complainant as a shareholder, director, or officer as such.[50]

---

44   *First Edmonton Place Ltd.* v. *315888 Alberta Ltd.* (1988), 40 B.L.R. 28 at 60–62 (Alta. Q.B.) [*First Edmonton*], rev'd on other grounds (1989), above note 18.

45   An additional point addressed by the courts is whether the interests alleged to be oppressed must be those of the complainant. This is discussed below in section D(5)(b)(v), "What Interests Are Protected?"

46   See, for example, *Naneff* v. *Con-Crete Holdings Ltd.* (1993), 11 B.L.R. (2d) 218 (Ont. Gen. Div), rev'd in part (1994), 19 O.R. (3d) 691 (Div. Ct.), rev'd (1995), 23 O.R. (3d) 481 (C.A.).

47   *Ibid.*

48   *Ibid.* at 250 (Ont. Gen. Div.).

49   *Ibid.* at 254.

50   See also *West* v. *Edson Packaging Machinery Ltd.* (1993), 16 O.R. (3d) 24 (Gen. Div.); and *Deluce*, above note 20, in which the termination of an employee for the purpose of triggering a share purchase option as part of a strategy by Air Canada to acquire 100 percent control of the corporation was held to be oppressive of the interests of the minority shareholder (a holding corporation controlled by the members of the employee's family) on the basis that the shareholder had a reasonable expectation that, in the absence of the termination of the employee for reasons having to do with the interests of the corporation, it would continue as a shareholder.

By contrast, in *Murphy* v. *Phillips*,[51] the general manager of a car dealership, who was not a shareholder,[52] was held to be an officer and so a complainant who could pursue a wrongful dismissal claim through the oppression remedy. Unfortunately, the court did not cite any authority in support of its conclusion, and the reasoning in *Naneff* is probably to be preferred.

Pursuant to section 238(c), the Director appointed under the *CBCA* has status as a complainant to commence oppression actions. The Director has used this status sparingly,[53] consistent with the expressed intention of the Dickerson Committee that the *CBCA* be largely "self-enforcing."[54]

c) Discretionary Complainants, Section 238(d)

i) General

The class of complainant contemplated by section 238(d) of the *CBCA* is "any other person who, in the discretion of a court, is a proper person to make an application" for relief from oppression. Courts have been asked to exercise this discretion by creditors in a number of cases with varying success and, in a few cases, by the corporation itself.

ii) Creditors

The courts have been reluctant to exercise their discretion to permit an oppression action to be brought by a creditor, notwithstanding the express reference to the interests of creditors in section 241(2). This reluctance was expressed in a recent case, *Royal Trust Corp. of Canada* v. *Hordo*:[55]

> The court may use its discretion to grant or deny a creditor status as a complainant under s. 238(d). It does not seem to me that debt actions should be routinely turned into oppression actions: . . . I do not think that the court's discretion should be used to give "complainant" status to a creditor where the creditor's interest in the affairs of a corporation is too remote or where the complaints of a creditor have nothing to do

---

51 (1993), 12 B.L.R. (2d) 58 (Ont. Gen. Div.).

52 The officer, with his wife, owned all the shares of a corporation that was a minority shareholder.

53 For example, *Sparling v. Javelin International Ltée.*, [1986] R.J.Q. 1073 (S.C.), aff'd (*sub nom. Doyle v. Sparling*) [1987] R.D.J. 307 (Que. C.A.) [*Javelin*]; *Sparling*, above note 16. Other Canadian corporate law regulators have been similarly reticent. The Ontario Securities Commission did commence an oppression action in *McLaughlin*, above note 34.

54 Dickerson, above note 2 at 160–62.

55 Above note 32.

with the circumstances giving rise to the debt or if the creditor is not proceeding in good faith. Status as a complainant should also be refused where the creditor is not in a position analogous to that of the minority shareholder and has no "particular legitimate interest in the manner in which the affairs of the company are managed."[56] [Citations omitted.]

Though the passage quoted makes the court's reluctance clear, it is difficult to give operational content to most of the criteria articulated for refusing to grant complainant status to creditors: the creditor's interest in the affairs of the corporation is too remote; the creditor is not in a position analogous to that of a minority shareholder; or the creditor has no particular legitimate interest in the manner in which the affairs of the company are managed. The final criterion mentioned in *Royal Trust*, though also vague, does suggest a more workable standard: where the complaints of the creditor have nothing to do with the circumstances giving rise to the debt.

This standard was more fully elaborated in *First Edmonton Place*,[57] a case involving an oppression claim by an unpaid lessor. In a very thorough judgment, McDonald J. made clear that to grant complainant status there must be some evidence of oppression. He identified two kinds of circumstances where this would occur, though he acknowledged that others were possible:

- an act of the directors or management of the corporation which constitutes using the corporation as a vehicle for committing fraud upon the applicant; and
- an act or conduct of the directors or management of the corporation which constitutes a breach of the underlying expectations of the applicant arising from the circumstances in which the applicant's relationship with the corporation arose.[58]

As an example of the second circumstance, McDonald J. suggested something in the circumstances in which the credit was granted, which prevented the creditor from taking adequate steps to protect its interest against the occurrence in respect of which it is now claiming oppression. In *First Edmonton* the applicant was an unpaid landlord of some office space. No such impediment prevented the landlord from seeking some form of protection and the applicant was denied complainant status.

---

56   *Ibid.* at 92.
57   Above note 44 at 63 (Alta. Q.B.).
58   *Ibid.* at 63–64.

The cases in which the courts have granted complainant status to creditors include no such principled analysis and appear to be based simply on the difficulty facing the creditor in enforcing its claim. In one of the first cases to grant complainant status to a creditor, *R. v. Sands Motor Hotel Ltd.*,[59] the Crown was given status as a complainant on the basis of being a creditor under the *Income Tax Act* where the ability of the Crown to recover income taxes owed by a corporation was impaired by dividends the corporation had paid to shareholders. The Crown sought and obtained an order setting aside the dividend payments. In *Canadian Opera Co. v. 670800 Ontario Inc.*,[60] the court granted complainant status to a creditor who had purchased a car, but not obtained possession, where the funds paid by the creditor had "gone south" from the corporation to an associate of the controlling shareholder. In another case, *Prime Computer of Canada Ltd. v. Jeffrey*,[61] a judgment creditor with no hope of recovery against a corporation because of excessive salary payments to the controlling shareholder was permitted to be a complainant. In both *Canadian Opera* and *Prime Computer*, on a finding of oppression, the complainant obtained an order directly against the controlling shareholder of the corporation.[62]

These decisions appear to open up the oppression remedy as a flexible alternative to commencement of an ordinary civil action to pursue a creditor's claim. There are two main advantages of an oppression action over an ordinary civil action for a creditor. Because oppression actions may be commenced by way of application, without the pleadings and discovery required for a civil action, an oppression action can probably be brought to court faster than a civil action, provided there are no significant factual issues in dispute requiring the trial of an issue. Also, the discretionary powers granted to the court under the oppression remedy are much broader than those available in a civil action, expressly contemplating the kind of remedy granted in *Canadian Opera* and *Prime Computer*.

---

59   *R. v. Sands Motor Hotel Ltd.* (1984), 36 Sask. R. 45 (Q. B.).

60   *Canadian Opera Co. v. 670800 Ontario Inc.* (1989), 69 O.R. (2d) 532 (H.C.J.).

61   (1991), 6 O.R. (3d) 733 (Gen. Div.). See also *Tropxe Investments Inc. v. Ursus Securities Corp.*, [1991] O.J. No. 2116 (Gen. Div.) (QL) [*Tropxe*], a case with essentially the same facts where the same relief was ordered. In *Royal Bank of Canada v. Amatilla Holdings Ltd.*, [1994] O.J. No. 198 (Gen. Div.) (QL), in similar circumstances, the shareholders were ordered to repay dividends to the corporation for the benefit of the creditor.

62   See also *Tavares v. Deskin*, (25 January 1993), (Ont. Gen. Div.) [unreported] [summarized at (1993), 38 A.C.W.S. (3d) 71], where an application to strike an oppression claim by a wrongfully dismissed employee was denied on the basis that the employee was entitled to complainant status where the corporation was stripping itself of assets in order to make it judgment proof.

iii) The Corporation

Two Alberta decisions have held that the corporation itself may be a complainant.[63] The classes of persons identified in section 238 as entitled to bring an oppression application under section 238 make no reference to the corporation. Nevertheless, in *Kredl*,[64] the Alberta Court of Queen's Bench held that the corporation was a proper person to be a complainant where all the shareholders, other than the respondent who was alleged to have committed the oppression, were joined as plaintiffs in the action. The shareholders had only recently gained effective control of the corporation and were seeking to recover funds on its behalf. This decision confirmed the earlier one in *Pocklington*,[65] in which Mac-Donald J. had refused an application to strike out a statement of claim on the ground that the corporation was not a proper person to be a complainant. In *Pocklington*, the Crown had taken over control of the corporation and the complaint related to the acts of a director.

A contrary result was reached, in effect, in *Canada (A.G.) v. Standard Trust Co.*[66] In this case, Houlden J.A. (*ad hoc*) refused to grant leave to a trustee in bankruptcy to pursue an oppression claim on the basis that the trustee succeeded to the rights of the corporation and the transaction had been unanimously approved by the board of the corporation such that, in the view of the court, the corporation could not have claimed oppression. The court expressly rejected an argument that the trustee should be given status as a complainant as a representative of the collective interests of creditors. *Standard Trust Co.* was distinguished in *Pocklington* on the basis that the claim did not relate to an action by the corporation, but to an action by one of the directors.

Given the broad fairness standard represented by the oppression remedy, granting the corporation status to claim oppression creates the risk that the oppression remedy will completely replace the fiduciary duty, a narrower standard, and, by virtue of many years of judicial consideration, a more certain one. In this regard it is important to note that even if the corporation were not permitted to seek relief from oppres-

---

63   *Calmont Leasing Ltd. v. Kredl* (1993), 142 A.R. 81 at 105 (Q.B.), aff'd (1995), 165 A.R. 343 (C.A.) [*Kredl*], and *Gainers Inc. v. Pocklington* (1992), 132 A.R. 35 at 65–66 (Q.B.) [*Pocklington*].

64   *Kredl, ibid.*

65   Above note 63.

66   (1991), 5 O.R. (3d) 660 (Gen. Div.) [*Standard Trust Co.*].

sion directly, the remedies expressly enumerated in section 241(3) include "an order compensating an aggrieved person," which would apparently include the corporation in any event.[67]

d) Summary

The intention of the Dickerson Committee in proposing the inclusion of the oppression remedy in the *CBCA* was the protection of minority shareholders in their capacities as shareholders, creditors, directors, and officers.[68] Enhanced protection for shareholders was needed because of the inadequacy of the existing corporate law, which was characterized by a high degree of judicial deference to management decision making and provided only very restricted access to limited kinds of remedies.[69] But, as the foregoing survey of cases makes clear, the categories of person who have standing as complainants to seek relief from oppression under section 238 of the *CBCA*, which tracks the language recommended by the Dickerson Committee, is much broader. Section 238 expressly provides that all security holders, not just shareholders, as well as directors and officers and the Director appointed under the *CBCA* have standing; it also permits a court to grant standing to any other person it determines is a "proper person" to seek relief (*CBCA*, s. 238(d)). In *First Edmonton Place*, the court described this discretion as "a grant to the Court of a broad power to do justice and equity in the circumstances of a particular case where a person who otherwise would not be a 'complainant' ought to be permitted to bring an action . . . to obtain compensation."[70] The primary category of person seeking to have the courts exercise this "power" has been creditors.

Though there are still too few cases to draw definitive conclusions, and although they have proceeded cautiously for the most part, the courts have been willing to grant complainant status to various groups that would not have had any status to seek relief under corporate law before the introduction of the oppression remedy: former shareholders, persons with contractual claims to be issued shares, creditors, and

---

67 This view is adopted by Welling, above note 20 at 561. It should be noted that approval by the directors does not relieve the directors from their duty to act in accordance with the *CBCA*, nor from liability for any breach of the Act (above note 19, s. 122(3)). The effect of this provision was apparently not argued before Houlden J.A. in *Standard Trust Co.*, *ibid.*

68 Dickerson, above note 2 at 160–63.

69 *Ibid.*

70 Above note 44 at 62 (Alta. Q.B.).

dismissed employees.[71] Potentially, this development represents a fundamental reordering of the responsibilities of corporate management under corporate law.

5) The Substantive Standard

a) Introduction

Any effort to describe what constitutes oppression without regard to the facts of a particular case is inherently problematic. As Brooke J.A. said in one of the leading cases on oppression, *Ferguson* v. *Imax Systems Corp.*,[72] " . . . each case turns on its own facts. What is oppressive or unfairly prejudicial in one case may not necessarily be so in the slightly different setting of another." The section that follows will attempt to set out some of the overriding principles identified by the courts as governing the availability of the oppression remedy.

b) General Principles

i) *General Approach to Interpretation*

From the earliest cases following the enactment of the *CBCA*, the courts have uniformly expressed the view that the oppression remedy should be interpreted broadly to carry out its purpose: to reform the law applicable to business corporations with a view to improving the protection of minority shareholders.[73] In this regard, various courts have made it clear that the oppression remedy is intended to protect not just the strict legal rights of shareholders but also their interests.[74] Mr. Justice Farley explained this concept of shareholder interests in the following widely cited passage in *820099 Ontario Inc.* v. *Harold E. Ballard Ltd*:[75]

---

71   Those with contractual claims to be issued shares, creditors, and dismissed employees did have and continue to have other legal means of seeking redress.

72   (1983), 43 O.R. (2d) 128 at 137 (C.A.) [*Ferguson*].

73   Regarding the purpose of the *CBCA*, above note 19, in general see above section 4, and regarding the oppression remedy, in particular, see Dickerson, above note 2. The leading authority for a broad interpretation of the oppression provisions is *Ferguson, ibid.*, cited in *Deluce*, above note 20; *Mason* v. *Intercity Properties Ltd.* (1987), 59 O.R. (2d) 631 at 635–36 (C.A.) [*Mason*]. See also *Stech* v. *Davies*, (1987), 80 A.R. 298 (Q.B.) [*Stech*]; *First Edmonton*, above note 44 at 140 (Q.B.).

74   *Westfair Foods Ltd.* v. *Watt* (1991), 115 A.R. 34 (C.A.), leave to appeal refused, [1992] 1 W.W.R. lxv (note) (S.C.C.) [*Westfair*].

75   (1991), 3 B.L.R. (2d) 113 at 185–86 (Ont. Div. Ct.) [*820099*]; cited in *Deluce*, above note 20; *Beazer* v. *Hodgson Robertson Laing Ltd.* (1993), 12 B.L.R. (2d) 101 (Ont. Gen. Div.); *M.* v. *H.* above note 42; *Sexsmith* v. *Intek*, [1993] O.J. No. 711 (Gen. Div.) (QL) [*Sexsmith*]. This approach derives from the decision of the House of Lords in *Ebrahimi* v. *Westbourne Galleries Ltd.* (1972), [1973] A.C. 360 (H.L.) [*Ebrahimi*].

Shareholder interests would appear to be intertwined with shareholder expectations. It does not appear to me that the shareholder expectations which are to be considered are those that a shareholder has as his own individual "wish list." They must be expectations which could be said to have been (or ought to have been considered as) part of the compact of the shareholders. Expectations were discussed in B. Welling, *Corporate Law in Canada: The Governing Principles* (Toronto: Butterworths, 1984), pp. 533 and 535:

> "Thwarted shareholder expectation is what the oppression remedy is all about. Each shareholder buys his [or her] shares with certain expectations. Some of these are outlandish. But some of them, particularly in a small corporation with few shareholders, are quite reasonable expectations in the circumstances."

In *Westfair Foods Ltd.* v. *Watt*, the Alberta Court of Appeal endorsed this approach, adding that the reasonable expectations of shareholders relevant to a determination of oppression should not be limited to those existing when the relationship first arose.[76]

ii) The Statutory Language

The oppression remedy is available on proof of an act or omission in respect of a corporation that is "oppressive or unfairly prejudicial to or that unfairly disregards the interests of any security holder, creditor, director or officer." Some courts have defined these three characterizations as establishing different standards.

The classic statement of the meaning of "oppression" comes from the House of Lords' decision in *Scottish Co-operative Wholesale Society Ltd.* v. *Meyer:*

> [The society] had the majority power and . . . [it] exercised . . . [its] authority in a manner "burdensome, harsh and wrongful" — I take the dictionary meaning of the word. [Per Viscount Simonds.]

and

> Oppression under section 210 may take various forms. It suggests, to my mind . . . a lack of probity and fair dealing in the affairs of a company to the prejudice of some portion of its members. [Per Lord Keith of Avonholm.][77]

---

76 Above note 74.
77 (1958), [1959] A.C. 324 at 342 & 363–64 (H.L.) [*Meyer*].

This construction, requiring a finding of bad faith, has been adopted in numerous Canadian decisions.[78] One commentator, however, has suggested that many courts have inferred bad faith from what was perceived as an unfair result.[79]

Ferguson has suggested the following general description of the kind of conduct which is likely to be found oppressive:

> . . . something amounting to a direct or indirect expropriation, or substantial diminishment, of the value of the complainant's investment in the corporation in question. Frequently the conduct of the respondent involves an abuse of position, where the individual moves arbitrarily outside the recognized structure of corporate decision making.[80]

The courts have determined that "unfairly prejudicial" and "unfairly disregards" create a somewhat lesser standard. In particular, it is now clear, based on the Ontario Court of Appeal's decision in *Brant Investments Ltd.* v. *KeepRite Inc.*,[81] that a finding of bad faith is not required, though, of course, such a finding would be highly probative.[82] Indeed, the court in *Brant Investments Ltd.* v. *KeepRite Inc.* went so far as to say that "there will be few cases where there has not been some 'want of probity' on the part of the corporate actor where a remedy pursuant to s. 234 [now 241] will be appropriate." Several courts have expressed the view that by referring to *unfairly* prejudicial and *unfairly* disregards, Parliament was expressing an intention to permit some prejudice or some disregarding.[83] Otherwise, however, the courts have given us only general statements about the meaning of these terms. For example, in *Stech* v. *Davies* the court offered the following: ". . . unjustly or without cause . . . pay no attention to, ignore or treat as of no importance . . ."[84]

In *Westfair Foods Ltd.* v. *Watt*,[85] the Alberta Court of Appeal rejected the idea that the different terms used to define the oppression standard

---

78   *Bank of Montreal v. Dome Petroleum Ltd.* (1987), 54 Alta. L.R. (2d) 289 (Q.B.) [*Dome*]; *Brant*, above note 35 at 303 (C.A.); *Tesari*, note 42. On the meaning of bad faith, see, generally, J.G. MacIntosh, "Bad Faith and the Oppression Remedy: Uneasy Marriage or Amicable Divorce?" (1990) 69 Can. Bar. Rev. 276.

79   MacIntosh, *ibid.*, at 297.

80   K.A. Ferguson, *The Oppression Remedy: Trends Anyone?* (Edmonton: Legal Education Society of Alberta, 1992) at 461.

81   Above note 35.

82   *Ibid.* at 311 (Ont. C.A.); *Tesari*, above note 42.

83   *Brant*, above note 35 at 761 (H.C.J.). See also cases cited by D.H. Peterson, *Shareholder Remedies in Canada* (Toronto: Butterworths, 1989) at para. 18.60.

84   Above note 73 at 302.

85   Above note 74 at 38.

could sensibly be given distinctive, operationally useful meanings, favouring instead a general fairness standard:

> I cannot put elastic adjectives like "unfair", "oppressive" or "prejudicial" into watertight compartments. In my view, this repetition of overlapping ideas is only an expression of anxiety by Parliament that one or the other might be given a restrictive meaning. . . . Recent changes adding words like "unfairly disregard" reflect just that concern . . . [I]n Peterson, *Shareholder Remedies in Canada*, (Butterworths, 1989), paragraph 18.60, the author contends that "unfairly disregards" implies that *some* "disregarding" is fair! I reject that kind of parsing. The original words, like the new additions, command the courts to exercise their duty "broadly and liberally" . . . the words charge the courts to impose the obligation of fairness on the parties, I must admit that the admonition offers little guidance to the public, and Parliament has left elucidation to us.

Kerans J.A. went on to say that he did not understand that the delegation of this duty permits a judge to impose personal standards of fairness. The standard must be based on values that have gained wide acceptance as "principles adopted in precedent." Kerans J.A. identified the determination of fairness based on the reasonable expectations of the parties considering all their "words and deeds" as a principle running through all the cases on oppression.

The approach taken by Kerans J.A. would seem to be the most appropriate. While there may be some kinds of conduct where relief may be claimed because they are oppressive, all such conduct is likely to meet the standard of "unfairly prejudicial" or "unfairly disregards." This was the view of the drafters of the *CBCA*.[86] Accordingly, in every case one must consider the legal rights and reasonable expectations of the applicant for relief from oppression and the extent to which they have been affected. The following sections identify some of the other principles the courts have developed in considering claims for relief from oppression.

iii) Indicia of Oppressive Conduct

Although the highly fact-specific nature of the oppression remedy precludes anything like an exhaustive list of the factors suggesting oppression, Mr. Justice Austin in *Arthur v. Signum Communications Ltd.* set out the following helpful catalogue:

---

86 Dickerson, above note 2 at 162–63.

- lack of a valid corporate purpose for the transaction;
- failure on the part of the corporation and its controlling shareholders to take reasonable steps to simulate an arm's-length transaction;
- lack of good faith on the part of the directors of the corporation;
- discrimination among shareholders, with the effect of benefiting the majority shareholder to the exclusion or the detriment of minority shareholders;
- lack of adequate and appropriate disclosure of material information to minority shareholders; and
- a plan or design to eliminate a minority shareholder.[87]

This listing has been cited with approval in several recent cases.[88]

iv) Personal and Derivative Claims

As mentioned above in *Farnham* v. *Fingold*,[89] the Ontario Court of Appeal held that where an injury was an injury to the corporation, and any injury to the shareholder was only incidental to the corporate injury, such as where a breach of fiduciary duty was alleged, relief could be claimed only by the corporation itself or by a shareholder, with leave of the court, by way of a derivative action. In *Farnham,* the Court of Appeal dismissed the plaintiff's action to the extent that it was derivative in nature.

This position has subsequently been rejected by many courts considering claims for relief from oppression, citing the broad scope of the statutory language creating the oppression standard.[90] One of these cases expressly distinguished *Farnham* on the basis that it was decided with regard to the Ontario corporate statute before the introduction of the oppression remedy.[91]

A contrary view was taken in one recent case, *Pappas* v. *Acan Windows Inc.*[92] The court determined that where an applicant sought derivative and personal relief, including personal relief by way of the oppression remedy, and leave of the court had not been obtained to commence

---

87 (1991), 2 C.P.C. (3d) 74 (Ont. Gen. Div.), aff'd [1993] O.J. No. 1928 (Div. Ct.) (QL).
88 For example, *Millar* v. *McNally* (1991), 3 B.L.R. (2d) 102 (Ont. Gen. Div.); [*Millar*]; *M.* v. *H.* above note 42.
89 [1973] 2 O.R. 132 (C.A.).
90 For example, *Deluce*, above note 20; *McLaughlin*, above note 34; *Javelin*, above note 53; *Jackman* v. *Jackets Enterprises Ltd.* (1977), 2 B.L.R. 335 (B.C.S.C.) [*Jackman*]; *Peterson* v. *Kanata Investments Ltd.* (1975), 60 D.L.R. (3d) 527 (B.C.S.C.) [*Kanata*]; *Diligenti* v. *RWMD Operations Kelowna Ltd.* (1976), 1 B.C.L.R. 36 (S.C.). See generally J.G. MacIntosh, "The Oppression Remedy: Personal or Derivative?" (1991) 70 Can. Bar Rev. 29.
91 *McLaughlin*, *ibid.*
92 Above note 15.

a derivative action, the court had to exercise a discretion whether to permit the claim for personal relief to proceed. The court stated that a claim for personal relief should not be premitted to proceed if the claim overall was "so saturated by derivative claims that it cannot be allowed to stand."[93] The court examined each of the applicant's claims, permitting some to proceed but not others. In reaching its conclusion, the court engaged in an extensive case law analysis and concluded that oppression does not arise where the only injury to an applicant is incidental to an injury to the corporation. In the court's view, this conclusion was necessary if the other provisions of the corporate statute, including, in particular, the derivative action provisions, were to have any rationale.[94]

This case seems inconsistent with the clear weight of authority permitting shareholders to claim relief from oppression arising from an injury to the corporation cited above. It also seems inconsistent with the cases referred to above, holding that in some circumstances the corporation may be a proper person to be a complainant.[95] If the allegedly oppressive behaviour falls within the prohibition in the statute, an application should be permitted to proceed.

A related point that the courts have addressed is the relevance of a director's fiduciary duty to a finding of oppression. In this regard it has been held that the fiduciary standard may inform what constitutes oppression, but compliance with fiduciary duty's requirement for good faith does not mean that no oppression may be found.[96]

v) What Interests Are Protected?

Section 241 identifies the interests that may not be oppressed as those of "any security holder, creditor, director or officer." A preliminary point addressed by the courts is whether the interests alleged to be oppressed must be those of the complainant. In *Re Abraham and Inter Wide Investments Ltd.*,[97] Griffiths J. expressed the following view:

---

93 *Ibid.* at 155.

94 *Ibid.* See also *Pak Mail Centers of America v. Flash Pack Ltd.*, [1993] O.J. No. 2367 (Gen. Div.) (QL), where it was held that a minority shareholder could not claim oppression based on an agreement transferring certain intellectual property rights from the corporation to a third party. The court indicated that in its view the oppression remedy was primarily designed to fight oppression by other shareholders. The court cited *Olympia & York Enterprises Ltd. v. Hiram Walker Resources Ltd.* (1986), 59 O.R. (2d) 254 (Div. Ct.) in support of this proposition.

95 See above, section D(4)(c)(iii).

96 *Deluce*, above note 20 at 310; *820099*, above note 75 at 178. In *Kredl*, above note 63, it was held that a breach of fiduciary duty constituted oppression (at 462).

97 (1985), 51 O.R. (2d) 460 at 468 (H.C.J.).

"Essential to the right to relief is the requirement that the company or directors in carrying out the company's business or exercising the powers of the directors have been guilty of conduct oppressive or unfairly prejudicial or that unfairly disregards the interests of the *complainant*."[98] [Emphasis added.] This requirement was satisfied on the facts before Griffiths J. Though one may be attracted by the requirement that a complainant have a personal stake in the oppression alleged, Welling has pointed out that such a requirement is not part of the statutory scheme.[99] This interpretation has been confirmed recently in *Themadel Foundation* v. *Third Canadian Trust Ltd.*[100]

A related point was raised in *Csak* v. *Aumon*,[101] in which it was alleged that even if a person with a contractual claim to be issued a share was entitled to complainant status as a "beneficial owner" of a security under section 238(a), such a person did not have an interest as a "security holder" which was protected under section 241(2), since that section refers only to "security holder," not "beneficial owner." Lane J. rejected this argument, holding, in effect, that if a person was entitled to complainant status under section 238(a), her interests were deserving of protection under section 241.

A further point of interpretation was addressed in *PMSM Investments Ltd.* v. *Bureau.*[102] In that case the court held that although a shareholder of an affiliate had status as a complainant, it could only claim relief from oppression of its interest as a "security holder, creditor, director or officer" of the corporation, not its interest in the affiliate.

Some cases have held that the interests of a security holder must be presently oppressed and that neither anticipated oppression nor past oppression entitles relief under the *CBCA*.[103] Under the *CBCA*, the language of section 239 does not expressly contemplate future acts or omissions. In *First Edmonton Place* v. *315888 Alberta Ltd.*,[104] it was held that the interests of a lessor to whom no rent was owed at the time of the allegedly oppressive act could not be oppressed. In that case, the alleged oppressive act was the distribution by the corporation to its

---

98   See also *Stone* v. *Stonehurst Enterprises Ltd.* (1987), 80 N.B.R. (2d) 290 at 305 (Q.B.).

99   Above note 20 at 555, n. 307.

100   (1995), 23 O.R. (3d) 7 at 24 (Gen. Div.); *PMSM*, above note 33.

101   Above note 36.

102   Above note 33.

103   *Dome*, above note 78; *Michalak*, above note 34 at 9–11; *Goldbelt Mines (N.P.L.)* v. *New Beginnings Resources Inc.* (1984), 28 B.L.R. 130 (B.C.C.A.). A contrary view was expressed in *McLaughlin*, above note 34 at 449. The *BCCA* (above note 21, s. 224) and the *OBCA* (above note 21, s. 248) expressly contemplate threatened behaviour.

104   Above note 44.

shareholders of a cash advance the landlord had made to the corporation. At the time of the distribution, no rent was owed to the landlord.

vi) Actions against Shareholders

Because section 241 refers to oppressive acts by affiliates of the corporation, it apparently contemplates that relief may be obtained against corporations that control, are controlled by, or are under common control with the corporation in which the shareholder has his interest.[105] The obvious implication is that oppression by non-corporate shareholders and corporate shareholders other than affiliates is not caught. In at least one case, claims against non-affiliated shareholders have failed.[106] Nevertheless, in other cases courts have not been careful to distinguish between oppression inflicted by the corporation or the shareholders.[107] Ultimately, this conflict may reduce to a matter of pleading in cases where the actions of the corporation or its directors or officers are somehow implicated in the action by the shareholder. Under section 241, it is clear that once a finding of oppression is made an order may be made against a shareholder.

vii) Oppression and Shareholders' Agreements

A number of cases have considered whether actions under the provisions of shareholders' agreements may be oppressive. Several cases have held that a breach of a shareholders' agreement may be oppressive.[108] Compliance with the strict terms of a shareholders' agreement, however, does not guarantee that no oppression has taken place. In *Deluce Holdings Ltd.* v. *Air Canada*[109] it was held that even the exercise of a share purchase option in strict compliance with the terms of a shareholders' agreement might be oppressive where it was part of a larger strategy to get rid of a minority shareholder without regard to the best interests of the corporation. Nevertheless, the courts have generally been unwilling

---

105   See definitions of "affiliate" and "affiliated body corporate" in sections 2(1) and 2(2) of the *CBCA*, above note 19. In *Deluce* (above note 20) the actions of Air Canada as an affiliate of the corporation and the actions of its nominee directors were found to be oppressive. This case is discussed below, notes 109 to 114, and accompanying text.

106   *Ruffo* v. *IPCBC Contractors Canada Inc.* (1988), 33 B.C.L.R. (2d) 74 (S.C.), aff'd (1990), 44 B.C.L.R. (2d) 293 (C.A.).

107   For example, *Ferguson*, above note 72. This approach was also followed in *Meyer*, above note 77.

108   For example, *Lyall* v. *147250 Canada Ltd.* (1993), 106 D.L.R. (4th) 304 (B.C.C.A.).

109   Above note 20.

to find oppression where the alleged act of oppression is pursuant to a right accorded by the applicant to the alleged oppressor in a contract, such as the right to buy the applicant out.[110]

An interesting related issue that has arisen in some cases is whether it is appropriate to provide a remedy where the matter in dispute is governed by the terms of a shareholders' agreement. In *Beazer* v. *Hodgson Robertson Laing Ltd.*,[111] an application for an order directing the purchase of shares was denied on the ground that the parties had addressed share purchases, in the circumstances that had arisen, in their shareholders' agreement.[112]

In *Deluce Holdings Ltd.* v. *Air Canada*, mentioned above, Air Canada argued that an application for relief from oppression was precluded by the shareholders' agreement, which required arbitration if the parties could not agree on the valuation of the shares to be purchased. In accordance with the provisions of the *Arbitrations Act*,[113] an application relating to a matter the parties agreed to submit to arbitration must be stayed. The court determined that the real subject matter of the oppression action was not the share valuation that the parties had agreed to submit to arbitration, but other acts of oppression, so that the *Arbitrations Act* did not bar the application.

Interestingly, the court suggested that if there had been a term providing for a general resort to arbitration, the result might have been different.[114] This suggestion would seem to indicate a planning opportunity for drafting shareholder agreements. It may be possible to minimize the uncertainties associated with potential oppression applications by providing that all disputes between shareholders be submitted to arbitration.

6) Remedies

a) Introduction
One of the most innovative features of the oppression remedy provisions is the unlimited flexibility granted to the court to fashion remedies. Under section 241(2) the court is generally empowered to make an

---

110   For example, *Camroux* v. *Armstrong* (1990), 47 B.L.R. 302 (B.C.S.C.). In *obiter* the court suggested an alternative rationale for refusing to provide relief: even if the shareholders' agreement had been breached, "a breach of private arrangement outside the carrying on of the company's affairs cannot be oppressive conduct of the company's affairs" (at 308).

111   Above note 75.

112   See also *Korogonas* v. *Andrew (No. 1)* (1992), 128 A.R. 381 at 388 (Q.B.).

113   R.S.O. 1990, c. A.24, s. 7.

114   *Deluce*, above note 20 at 150–51.

order "to rectify the matters complained of." In section 241(3) the breadth of this grant of remedial power is confirmed: the court may make "any interim or final order it thinks fit." There follows a lengthy shopping list of orders a court may consider which overlap virtually all the other remedial provisions in the *CBCA*[115] as if to encourage courts to exercise their remedial powers.[116]

Courts have shown their willingness to use their broader remedial powers to tailor the remedy to the nature of the oppressive act or omission found.[117] Given the fact-specific nature of oppression actions, it is difficult to articulate a principled basis for determining how remedies may be tailored to address precisely the seriousness of the oppression. Some examples of remedies employed, however, may be instructive.

b) Share Purchase

By far the most common remedy requested in oppression actions is the purchase by a corporation or a majority shareholder of the applicant's shares.[118] This remedy has been found to be appropriate where the parties have lost confidence in each other and their relationship has become unworkable.[119] A share purchase may not be appropriate if neither the corporation nor the controlling shareholders are in a financial position to purchase the applicant's shares. In such circumstances, where the parties' relationship has completely broken down, liquidation and dissolution may be appropriate.[120] A share purchase was held not to be appropriate where the oppression consisted of a failure to comply with various obligations under the *BCCA*, such as the requirements to appoint auditors and to hold annual meetings. The court determined that an order to comply with the *BCCA* would be sufficient.[121] Various

---

115 Above note 19. For example, compliance and restraining orders under section 247 are contemplated in section 241(3)(a); investigations under Part XIX are contemplated in section 241(3)(m); liquidation and dissolution, which is available under Part XVIII, are permitted under section 241(3)(l); the purchase by a corporation of a shareholder's shares, which is addressed in section 190, is contemplated in section 241(3)(f).

116 Welling characterizes these provisions as a "striking example of legislative overkill," above note 20 at 563.

117 The need to tailor the remedy granted to the seriousness of the oppressive act was expressly recognized in *Jackman*, above note 90, as well as in *Tropxe*, above note 61.

118 For example, *Loveridge Holdings Ltd. v. King-Pin Ltd.* (1991), 5 B.L.R. (2d) 195 (Ont. Gen. Div.)[*Loveridge*]; *Millar*, above note 88; *Mason*, above note 73.

119 *Redekop v. Robco Construction Ltd.* (1978), 5 B.L.R. 58 (B.C.S.C.).

120 *Millar*, above note 88.

121 *Jackman*, above note 90.

valuation issues that arise in the context of such buy-outs have been the subject of extensive judicial consideration.[122]

c) Liquidation and Dissolution

As noted above, where the parties' relationship has completely broken down, liquidation and dissolution of the corporation may be the only remedy. The courts have shown great reluctance to use this remedy.[123] Indeed, the courts have acknowledged that one of the reasons the flexible remedial regime in section 241 was introduced was to permit relief to be provided without winding up the corporation.[124] In one case, dissolution was ordered subject to a thirty-day stay to permit the parties to find a less disruptive solution.[125] Dissolution may also be sought by application under section 214 of the *CBCA*. Such applications are considered at the end of this chapter under the heading "Termination of the Corporation — Winding Up."

d) Remedies against Shareholders

As indicated above under the heading "Discretionary Complainants," the courts have been willing to grant remedies for oppression directly against shareholders at the instance of creditors where the shareholder has participated in rendering the corporation unable to satisfy the creditor's claim, though one judge called this a "drastic remedy."[126] Courts have also ordered other sorts of remedies against shareholders, including share buy-backs.[127]

e) Compliance

In several cases, where there was a failure to prepare and distribute annual financial statements, hold annual meetings, or act in some other way required by the governing corporate statute, all of which effectively excluded a shareholder from a corporation, compliance with the statute was ordered.[128] Compliance orders may also be obtained by application

---

122   *Brant*, above note 35, is one of the leading cases on the principles appropriate to valuation. Regarding valuation generally, see section H below, "Corporate Purchase of Shares of Dissenting Shareholder."

123   For example, *Loveridge*, above note 118; *Rivers v. Denton* (1992), 5 B.L.R. (2d) 212 (Ont. Gen. Div.) [*Rivers*].

124   *Rivers, ibid.* at 203. See also *Mason*, above note 73.

125   *Rivers, ibid.*

126   *Tropxe*, above note 61.

127   *Loveridge*, above note 118; *Lajoie v. Lajoie Brothers Contracting Ltd.* (1989), 45 B.L.R. 113 (Ont. H.C.J.).

128   For example, *Millar*, above note 88; *Jackman*, above note 90. In *Sexsmith*, above note 75, however, the court refused to make an order under the oppression provisions to direct compliance with the *OBCA*, above note 21, where the irregularities were not accompanied by financial loss.

under section 247 of the *CBCA*. Such applications are discussed under "Compliance and Restraining Orders" below.

f) Other

Courts have made a bewildering variety of other kinds of orders to address the particular acts or omission constituting oppression in individual cases, including orders directing the amendment of by-laws and the replacement of management,[129] the appointment of receivers,[130] the amendment of shareholder agreements,[131] and the creation of a preemptive right.[132]

7) Summary

The foregoing survey has attempted to sketch some of the evolving contours of the oppression remedy through a discussion of recent cases in which the courts have considered claims for relief from oppression. It is by no means exhaustive. It was not possible to catalogue fully the avalanche of cases decided in the last several years, nor to address all issues relating to the application of the oppression remedy.

Nevertheless, this survey was intended to demonstrate two aspects of the revolutionary change being wrought by the application of the oppression remedy. First, the enactment of the oppression remedy has successfully convinced judges to shake off the restrictions imposed on the remedies available to minority shareholders under Canadian corporate law regimes before the *CBCA* and its provincial progeny. This was one of the express intentions of the Dickerson Committee in drafting the *CBCA*.[133] Indeed, the range of circumstances in which courts have provided relief and the enormous variety in remedies ordered threatens to displace other remedial routes, such as the derivative action, compliance, and liquidation and dissolution. This trend has implications for both corporate lawyers and litigators.

Second, the scope of the remedy is potentially exceedingly broad and, while the proliferation of cases is steadily clarifying how the oppression remedy will work, there are still many issues remaining to be resolved. Unfortunately these issues, such as when relief can be claimed for injuries to the corporation, when relief can be claimed

---

129   *Trnkoczy*, above note 42.
130   *Kanata*, above note 90.
131   *Tesari*, above note 42.
132   *Mazzotta v. Twin Gold Mines Ltd.* (1987), 37 B.L.R. 218 (Ont. H.C.J.).
133   Dickerson, above note 2 at 153.

against a shareholder, when a creditor qualifies as a complainant as well as various procedural issues, are unlikely to be resolved until more cases get to the courts of appeal.

E. COMPLIANCE AND RESTRAINING ORDERS

The *CBCA* and most other modern corporate statutes[134] allow a complainant or a creditor to apply for a court order requiring compliance with or restraining a breach of the Act, the regulations, the corporation's articles or by-laws, or a unanimous shareholder agreement (*CBCA*, s. 247). Such an order may be made against the corporation itself as well as against any director, officer, employee, agent, auditor, trustee, receiver, receiver-manager, or liquidator of a corporation. Although, as noted above, a compliance order could be a remedy in an oppression action, the chief benefit of the compliance action is that it provides a summary procedure to deal with discrete problems of non-compliance. It has been used, for example, to require a corporation to act on the statutory rights of a dissenting shareholder to have his shares bought out.[135] The compliance remedy cannot be used, however, if making a finding of non-compliance requires a determination of complex issues of fact or law, such as a claim that there has been a breach of fiduciary duty.[136]

The compliance remedy is noteworthy in several respects. First, creditors have a right to make an application, unlike the derivative action and oppression remedies where they can make an application only with permission of the court. Also, the compliance remedy extends to a very wide range of people, much wider than any other remedy under the *CBCA*. Finally, as noted in chapter 7, it is possible to use this remedy to enforce compliance with a unanimous shareholder agreement.

F. RECTIFICATION OF CORPORATE RECORDS

Where a person's name has been wrongly entered or retained in the shareholder registers or other records of a corporation, a security holder or any other aggrieved person may apply to a court to have any register

---

134   *ABCA*, above note 21, s. 240; *BCCA*, above note 21, s. 25; *MCA*, above note 21, s. 240; *NBBCA*, above note 21, s. 172; *NCA*, above note 21, s. 373; *OBCA*, above note 21, s. 252; *SBCA*, above note 21, s. 240.

135   *Skye Resources Ltd. v. Camskye Holdings Inc.*(1982), 38 O.R. (2d) 253 (H.C.J.). See also *Goldhar v. D'Aragon Mines Ltd.* (1977), 15 O.R. (2d) 80 (H.C.J.).

136   *Goldhar v. Quebec Manitou Mines Ltd.* (1975), 9 O.R. (2d) 740 (Div. Ct.).

or record rectified (*CBCA*, s. 243).[137] Because the records of the corporation may be used to identify who should be given notice of meetings or receive dividends, the court may also restrain the calling or holding of any meeting or the payment of any dividend until the register or record is rectified to ensure that any wrongfully excluded shareholder may participate (*CBCA*, s. 243(3)).

In addition to ensuring that notices of meetings and dividends are sent to the correct persons, the right to obtain the rectification of records on an expeditious summary basis is important because corporate registers and other records are, in the absence of evidence to the contrary, proof of what they disclose (*CBCA*, s. 257).

G. INVESTIGATIONS

Part XIX of the *CBCA* sets out a comprehensive scheme under which investigations may be carried out into the business and affairs of a corporation or any of its affiliates. A court may order an investigation on the application of a security holder or the Director where it appears to the court that any of the following grounds has been made out:

- the business of the corporation or any of its affiliates is or has been carried on with intent to defraud any person;
- the business or affairs of the corporation or any of its affiliates are or have been carried on or conducted, or the powers of the directors are or have been exercised, in a manner that is oppressive or unfairly prejudicial to or that unfairly disregards the interests of a security holder;
- the corporation or any of its affiliates was formed for a fraudulent or unlawful purpose; or
- persons concerned with the formation, business, or affairs of the corporation or any of its affiliates have in connection therewith acted fraudulently or dishonestly.[138]

---

137   *ABCA*, above note 21, s. 246; *BCCA*, above note 21, s. 68; *MCA*, above note 21, s. 236; *NBBCA*, above note 21, s. 168; *NCA*, above note 21, s. 349; *OBCA*, above note 21, s. 249; *SBCA*, above note 21, s. 236.

138   Other statutes also provide investigation rights: *ABCA, ibid.*, s. 223; *BCCA, ibid.*, s. 233; *MCA, ibid.*, s. 222; *NBBCA, ibid.*, s. 155; *NCA, ibid.*, s. 354; *NSCA, ibid.*, s. 115, *OBCA, ibid.*, s. 160; *Quebec Companies Act*, R.S.Q. 1977, c. C-38, s. 110; *SBCA, ibid.*, s. 160.

H. CORPORATE PURCHASE OF SHARES OF DISSENTING SHAREHOLDER

The *CBCA* and the statutes modelled after it provide that shareholders who dissent in relation to a shareholder vote on certain matters of fundamental importance to the corporation may require the corporation to buy their shares.[139] Shareholder votes on the following fundamental changes trigger this right, which is referred to as the shareholder's dissent and appraisal right:

- amendment to the corporation's articles to add, change, or remove any provision restricting or constraining the issue, transfer, or ownership of shares of the class held by the dissenter or to add, change, or remove any restriction on the business or businesses that the corporation may carry on;
- amalgamation with other corporations;[140]
- continuation of the corporation under the laws of another jurisdiction, with the result that the corporation becomes governed under a corporate statute other than the *CBCA*; or
- the sale, lease, or exchange of all or substantially all of the corporation's property other than in the ordinary course of business (*CBCA*, s. 190(1)).

Also, the holder of any shares entitled to vote separately as a class on any matter has dissent and appraisal rights in relation to that vote (*CBCA*, ss. 176 & 190(2)).

All these triggering events are fundamental changes to the nature of a shareholder's investment. Since they will affect significantly the risk and return characteristics of the shares, the shareholder is given an exit right if he does not agree with the change. At the same time, the majority is not prevented from changing the corporation to respond to changing circumstances. The existence of the right, however, also indirectly gives minority shareholders enhanced power to determine whether the corporation goes ahead with one of these fundamental changes. If many shareholders will dissent, the resulting purchase obligation may require a substantial expenditure for the corporation. With this in mind, management may decide not to put a fundamental change to a shareholder

---

139   *CBCA*, above note 19, s. 190; *ABCA*, *ibid.*, s. 184; *BCCA*, *ibid.*, s. 231; *MCA*, *ibid.*, s. 189; *SBCA*, *ibid.*, s. 184; *NBBCA*, *ibid.*, s. 131; *OBCA*, *ibid.*, s. 184; *NCA*, *ibid.*, ss. 300–1.

140   So called "short form" amalgamations between corporations under common ownership. These are discussed in chapter 10.

vote, even in circumstances where it knows there will be sufficient votes to pass the special resolution approving it. As a result, minority share-holders may have more leverage to prevent fundamental changes than their votes would indicate.

Although some issues arise in connection with the rather cumber-some procedure for the exercise of dissent and appraisal rights provided for in the corporate legislation, the most significant issue relating to the exercise of dissent and appraisal rights is the price at which the corpora-tion buys the dissenting shareholders' shares. The corporation's obliga-tion is to purchase the shares of dissenting shareholders for "fair value." Although it is beyond the scope of this book to present an analysis of the determinants of fair value, some general comments may be made.[141]

The basic approach to calculating fair value is to determine the value of all the shares of the corporation, then allocate to the dissenting shareholder her *pro rata* share of that value. The significance of this approach is that it values minority shareholder interests on the same basis as majority holdings. Because of the operation of shareholder democracy, it is usually possible to obtain a higher price per share for a block of shares that represents control of the corporation, whether this is defined as the power to elect the majority of the board of directors or otherwise. The higher incremental value of a control block is referred to as a "premium for control," and the corresponding reduction in value attributed to minority holdings is called a "minority discount." In some early cases it had been held that a minority discount should be applied to determine the fair value of dissenters' shares. In *Brant Investments Ltd. v. KeepRite Inc.*,[142] the Ontario Court of Appeal authoritatively deter-mined that this was not the correct approach, at least in Ontario.

In the same case, the Court of Appeal identified four widely accepted methods for valuing all the shares of the corporation:

- Market Value: The value determined by reference to the price at which shares trade on some market — for example, the Toronto Stock Exchange.
- Asset Value: The value of the assets of the corporation, either on a going concern basis or as though the corporation's assets were being sold as part of a liquidation.
- Earnings Value: Some maintainable level of earnings is established (such as the average over the last five years) and the value of the

---

141   See V. Krishna, "Determining the 'Fair Value' of Corporate Shares" (1988) 13 Can. Bus. L.J. 132.

142   Above note 35 (Ont. C.A.).

corporation is calculated as the value today of those earnings received by the corporation in an indefinite number of future years.

- Combination Method: The fourth method is simply to determine value based on the consideration of the value generated by the other three methods. A common way of doing so is to assign a weight to the value generated by each method and to calculate the average.

The Canadian courts have used each of these methods and have stated that no rigid rule can be adopted about which method is appropriate. In each case, the choice of method will depend on the facts of the case, including, in particular, the nature of the corporation's business and its share holdings. For example, where a corporation's shares are widely held and actively traded, the best method may be to take the market value.[143] On the other hand, the market value approach will not be appropriate where the trading is thin and dominated by a controlling shareholder.[144] Where a corporation has sold most of its assets and ceases to carry on an operating business, the value of the corporation will be best determined by the value of its assets as if they were sold on a liquidation.[145] If the business will continue to be carried on, it may be more appropriate to value the assets on a going concern basis or to use the earnings value. Finally, where a corporation's sole asset is a large land holding with little income flow, it will not be appropriate to determine fair value based on earnings.[146]

There are some additional general rules about valuation. Valuations must be conducted as of particular date with reference only to the facts as they were known at that time.[147] The valuation date for fair value determinations is as of the close of business on the day before the resolution from which the shareholder dissents is adopted (*CBCA*, s. 190(3)). The purpose of this provision is to ensure that the effect of the change dissented from is not taken into account in determining fair value.[148] Also, dissenting shareholders are not entitled to a special premium just because they are dissenting.[149] Some early cases had held that dissenters

---

143   *Montgomery v. Shell Canada Ltd.* (1980), 3 Sask. R. 19 (Q.B.). Note that market prices incorporate an inherent minority discount, since the market price is the price at which minority interests trade in the market.

144   *Manning v. Harris Steel Group Inc.* (1986), 7 B.C.L.R. (2d) 69 (S.C.).

145   *Kelvin Energy Ltd. v. Bahan* (1987), 79 A.R. 259 (Q.B.).

146   *LoCicero v. B.A.C.M. Industries Ltd.*, [1988] 1 S.C.R. 399 [*LoCicero*].

147   *New Quebec Raglan Mines Ltd. v. Blok-Andersen* (1991), 4 B.L.R. (2d) 71 (Ont. Gen. Div.).

148   *LoCicero*, above note 146; *Neonex International Ltd. v. Kolasa* (1978), 84 D.L.R. (3d) 446 (B.C.S.C.).

149   *Brant*, above note 35.

were in a position similar to that of people whose property is expropriated and so should receive additional compensation because of the involuntary nature of the sale of their shares.[150] The Ontario Court of Appeal in *Brant Investments Ltd.* v. *KeepRite Inc.* held that no such premium should be paid to dissenters as an element of fair value.[151]

I. TERMINATION OF THE CORPORATION: WINDING UP

One of the remedies that a court may grant on an application for relief from oppression is to terminate the corporation's existence, sometimes referred to as "winding up" the corporation. This involves selling off or liquidating all the assets of the corporation, using the proceeds to pay off all the corporation's liabilities, and paying out any surplus to the corporation's shareholders in accordance with the scheme for the distribution of assets on dissolution set out in the corporation's articles. Any shares with a preference on dissolution will be paid first, and any remaining surplus will be paid to the shares with a claim to the residual assets of the corporation on dissolution — typically, the common shares.

In addition to obtaining a winding-up order in an oppression action, the *CBCA* separately provides for an application for a winding up (*CBCA*, ss. 213 & 214). The process for obtaining a court order to wind up a corporation under these provisions is described in chapter 10 under the heading "Dissolution of the Corporation." In this chapter we briefly discuss the grounds for such an order.

The separate provisions relating to winding up restate, in a somewhat duplicative way, that winding up may be obtained if oppression, defined in the same way as in section 241, is found. Since winding up is the ultimate form of shareholder relief, it will not be granted in all cases of oppression. Consistent with the general approach developing in the courts of seeking to balance the remedy granted with the specific problem creating the oppression, it is to be expected that a court will only

---

150 For example, *Domglas Inc.* v. *Jarislowsky, Fraser & Co.* (1982), 138 D.L.R. (3d) 521 (Que. C.A.).

151 *Ibid.* A premium may be appropriate where shareholders are forced to sell as a result of a going-private transaction or the exercise of the statutory compulsory acquisition rights described in chapter 11. See *Investissements Mont-Soleil Inc.* v. *National Drug Ltd.*, [1982] C.S. 716 (Que. S.C.) (premium ordered on amalgamation squeeze out).

order winding up where the oppression is very serious. Resort to winding up in cases of oppression was discussed above.

The other general ground on which a court may order winding up is when "it is just and equitable that the corporation should be liquidated and dissolved" (*CBCA*, s. 214(b)(ii)). This was the primary ground on which the courts would order winding up prior to the creation of the oppression remedy. The courts have made it clear that the circumstances in which this requirement may be satisfied may not be defined exhaustively; each case must be judged based on its own facts. Nevertheless, several categories of cases may be identified.

First, courts have been willing to order winding up where it is no longer possible for the corporation to carry on the business for which it was created. Second, winding up has been ordered where the shareholder seeking winding up has a "justifiable lack of confidence" in the conduct of the management of the corporation.[152] Such a lack of confidence cannot consist only of a disagreement about the policies of the management. Rather, there must be some serious misbehaviour on the part of management. This would include not only fraud but also deliberate violations of corporate policy, such as failing to hold annual meetings and attempting to exclude shareholders from exercising their rights to participate in the corporation. Third, courts have ordered winding up where the corporation is, in effect, a partnership between two or more persons with more or less equal power in the corporation who have come to disagree fundamentally on how the business should be operated.[153] The courts have been particularly sympathetic where, because of the decision-making structure in place in the corporation, the disagreement has made it impossible for the corporation to act.[154] This situation is referred to in the cases as a "deadlock."

The purpose of the drafters of the *CBCA* in including the oppression ground in the winding-up section was to try to ensure that the courts would grant winding up in more liberal circumstances than they had under the "just and equitable" rule.[155] In some respects, however, precisely the opposite has occurred. Because of the flexibility under the oppression remedy to fashion remedies to address the oppressive behaviour, courts have been willing to order a winding up only as a last resort. Many of the cases in which winding up has been ordered have been in

---

152   *Loch v. John Blackwood Ltd.*, [1924] A.C. 783 at 788 (P.C.).
153   *Ebrahimi*, above note 75.
154   For example, *Re Yenidje Tobacco Co. Ltd.*, [1916] 2 Ch. 426 (C.A.).
155   Dickerson, above note 2 at 158–63.

one of the three categories mentioned above and where a less intrusive order will not work.[156]

J. CHAPTER SUMMARY

In this chapter we looked at the various ways in which shareholders may seek relief from actions by the corporation, management (including the directors), and other shareholders. Historically, the ability of shareholders to obtain relief in such circumstances was very limited, but now a variety of effective options are available.

In addition to attempting to sue personally where an individual shareholder right has been infringed, shareholders may seek leave of the court for injuries caused to the corporation resulting from the breach of duties owed by directors and officers to the corporation. Leave will be granted so long as the action appears to be in the interests of the corporation, the shareholder has given reasonable notice to the directors to permit them to decide whether they should cause the corporation to take action, and the shareholder is acting in good faith.

Perhaps the most significant enhancement in shareholder remedies is the oppression remedy. Shareholders may now claim relief in a wide range of circumstances where their interests have been oppressed or unfairly disregarded or prejudiced. The courts have interpreted their mandate to provide relief broadly and have sought to tailor remedies to the precise problem arising in each case. Though the case law is still developing, the oppression remedy seems to be changing corporate law in several significant ways. First, as courts grant complainant status to creditors of various kinds, the courts are changing the categories of stakeholders to whom management is directly responsible. As discussed in chapter 12, the courts have generally considered management's obligations to flow only to the corporation and, for the purpose of defining what the corporation's interests are, they have refused to consider interests of stakeholders other than shareholders. Second, it seems that, by

---

156   For example, *Re Cravo Equipment* (1982), 44 C.B.R. (N.S.) 208 (Ont. H.C.J.) (partnership-like relationship broken down, lack of confidence based on absence of good faith and improper conduct); *Re Alf's Roofing & Contracting Ltd.* (1985), 61 A.R. 16 (Q.B.) (irreconcilable differences between two equal shareholders); *Di Giacomo* v. *Di Giacomo Canada Inc.* (1989), 28 C.P.R. (3d) 77 (Ont. H.C.J.), additional reasons at (1990), 28 C.P.R. (3d) 447 (Ont. H.C.J.) (corporation had ceased operations and licence to use confidential trade secrets terminated). Other Canadian statutes also have winding-up remedies: *ABCA*, above note 21, s. 207; *BCCA*, above note 21, s. 224; *MCA*, above note 21, s. 207; *NBBCA*, above note 21, s. 143–45; *NCA*, above note 21, ss. 339 & 341; *OBCA*, above note 21, s. 206; *SBCA*, above note 21, s. 207.

beginning to impose remedies on shareholders, the courts are developing a kind of duty owed by shareholders to each other.

The *CBCA* and other modern corporate statutes provide various other remedies, including compliance orders, orders to rectify corporate records, investigations, dissent and appraisal remedies on the occurrence of fundamental changes to the corporation, and winding up of the corporation.

FURTHER READINGS

BECK, S.M., "Minority Shareholders' Rights in the 1980s" [1982] Spec. Lect. L.S.U.C. 311

BECK, S.M., "The Shareholders' Derivative Action" (1974) 52 Can. Bar Rev. 159

BUCKLEY, F., M. GILLEN, & R. YALDEN, *Corporations: Principles and Policies*, 3d ed. (Toronto: Emond Montgomery, 1995) at 700–96

CHEFFINS, B.A., "An Economic Analysis of the Oppression Remedy: Working Toward a More Coherent Picture of Corporate Law" (1990) 40 U.T. L. J. 775

KRISHNA, V., "Determining the 'Fair Value' of Corporate Shares" (1988) 13 Can. Bus. L.J. 132

MacINTOSH, J.G., "Bad Faith and the Oppression Remedy: Uneasy Marriage or Amicable Divorce?" (1990) 69 Can. Bar Rev. 276

MacINTOSH, J.G., "Minority Shareholder Rights in Canada and England, 1860–1987" (1988) 27 Osgoode Hall L.J. 1

MacINTOSH, J.G., "The Oppression Remedy: Personal or Derivative? (1991) 70 Can. Bar Rev. 29

MacINTOSH, J.G., "The Shareholders' Appraisal Right in Canada: A Critical Reappraisal" (1986) 24 Osgoode Hall L.J. 201

MacINTOSH, J.G., J. HOLMES, & S. THOMPSON, "The Puzzle of Shareholder Fiduciary Duties" (1991) 19 Can. Bus. L.J. 86

PETERSON, D.H., *Shareholder Remedies in Canada* (Toronto: Carswell, 1989) (looseleaf)

VANDUZER, J.A., "Who May Claim Relief from Oppression: The Complainant in Canadian Corporate Law" (1993) 25 Ottawa L. Rev. 463

WALDRON, M.A., "Corporate Theory and the Oppression Remedy" (1982) 6 Can. Bus. L.J. 129

ZIEGEL, J.S., et al., *Cases and Materials on Partnerships and Canadian Business Corporations*, 3d ed. (Toronto: Carswell, 1994) c. 12

CHAPTER 10

CORPORATE CHANGES

A. CHANGES IN CORPORATE CHARACTERISTICS

1) Introduction

After a corporation is incorporated, it may be necessary to change its characteristics for a variety of reasons. Perhaps a new class of shares must be created to meet the needs of a new investor, or the number of directors needs to be increased. Changing these characteristics involves amending the articles of the corporation, and in this chapter we discuss how this may be done. This chapter also sets out what is required to effect various other corporate changes, including adjustments to a corporation's stated capital, continuing the corporation under the laws of another jurisdiction, amalgamating the corporation with other corporations, selling substantially all the corporation's assets, and terminating the corporation's existence under the *CBCA*.

2) Amendment of Articles

The articles of the corporation must be amended to add, change, or remove any provision contained in the articles (*CBCA*, ss. 173–79). Specifically, amendment is required to do any of the following:

- change the corporate name;
- change the municipality or address of the corporation's registered office;

- add, change, or remove provisions relating to the classes of shares of the corporation;
- add, change, or remove any restriction on the issue, transfer, or ownership of shares;
- change the number or the minimum or maximum number of directors;
- add, change, or remove any restriction on the business the corporation may carry on or on the powers the corporation may exercise; or
- add any provision that might have been set out in articles or by-laws at incorporation but was not.

Subject to the exceptions described below, amendment of the articles requires approval by special resolution. As outlined in chapter 7, this is a resolution passed at a meeting of shareholders by a majority of not less than two-thirds of the votes cast at the meeting or consented to in writing by all shareholders. A level of approval higher than two-thirds may be specified in a shareholder agreement or in the corporation's articles. As with all shareholder meetings, notice of a meeting to consider a resolution to amend the articles must be sent to shareholders. The notice must state the nature of the proposed amendment in sufficient detail to permit shareholders to form a reasoned decision whether to vote for or against the amendment and must include the text of the special resolution on which the shareholders will be asked to vote (*CBCA*, s. 135(6)). In addition, if the corporation has more than fifteen shareholders, the management must send shareholders a form of proxy and a management proxy circular that provide further information (*CBCA*, s. 149(1)).[1] Shareholders may initiate amendments to articles themselves by making a shareholder proposal (*CBCA*, s. 182). These proposals were discussed in chapter 7.

At the meeting, only those shareholders who would otherwise be entitled to vote are permitted to do so. Any class or series of shares that is affected by the amendment in a manner set out in section 176 of the *CBCA* are entitled to vote separately as a class. Section 176 lists exhaustively the specific circumstances when such a separate vote is required. Essentially, a class or series is entitled to a separate vote whenever it will be more prejudicially affected by the adoption of the amendment than other classes or series. This might occur, for example, where an amendment would create a new class that would be entitled to receive dividends before any dividends were paid to an existing class. A separate

---

1   Under the Ontario *Business Corporations Act*, R.S.O. 1990, c. B.16 [*OBCA*], this obligation applies only to offering corporations (*OBCA*, s. 11).

vote is required even if the class or series of shares would not otherwise have the right to vote (*CBCA*, s. 176(5)). If a separate vote is required, the amendment is not passed unless it is approved by a special resolution of the class or series entitled to vote separately, in addition to any other required approval (*CBCA*, s. 176(6)).

If an amendment is approved by special resolution in circumstances where a class or series was entitled to vote separately, the shareholders of that class or series who voted against the amendment are entitled to have the corporation buy them out for fair value. This so-called "dissent and appraisal right" is also available to *all* shareholders who vote against an amendment to add, change, or remove any provision restricting the issue, transfer, or ownership of shares of the class held by them or restricting the business the corporation is permitted to carry on (*CBCA*, s. 190).[2] The dissent and appraisal right was discussed in chapter 9.

Once the amendment is approved, the directors must file articles of amendment with the relevant corporate authority. Under the *CBCA*, this is the Director appointed under the Act. On receipt of the articles of amendment, the Director issues a certificate of amendment. The amendment is effective from the date of the certificate. The resolution authorizing the amendment may provide that the directors may revoke the resolution before they file articles of amendment without further authorization from the shareholders (*CBCA*, s. 173(2)). Such a provision might be useful to include in a resolution amending the articles if the directors wanted to see how many dissenters would have to be bought out by the corporation if the resolution passed. If the number of dissenters was significant and the cost of buying them out was too high as a result, the directors could decide not to go ahead with the amendment.

Several amendments may be made without the approval of shareholders. The names of first directors and the address of the registered office may be changed without shareholder approval (*CBCA*, s. 6(3)). A corporation that gave only a number name when it incorporated (such as 123456 Canada Inc.) may adopt a new name without shareholder authorization (*CBCA*, s. 173(3)). Finally, as noted in chapter 6, fixing rights privileges, conditions, and restrictions of series of shares within a

---

2   In order to exercise the dissent and appraisal right, a shareholder must satisfy the procedural requirements of *Canada Business Corporations Act*, R.S.C. 1985, c. C-44, s. 190 [*CBCA*], including giving notice to the corporation of her intention to dissent before the meeting at which the vote will take place.

class may be done by the directors alone (*CBCA*, s. 27). In each case the directors must file articles of amendment.

3) Changes to Stated Capital

As outlined in chapter 6, a stated capital account must be maintained for each class and series of shares which records the full amount of any consideration received by the corporation in return for issuing shares of the class or series. The stated capital account must be reduced when shares are acquired by the corporation. In addition, the corporation may want to reduce its stated capital for a variety of reasons. A reduction might be desirable in connection with a dividend that is to constitute a repayment of capital to shareholders. In general, capital dividends may be received by shareholders tax free. Also, where there has been a decline in the value of a corporation's assets, a reduction in stated capital may be desirable to permit the corporation to do certain other things, such as paying dividends or giving financial assistance to insiders of the corporation or acquiring its shares, which are prohibited unless the realizable value of the corporation's assets will exceed the aggregate of its liabilities plus the stated capital of all classes of shares. These financial tests are discussed in chapter 6.

If a corporation's stated capital is set out in its articles, then a reduction can only be accomplished by articles of amendment (*CBCA*, s. 173((1)(f)). In practice, this is rarely done. In all other circumstances a reduction in stated capital must be approved by a special resolution of the shareholders. A corporation cannot reduce its stated capital if it is insolvent, or, where a dividend to shareholders will be paid out of capital, if there are reasonable grounds for believing that the realizable value of the corporation's assets will be less than its liabilities after the dividend is paid (*CBCA*, s. 38(3)).

Where shares are redeemed or purchased, the stated capital account for the class or series of shares redeemed or acquired must be reduced *pro rata* (*CBCA*, ss. 30, 31, & 32). No shareholders' resolution is required. All that is needed is for the directors to pass a resolution authorizing the redemption or purchase. The requirements to be satisfied before a redemption or acquisition is permitted are discussed in chapter 6.

A corporation must increase its stated capital account for a class or series of shares if it pays a stock dividend on shares of the class or series. The declared amount of the dividend in money must be added to the stated capital account for the class or series (*CBCA*, s. 43(2)). Stated capital accounts may have to be adjusted in certain other circumstances discussed later in this chapter, including amalgamations and arrangements as well as the conversion of shares from one class into another (*CBCA*, s. 39(5)).

4) By-laws

The directors may make, amend, or repeal by-laws. Their action is effective as soon as the directors' resolution is passed, but the directors must submit their action to the shareholders at their next meeting. The shareholders may confirm, reject, or amend the directors' action. If the directors' action is rejected by the shareholders or if the directors fail to submit it to the shareholders, the action ceases to have effect on the date of rejection or on the date of the meeting when it should have been submitted. In such a case, no subsequent resolution of directors to make, amend, or repeal a by-law having substantially the same purpose or effect is effective until it is confirmed by shareholders (*CBCA*, s. 103).

New by-laws, as well as changes to and the repeal of by-laws, can also be initiated by shareholders in a shareholder proposal (*CBCA*, s. 103(5)). Such an action becomes effective as soon as it is approved by the shareholders. No action from the directors is needed. Proposals are discussed in chapter 6.

Regardless of who initiates a new by-law or the amendment or repeal of a by-law, shareholder approval need be by ordinary resolution only (*CBCA*, s. 103(2)). If some greater majority is considered desirable, it can be specified in the corporation's articles. Alternatively, a higher approval level may be specified in a unanimous shareholders' agreement.

B. CONTINUANCE

1) Introduction

The corporate law of most jurisdictions in Canada permits corporations governed by its laws to leave the jurisdiction (the "exporting jurisdiction") and to be continued under and governed by corporate laws of another jurisdiction (the "importing jurisdiction") (*CBCA*, ss. 187–88). The basic requirement for doing so is the permission of the exporting jurisdiction and, in the case of export from the *CBCA* and other Canadian jurisdictions, shareholder approval. A continuance may be desirable to take advantage of some particular provision of the corporate law of the importing jurisdiction, though this has little relevance in the Canadian context because of the substantial similarity of all Canadian corporate laws.[3] The most common reason to continue is to permit an amalgamation since, in order to effect this statutory procedure, all the corporations must be governed under the same corporate law.

2) Import

If a corporation wanted to become governed by the *CBCA*, it must make an application in the form of articles of continuance (*CBCA*, Form 11), which require information similar to that required in articles of incorporation (*CBCA*, s. 187). The articles of continuance become the articles of incorporation on continuance. The articles of continuance require some additional information as well: the name of the exporting jurisdiction and the date of incorporation. In the articles of continuance it is also necessary to make any changes needed to conform the characteristics of the corporation to the *CBCA*. Any other amendments that are desired may also be made to the corporation's characteristics so long as the same shareholder approval as would be required under the *CBCA* for such a change is given to the continuance (*CBCA*, s. 187(2)).

In addition to the articles of continuance, it is necessary to file a letter of satisfaction or some other document issued by the exporting jurisdiction indicating that the corporation is authorized to apply for continuance under the *CBCA*, a notice of directors, a notice of registered office, a list of the provinces in which the corporation is registered as an extraprovincial corporation, the required fee of $200, and a name search report. Unless the corporation is incorporated under the laws of Alberta, British Columbia, Manitoba, Saskatchewan, or Ontario, it is also necessary to file a legal opinion that the laws of the exporting jurisdiction allow the corporation to apply for continuance under the *CBCA*.

---

3   There are, however, differences, particularly between *CBCA* model and non-*CBCA* model jurisdictions, which may be extremely important in particular circumstances. For an example of a continuance to take advantage of a difference between the corporate law of Nova Scotia and the *CBCA*, see *Jacobsen v. United Canso Oil & Gas Ltd.* (1980), 40 N.S.R. (2d) 692 (S.C.T.D.), discussed in chapter 6.

3) Export

Under the *CBCA*, the export of a corporation must be authorized by special resolution of the shareholders (*CBCA*, s. 187(5)). The resolution should contain authority for the directors to do the following:

- to apply for continuance under laws of the importing jurisdiction;
- to apply to the Director under the *CBCA* to authorize the continuance; and
- to make all necessary amendments to conform to the laws of the importing jurisdiction.

All shareholders have the right to vote on a resolution authorizing a continuance, even if they do not otherwise have the right to vote (*CBCA*, s. 188(4)). Shareholders also have the right to have their shares bought by the corporation for fair value if they vote against the continuance, but it is nevertheless adopted (*CBCA*, s. 190(1)(d)). The notice of meeting must refer to this right to dissent and be bought out (*CBCA*, s. 188(3)).

The resolution authorizing continuance may permit the directors to abandon the continuance. Again this may be desirable, for example, to guard against the risk that so many shareholders exercise their dissent rights that the continuance becomes too expensive for the corporation.

Once the shareholders have approved the continuance, the directors must file an application for permission to continue. Under the *CBCA*, there is no prescribed form for this purpose, so a letter to the Director is sufficient.[4] A legal opinion must be provided that the laws of the importing jurisdiction meet certain requirements specified in section 188(10) of the *CBCA*. Essentially, these requirements are intended to ensure that both the rights and the obligations of the corporation will continue, so that no one is prejudiced by the continuance. A fee of $200 must also be paid.

Once these requirements have been satisfied, the Director issues a document to that effect. This document is submitted to the importing jurisdiction. Once the importing jurisdiction has given effect to the continuance, the corporation must file a notice to this effect with the

---

4   Under the *OBCA*, above note 1, Form 7 must be used. In Ontario, several other items must be filed to get permission to leave Ontario: under the *Corporations Information Act*, R.S.O. 1990, c. C.39, filings must be up to date; consent must be obtained from the Ontario Corporations Tax Branch; and, if the corporation was offering its securities to the public, a consent must be obtained from the Ontario Securities Commission.

Director. Then the Director issues a certificate of discontinuance (Form 14). The *CBCA* ceases to apply to the corporation on the date shown in the certificate of discontinuance (*CBCA*, s. 187(9)).

C. AMALGAMATION

1) Introduction

Amalgamation is a procedure provided for under corporate statutes by which two or more corporations (the "amalgamating corporation[s]") are combined into one corporation (the "amalgamated corporation") (*CBCA*, ss. 181–86). Amalgamations may be motivated by a variety of business or tax reasons. One common tax reason is to combine a corporation earning taxable income with one that has tax losses, so as to permit the losses to be deducted against the income.

The effect of an amalgamation is that the amalgamated corporation is subject to all the liabilities, owns all the property, and has all the rights of the amalgamating corporations.

As noted in the previous section, to carry out an amalgamation all the amalgamating corporations must be governed by the same corporate law. Where the amalgamating corporations have different shareholders, a "long-form" amalgamation is required. Where amalgamating corporations are affiliated,[5] a simpler "short-form" amalgamation is permitted in some circumstances. A short-form *vertical* amalgamation may be effected between a corporation and one or more subsidiaries which are either wholly owned by the corporation or where the only shares not held by the corporation are owned by one or more of the other amalgamating subsidiaries. Similarly, a short-form *horizontal* amalgamation may be effected between subsidiaries which are either wholly owned or where any shares not held by the parent corporation are held by one of the other amalgamating subsidiaries.

2) Long Form

To complete a long-form amalgamation, the amalgamating corporations need to enter into an amalgamation agreement setting out the terms of the amalgamation. Although this agreement will take the form of a con-

---

5   Under the *CBCA*, above note 2, corporations are affiliated with each other if one of them is a subsidiary of the other or they are controlled by the same person or corporation (s. 2(2) to (5)).

tract between the amalgamating corporations, some of the items that must be addressed are stipulated in the statute (*CBCA*, s. 182). The agreement must set out the provisions of the articles of the amalgamated corporation which must include all the same elements as the articles of incorporation, as well as the names and addresses of the directors of the corporation. In addition, the agreement must set out the basis on which the holders of shares in the amalgamating corporations will receive money or securities in the amalgamated corporation in exchange for their shares. Where the amalgamating corporations cannot agree on the values to be attributed to their own shares or those of the other amalgamating corporations, it may be necessary to obtain independent valuations. If valuations cannot be completed by the date contemplated for the amalgamation, adjustments may have to be made after the amalgamation is completed. Consistent with the rule that a corporation may not hold shares in itself, any shares of one of the amalgamating corporations held by another must be cancelled upon the amalgamation (*CBCA*, s. 182(2)).

There is one other matter that must be addressed in the amalgamation agreement. The amalgamating corporations will have to set out arrangements for the management and operation of the amalgamated corporation, including whether the by-laws of the amalgamated corporations will be those of one of the amalgamating corporations or whether new by-laws are needed (*CBCA*, s. 182(1)(f) & (g)).

If the shareholders in the amalgamating corporations are not closely related, then each amalgamating corporation may insist on the other making representations and warranties regarding their assets, liabilities, and business. What these representations and warranties consist of will depend on the nature of the transaction and the businesses being carried on by the amalgamating corporations. In this regard, it may be helpful to point out that an amalgamation may be one way of giving effect to the combination of two or more businesses in a form of joint venture. In this case, the parties will want to know what each is bringing into the joint venture through the amalgamating corporation. An amalgamation may also be used to give effect to an acquisition of a business. For example, if Jane owns all the shares of Jane Inc. and Tom owns all the shares of Tom Inc., an amalgamation of Tom Inc. with Jane Inc. could be used to acquire the business of Tom Inc. In the amalgamation, Jane could be given all the shares in the amalgamated corporation. Tom could receive cash. When this amalgamation is complete, the result will be functionally similar to Jane buying all of Tom's shares in Tom Inc. or Jane Inc. acquiring all the assets of Tom Inc., in the sense that Jane has acquired control of the business of Tom Inc. There are certain tax, liability, and other differences that would have to be taken into account in determining whether this form of acquisition is desirable.

In order to proceed with an amalgamation, the board of each amalgamating corporation must approve the amalgamation on the terms of the amalgamation agreement, then submit the agreement to the shareholders for approval by special resolution (*CBCA*, s. 183(1)). There must be a separate class vote only if the amalgamation agreement contains a provision that, if it was in the articles of amendment, would require a class vote under section 176 of the *CBCA* (*CBCA*, s. 183(4)). All shareholders have the right to vote on the resolution to approve the amalgamation, even if they do not otherwise have the right to vote (*CBCA*, s. 183(3)). The notice of the meeting must include a copy of the amalgamation agreement or a summary of it (*CBCA*, s. 184(2)(a)).

All shareholders have dissent and appraisal rights if they vote against an amalgamation, but the amalgamation is nevertheless approved (s. 190(1)(c)). The availability of the dissent and appraisal right must be stated in the notice of the meeting (*CBCA*, s. 184(2)(b)).

3) Short Form

a) Introduction
Amalgamations may be done on a "short-form" basis between certain corporations that are affiliated without the approval of their shareholders. For a short-form amalgamation, approval is required from the directors only and no amalgamation agreement is necessary (*CBCA*, ss. 184(1)(a) & (2)(a)). Short-form amalgamations do not trigger dissent and appraisal rights.

b) Vertical
A vertical short-form amalgamation may be used if the proposed amalgamation is between a corporation (the "parent corporation") and one or more wholly owned subsidiaries. A vertical short-form amalgamation may also be used if the subsidiaries are not wholly owned, so long as all the shares of each amalgamating subsidiary are held by either the parent or one of the other amalgamating subsidiaries. In such an amalgamation, the shares of each amalgamating subsidiary are cancelled without any repayment of capital or any other payment of any kind to the shareholders. No securities are issued and no assets are distributed by the amalgamating corporations. Also, the stated capital of the amalgamated corporation is the same as that of the parent corporation (s. 184(1)).

The articles of amalgamation of the amalgamated corporation must be the same as the articles of the parent corporation (*CBCA*, s. 184(1)(b)(ii)). So, if the intention of the parties is for the articles to be different from the parent's, a short-form amalgamation alone cannot be used. In such a case, it would be necessary to amend the articles of the parent corporation before the amalgamation, amend the articles of the amalgamated corporation after the amalgamation, or use a long-form amalgamation. The vertical short-form amalgamation is thus a simple way to reorganize a corporate group to eliminate unnecessary subsidiaries.

c) Horizontal

A horizontal short-form amalgamation may be used if the proposed amalgamation is between two or more wholly owned subsidiaries of one corporation. In such an amalgamation, the shares of all but one of the subsidiaries are cancelled without repayment of capital or any other payment to the shareholders. The stated capital of the shares of the amalgamating subsidiaries whose shares are cancelled must be added to the stated capital of the subsidiary whose shares are not cancelled (*CBCA*, s. 184(2)).

The articles of the amalgamated corporation are the same as the articles of incorporation of the amalgamating subsidiary whose shares are not cancelled (*CBCA*, s. 184(2)(b)(ii)). Accordingly, if different articles are needed, some additional or alternative procedure similar to that described above will be necessary.

4) Procedure after Approval of Long- and Short-Form Amalgamations

Under the *CBCA*, after approval by the shareholders of a long-form amalgamation or approval by the directors of a short-form amalgamation, articles of amalgamation (*CBCA*, Form 9) must be prepared and filed with the Director, along with the required fee of $200, a notice of directors, and a notice of registered office (*CBCA*, s. 185(1)). A name search report must also be filed if the name of the amalgamated corporation is not the same as the name of one of the amalgamating corporations. The required name search is identical to that required on incorporation. Name searches filed on incorporation are discussed in chapter 4.

The articles of amalgamation must have attached to them a statutory declaration by an officer or director of each amalgamating corporation that there are reasonable grounds for believing the amalgamating corporation is and the amalgamated corporation will be solvent and that the realizable value of the amalgamated corporation's assets will be greater than its liabilities and the stated capital of its shares. Also, the declarations must address the risk of prejudice to creditors. Each declaration must state that either (i) there are reasonable grounds for believing that no creditor will be prejudiced by the amalgamation or (ii) that adequate notice has been given to all known creditors of the amalgamating corporations and no creditor objects, except on grounds that are frivolous or vexatious (*CBCA*, s. 185(2)). There is no case on what constitutes pre-judice. One could argue that the creditors of the financially stronger amalgamating corporation will always be prejudiced. This, however, would make it impossible to amalgamate under the statute without notice to creditors except in the rare case where all amalgamating corporations are financially equal. It would seem more sensible to adopt the view that no prejudice occurs so long as it is reasonable to believe that all creditors will be paid on the same terms and conditions to which they were entitled prior to the amalgamation.

The *CBCA* spells out what will be considered adequate notice. The statute requires that notice be given to each creditor with a claim exceeding $1000; and that notice be published once in a newspaper published or distributed in the place where the corporation has its registered office, that each notice names the corporations with which the corporation intends to amalgamate, and that a creditor may object to the amalgamation within thirty days from the date of the notice (*CBCA*, s. 185(3)). Under the *OBCA*, in order for notice to creditors to be adequate, it must state as well that a creditor has the status of complainant for the purpose of seeking relief from oppression (*OBCA*, s. 178(2)(d)(ii)).

Once these documents are filed, the Director will issue a certificate of amalgamation. The amalgamated corporation will then have to be organized in much the same way as a newly incorporated corporation must be. Post-incorporation organization is discussed in chapter 4. There are some additional issues to be considered. New by-laws may be required. A certificate should be filed in any land registry office where any land held by the corporation is registered recording the amalgamation. Some agreements provide that certain things, such as giving notice to the other parties, must be done on amalgamation. Notices should be given to governmental authorities, including the Unemployment Insurance Commission and the Canada Pension Plan. And it will be necessary to file final tax returns for the amalgamating corporations. Under the *Income Tax Act*,[6] a year end is deemed to occur for tax purposes on the date the amalgamation becomes effective.

---

6   R.S.C. 1985 (5th Supp.), c. 1. See Interpretation Bulletin IT-474R, "Amalgamations of Canadian Corporations" (March 14, 1986).

D. ARRANGEMENTS

An arrangement under the *CBCA* is a procedure used to effect some change to the corporation which is not contemplated in the Act or, if such a change is contemplated, where it is not practicable to follow the procedure contemplated in the Act for some reason. One example of the first case is a reorganization of share capital of two corporations where some share interests in one corporation are exchanged for share interests in another. An example of the second is the transfer of all the property of a corporation in circumstances where it is impossible to obtain the necessary approval by special resolution, but the transaction is in the interests of the corporation (*CBCA*, s. 192). In addition, complex reorganizations may be effected through arrangements where there would be simply too many corporate steps to complete the reorganization in the manner contemplated in the *CBCA*.[7]

To implement an arrangement, it is necessary to obtain court approval. In connection with the approval the court may make any order it thinks fit, including requiring that the arrangement be approved by shareholders or that shareholders be granted dissent and appraisal rights (*CBCA*, s. 192(4)). Under the *OBCA*, subject to court order, an arrangement must be approved by a special resolution of shareholders (*OBCA*, s. 182). Also, each separate class is entitled to a class vote if the arrangement contains anything that, if it was in the articles of amendment, would require a class vote under section 170 of the *OBCA*.

Under the *CBCA*, after the requirements of any court order have been satisfied, articles of arrangement (*CBCA*, Form 14.1) must be prepared and filed with the Director, along with the required fee of $200 and a notice of change of registered office and notice of change of directors, if relevant.

Arrangements are relatively rare. This is due, in part, to the extraordinary nature of the circumstances in which an arrangement is needed. Also, in many cases in which an arrangement might otherwise be a useful procedure, the corporation is in financial difficulty. In general, where a corporation is insolvent or the realizable value of its assets is less that the aggregate of its liabilities and stated capital, however, an arrangement is not permitted (*CBCA*, s.192(2)). It is necessary to proceed under the *Bankruptcy and Insolvency Act*[8] or

---

7   Under the *OBCA*, above note 1, it is not necessary to show that the other procedures in the Act are not practicable.

8   R.S.C. 1985, c. B-3 [*BIA*].

the *Companies' Creditors Arrangement Act.*[9] In some circumstances, arrangements have been permitted where the applicant is solvent but other corporations involved in the arrangement are not.[10]

E. SALE OF ALL OR SUBSTANTIALLY ALL OF THE CORPORATION'S ASSETS

The "sale, lease or exchange of all or substantially all the property of a corporation other than in the ordinary course of business of the corporation" is a fundamental change affecting shareholders' investments and cannot be completed without the approval of the shareholders by special resolution (*CBCA*, ss. 189(3)–(9)).

The notice of the shareholders' meeting must include a copy or summary of the agreement giving effect to the transaction and a statement that shareholders are entitled to dissent from the resolution approving the transaction and to require the corporation to buy their shares for fair value. At the meeting, the shareholders may authorize the transaction and may fix, or authorize the directors to fix, any of the terms and conditions of the transaction. The shareholders may authorize the directors to abandon the transaction without any further approval of the shareholders.

On a resolution, each share has the right to vote whether or not it otherwise has the right to vote, and any class or series of shares is entitled to a class vote if it is affected differently from another class or series.

F. GOING-PRIVATE TRANSACTIONS

1) Introduction

The *OBCA* has special provisions to deal with certain transactions called "going-private transactions," the result of which is the extinguishing of a shareholder's interest in an offering corporation (s. 190). Special procedures, including enhanced levels of shareholder approval, must be followed to give effect to such a transaction. Similar, but more detailed, procedures must be observed by all corporations subject to the *Securities Act* (Ontario),[11] as provided in the Ontario Securities Commission Policy 9.1. Although there are no equivalent provisions in the *CBCA*,

---

9   R.S.C. 1985, c. C-36.

10   *Savage v. Amoco Acquisition Co.* (1988), 61 Alta. L.R. (2d) 279 (C.A.). The Director has issued a policy statement on arrangements (*CBCA Arrangements Transactions Policy*).

11   R.S.C. 1990, c. S.5.

the Director issued a policy statement in September 1994 indicating that, so long as procedures similar to those in section 190 of the *OBCA* were followed, she would not initiate an oppression action in relation to the transaction.

Under the *OBCA* scheme, a going-private transaction is defined as any amalgamation, arrangement, amendment of articles, or other transaction carried out under that Act which would cause the interest of a holder of a "participating security" to be terminated without the consent of the holder and without the substitution of an interest of equivalent value in another participating security. A participating security usually means one that has some right to participate in earnings, such as securities that carry a dividend right and a right to receive the remaining property of the corporation on dissolution, as such common shares (*OBCA*, s. 190). Two examples of going-private transactions are set out in figure 10.1.

Figure 10.1   Examples of Going-Private Transactions

Amalgamation Squeeze-Out of Minority Shareholder
Corporation A has one shareholder who holds 75 shares and a minority shareholder who holds the remaining 25. The controlling shareholder of Corporation A incorporates Corporation B and transfers to it all shares he owns in Corporation A. He then causes Corporation A to amalgamate with Corporation B. The amalgamation agreement provides that the controlling shareholder gets common shares in the amalgamated corporation, and the minority shareholder gets cash or redeemable shares, which are subsequently redeemed, thus terminating the minority shareholder's interest in Corporation A.

Consolidation at High Ratio
Assume the facts from the previous example. Instead of an amalgamation, the controlling shareholder approves articles of amendment which consolidate all issued shares on the basis of 75 shares for one and provides that any outstanding fractional shares are to be repurchased by the corporation. This arrangement leaves the minority shareholder with only one-third of a share. The corporation buys back the fractional share, and the minority shareholder's interest in the corporation is terminated.

2) Approval Process

In order to implement a going-private transaction, it is necessary to obtain an independent valuation of the securities affected. If the transaction contemplates giving securities in exchange for those extinguished, a valuation is required to show whether the value of the securities, combined with any cash, to be received by the person whose interest will be extinguished is greater or lesser than that of the affected security.

Each class of affected securities must approve the transaction. Management must send notice of the meeting and a management information circular to shareholders not less than forty days before the meeting. The circular must contain the following material:

- a summary of the valuation;
- a statement that the valuation may be inspected at the registered office of the corporation and that a shareholder may obtain a copy;
- a certificate that no material fact relevant to the valuation was not disclosed to the valuer;
- what shareholder approval is required;
- what securities are affected; and
- what votes will not be taken into account for the purposes of the shareholder approval.

The most complex rules governing going-private transactions relate to the level of shareholder approval required to give effect to the transaction. In addition to any other approval that may be required, approval need only be by ordinary resolution of each class of affected securities unless non-cash consideration is being offered to shareholders whose interests are being extinguished or the price being offered is less than the amount of the valuation, in which case a special resolution is required. The votes of certain security holders with an interest in the transaction are not counted. The most common type of going-private transaction results in the controlling shareholder owning 100 percent of the issued shares of a corporation and the minority shareholders being bought out for cash. Such a transaction must be approved without counting the votes of the controlling shareholder.[12] Approval will require a resolution to be passed by a majority of the minority shareholders. For this reason, the going-private transaction approval requirement is often referred to as the "majority of the minority" test, where the minority means the shareholders other than the controlling shareholder.

---

12   Another kind of interested party is any person who receives a per security consideration greater than that available to other security holders of the same class.

In some circumstances the Ontario Securities Commission may grant an exemption from the application of this procedure (*OBCA,* s. 190(6)). If a going-private transaction is approved by shareholders, any dissenting shareholder may exercise a right to have her shares bought by the corporation for fair value (*OBCA,* s. 190(7)). Also, notwithstanding that the corporation may have complied with the approval procedure described above, a shareholder is not precluded from claiming that the transaction is oppressive (*OBCA,* s. 248; *CBCA,* s. 241). Both the dissent and appraisal right and the oppression remedy are described in chapter 9.

G. TERMINATION OF THE CORPORATION'S EXISTENCE

1) Introduction

There are a variety of circumstances in which it may be desirable to terminate the existence of a corporation. Perhaps its business may have ceased or been sold, the corporation was being used for a tax-planning purpose that is no longer relevant, or the shareholder/managers can no longer agree on how to carry on business together and have decided to go their separate ways. The *CBCA* and other Canadian corporate statutes provide several methods by which a corporation may be terminated. Which one is most appropriate will depend on whether the corporation has many assets to dispose of, whether the directors will supervise the termination or an outside professional is needed, whether the shareholders all agree that termination is desirable, and various other factors. If the reason termination is necessary is that the corporation is insolvent, however, the corporate law procedures may not be used (*CBCA,* s. 208). In such a case the corporation may only be terminated under the *Bankruptcy and Insolvency Act*[13] or the *Winding Up Act*.[14] In some cases where the corporation is inactive or is in default of some requirement under its governing statute or some other legislation, the corporation's existence may be terminated by the corporate regulators. The following sections outline the termination options available under the *CBCA.*

---

13 Above note 8.
14 R.S.C. 1985, c. W-11.

2) Voluntary Dissolution

Voluntary dissolution is the simplest and most common form of termination. It is handled by corporate management or by another person appointed for that purpose.

If the corporation has never issued any shares, it may be dissolved at any time by its directors (CBCA, s. 210(1)). A corporation that has issued shares but has no property and no liabilities may be dissolved by special resolution of the shareholders or, if the corporation has more than one class of shares, by special resolutions of the shareholders of each class, whether they are otherwise entitled to vote or not (CBCA, s. 210(2)). If the corporation has assets or liabilities or both, it may be dissolved with the same level of approval so long as the shareholders also authorize the directors to discharge all the liabilities and distribute any remaining assets (CBCA, s. 210(3)). In any of these three cases, once the appropriate approval has been obtained and, in the last case, the liabilities of the corporation have been discharged and the assets distributed, articles of dissolution (Form 17) may be sent to the Director, who shall issue a certificate of dissolution dissolving the corporation (CBCA, s. 210(4)–(6)).

Where the assets and liabilities cannot be dealt with easily, which will often be the case if the corporation carried on any substantial business, the CBCA provides a more complex procedure (CBCA, s. 211). On the proposal of any director or shareholder, a special meeting of shareholders must be held to consider liquidating the corporation's assets and dissolving the corporation. Once liquidation and dissolution is approved, as described in the preceding section, the corporation must send a statement of intent to dissolve (Form 19) to the Director. The Director must then issue a certificate of intent to dissolve. From the date of the certificate, the corporation may not carry on business except to the extent necessary to complete the liquidation and dissolution.

After the issuance of the certificate, the corporation must do the following:

- send a notice to each known creditor;
- publish notice of its intent to dissolve once a week for four consecutive weeks in a newspaper published or distributed in the place where the corporation has its registered office, and take reasonable steps to give public notice in each province in which the corporation does business;
- liquidate the business by collecting all the corporation's property, discharging its liabilities, and selling off any assets not to be distributed to the shareholders; and

- after completing the foregoing, distribute the remaining assets to the shareholders.

Any interested party may apply to have the liquidation supervised by the court (*CBCA*, ss. 211(8) & 215).

Once these steps have been completed, the corporation may prepare and file articles of dissolution with the Director. No fee is required to be filed with the articles of dissolution. On receipt of articles of dissolution, the Director issues a certificate of dissolution.

Although it is not required by the *CBCA*, it is advisable to obtain the consent of Revenue Canada to the dissolution. If no consent is obtained, directors will be personally liable for any unpaid corporate tax or any other amount owed to Revenue Canada up to the amount distributed to shareholders on dissolution. It is also useful to obtain consents from provincial taxation authorities in provinces where the corporation carried on business.

3) Involuntary Dissolution

a) By Court Order

Any shareholder, the Director, or any other interested person, such as a liquidator or a creditor, may apply to have a corporation liquidated and dissolved on a variety of grounds set out in the *CBCA* (ss. 213 & 214). Such an action is sometimes referred to as "winding up" the corporation. The grounds include failing to comply with certain provisions of the Act, the occurrence of an event that entitles a complaining shareholder to demand dissolution in accordance with a unanimous shareholder agreement, and circumstances in which it is just and equitable to dissolve the corporation. The *CBCA* also expressly provided that a court may order dissolution in the same circumstances as relief for oppression may be granted under section 241. Consistently, liquidation and dissolution may be ordered if oppression is found in an application under the oppression section (*CBCA*, s. 241(3)(l)). These grounds for winding up are discussed in chapter 9 under the heading "Winding Up."

The court may make any order it thinks fit in connection with the dissolution or the liquidation of a corporation, including appointing a liquidator and directing that notice be given or payments be made to identified parties (*CBCA*, s. 217). Any liquidator appointed by the court has certain statutory powers to assist with the liquidation as well as certain duties, such as giving notice to creditors (*CBCA*, ss. 221 & 222). Once the liquidation process is complete, the liquidator has submitted its final accounts, and the court has approved these accounts, the court must order that articles of dissolution be filed (*CBCA*, s. 223(5)). The liquidator then prepares and files the articles, and the Director issues a certificate of dissolution (*CBCA*, ss. 223(6) & (8)).

b) Dissolution by the Director

Under the *CBCA* there are two grounds on which the Director can issue a certificate of dissolution on her own initiative and dissolve a corporation: the corporation has not carried on business for three years, or the corporation is in default in filing any document required to be filed under the Act for one year (s. 212). Before dissolving the corporation, the Director must give at least 120 days' notice to the corporation, publish notice in the *Canada Gazette,* and publish notice in the bulletin published by the Director.

4) Effect of Dissolution

If, as a result of any of the procedures described above, a certificate of dissolution is issued by the Director, the corporation ceases to exist on the date of the certificate. Nevertheless, legal proceedings existing at the date of dissolution may be continued and new ones commenced within five years. Each shareholder remains liable for property received on the dissolution (*CBCA*, s. 226).

Any property not disposed of at the time of dissolution vests in the Crown. Under the corporate laws of most Canadian jurisdictions, there is a procedure by which corporations may be revived in some circumstances (e.g., *CBCA*, s. 209). Where a corporation is revived, any assets vesting in the Crown on dissolution are returned to it or, if the property has been disposed of, a payment of money equal to the value at the date of dissolution is made (*CBCA*, s. 228).

H. CHAPTER SUMMARY

In this chapter we discussed the various ways in which a corporation may change after it is incorporated, and the procedures required to be followed to effect such changes.

It is possible to change any of a corporation's characteristics set out in its articles by articles of amendment approved by the shareholders by special resolution. By-laws may be made, amended, or repealed by directors or shareholders, though in the former case, for a new by-law or a change to a by-law to continue to be effective, the shareholders must approve it by an ordinary resolution. A corporation's stated capital account must be adjusted in certain circumstances, such as the redemption by the corporation of shares, and may be changed by special resolution in some circumstances. A corporation might want to reduce its stated capital where there has been a decline in the realizable value of its assets.

The laws of most Canadian jurisdictions permit corporations to migrate in and out of the jurisdiction. Such a migration is called a "continuance." We discussed the process by which a corporation governed by the *CBCA* can cease to be so governed by continuing under the laws of another jurisdiction. We also discussed how a corporation governed under the laws of another jurisdiction can become continued and therefore governed under the *CBCA*.

One reason to continue a corporation under the laws of a particular jurisdiction is to merge with another corporation governed under the same jurisdiction through a statutory procedure called "amalgamation." The corporations who are to be the parties to the amalgamation must enter into a detailed amalgamation agreement setting out the terms of the transaction, and the amalgamation must be approved by a special resolution of shareholders. Certain affiliated corporations can use a "short-form" amalgamation, which requires the approval of the directors only and does not require an amalgamation agreement.

Sometimes, usually at the instigation of a controlling shareholder, corporations will engage in an amalgamation or some other transaction that results in the interest of one or more shareholders being extinguished. Because of the potential for such transactions to be inconsistent with minority shareholders' interests, the *OBCA* imposes strict requirements on them regardless of the form they take. The most significant is that the transaction must be approved by a majority of shareholders other than the controlling shareholder and any shareholders who receive consideration of higher value than other shareholders of the same class. The Director appointed under the *CBCA* has indicated that she expects these same procedures to be followed for *CBCA* corporations.

We also discussed restructuring transactions that cannot be completed in accordance with the requirements of the relevant corporate legislation. Under the *CBCA,* these transactions are called "arrangements." An arrangement may be used because there is no provision for the kind of transaction desired under the corporate statute, or because the particular requirements of the statute cannot be met for some reason. In either case, the corporation may complete the transaction through an arrangement with the approval of the court.

Finally, we discussed the various ways in which a corporation's existence may be terminated. Where a corporation has no assets to sell off and no liabilities to pay, this may be done by a special resolution of shareholders. If the corporation has assets and liabilities, the process will be more complex involving, in addition to shareholder approval, the appointment of a liquidator, notices to creditors, sale of all the corporation's assets, payment of all its liabilities, and distribution of any remaining assets to the shareholders — possibly all under court supervision. Termination may also occur involuntarily by court order on the application of any interested party, including a creditor, or by the Director, if the corporation has been inactive for three years or is in default of certain filing requirements.

FURTHER READINGS

BUCKLEY, F.H., M. GILLEN, & R. YALDEN, *Corporations: Principles And Policies,* 3d ed. (Toronto: Emond Montgomery, 1995) c. 11

Canadian Corporate Law Reporter (Toronto: Butterworths) (looseleaf)

GILLEN, M.R., *et al., Corporations and Partnerships: Canada* (Boston: Kluwer, 1994)

GRAY, W.D., *Canada Business Corporations Act, 1996* (Toronto: Carswell, 1996)

KINGSTON, R.A., & W. Grover, *Canada Corporation Manual* (Toronto: Carswell, 1996) (looseleaf)

LAW SOCIETY OF UPPER CANADA, *Bar Admission Course Reference Materials: Business Law* (Toronto: Law Society of Upper Canada, 1995) c. 9

VANDUZER, J.A., "Shareholder Approval of Asset Sales: The 'All or Substantially All' Threshold" (1991) 4 Can. Corp. L.R. C145

CHAPTER 11

THE PUBLIC CORPORATION

A. INTRODUCTION

Often throughout this book we have referred to the different rules which apply to large corporations that offer their shares to the public and those which apply to smaller, closely held corporations. We have also discussed the differing ways in which the same rules operate, depending on the scale of the corporation. In this chapter we focus, in more detail, on some areas of particular concern when one is dealing with a public corporation.

First, the basic scheme of securities regulation will be discussed, based on the Ontario model. Securities legislation in each province seeks to regulate both the issuance of securities by businesses and the marketplace in which securities are traded once securities are issued. The *CBCA* also contains provisions that parallel many of the provisions of provincial securities laws. These provisions are enacted under the federal government's jurisdiction over corporate law and apply only to corporations governed by the *CBCA*.[1] If a *CBCA*-incorporated corporation has a shareholder in a province, both the *CBCA* and the provincial securities laws will apply. In June 1996 the federal government and the governments of all provinces, other than Quebec and British Columbia, announced an agreement in principle to establish a national securities

---

1   See chapter 3 for a discussion of federal jurisdiction in this regard.

regulator to replace the provincial regulators.[2] If implemented, this agreement will greatly simplify compliance with securities requirements in Canada.

Securities law is complex, and a thorough discussion of securities law is far beyond the scope of this book.[3] We will look briefly at the way participants in the securities markets, such as investment advisers and securities dealers, are regulated by securities law, as well as the manner in which securities legislation seeks to protect investors by requiring disclosure about the business of issuers of securities and the securities they are offering.

We will look also at trading by directors, officers, significant shareholders, and other insiders of corporations. Because of the special knowledge such people have about the corporations they are associated with, their trading of securities is closely regulated under both provincial securities laws and the *CBCA*.

Finally, we will consider the regulation of efforts to take over a corporation by acquiring its shares. In closely held corporations, the selling of shares is always a negotiated transaction between the buyer and the seller or sellers. Because of the large number of shareholders in a widely held corporation, such negotiation is not possible. A bid must be made through communication of a "take it or leave it offer" to shareholders. Such takeover bids are regulated under provincial securities laws and the *CBCA* to ensure that shareholders have a reasonable opportunity to participate in any bid that is made.

B. SECURITIES REGULATION

1) Introduction

As noted in chapter 3, each province has a law concerned with regulating the marketplace for the trading of securities. The fundamental objective of these securities laws is to ensure that participants in the market act honestly and that buyers and sellers have sufficient information to make decisions about investing in securities. The basic approach taken in securities laws to accomplish this objective has four aspects.

---

2   B. McKenna & A. Freeman, "Eight Premiers Endorse National Securities Commission: Quebec, B.C. Want No Part of Federal Agency" Toronto *Globe and Mail* (22 June 1996) B1.

3   See generally, M.R. Gillen, *Securities Regulation in Canada* (Toronto: Carswell, 1992), and J.G. MacIntosh, *Essentials of Securities Law*, (Toronto: Irwin Law) (forthcoming).

The first is to require securities dealers, such as Nesbitt Burns and ScotiaMcleod, and others who make a business of being involved in securities transactions to be registered and subject to regulation. The second is to require businesses issuing securities to disclose information about the securities and their business both when the securities are first offered for sale, and thereafter on a regular basis, as well as whenever something happens that is likely to affect the value of the securities. As noted in chapter 3, in pursuing this approach securities laws address some of the same areas as corporate law. For example, both deal with the disclosure that must be made to shareholders in connection with shareholder meetings and, more generally, with ensuring that corporate decisions are not made without regard for the interests of minority shareholders. The third and fourth aspects are the regulation of insider trading and of takeover bids, both of which are discussed in this chapter.

The administration and enforcement of securities laws of each province is the responsibility of some specialized agency of the government of that province. In Ontario it is the Ontario Securities Commission (the OSC). One of the challenges for securities administrators, like the OSC, is to ensure that they are able to discharge their responsibilities effectively, given the constantly changing nature of the transactions in securities markets. In recent years, for example, securities administrators have had to grapple with how to regulate the exploding market for derivatives, securities whose value is not determined in relation to any direct claim to an interest in a business or asset. To be responsive to changes in the marketplace, securities administrators have tried to augment provincial legislation and regulations with policy statements that can be more quickly modified to address new conditions. Individual securities administrators also issue notices about the way they interpret the legislation that applies to particular types of transactions or investments. Finally, there are National Policy Statements that have the approval of securities administrators from all Canadian jurisdictions. Anyone engaged in securities practice must be familiar with all these sources of law and interpretation.

Recently, the authority of the OSC to enforce its policy statements was successfully challenged in the courts.[4] In response, in 1994 the Ontario government gave the OSC power to make binding rules.[5]

---

4   *Ainsley Financial Corp. v. Ontario (Securities Commission)* (1994), 18 O.S.C.B. 43 (C.A.), aff'g (1993), 14 O.R. (3d) 280 (Gen. Div.).

5   *An Act to Amend the Securities Act*, S.O. 1994, c. 33, implementing the recommendations of a task force struck to consider the issue (Ontario, *Final Report of the Ontario Task Force on Securities Regulation: Responsibility and Responsiveness* (Toronto: Queen's Printer, 1994).

2) What Is a Security?

In general, in order for securities legislation to have any application to a transaction, the transaction must involve a "security."[6] In recognition of the wide and continually expanding ways in which businesses raise money, "security" is defined very broadly to ensure that the protection for investors provided by securities legislation is not avoided. Indeed, the definition in the Ontario *Securities Act* (*OSA*) is not exhaustive. Securities are not restricted to shares and debt obligations, such as bonds, which are traded in public markets at prices reported in the business pages of any newspaper. In general, a security is any "evidence of title to or interest in the capital, assets, property, profit, earnings or royalties of any person or company."[7] The *OSA* definition then goes on to provide a list of sixteen examples of securities. The last example is an "investment contract," which is a kind of catch-all. An investment contract exists whenever the following criteria are met: an investment of money is made in a common enterprise with an expectation of profit solely from the efforts of others.[8] The "common enterprise" requirement means that the return to the investor is related to the ability and skill of the person to whom the investor entrusts his funds. A pooling of funds for a common purpose indicates a common enterprise. Although the scope of this definition of security is very wide, the effective scope of many of the obligations under securities legislation is cut back by the many exemptions provided for. These exemptions will be discussed below.

3) Regulation of Securities Dealers and Other Participants in the Market

As noted above, one way in which securities legislation attempts to ensure that securities markets function effectively is to regulate those who participate in the buying and selling of securities. The primary method of regulation is to require securities market participants to register as a condition of their participation. To obtain registration, a participant must meet certain standards of honesty, competence, and financial solvency. To ensure continuing compliance with the last requirement, registrants must provide

---

6   The Ontario Securities Commission has asserted a jurisdiction to regulate in some circumstances, even where there is no security, where it feels the public interest requires it. See *Re Albino* (1991), 14 O.S.C.B. 365, a case involving stock appreciation rights.

7   *Securities Act*, R.S.O. 1990, c. S.5, s. 1(1) [*OSA*].

8   *Pacific Coast Coin Exchange of Canada* v. *Ontario* (*Securities Commission*) (1975), 7 O.R. (2d) 395 (Div. Ct.), aff'd (1975), 8 O.R. (2d) 257 (C.A.), aff'd [1978] 2 S.C.R. 112 applying *S.E.C.* v. *W.J. Harvey Co.*, 328 U.S. 293 (1946).

financial reports to the OSC on a regular basis and maintain a minimum level of capital. In addition, registrants must comply with certain requirements for record keeping and most must participate in an investor compensation fund. In Ontario the OSC has a broad discretion to suspend, cancel, restrict, and impose terms and conditions on the registration of participants where it determines that it is in the public interest to do so.

Registration is required for all persons who trade in securities or act as an adviser or underwriter of securities (*OSA* s. 34(b)). An adviser is anyone who provides investment advice or has a discretion with respect to the investment of someone else's securities. An underwriter is a person who purchases securities for resale. For example, when a corporation wants to issue shares to the public, it usually enters into a contract with an underwriter, such as ScotiaMcleod, who agrees to buy all the shares a corporation wants to issue and then tries to resell the shares to the public through its network of account executives.

Certain categories of people benefit from a limited exemption from these requirements. Lawyers and accountants do not need to register as advisers so long as any investment advice provided by them is solely incidental to their principal business or occupation (*OSA*, s. 34(b)). The *OSA* also contains exemptions for certain kinds of trades in relation to which the participants do not need the protection provided by the Act, — for example, financial institutions (*OSA*, s. 35(1)).

Further exemptions are provided, based on the nature of the security (*OSA*, s. 35(2)). If the security is being issued by the federal government, no registration is necessary since there is no risk of default on such a security. Practically the most important exemption of this kind is for securities of a "private company" which are not offered for sale to the public (*OSA*, s. 35(2)10). As noted in chapter 4, section 1(1) of the *OSA* defines "private company" as a corporation whose articles restrict the transfer of shares, limit the number of shareholders (exclusive of employees) to fifty, and prohibit any invitation to the public to subscribe for securities.

It is also possible to apply to the securities administrators for an exemption from registration if the security or the purchaser does not otherwise qualify for an exemption (*OSA*, s. 74). In Ontario the OSC has the power to grant an exemption from the registration requirements if to do so would not be prejudicial to the public interest.

4) Regulation of the Distribution of Securities

a) Prospectus Requirements

In order to issue securities to the public, a business must provide substantial disclosure about both its business and the securities to be issued in a document called a "prospectus." Under the Ontario Act, a prospectus must be prepared and filed whenever a business intends to trade in a security, if the trade constitutes a "distribution," unless an exemption is available, as discussed in the next section (*OSA*, s. 53).

Each of the following kinds of trade is a distribution:

- an issue of previously unissued securities;
- a disposition of any securities by a control person (that is, in general, any person who owns more than 20 percent of the voting securities of the issuer); and
- a trade in previously issued securities that have been redeemed, purchased, or otherwise acquired by the issuer.

The securities regime is called a "closed system" because either a prospectus must be filed by an issuer or a specific exemption must be found as described below, in order for securities to be issued. Once securities are issued and the prospectus requirements have been met, they may be resold freely.[9] If no prospectus was filed and the securities were issued under an exemption, they may only be resold pursuant to another exemption. The only exception to the requirement for an exemption is if a prospectus was filed by the issuer of the securities after the securities were issued, and the person holding the securities has done so for a specified length of time. These resale restrictions are discussed below in more detail.

To fulfil the prospectus requirements, it is necessary to prepare and file a prospectus with the securities administrators in each provincial and territorial jurisdiction in which it is intended to offer the securities for sale. The prospectus is a long, detailed document that must provide "full, true and plain disclosure of all material facts" about the securities offered (*OSA*, s. 56). In addition to a description of the business of the issuer and the characteristics of the securities to be offered, the prospectus must specifically identify the risks associated with an investment in the securities and include complete audited financial statements (see *Regulation* under the *OSA*, ss. 53–62).

The *OSA* imposes civil liability on the issuing corporation, the underwriter, and the directors, any officer who signed the prospectus, and any expert who gave consent to the use of his or her opinion in the prospectus for any misrepresentation in the prospectus (*OSA*, s. 130). A purchaser may claim recision or damages against the issuer or underwriter and damages against the other possible defendants. A defence is available for persons, other than the issuer, if they made adequate

---

9   Sales by a control person of securities bought on the market can only be made under a prospectus or pursuant to an exemption (see *OSA*, s. 72(7)).

inquiries such that they could entertain a reasonable belief that there was no misrepresentation (*OSA*, ss. 130(3)–(5) & 131). This defence is referred to as a "due diligence" defence. The risk of liability encourages all those engaged in the process of preparing the prospectus to conduct an intensive investigation to ensure that all material information is properly disclosed.

Once the prospectus is drafted, it is filed with the securities administrators, who issue a receipt for it. At this stage the prospectus is called a "preliminary prospectus." The securities administrators will review the preliminary prospectus to ensure that the disclosure is adequate. A deficiency letter will be issued indicating the areas in the preliminary prospectus where more or better disclosure is required. Once the deficiencies have been addressed, which often involves some discussions between the issuer's lawyers and the administrator, a final prospectus is prepared and filed and a receipt is issued by the administrator. Once the receipt has been issued, the securities can be sold.

After the preliminary prospectus has been filed, but before the receipt is issued for the final prospectus, the issuer and anyone acting on its behalf, such as the underwriter, can solicit expressions of interest from prospective purchasers based only on the preliminary prospectus. The preliminary prospectus must have a warning printed on it in red ink indicating it is a preliminary prospectus and has not been reviewed by any securities administrator. Before a purchaser can enter into a legally binding commitment to purchase securities, she must have received a copy of the final prospectus (*OSA*, s. 65). A purchaser has two days to withdraw from any commitment made to purchase securities after receiving the final prospectus (*OSA*, s. 71).

It is important to note that the primary purpose of securities administrators is not to review the terms on which securities are offered to ensure that the price is appropriate or that the terms are otherwise fair. Their main concern is to ensure that the disclosure is adequate, so that investors may make an informed choice. Securities laws in most jurisdictions do, however, provide some scope for administrators to review the merits of the transaction (e.g., *OSA* s. 61(2)).

b) Exemptions from Prospectus Requirements

Securities laws provide various exemptions from the requirement to provide prospectus disclosure. These exemptions are a critical part of the scheme of securities regulation because any issuance of shares will be a distribution, no matter how few investors are involved or how little capital is being raised, and compliance with the prospectus is time consuming and expensive. In the absence of the exemptions, the prospectus requirements would make it impractical for small- and medium-sized businesses to raise money other than by borrowing from a financial institution.[10]

Many of the exemptions for distributions have the same rationale as the exemptions from registration. So, for example, an exemption is available if the purchaser does not need the protection of the securities legislation, perhaps because it is a registered securities dealer, a financial institution, or the government (*OSA*, s. 72(1)(a)). Similarly, a prospectus is not required if the acquisition cost to the purchaser of the securities is greater than $150,000 (*OSA*, s. 72(1)(d)); *OSA, Regulation*, s. 27(1); OSC Policy 6.1). This exemption, called the private placement exemption, is premised on the assumption that anyone paying more than $150,000 is sufficiently sophisticated that they do not need the protection of prospectus disclosure.

To ensure that distributions made in reliance on the private placement exemption are to purchasers who have sufficient information, some conditions are placed on its availability. If securities are advertised in print media or on radio or television, prospective investors must be provided with an "offering memorandum" (*OSA Regulation*, s. 32(2)). There is no prescribed content for the memorandum but, in practice, the level of disclosure is similar to that of a prospectus. This openness is encouraged by the requirement to provide investors with a "contractual right of action" that entitles investors to claim recision or damages if there is a misrepresentation in the offering memorandum. This right may be exercised within ninety days of the date on which payment is made (*OSA Regulation*, s. 32(1)). As a matter of practice, an offering memorandum is prepared and delivered to prospective investors in most situations where this exemption is relied upon.

As noted above, there is an exemption from registration in connection with securities of a private company that is not offering its shares to the public. Section 73(1)(a) of the *OSA* creates an identical exemption from the prospectus requirements. Although it is straightforward to determine if a corporation has the provisions required in its articles to make it a "private company" for the purposes of the Act, it may be difficult to know if a trade in securities is a distribution to the public in particular situations. One test the courts have used to determine who the public is in this context is to ask whether the person to whom the securities are offered needs the disclosure required by the securities regime's

---

10   On the financing problems faced by such businesses and some proposals for law reform, see J.G. MacIntosh, *Legal and Institutional Barriers to Financing Innovative Enterprise in Canada* (Kingston: Queen's University, Policy Studies, 1994).

prospectus requirements.[11] Applying this test involves assessing the knowledge and sophistication of the offerees. Another test used in Canada focuses instead on the relationship between the issuing corporation and the offerees. Under this test, if there are "common bonds of interest or association" between the issuer and the offerees, the offerees are not the public. The required bonds may be found to exist as a result of access to information about the issuer, control over the issuer, or family or business relationships. This test was applied in *R. v. Piepgrass*.[12] In that case the Alberta Court of Appeal held that a promoter soliciting funds from farmers who were not friends or business associates was offering securities to the public.

One other exemption that is often relied on is the so-called seed capital exemption. The purpose of the exemption is to give small businesses a one-time opportunity to raise capital to facilitate the initial development or expansion of their business. An issuer is permitted to solicit up to fifty prospective purchasers and to sell its securities to as many as twenty-five purchasers if certain requirements are met (*OSA*, s. 72(1)(p)). In Ontario, the exemption may be used only once, and the purchasers are limited to senior officers and directors of the issuer, their parents, spouses, brothers, sisters, and children and any person who, by virtue of his net worth or investment experience or advice from a registered adviser or securities dealer, is in a position to be able to evaluate the investment. Each purchaser must be given access to substantially the same information concerning the issuer that a prospectus would provide. This information is included in an offering memorandum that is subject to the same requirements as discussed above in relation to the private placement exemption.

Where a trade is made in reliance on any of the exemptions described above or certain of the other exemptions, a report must be filed with the securities administrators (e.g., *OSA Regulation*, Form 20) within ten days of the trade. The report includes the identity of the parties, the securities sold, and the price at which the transaction took place. As with the registration obligations, it is possible to apply for an exemption from the prospectus requirements if a trade does not fit within any of the specific exemptions (*OSA*, s. 74).

---

11   The leading case on this "need to know" test is *S.E.C. v. Ralston Purina Co.*, 346 U.S. 119 (1953). It has been adopted in many Canadian decisions (e.g., *R. v. McKillop* (1971), [1972] 1 O.R. 164 (Prov. Ct.)). The applicability of this test was questioned in *R. v. Buck River Resources Ltd.* (10 February 1988), (Alta. Q.B.) [unreported], aff'g (1984), 25 B.L.R. 209 (Alta. Prov. Ct.).

12   (1959), 23 D.L.R. (2d) 220 (Alta. C.A.).

c) Resale Restrictions

If securities are sold under an exemption, they cannot be resold except under an exemption or after the issuer has become a "reporting issuer" and certain hold periods have expired. A corporation becomes a reporting issuer by preparing and filing a prospectus. This requirement is what makes the securities regime a closed system, as mentioned above. In effect, securities cannot be distributed unless a prospectus has been filed or an exemption can be relied on. Restrictions on resale are necessary since exactly the same considerations apply to the resale of securities sold under an exemption as to the issuance of shares. The protection of the prospectus requirements is needed unless the circumstances exist in which an exemption is available. In general, however, so long as the issuing corporation is a reporting issuer, securities sold pursuant to an exemption may be resold within six to eighteen months after the initial exempt trade, depending on which exemption was relied on for the initial trade. In some circumstances, resales may occur immediately so long as the issuer has been a reporting issuer for at least twelve months (*OSA*, ss. 72(4), (5), & (6)).

d) Continuous and Timely Disclosure

Once a corporation has become a reporting issuer, it has certain mandatory "continuous" disclosure obligations which are designed to ensure that buyers and sellers in the market have sufficient information to make informed decisions. Continuous disclosure requires issuers to distribute to security holders certain financial information as well as certain information in connection with annual and special meetings of security holders. These requirements are similar to those imposed under the *CBCA* described in chapter 6.

Within 140 days of the end of each financial year, the corporation must file with the OSC and distribute to security holders audited financial statements showing the results of that year and comparative information for the previous year, as well as management's discussion and analysis of the financial results (*OSA*, s. 78; *OSA Regulation*, ss. 10–11, OSC Policy 5.10). Usually these statements are included in a more or less glossy annual report in which management describes the firm's business and its expectations for the future. Reporting issuers must also file and distribute to security holders unaudited interim financial statements showing the results for each three-month period (*OSA*, s. 77; *OSA Regulation*, ss. 7–9).

In addition to these continuous disclosure obligations, securities law imposes "timely" disclosure obligations that arise each time a material change occurs in the affairs of a reporting issuer (*OSA*, s. 75). In each case the issuer must issue a press release disclosing the nature and substance of the change and file a material change report with the OSC.

A change is material if it reasonably would be expected to have a significant effect on the market price or value of the securities of the reporting issuer (see National Policy 40, "Timely Disclosure").[13]

C. INSIDER TRADING

1) Introduction

An additional aspect of disclosure in relation to reporting issuers is the filing of reports by certain "insiders" of the issuer,[14] such as a director or officer, whenever such insiders trade securities. A broader class of persons may not trade where they have knowledge of a material fact in relation to an issuer if the fact has not been disclosed to the public. This broader class includes persons whose relationship with the issuer is such that they are likely to have access to relevant material information concerning the issuer which is not known to the public. At common law there was no prohibition on trading by such persons; they had no duty to disclose such information to people they buy from or sell to.[15] The genesis of statutory regulation of insider trading was the Kimber Report completed for the Ontario government in 1965.[16] The Report recommended that regulation of trading by insiders was necessary to prevent them from making profits from their inside information and to ensure public confidence in the securities markets.[17] As will be discussed below, there are many commentators who have challenged the way in which insider trading is regulated and the basis for such regulation, but before we discuss these criticisms of the statutory scheme we will outline the scheme itself.

2) The Statutory Scheme

The statutory schemes governing insider trading are extraordinarily complex; the following is only an outline. In most jurisdictions the scheme has the following elements: an obligation to report trades, liability to the issuer for profits made by insiders from insider trading, liability to other traders in the market place for damages suffered as a result of

---

13 Stock exchanges on which securities of a corporation are listed also impose disclosure obligations.

14 The securities regime applies to insiders of all reporting issuers, corporate and otherwise.

15 *Percival v. Wright*, [1902] 2 Ch. 421.

16 Ontario, *Report of the Attorney General's Committee on Securities Legislation in Ontario* (Toronto: Queen's Printer, 1965) (Chair: J.R. Kimber).

17 *Ibid.* at para. 2.02.

insider trading, and criminal liability in some circumstances. Depending on the jurisdiction, insider trading rules may be found in corporate statutes, in securities statutes, or in both. As noted above, securities legislation in each jurisdiction applies to business entities that have distributed securities in that jurisdiction. Trading by insiders of such entities is regulated under the securities laws of many jurisdictions in Canada, including Ontario. Trading by insiders of non-offering corporations incorporated in Ontario is dealt with in the *OBCA* (Part X). The *CBCA* provides a complete scheme for the regulation of insider trading which applies only to insiders of corporations incorporated under the *CBCA* (Part XI). The various provincial schemes for the regulation of insider trading often overlap for corporations doing business outside the province in which they were incorporated. Insiders in such corporations may be subject to regulation in the jurisdiction of incorporation as well as in the other provinces in which they are doing business. Insiders of federally incorporated corporations will be subject to the *CBCA* as well as provincial rules in each province where they offer securities. The following discussion is based on the Ontario *Securities Act* and the *CBCA*.

The first, and perhaps the most complex element of the statutory schemes regulating insider trading is the definition of those to whom the scheme applies. The starting point for the application of insider trading rules is the following group of persons, all of whom are defined to be insiders:

• the corporation issuing the securities;
• directors and senior officers of the corporation;
• directors and senior officers of subsidiary corporations and corporations that are themselves insiders; and
• persons who own more than 10 percent of the shares of the corporation or who exercises control over more than 10 percent of the votes attached to shares of the corporation (*OSA*, s. 1(1); *CBCA* s. 126).[18]

The scope of this definition is extremely wide and may result in a heavy burden on businesses. It is possible to obtain an exemption from the reporting obligations, though not from civil liability as will be discussed later in this chapter (*OSA*, s. 121(2); OSC Policy 10.1; *CBCA*, s. 127(8))

Insiders have a duty to report all trades, whether based on undisclosed information or not (*OSA*, s. 107; *CBCA*, s. 127). Under the *CBCA*, the reporting obligations apply only to insiders of *distributing* corporations, while the civil liability provisions apply to a broader class of insiders of all

---

18   Ontario *Business Corporations Act*, R.S.O. 1990, c. B.16, s. 138(1) [*OBCA*]. The *OBCA* definition includes all officers and employees of the corporation, all persons retained by the corporation, and all affiliated corporations, not just subsidiaries.

corporations under the *CBCA*. Under the *OSA*, reporting obligations apply only to insiders of reporting issuers.[19] For simplicity, the balance of this section will refer only to reporting issuers. In Ontario, reports must be filed with the OSC and with any other designated authority under any applicable corporate law within ten days of the end of the month in which a trade is made by an insider or by which a person became an insider (*OSA*, ss. 107(1) & (2); *CBCA*, ss. 127(1) & (4)). The purpose of disclosure is to inhibit trading on undisclosed information. Failure to file when required is an offence (*OSA*, ss. 122(1) – (3); *CBCA*, s. 127(9)(10)).

The *CBCA* and the *OSA* impose civil liability for trading with information that has not been generally disclosed.[20] For the purpose of attaching civil liability, the definition of who is liable is much broader than for the reporting requirements set out above. Civil liability attaches to any person or corporation in a "special relationship" with a reporting issuer. Such a special relationship may arise in a wide variety of circumstances, including the following:

- a person is associated with or an affiliate of the reporting issuer;[21]
- a person is proposing to make a takeover bid for the reporting issuer;
- a person is proposing to become a party to a reorganization involving the reporting issuer;[22]
- a person is an officer or an employee of the issuer, or is retained by the corporation or any affiliated corporation;
- a person is engaged in or proposes to engage in any business or professional activity with or on behalf of the reporting issuer, or with or on behalf of a takeover bidder or a party to a reorganization involving the reporting issuer; and
- a person (a "tippee") learns of a material fact or a material change with respect to the reporting issuer from an insider or any other person referred to above, including a person who receives such information from a tippee (*OSA*, ss. 76(5) & 134(7); *CBCA*, s. 131).

Every person in such a special relationship with a reporting issuer who purchases or sells the issuer's securities and has knowledge of a material fact or a material change concerning the issuer that has not been generally disclosed is liable to compensate the seller or the purchaser,

---

19   Reporting issuers were discussed in the previous section, B(1)(c).

20   The *OBCA* imposes civil liability in such circumstances in relation to non-offering corporations (*OBCA*, above note 18, s. 138(5)).

21   "[A]ssociate" is defined in section 1(1) of the *OSA*, above note 7; "affiliated companies" is defined in sections 1(2), (3), & (4) of the *OSA*.

22   A reorganization includes an amalgamation, merger, or similar business arrangement (*OSA*, *ibid.* s. 76(5)(a)(ii)).

as the case may be, for damages resulting from the trade (*OSA*, s. 134(1); *CBCA*, s. 127(4(a)). Liability may be avoided if the person in the special relationship can prove that she reasonably believed that the material fact or change had been generally disclosed or the material fact or change was known or ought reasonably to have been known to the seller or purchaser.

Similar rules govern "tipping" by persons in a special relationship. A reporting issuer or a person in a special relationship who informs another person of a material fact or change that has not been generally disclosed is liable to compensate any person that thereafter sells securities of the reporting issuer to or buys such securities from the person who received the information. The same defences mentioned above are available (*OSA*, s. 134(2); *CBCA*, s. 127(1)). Under the *OSA*, the tipper may also avoid liability if the information was given in the necessary course of business (s. 134(2)(f)).

In addition to this liability to sellers and purchasers of securities from persons with inside information, an insider or an affiliate or associate of a reporting issuer who trades with insider information or gives a tip is accountable to the corporation for any advantage received as a result of the purchase, sale, or tip, unless the person reasonably believed that the inside information had been generally disclosed (*OSA*, s. 134(4); *CBCA*, s. 127(4)). It is not clear whether the advantage would be reduced to the extent of any compensation required to be paid to a person with whom the insider associate or affiliate dealt. Under the *OSA*, this liability to the corporation does not extend to everyone in a special relationship with the corporation but only insiders, affiliates, and associates. Under the *CBCA*, liability extends to all those in a special relationship.

The operation of this statutory scheme may be illustrated by an example. Assume that the shares of A Corporation are listed on the Toronto Stock Exchange and have been trading at an average price of $10 per share for the last month. The directors have been advised that someone will make a takeover bid for all the shares of a corporation at a price of $15 per share. On obtaining this information, one director buys 1000 shares for $10. The bid is made a few days later and the director sells his shares for $15 per share, for a profit of $5 per share. The director will be accountable to the corporation for the $5 profit per share and liable to those who sold him the 1000 shares for the same amount. If, instead of buying the shares himself, he told his dentist, who bought 1000 shares at $10 and sold them into the bid, the director would have the same liability to the seller of the shares, but may have no liability to the corporation because he received no benefit from the tip. The tippee, the dentist, would also be liable to the seller. Liability of the director and the tippee would be subject to the defences mentioned.

Where an insider trade or a tip has occurred and no action is being taken by the reporting issuer to seek relief, the OSC or any security holder at the time of the trade or the tip may apply to the court for an order directing the OSC or any other person to initiate an action on behalf of the reporting issuer (*OSA*, s. 135(1)). Under the *CBCA*, such an action could be taken in accordance with the procedure for commencing a derivative action discussed in chapter 9 (*CBCA* s. 239).

Any person in a special relationship who trades with insider information or gives a tip is guilty of an offence under the *OSA* and the *CBCA* (*OSA*, ss. 76 & 121; *CBCA*, s. 251). Under the *OSA*, where a person has made a profit by reason of the contravention, the fine shall be not less than the profit made by the person and not more than the greater of three times the profit and $1,000,000 (*OSA*, ss. 76 & 122(4)). Criminal enforcement has been rare.

3) Some Observations on Insider Trading Regulation

While the approach recommended by the Kimber Commission and adopted in Canadian legislation has some intuitive appeal in that it seeks to prevent insiders from taking advantage of information denied to others in the marketplace, there is a substantial academic literature claiming various benefits from insider trading and arguing for less onerous regulation.[23] All this literature is based on certain assumptions about the way securities markets work, which may be summarized as follows. Investors buy securities to receive returns in both the form of dividends and the increase in the value of the securities over time. The price investors are willing to pay is a function of these returns and the risk associated with these returns. An assessment of these variables is based on all available information about the corporation and its business. An investor's buying and selling decisions are based on whether the price in the market is above or below what she calculates is the value of the shares or, more practically, the price she is prepared to pay. To oversimplify, if the calculated price of a share is more than the market price, she will buy (or hold the share if she already owns it); if it is less than the market price, she will not buy (or sell the share if she already owns it). Transactions in the market place between investors making these calculations is what determines the price in the market. Based on these assumptions, the price should change only when new information causes investors to redo their calculations of risk and return and make different buy or sell decisions.

---

23   For the purposes of the discussion in this section, "insider" refers to all those whose behaviour is subject to the insider trading regime (i.e., defined insiders and those in a special relationship with the issuer).

Assume, for example, that the shares of a gold mining corporation trade on the Toronto Stock Exchange. Investors will buy the shares up to the point at which, in their calculations, the price represents a fair approximation of the present value of the future returns on the share, taking into account the risk associated with those returns, meaning how likely it is that they will be received. The price should stay at this equilibrium level until some new information, good or bad, is disclosed which will cause investors to do their present value calculations differently. So, if it was disclosed that the corporation had made an enormous gold find, investors would increase their expected returns and be prepared to pay more for the shares. Their purchases would push up the price of the shares. By contrast, if certain claims in which the corporation had expected to find gold turned out not to have any deposits that were commercially feasible to extract, the disclosure of this news would cause investors to reduce the price they would be willing to pay for the shares. If such investors were holding the shares, they would try to sell them. This sale, in turn, should cause the price to decline. Needless to say, this process of re-evaluating share price based on new information is going on constantly. It is because of the importance of information to the working of the market that the continuous and timely disclosure obligations described above were imposed.

It is also because of this link between information and securities price that insider trading is regulated. To ensure that trading in markets is fair, in the sense that no one is making a buying or selling decision without access to information that the other person involved in the transaction has, insiders are not permitted to trade with information that is not disclosed generally, and, if they do, they must pay compensation to those with whom they trade. This claim that insider trading needs to be regulated in the interests of equal access to information can readily be challenged, however, since it is obvious that not all participants have equal access even to publicly available information. The full-time professional investment adviser will have access to information and, more important, analysis that will not be shared with the investor who reads only the financial pages of the local newspaper. In this context it is possible to ask why insider information may not be used when other information not universally shared may be. Also, if securities markets function efficiently there is no obvious reason to suppose that, if insider trading were permitted, prices would not adjust to reflect any risk associated with such trading. Nevertheless, insiders' access to undisclosed information is the main basis on which insider trading regulation is justified.[24]

---

24   *Green v. Charterhouse Group Canada Ltd.*, [1973] 2 O.R. 677 at 741 (H.C.J.), aff'd (1976), 12 O.R. (2d) 280 (C.A.).

Insider trading regulation is justified also on the basis that the inside information is the property of the corporation which cannot be appropriated by the insider for her own benefit. This position suffers from some obvious conceptual weaknesses: it can justify compensation only to the corporation, not people who trade with insiders, and presumably would permit a corporation to issue and purchase its own shares based on insider information which, as discussed, is not permitted.

Even if the regulation of insider trading were justifiable in principle, it is possible to criticize the current scheme of insider trading regulation on the basis of the arbitrary way it operates in modern securities markets. The scheme gives a claim only to the person who bought from or sold to the insider, even though it is completely arbitrary whose buy or sell order is matched with the insider's in the marketplace. All sellers and buyers in the marketplace arguably suffer a loss when an insider trades. For example, assume that a shipment of a corporation's gold has been stolen, that the price of the corporation's shares will fall when this information reaches the market, and that the corporation's president sold 1000 shares of the corporation before the information was disclosed to avoid a personal loss. The person who bought the president's shares would suffer a loss when the news was disclosed and the price dropped to $5, but so would anyone else buying after the theft but before its disclosure.[25]

In addition to attacking the conceptual underpinnings and the practical operation of current insider trading regulation, commentators have attributed some benefits to insider trading. The main benefit claimed is that insider trading facilitates the operation of securities markets by tending to push securities prices towards fair prices. Because insiders trade on information not generally available, their buying and selling decisions will be better informed and more accurately reflect the true price of the security. Even where the volume of securities traded by insiders is relatively small and the direct effect on supply and demand correspondingly limited, insider trading may still have a significant effect on price because the insider trading itself is information that other participants in the market will respond to. So, for example, when the president in the example above sells her shares, this sale signals to other participants in the marketplace that she, based on her inside information, expects share price to fall. It should encourage other traders to sell as well, driving down the price towards

---

25   While one option might appear to be imposing liability to compensate all such traders, it would be impractical to administer. Under such a regime, an insider trading even one share would thereby potentially be subject to almost unlimited liability.

where it should be, given the change in the corporation's circumstances, even before the change is disclosed to the public. In this way it is said that insider trading speeds the transition from one equilibrium price to another.

Accurate pricing of securities encourages investor confidence in the securities markets, facilitating the raising of capital and liquidity in securities markets. The policy implication of this analysis is that insider trading should not give rise to criminal or civil liability. The magnitude of the benefits of insider trading has been questioned, however, on the basis that, given continuous and timely disclosure requirements, insider information should be disclosed and impounded into share price relatively quickly in any event.

In conclusion, finding the optimal scheme for the regulation of insider trading is problematic. There appear to be benefits and costs associated with insider trading in principle. Some greater accuracy in securities pricing must be balanced against a concern about some notion of fairness in securities markets if markets are to work most efficiently. Also, even acknowledging that some regulation is desirable, defining the class of person who should be eligible for compensation is both conceptually and practically difficult.

D. TAKEOVER BIDS

1) Introduction

One of the most written about situations involving public corporations is the hostile takeover bid. In chapter 7 we mentioned that the operation of the market for corporate control is one of the non-legal mechanisms that tends to reduce the incentives for directors and officers to engage in behaviour to benefit themselves at the expense of the corporation. Takeover bids and, perhaps more important, the threat of them reduce agency costs in this way. In chapter 8 we briefly discussed the ways in which this market mechanism was complemented by the fiduciary duty.

In this section we briefly discuss the framework for the regulation of takeover bids and the ways it seeks to ensure that bids are conducted in a manner that is fair to all shareholders. We will also revisit the question raised in chapter 8: What is the best way to balance the general interest in maintaining an effectively functioning market for corporate control against permitting directors to take action to try to defeat bids that are not in the corporation's interests?

2) The Statutory Framework

a) The Basic Scheme

Takeover bids are regulated under the *CBCA* as well as under provincial securities law. The requirements are broadly similar. In each jurisdiction the law requires certain disclosure regarding the bid, establishes a procedure that the bid must follow, imposes certain rules to ensure that all security holders are treated equally, and provides certain exemptions. Where a bid is made for a *CBCA*-incorporated corporation, the requirements of the *CBCA* and the securities legislation in any province where persons holding securities subject of the bid reside must all be satisfied. Although the laws are similar they are not the same, so this overlap may impose different and sometimes conflicting requirements. In general, it is sufficient to comply with the more onerous requirements. The following discussion describes the scheme under the *OSA* and the *CBCA*.

Takeover bid requirements apply only when there is a "takeover bid" as defined in the relevant legislation. Under the *OSA* and the *CBCA* schemes, a takeover bid occurs when an "offer to acquire" voting or equity[26] securities of a class is made and the acquisition will result in the bidder ending up with more than 20 percent of the outstanding securities of that class (*OSA*, s. 89(1)).[27] An "offer to acquire" is made not only where the bidder makes an offer to purchase shares but includes a solicitation of an offer and an acceptance of an offer to sell shares (*OSA* s. 89(1)).[28] An offer by a corporation to acquire its own shares is also a takeover bid, usually referred to as an "issuer bid."

In order to make a takeover bid, the bidder must prepare a disclosure document called a takeover bid circular and send it to all shares holders to whom the bid is made, the corporation whose shares are the subject of the bid (the "target"), and the securities authorities in each provincial jurisdiction in which there are persons holding shares subject of the bid (*OSA*, ss. 98 & 100; *OSA Regulation*, s. 170, Form 32; *CBCA*, ss. 198 & 200; *CBCA Regulations*, ss. 59–62).[29] The bidder must

---

26 An equity security is defined as any right to participate in the earnings of the issuer and, on liquidation or dissolution, in its assets (*OSA*, above note 7, s. 89(1)). The *Canada Business Corporations Act*, R.S.C. 1985, c. C-44 [*CBCA*] scheme applies only to voting shares. In this section we will refer only to shares.

27 Under the *CBCA* the threshold is 10 percent (*ibid.*, s. 194).

28 The *CBCA* does not include an acceptance of an offer (*ibid.*, s. 194).

29 The *CBCA* requires that the takeover bid circular be sent to all shareholders in Canada, the directors of the corporation, and the Director appointed under the *CBCA*.

make its offer to all holders of securities of the class of shares subject of the bid in each provincial jurisdiction in which such shares' holders are resident (*OSA*, s. 95(1)). The *CBCA* simply provides that the offer must be made to all shareholders of the class subject of the bid in Canada (*CBCA*, s. 198(1)).

The directors of the target must send all offeree shareholders a director's circular within ten days of the bid being made. In their circular, the directors must recommend acceptance or rejection of the bid or state that they make no recommendation; whatever their recommendation, they must provide their reasons (*OSA*, s. 99; *OSA Regulation*, ss. 172 & 173, Forms 34 & 35; *CBCA*, s. 201; *CBCA Regulations*, ss. 64, 68, & 69). Under the *OSA*, offeree shareholders have a civil right of action for a misrepresentation in a takeover bid circular or a directors' circular (*OSA*, s. 131).

Once the bid is made it must remain open for acceptance by the offerees for at least twenty-one days (*OSA*, s. 195; *CBCA*, s. 197(c)). If a variation is made in the terms of the bid, it must be extended for an additional ten days (*OSA*, s. 98(5)).[30] These time periods are to ensure that shareholders have a reasonable opportunity to consider the bid. Also, where a bid is expressed to be made for less than all the shares of a particular class, the bidder cannot simply accept the first shares that are tendered. If this were permitted, shareholders might feel stampeded into tendering their shares as soon as possible to ensure that they will be able to sell to the bidder. Where a bid is made for less than all the shares of a class and more shares are tendered than the bidder sought, the bidder must acquire shares on a *pro rata* basis from each shareholder who tendered up to the maximum amount sought (*OSA*, s. 95(7); *CBCA*, s. 196(c)).

Sometimes competitive takeover bids will be made for a target corporation. For offeree shareholders such competition is highly desirable, since the competition for their shares typically will result in better terms being offered to them. In order to facilitate the competitive process, shareholders who tender their shares under one bid retain the right to withdraw them and tender them to another bidder any time up to the expiry of the twenty-one day period (*OSA*, ss. 95(4)–(6)).[31] If the terms of the bid are varied by the bidder, the withdrawal rights period cannot expire until at least ten days after notice of the variation is delivered to all persons who were sent the takeover bid circular (*OSA*, s. 95(4)). If only cash is being offered to the offerees and the change is either a

---

30   There is no equivalent *CBCA* requirement.
31   Under the *CBCA*, a shareholder may withdraw only within ten days of the date of the bid (*ibid.*, above note 26, s. 197(a)).

waiver of a condition imposed by the bidder, such as the tendering of a minimum percentage of shares in a class, or an increase in the consideration being offered, no such increase in the withdrawal rights period is required (*OSA*, ss. 95(4), (5), & 98(6)).[32]

Shares tendered under a takeover bid must be taken up by the bidder within ten days of the expiry of the bid and must be paid for within three days thereafter (*OSA*, ss. 95(9) & (10)).[33]

Takeover bid rules are designed to ensure that shareholders are treated equally by bidders. All shareholders must be offered identical consideration (*OSA*, ss. 97(2) & (3)).[34] If the consideration to be paid to shareholders is increased after the bid is made, the increased consideration must be paid to all shareholders, including those who had already tendered their shares before the increase. Also, the bidder's ability to purchase shares on the open market, such as through a stock exchange, is restricted during the period of the bid. If the bidder intends to make such purchases, it must announce its intention to do so in the takeover bid circular and cannot start to do so until at least three days after the commencement of the bid. The purchases must be made through the facilities of a stock exchange and the bidder must issue a press release at the close of business of the exchange on each day that it makes purchases (*OSA*, ss. 94(2) & (3); *CBCA*, s. 197(e) & (f)).[35] Finally, while a bid is open the bidder cannot tender shares into another bid (*OSA*, s. 94(8)).[36]

b) Exemptions

A variety of transactions that would otherwise be takeover bids are exempt from the requirements described above. Some of the exemptions most commonly relied on are described in this section.

Perhaps the most important exemption is for the acquisition of shares of a closely held corporation. Securities laws generally exempt a bid to acquire securities where there are fewer than fifty holders of securities of that class, the target has not distributed its shares to the public, and there is no published market for the securities (*OSA*, s. 93(1)(d)). Under the

---

32   There is no equivalent provision in the *CBCA*.
33   Under the *CBCA*, shares must be taken up and paid for within fourteen days of the expiry of the bid (above note 26, s. 197(b)).
34   There is no equivalent provision in the *CBCA*.
35   The *CBCA* does not specify a waiting period before open market purchases can commence. Also, the federal Act provides that if a price is paid in an open market purchase that is higher than the bid price, the bid price is deemed to be increased to this higher price (above note 26, s. 197(f)).
36   There is no equivalent requirement under the *CBCA*.

CBCA, offers to purchase shares of a *CBCA* corporation are exempt if the corporation has fewer than fifteen shareholders (*CBCA,* s. 194(c)).

An exemption is also available for the acquisition of a controlling block of shares from up to five shareholders so long as the offer price does not exceed the market price by more than 15 percent (*OSA,* s. 93(1)(c); *CBCA,* s. 194(a)(no 15 percent premium restriction)).

Another important exemption is for what are referred to as "normal course purchases." Any acquisition of shares by a person with 20 per-cent of the shares of a particular class falls within the definition of take-over bid and so would be subject to the full requirements described above. Since, for small purchases, this would serve no useful purpose, securities laws exempt purchases of up to 5 percent of the shares of a class within any twelve month period at the market price (*OSA,* s. 93(1)(b); *CBCA,* s. 194(b); *CBCA Regulations,* s. 58, contains a somewhat broader exemption).

Bids made through a recognized stock exchange, such as the Toronto Stock Exchange, are exempt, though stock exchanges have their own requirements that are more or less similar to those under securities leg-islation (*OSA,* s. 93(1)(a); *CBCA,* s. 194(b), *CBCA Regulations,* s. 58; e.g., *Toronto Stock Exchange By-law,* ss. 23.01–23.15).

Finally, in all jurisdictions it is possible to make an application to the relevant authority for an exemption for a bid that does not fit within any of the available exemptions (*OSA,* s. 192)(c); *CBCA,* ss. 194 & 204).

c) Compulsory Acquisitions

In some jurisdictions, where a takeover bidder has successfully acquired the overwhelming majority of the shares of the class subject of the bid, the bidder has a right to acquire the remaining shares it does not own. Under the *CBCA* and the *OBCA,* if a bidder has acquired more than 90 percent of the shares of a class subject to a takeover bid, not counting those held by the bidder when the bid was made, the bidder is entitled to put the holders of shares not tendered to an election: the shareholders must either transfer their shares to the bidder on the terms of the bid or notify the bidder that they demand to be paid fair value for their shares (*CBCA,* s. 206; *OBCA,* s. 188). "Fair value" is discussed in chapter 9 under "Dissent and Appraisal Rights." It may be more or less than the amount offered by the bidder. At the request of either the bidder or the dissenting shareholder, a court will determine fair value.

In addition, for Ontario corporations where a bidder has acquired 90 percent of a class of shares, any shareholder who has not tendered her shares is entitled to require the target corporation to acquire her shares for fair value (*OBCA,* s. 189). Where the 90 percent threshold has been exceeded, the corporation must send all security holders so entitled a notice informing them of their right and offering a price that the corporation is willing to pay. If the security holder is not satisfied with the price, he may require the corporation to apply to a court to have the fair value of the securities fixed.

d) Fiduciary Duties and Actions by Management to Defend against Takeover Bids

The statutory scheme, for the most part, does not address what is acceptable behaviour on the part of management when confronted with a takeover bid. In large part, what people think should be permitted behaviour will depend on what kind of economic function they think takeover bids serve; whether they think they are efficiency and value-creating transactions or transactions without economic value.

Why do takeover bids get made? As discussed previously, one of the reasons is that the bidder believes the value of the corporation can be increased by some changes in management, including, probably, the replacement of existing directors and senior managers. In such circumstances, the self-interest of directors and senior managers in preserving their positions may lead them to try to defeat the takeover bid. Their opposition will often be contrary to the interests of shareholders. Those who sell their shares to the bidder will usually receive a substantial premium over the market price. Those who do not sell will reap the benefit of the improvements made by the bidder. To the extent that directors and management may take action to try to defeat the bid, not only will the shareholders lose the immediate benefits of the bid but also the general disciplinary effect of the market for corporate control, described in chapter 7, will be impaired. Hostile takeover bids will be made more expensive, and the incentive to launch a hostile bid will be reduced. As a result, fewer bids will be made, and directors and officers will not need to worry about them. On the other hand, if no defensive tactics are permitted, the only way directors and management can prevent a takeover bid would be to manage the corporation so effectively that no bidder could improve value by making the bid. Following this argument, the courts should apply the fiduciary duty to prevent all defensive measures.

There are, however, motivations for takeovers other than changing management to increase value. Some of them are less threatening to management and may even encourage management to cooperate in the completion of the bid. There may be what is referred to as synergy between the bidder and the target. For example, the combination of the two enterprises may lead to more efficient operations through more intensive use of available resources, such as plants. It may be that the combination will result in a diversified combined entity which will have more stable returns. For example, a bid might be launched to combine a heating business with an air conditioning business to overcome the opposite seasonal downturns in each business. There are also other motivations that are less obviously positive. A bid might be made to eliminate a competitor. Finally, there are other non-economic reasons that may encourage takeovers, such as managerial self-aggrandizement.

The diversity of possible motivations for takeover bids means there is a wide range of possible consequences of a particular takeover bid. This range makes it difficult to formulate rules to govern the behaviour of directors and managers when a bid is made or in anticipation of a bid. Some takeover transactions will be in the best interests of the corporation, its shareholders and other stakeholders, while others will not be. While permitting management to defend against takeover bids puts them in the kind of conflict of interest the common law has sought long to avoid, prohibiting them from doing so means that takeovers which are not in shareholders' interests will be permitted to go ahead. The simplest example of the problem raised by a prohibition on defensive tactics is a bid at a price that the directors and officers correctly believe is less than the actual value of the corporation.[37] In such circumstances, defensive measures by management will be in the best interests of the corporation and its shareholders.

Another factor complicating the regulation of defensive measures is the huge and constantly expanding range of measures in use. Historically, the most common method was for directors to issue shares to persons who will not tender into the bid.[38] More recently, corporations have amended their articles to adopt what management call "shareholder rights plans" and their opponents call "poison pills." These provisions work in various ways, but the archetypal model is that the shareholders receive rights to purchase additional shares of the corporation at some price much higher than the current market price of the shares. If a bidder purchases in excess of a specified percentage of the target's shares, the price at which the rights are exercisable drops to a level much below the market price. The bidder itself is precluded from exercising these rights. Management is given some power to waive the exercise of these rights. The result is that the bidder must either negotiate with

---

37   In order for this to be the case there would have to be some inefficiency in the way in which the market priced the shares of the corporation. The most likely situation in which this might occur is where the directors possess inside information that suggests a higher value.

38   For example, *Hogg v. Cramphorn Ltd.* (1966), [1967] Ch. 254 [*Hogg*].

management to exercise its waiver or face a dramatic increase in the cost of the bid as shareholders exercise their rights. It is far beyond the scope of this book to describe these measures much less analyse what the appropriate scope of management's use of them should be.[39] Doing so would necessitate dealing with the substantial theoretical and empirical literature on defensive measures.[40]

Nevertheless, it is possible to summarize the general position established in the few English and Canadian cases on the actions of directors to defend against takeovers. A number of old cases had held that it was improper for directors to issue shares for the sole purpose of defeating an attempt by someone to gain control of the corporation even if they *bona fide* believed such an action to be in the best interests of the corporation.[41] This approach was rejected in *Teck Corp.* v. *Millar*[42] on the basis that directors must be able to act in the best interests of the corporation in responding to a takeover bid. They should be able to consider the consequences of a takeover bid and exercise their powers to defeat it if they genuinely believe that the success of the bid would not be in the corporation's best interests. This, of course, raises a significant problem: How is the court to determine if the purpose of the directors' action is to protect the interests of the corporation? In *Teck Corp.* v. *Millar*, Berger J. suggested that the courts should ask if there were reasonable grounds for the director's belief that they were acting in the corporation's best interests. This approach has been applied in some subsequent cases even where it has been acknowledged that one of the effects of the directors' actions has been incidentally to benefit the directors themselves, by maintaining their positions.[43] Indeed, in *Olympia & York Enterprises Ltd.* v. *Hiram Walker Resources Ltd.* the court seemed to suggest that the fiduciary duty to act in the best interests

---

39 See J.S. Ziegel, *et al.*, *Cases and Materials on Partnerships and Canadian Business Corporations*, 3d ed. (Toronto: Carswell, 1994) at 645–59, for a selection of excerpts from the extensive literature on this subject.

40 Ziegel, *ibid.*, sets out a selected bibliography and useful excerpts from this literature at 643–83. See also F.H. Buckley, M. Gillen, & R. Yalden, *Corporations: Principles and Policies*, 3d ed. (Toronto: Emond Montgomery, 1995) at 1052–1167.

41 *Bonisteel v. Collis Leather Co.* (1919), 45 O.L.R. 195 (H.C.J.). This approach was also followed in the leading English case of *Hogg*, above note 38.

42 (1972), 33 D.L.R. (3d) 288 (B.C.S.C.). A similar approach had been followed in *Spooner v. Spooner Oils Ltd.*, [1936] 2 D.L.R. 634 (Alta. C.A.), and the Australian case *Ashburton Oil No Liability v. Alpha Minerals No Liability* (1971), 45 A.L.R.J. 162 (Austl. H.C.).

43 *Olympia & York Enterprises Ltd.* v. *Hiram Walker Resources Ltd.* (1986), 59 O.R. (2d) 254 (Div. Ct.).

of the corporation imposed a positive duty to take defensive measures if the board believed the successful completion of the bid would not be in the interests of the corporation.[44]

Other cases have taken a more restrictive view. In *Exco Corp.* v. *Nova Scotia Savings & Loan Co.*,[45] the court held that the proper test was whether an action taken by the directors was not only in the best interests of the corporation but also inconsistent with any other interests, including the directors' personal interests.[46]

Accordingly, even the general criteria by which the actions of directors' and officers' conduct are to be judged are unclear. The cases provide no guidance on the many second-level questions that must be addressed before either test can be applied with confidence to particular situations. For example, they provide no guidance regarding how to determine if the defensive measure was reasonable, given the threat of injury to the corporation posed by the bid. Perhaps more important, the tests do not seek to reconcile what directors may do with the principle that shareholders rather than directors should have the right to determine to whom and on what terms they may sell their shares.[47]

Some guidance in this regard may be taken from National Policy 38, which specifically addresses defensive tactics in takeover bids. Although the policy statement does not purport to set out a code of behaviour for directors, it does express the policy basis for takeover bid regulation. It provides that the primary purpose of such regulation is to protect the *bona fide* interests of the shareholders of the target and to permit takeover bids to proceed in an open and even-handed environment. This policy suggests that defensive measures should not deny shareholders the ability to make a decision and that, whenever possible, prior shareholder approval should be obtained for proposed defensive measures. This policy was held to inform the content of directors' fiduciary duty in *347883 Alberta Ltd.* v. *Producers Pipelines Ltd.*[48]

---

44   *Ibid.* at 271–72.

45   (1987), 78 N.S.R. (2d) 91 (S.C.T.D.).

46   *Ibid.* at 271–72.

47   This principle was most forthrightly set out by the English Privy Council in *Howard Smith Ltd.* v. *Ampol Petroleum Ltd.*, [1974] A.C. 821 at 837–38 (P.C.), Lord Wilberforce.

48   (1991), 92 Sask. R. 81 (C.A.). In that case the same standard was applied to hold that a shareholder rights plan was oppressive of the interests of a minority shareholder.

E. CHAPTER SUMMARY

The focus of this chapter is a cluster of subjects of particular concern to corporations whose shares are publicly traded:

- the regulation of participants in securities markets;
- the requirements to qualify shares to be issued either by filing a prospectus or by relying on an exemption;
- insider trading regulation; and
- takeover bid regulation.

These subjects are regulated under provincial securities laws and, for federally incorporated corporations, the *CBCA*. The general purpose of such regulation is to ensure that participants in the market act honestly and that buyers and sellers have sufficient information to make decisions about investing in securities.

The general threshold requirement for the application of securities laws in relation to some activity is that the activity involve a "security." This requirement is easily met in most cases because the definition of security is extremely broad and open ended. It extends far beyond shares of corporations.

One of the ways in which securities laws seek to ensure that securities markets function effectively is to require securities dealers, investment advisers, underwriters, and others who make a business of participating in securities markets to meet certain standards of honesty, competency, and financial solvency. This certification is done by requiring such persons to register as a condition of their being eligible to participate. Certain exemptions from registration are available.

Securities laws also regulate the distribution of securities by requiring that a corporation desiring to issue securities prepare and distribute to prospective investors a prospectus which contains detailed disclosure about the corporation's business as well as the securities to be issued. Complying with the prospectus requirements is time consuming and expensive. Civil liability attaches to any misrepresentation in the prospectus.

The only way securities may be issued without complying with the prospectus requirements is if the transaction qualifies for one of the exemptions provided under securities laws. The general purpose of these exemptions is to waive the requirements where the nature of the purchaser or the security is such that prospectus-like disclosure is not required. Securities traded under an exemption can only be sold pursuant to another exemption unless the issuing corporation has filed a prospectus and certain other requirements, including the expiry of hold periods, are satisfied.

Once a corporation has issued its securities under a prospectus, it becomes a reporting issuer and must comply with certain continuous and timely disclosure obligations; these include sending financial statements to shareholders on a regular basis and disclosing any event that occurs and may affect the price of the corporation's shares.

An additional aspect of disclosure in relation to reporting issuers is that insiders of the corporation, including directors, senior officers, and significant shareholders, must report their trades in the corporation's securities. Also, if an insider, or anyone in a broadly defined group of people in a special relationship with the corporation, trade with information that has not been generally disclosed to the public, that person may be liable to the corporation and to everyone with whom she traded for any loss they incur. Anyone who trades on information from any such person will also be liable to the persons with whom she trades.

The regulation of insider trading is intended to ensure that people who have information denied to others are not permitted to profit from it by trading in securities markets. The regulation of insider trading has, however, been criticized on several bases. First, inside information is just one example of the information inequalities that characterize securities markets. Second, insiders should be encouraged to trade, since such trading reflects the best information available about a corporation and so leads to more accurate pricing of securities. Third, current liability schemes operate in an arbitrary way because they compensate only the person who actually traded with the insider or the person in a special relationship, while the persons injured by insider trading include anyone who trades before the disclosure of the insider information.

Finally, we discussed the regulation of takeover bids. Securities laws impose detailed requirements for how bids may be conducted to ensure that the bid is fair to all shareholders. Perhaps the most difficult issue in the context of takeover bid regulation is not addressed in securities law: What is the proper role of the directors and management in responding to a takeover bid? This issue is of great significance, since the ability of directors and management to defend against takeover bids will directly affect the likelihood of takeover bids being made, and an active market for control of corporations is one of the ways in which directors and managers will be discouraged from running the corporation in their own interests as opposed to those of the corporation, its shareholders, and other stakeholders. Unfortunately, the present law on the duties of directors and officers provides little guidance on what is acceptable behaviour on their part.

FURTHER READINGS

ALBOINI, V.P., *Securities Law and Practice*, 11 vols., (Toronto: Carswell, 1984) (looseleaf)

ANISMAN, P., J.L. HOWARD, & W. GROVER, *Proposals for a Securities Market Law for Canada*, 2 vols. (Ottawa: Consumer & Corporate Affairs, 1979)

BUCKLEY, F.H., M. GILLEN, & R. YALDEN, *Corporations: Principles and Policies*, 3d ed. (Toronto: Emond Montgomery, 1995), cc. 5, 8, and 11

GILLEN, M.R., "Sanctions against Insider Trading: A Proposal for Reform" (1991) 70 Can. Bar Rev. 215

GILLEN, M.R., *Securities Regulation in Canada* (Toronto: Carswell, 1992)

JOHNSTON, D., *Canadian Securities Regulation* (Toronto: Butterworths, 1977)

MACINTOSH, J.G., *Corporate Governance* (Toronto: Irwin Law) (forthcoming)

MACINTOSH, J.G., *Essentials of Securities Law* (Toronto: Irwin Law) (forthcoming)

MACINTOSH, J.G., *Legal and Institutional Barriers to Financing Innovative Enterprise in Canada* (Kingston: Queen's University, Policy Studies, 1994)

MACINTOSH, J.G., "The Poison Pill: A Noxious Nostrum for Canadian Shareholders" (1989) 15 Can. Bus. L J. 276

MANNE, H.G., *Insider Trading and the Stock Market* (New York: Free Press, 1966)

ONTARIO, *Report of the Attorney General's Committee on Securities Legislation in Ontario* (Toronto: Queen's Printer, 1965)

ZIEGEL, J.S., et al., *Cases and Materials on Partnerships and Canadian Business Corporations*, 3d ed. (Toronto: Carswell, 1994) at 643–739

CHAPTER 12

CONCLUSIONS

A. INTRODUCTION

In this chapter we try to draw together some of the themes that have been touched on throughout this book.

Beginning in chapter 1 we described a business organization as the intersection or locus of the claims of stakeholders, including owners, managers, creditors, customers, the public, government, and tort victims. All these groups have a stake in business decision making. In this context, both partnership law and corporate law have three principal functions. First, they represent an intervention in the marketplace which, to a greater or lesser extent, pre-empts bargaining between these groups and puts in place a regime that allocates the risk associated with the business activities of the corporation and the partnership between the stakeholders. As we have seen, in many respects the law of corporations favours the interests of shareholders over those of other stakeholders by allocating the risk associated with a business to other stakeholders for the benefit of shareholders, so as to encourage investment in the business. The second function of corporate and partnership law is to provide a scheme of default rules, which may be adopted by businesses, to govern the relationship between owners and managers and between members of each of these groups. The purpose of this second function is to reduce the costs of setting up a business: it permits some of the costs associated with negotiating such a governance scheme to be avoided. The third principal function of partnership and corporate law is to deal with agency costs: in the case of a corporation, those costs arising as a result of the corporation being managed by the directors and officers rather than by the shareholders directly; in the case of a partnership, those costs arising for a particular partner as a result of the partnership being managed by other partners or employees.

Most of the previous chapters focused on the relationship between management and shareholders in corporations incorporated under the *CBCA*. We discussed the allocation of responsibilities under the *CBCA* among shareholders, directors, and officers, as provided for in legislation and in practice, for both large and small corporations, as well as the mechanisms in place for shareholders to control management.

In this chapter we will revisit and expand on this previous discussion from the perspective of the interests of other stakeholders, by looking at the nature of management's obligations to shareholders and at the efficacy of the mechanisms to ensure that they are fulfilled. We will also examine the extent to which corporate law permits management to take the interests of other stakeholders into account in making decisions about the business and to what extent it requires management to do so. These are critically important issues, owing to the inherent conflicts between the interests of other stakeholders and shareholders. Once we have sketched out this broader legal context in which management must operate, we will discuss some of its implications for corporate governance. Finally, we will identify some of the trends in corporate governance drawing on this analysis.

B. MANAGEMENT'S OBLIGATIONS TO SHAREHOLDERS

1) The Nature of Shareholders' Interests in the Corporation

For most practical purposes, shareholders' interests are financial. Shareholders are interested in the dividends paid to them and the appreciation in the value of the claim that their shares represent against the corporation. Because the nature of the claim of at least one class of shares, typically common shares, is that they are entitled to any remaining property of the corporation on dissolution, holders of such shares may be prepared to forgo the receipt of dividends presently in favour of having the money that otherwise would have been paid out reinvested in the corporation to generate future growth in the corporation's assets. Such reinvestment increases the value of their residual claim. It is to get these two kinds of returns that people invest money in corporations.

People buy previously issued shares for the same reason. As a result, shareholders hope and expect that management will operate the corporation's business to the best of their ability to make profits either to be paid out as dividends or reinvested for future growth. In other words, shareholders want management to maximize their financial returns.

Canadian corporate law adopts this financial conception of shareholder interests. In chapter 7, for example, we saw that the shareholder's proposal right under the *CBCA* does not permit the making of a proposal "primarily for the purpose of promoting general economic, political, racial, religious, social or similar causes" (s. 137).[1]

2) Conflicts between the Interests of Shareholders and Other Stakeholders

It is not hard to identify circumstances in which the shareholders' interest in having management maximize their returns may conflict with the interests of other stakeholders. Corporate decision making will often have significant social and economic implications for stakeholders other than shareholders. Consider the following examples.

- A corporation decides to close a money-losing mine that is the single largest employer in a community, in the interests of maximizing returns to shareholders. Although such a decision will, in general, benefit those with a continuing economic interest in the health of the corporation, such as any remaining employees, creditors, and, of course, shareholders, the costs of such a decision will ripple throughout the community. Hundreds of people may be put out of work and the costs to the state of social assistance will skyrocket; businesses that supply goods and services to the workers will suffer; and so on. Under the current legal regime, most of these costs, referred to by economists as "externalities," are not borne by the corporation.
- A corporation that sells seeds to farmers decides to donate money for the development of rural health centres. Although the goodwill generated by such a donation may result in some economic benefits to shareholders

---

1   Canadian law is distinguished from American corporate law in this regard. See the American Law Institute, *Principles of Corporate Governance: Analysis and Recommendations* (Proposed Final Draft) (1992), which, while stating that the primary purpose of the corporation is enhancing corporate profit and shareholder gain, recognizes the appropriateness of corporations taking into account ethical considerations and the possibility of devoting a reasonable amount of resources to "public welfare, humanitarian, educational and philanthropic purposes" (§ 2.01).

and others interested in the economic health of the corporation, these benefits are indirect and hard to measure. The main effect, at least in the short term, will be a reduction in the pool of assets available to be paid out as dividends or reinvested. The donation may even marginally reduce the ability of the corporation to repay its creditors or meet its payroll. The reputational benefit may be reduced to the extent that the cause is politically controversial; for example, if the health centres were perceived to be advocating abortion.[2]

- A corporation puts in place a program to ensure its compliance with the minimum health and safety requirements imposed by law. Even complying with mandatory rules designed to protect certain stake-holders, such as occupational health and safety laws intended for the protection of employees, may be considered to require management to favour the protected group over others who have financial claims against the corporation which may be negatively affected. To the extent that moving to the legal standards imposes additional costs on the corporation, its profits will be reduced, as will the returns to shareholders. If the corporation has sufficient market power, some of these increased costs may be passed on to customers. Nevertheless, complying with the law will not be a difficult choice for management members to make, especially since, under many modern regulatory regimes, they will be personally liable if they do not.[3]

- A more difficult decision for management to make will be whether the minimum statutory standards should be exceeded. Although this choice will impose costs in the same way as complying with the minimum standards, such costs may be mitigated by several factors. Because of its experience and expertise in relation to its own business, a corporation may be better placed to determine how higher standards may be most effectively and efficiently implemented. As a consequence, not only would the protected group receive a higher level of protection but the protection may be more effective and may be provided at less cost than if it were to come as the result of some new mandatory regulation; moving to this level now may eliminate future adjustment costs when the minimum standards

---

2   This example is based on an actual case: R. Gibson, "Boycott Drive against Pioneer Hi-Bred Shows Perils of Corporate Philanthropy" *Wall Street Journal*, (10 June 1992) B1 & B5. For another example of a corporation responding to political concerns, see D. Fagan, "Petrocan Ending Drilling in Myanmar: Criticism of Brutal Regime Considered" *Globe and Mail* (3 November 1992) B11.

3   Indemnification by the corporation may undermine these incentives. See the discussion in chapter 7 under "Indemnification."

are increased in the future. Indeed, proactively setting higher standards may decrease the likelihood of additional regulation. It may even be possible to obtain some competitive advantage if one can successfully lobby to have one's own enhanced standard legislated as the new minimum standard. As well, there may be reputational benefits to being the first to increase standards that may work to enhance sales.

Apart from complying with specific mandatory rules imposed on directors and officers, what are the obligations of directors and officers when confronted with conflicting stakeholder interests, such as in the circumstances described above? This general question may be broken down into several more specific questions. To what extent does corporate law require managers to act in shareholders' interests? Is management permitted to favour other interests? Is it only to the extent that these other interests somehow coincide with shareholder interests? Is management ever required to act in the interest of non-shareholder stakeholders? As we will see, in general, corporate law in Canada is based on the notion that management's job is to work for the interests of shareholders.

3) Legal Mechanisms Encouraging Management to Look after Shareholder Interests

In addition to various market mechanisms discussed in chapter 7, a primary focus of this book has been the legal mechanisms by which management is encouraged to be responsive to the interests of shareholders. The main concern for shareholders in this regard is agency costs, which include the direct costs associated with directors and officers, the agents of the shareholders, acting to further their personal interests, in an opportunistic way, at the expense of the corporation. There are related costs associated with what shareholders must do to monitor their agents in performing their duties so as to guard against such opportunistic behaviour.

Of the legal mechanisms, perhaps the most direct is shareholders' power to vote. If management is not maximizing shareholder returns, the shareholders, acting collectively, can either replace the board of directors or refuse to elect them at the next annual meeting. We discussed in chapter 7 some of the impediments to the effectiveness of shareholder voting in practice in corporations with many shareholders. Voting remains an important right for shareholders, particularly where shares are held by a controlling shareholder or by large institutional shareholders who do not face the same impediments as shareholders with less knowledge and experience and smaller share holdings.[4]

Because of the ineffectiveness of voting in corporations with many shareholders, instead of trying to effect change by voting, shareholders will often "vote with their feet" — meaning they will simply sell their shares if they are dissatisfied with the policies of present management and the corresponding returns. This market alternative is only available for holders of shares for which there is a ready market, such as those listed on a stock exchange. For such shareholders, the ability to sell is an important option. Also, it will tend to have an effect on the exercise of voting rights by the remaining shareholders. By increasing the supply of shares on the market, sales by dissatisfied shareholders will depress the share price, further encouraging the remaining shareholders to vote to replace the directors. At the same time, as discussed in chapters 7 and 11, the exercise by shareholders of their right to vote with their feet and the resulting drop in price will create an incentive for others to make a takeover bid for the corporation. By acquiring a majority of the voting shares, the takeover bidder can exercise the voting rights attached to the shares it acquires for the purpose of changing management. Both these market dynamics operate to support the right to vote as a mechanism for shareholder control.

Corporate law also imposes standards of behaviour on directors and officers through the fiduciary duty and the oppression remedy, which require them to act in the interests of shareholders. The standard represented by the oppression remedy is still emerging, and the potential beneficiaries extend to non-shareholder stakeholders in some circumstances that have not been precisely defined by the courts. Nevertheless, the primary category of intended beneficiary is shareholders, and it is shareholders who have commenced the majority of oppression actions. As such, it has become an increasingly important mechanism for shareholders to control management. The fiduciary duty runs in favour of the corporation and so, conceptually, it might have been interpreted as requiring some reconciliation of stakeholder interests by directors and officers in their decision making. The courts, however, have consistently treated the interests of the corporation as virtually coextensive with the interests of shareholders; interests of other stakeholders may be considered only to the extent

---

4   These characteristics dominate the Canadian marketplace. We will discuss their implications below.

that they are reasonably incidental to carrying on business for the benefit of the shareholders.[5]

In *Dodge* v. *Ford Motor Co.*[6] the court held that the directors of a corporation could not operate the corporation's business for any purpose other than earning profits for the benefit of shareholders. While a court should not lightly interfere with management's decisions regarding how this purpose should be achieved, management may not abandon this purpose altogether. In that case the court refused to interfere with a plan by Henry Ford to expand the business by selling cars of better quality for cheaper prices, even though the immediate effect was to reduce profits. In the court's view, because such a plan ultimately might be in the interests of shareholders in that it increased profits in the long run, interference would be inappropriate.

The court did interfere with management decision making in the English case of *Parke* v. *Daily News Ltd.*[7] A corporation sold its principal business and the board decided to use the proceeds exclusively for the benefit of the employees and former employees by paying them for extra weeks of holidays, increased pensions, and other compensation that the corporation was under no obligation to pay. The court ordered that no such payments should be made. In the absence of a contractual commitment, payments could only be made if they could be considered to be reasonably incidental to carrying on the corporation's business. Here the court found that the payments were motivated by philanthropy and a desire to treat the employees generously, and so this test was not met. The court expressly held that the corporation had no duty to employees as a matter of law.

Thus management must always take into account shareholders' interests and ensure that what they do is reasonably incidental to carrying on the corporation's business for profit. How much room this leaves to take into account the interests of other stakeholders depends on how broadly one is willing to interpret "reasonably incidental." Although it is inherently problematic to try to articulate what the appropriate interpretation is, it is possible to identify some of the factors on which an

---

5   *Dodge* v. *Ford Motor Co.*, 170 N.W. 668 (Mich. S.C. 1919). The court did require the payment of uncommitted funds to the shareholders because the reason the board was withholding dividends was to be able to drop the price of cars and benefit the consuming population at large. This case represents a rare instance in which a court has required a corporation to pay dividends because of an improper motive for not paying them.

6   *Ibid.*

7   [1962] 1 Ch. 927.

assessment of reasonableness will depend. These factors include how far into the future the benefits may arise and how indirect the benefits may be. If one is prepared to consider as being incidental to the corporation's business actions that have no direct or immediate benefit in terms of profits, many actions primarily intended for the benefit of non-shareholder stakeholders may be upheld. For example, enhancing employee benefits may reduce short-term profits but may have benefits in terms of improved employee relations and fewer days lost to strikes; in addition a better public image may increase future profits. Although there have been statements by Canadian courts suggesting a broad view of what may be considered reasonably incidental,[8] the prevailing view has been a narrow one.[9]

4) Should Corporations Be Bound to Act in a Socially Responsible Way?

The conclusion of the foregoing analysis, that management is obliged to take into account the interests of shareholders alone, does not seem to reflect how corporate managers define their own roles. Many managers, if asked, will say that they are responsible to a wide range of stakeholders, including creditors, customers, and certainly the public.[10] In this section some of the considerations relevant to managers' obligation to take into account the interests of both shareholders and non-shareholder stake-

---

8   *Teck Corp.* v. *Millar* (1972), 33 D.L.R. (3d) 288 at 314 (B.C.S.C.):
    A classical theory that once was unchallengeable must yield to the facts of modern life. In fact, of course, it has. If today the directors of a company were to consider the interests of its employees no one would argue that in doing so they were not acting *bona fide* in the interests of the company itself. Similarly, if the directors were to consider the consequences to the community of any policy that the company intended to pursue, and were deflected in their commitment to that policy as a result, it could not be said that they had not considered *bona fide* the interests of the shareholders.
    See to similar effect *Miles* v. *Sydney Meat-Preserving Co. Ltd* (1913), 16 C.L.R. 50 at 64 (Austl. H.C.), aff'd (1914), 17 C.L.R. 639 (P.C.).
9   See Canada, *Report of the Industrial Inquiry Commission on Canadian National Railways "Run-Throughs"* (Ottawa: Queen's Printer, 1965) (Commissioner: S. Freedman).
10 For example, a vice-president of the Royal Bank was quoted as saying that contrary to the old belief that the shareholder is king, today's corporation is responsible to a wide variety of groups beyond shareholders — customers, employees, suppliers, and even the general public (D. Slocum, "Shareholder Activists Out of Line: Banker: Conference Probes Pension Funds' Role" *Globe and Mail* (8 December 1990) B6. The increasing currency of such views was recently described in L.D. Hebb, "Consider the Other Stakeholders" *Globe and Mail* (2 July 1996) B2.

holders will be discussed. To render the discussion more concrete, it will be based on one of the examples mentioned at the beginning of this section: the closure of a mine.

A management decision to close a mine will, in general, benefit those with a continuing economic interest in the health of the corporation, such as the shareholders, any remaining employees, and creditors, while the costs of such a decision will ripple throughout the community. The first ripple will be the loss of employment for the factory workers, followed by increases in the local cost of social assistance. Next, businesses that supply goods and services to the workers will begin to suffer and, in turn, more unemployment and demands for social services will result. The interests of creditors of the unemployed and such businesses will be prejudiced, as will the interests of the municipal, provincial, and federal governments in receiving tax revenue, and those with a stake in the local real estate market.

The magnitude of these effects will depend on various factors, including labour market mobility and the nature and strength of the local economy. If the local economy is otherwise strong and diversified, the effects of the closure will be mitigated. At the other extreme, if the local economy is entirely dependent on the continuation of the factory that closed, a "company town," these negative effects may well be dramatic.[11]

To assess the effect of a requirement that management should take the interests of other stakeholders into account, one would have to consider the aggregate costs and the aggregate benefits, as well as, in each case, the distributional consequences: Who will bear the costs and who will receive the benefits? Such assessments implicate contentious moral questions as well as complex calculations that management will often be ill equipped to make. An additional difficult question is, assuming such an obligation should be imposed: How should it be done? For example, should it be simply left up to the conscience of individual managers through a change to corporate law permitting non-shareholder interests to be considered, or should managers have a legally enforceable obligation to consider such interests? If so, should they be personally liable for failing to do so? Should the obligation take the form of a tax, the amount of which is related to the external social costs of the corporation's decision? Some would argue that requiring corporations to bear these costs directly is the only way to ensure that decision making is rational and efficient.

---

11 For example, J. Rochon, "Mining for Hearts of Stone" *Globe and Mail*, (28 February 1990) A7, which describes the effects of closing a mine that was the major employer in Kimberly, British Columbia, and proposes that corporations that take such decisions should pay a "community survival tax."

Whatever the policy instrument chosen to impose a requirement on corporations to take into account all the costs of their actions, management or, in the case of a tax, the state would be confronted with the difficult problem of defining when costs are too remote to be considered. As the example illustrates, the costs attending corporate decisions can be far reaching. Even if a satisfactory test of remoteness could be devised to define the relevant costs, the practical problem of assessing what those costs are would remain. Apart from these problems, the locus of claims nature of the corporation means that imposing responsibility for these costs on the corporation will ultimately impose costs on some of the stakeholders. Which classes of stakeholders will be affected will depend on the market power of the corporation.

If the corporation sells its products in a perfectly competitive market, it will have no ability to increase its prices to try to recover the increased costs because consumers will switch to another brand rather than pay the increased price. In such a case, the entire cost will be borne by shareholders as well as the remaining employees and creditors. To some extent, imposing costs on shareholders will mean imposing costs directly on individual investors, who are often supposed to be high net worth individuals capable of bearing the risk. In Canada, however, a large proportion of shares are held by financial institutions, such as mutual funds, pension funds, and insurance companies, whose ultimate beneficiaries are ordinary individuals who do not fit this stereotypical profile of the stock market investor. Whoever the investors are, the question must be asked: Are they the appropriate people to bear the costs? In today's global marketplace, inevitably some of the shareholders will be foreign. As a matter of Canadian government policy, should this make a difference? Any continuing employees and creditors of the corporation will also be negatively affected by the reduction in profits, in the sense that the risk that they will not get paid will increase. In the worst case, the corporation may be forced out of business and employees and creditors may not be paid at all.[12]

On the other hand, if the corporation has a monopoly on the products it sells or has some lesser degree of market power such that, even if it raises prices, it will keep some of its customers, it will be able to pass on some of the costs to its customers. How one views this result may well depend on the nature of the product. If it is a basic consumer product, such as food, the passing of these costs on to consumers may be viewed as an unaccept-

---

12 A much more thorough analysis of this kind is provided in R.A. Posner, *Economic Analysis of Law*, 3d ed. (Boston: Little, Brown & Co., 1986) at 394–97.

able regressive tax. If the product is industrial equipment, it may be another business that bears the cost, though the business, in turn, may be able to pass on such costs to its customers, to a greater or lesser extent.

The first point of the foregoing discussion is to demonstrate that corporate decision making affects a wide variety of stakeholder interests, and the position taken in Canadian corporate law, that management should have regard only for the interests of shareholders, means favouring their interests over those of other stakeholders. The second is that whether a corporation should be required to take into account other stakeholders, to what extent and by what means this should be done, are all questions that are very difficult to assess in the abstract. Arguably, in each case, one would have to determine who benefits and who loses from a particular decision, and by how much, as well as wrestling with whose interests should be preferred.

C. TRENDS IN CORPORATE LAW AND GOVERNANCE

1) Introduction

In this final section of the book we discuss some of the trends in the development of corporate law and the governance of corporations. In this discussion we draw on the analysis in the first part of the chapter and throughout the book. We will look at the implications of increasing share ownership by institutional investors, the increasing responsibilities of directors, and the ways in which the current discussions dealing with reform of the CBCA are responsive to these trends and some of the other issues raised throughout this book.

2) Institutional Ownership

Financial institutions own an increasingly large share of publicly traded shares in Canada.[13] Traditionally, most financial institutions carefully avoided playing any role in the management of the corporations in which they held shares. There are signs, however, that this is changing

---

13   Daniels and Waitzer suggest that between 50 percent and 60 percent of the shares of widely held companies traded in deep markets in Canada are held by institutional owners. (R.J. Daniels & E.J. Waitzer, "Challenges to the Citadel: A Brief Overview of Recent Trends in Corporate Governance" (1994) 23 Can. Bus. L.J. 23 at 33.)

and that institutional investors are becoming more active.[14] Most commentators have viewed this trend as a positive development because institutions should be able to overcome some of the impediments to the effective exercise of shareholder voting referred to in chapter 7. The investment departments of banks, pension funds, mutual funds, and insurance companies have a sophisticated understanding of business and the securities markets which they may bring to bear in exercising their voting rights. Also, because of the typically large stakes they hold, institutional investors may be prepared to gather and analyse the information needed to evaluate how management is performing and to try to coordinate shareholder action to vote on matters or to replace the board. Coordination among institutional investors is likely to be easier than among a large number of geographically disparate shareholders.

Increased institutional shareholder activism is, perhaps, especially important in Canada, given that one of the distinctive features of the Canadian marketplace is that most public corporations are controlled by a single shareholder or group of shareholders. While such control helps to ensure that management is responsive to shareholder concerns and reduce agency costs, at the same time it creates the potential for exploitive behaviour by the majority.[15] Such behaviour might include, for example, transactions between the corporation and the controlling shareholder on terms that are unfairly favourable to the shareholder.

The principal areas in which institutional shareholders have been active to date is in voting against the adoption of the so-called poison pill measures that permit management to defend against takeover bids.[16] As discussed in chapter 11, giving directors the power to block takeover bids will often not be in shareholders' interests. One result of increased institutional shareholder activism has been that many corporations now consult with their institutional shareholders before putting questions to a shareholder vote.[17] Although the actions of institutional shareholders appear to be still largely reactive and the degree of coordination between institutional investors limited, increased institutional shareholder activism

---

14 "Calpers Setting Governance Trend" *Globe and Mail* (1 July 1996) B3.
15 R.J. Daniels & P. Halpern, "Too Close for Comfort: The Role of the Closely Held Public Corporation in the Canadian Economy and the Implications for Public Policy" (1995) 26 Can. Bus. L.J. 11; R.K. Morck, "On the Economics of Concentrated Ownership" (1995) 26 Can. Bus. L.J. 63.
16 Daniels & Waitzer, above note 13 at 33–35.
17 *Ibid.* at 35–36.

has the potential to make directors and officers much more responsive to shareholder interests.

3) Directors' Liability

At the same time as institutional investors have been making directors and officers more accountable to the interests of shareholders, there has been an explosion in the range and scope of directors' liability in Canada to other stakeholders. It has resulted from the enactment of regulatory schemes, such as occupational health and safety laws and environmental laws that are designed to protect certain stakeholders, and from the judicial development of tort law[18] and the extension of relief under the oppression remedy to non-shareholder stakeholders. As a result, directors and officers have had to become sensitized as well as legally responsible to a range of interests that are much broader than and, as discussed above, often in conflict with those of shareholders.

Daniels and Waitzer suggest that the combination of these contradictory pressures leaves directors and officers in an intolerable situation.[19] The multiple, continuously changing sources of liability for directors and officers mean that it is increasingly difficult for them to know, with certainty, what their obligations are in particular circumstances. In turn, the absence of a clear standard against which directors and officers may be judged will tend to impair the effectiveness of shareholder oversight. Also, the risk of personal liability may discourage directors and officers from causing the corporation to engage in behaviour that presents or increases this risk. To the extent that this occurs, directors and officers may forgo attractive opportunities that would have been in the best interests of the corporation and desired by shareholders. The inadequacy or unavailability of liability insurance for directors and officers in Canada serves, it is argued, to exacerbate these problems.[20]

18   The former was discussed in chapter 8 while the latter was discussed in chapter 3.

19   Daniels & Waitzer, above note 13 at 42–43.

20   R.J. Daniels & S.M. Hutton, "The Capricious Cushion: The Implications of the Directors' and Officers' Insurance Liability Crisis on Canadian Corporate Governance" (1993) 22 Can. Bus. L.J. 182. As noted in chapter 7, the use of insurance and other forms of indemnification will blunt incentives for directors and officers to ensure compliance with statutory schemes imposing personal liability, contrary to the policy of such schemes.

The increased scope of director liability will make it harder for corporations to attract and keep highly qualified directors.[21] This was illustrated dramatically by the recent resignation of the entire board of directors, in an effort to avoid personal responsibility for employee wages and other liabilities, of three major Canadian corporations facing financial difficulties.[22] Unfortunately, it is when a corporation is facing financial difficulties and in other critical situations that a corporation's need for the leadership of an experienced board is the greatest. Also, if Canadian corporations do not have the benefit of talented board members, their prospects for thriving in increasingly competitive domestic and international markets will be diminished. As will be discussed in the next section, rationalizing directors' duties, which are imposed by corporate law, is a major objective of the current process of reforming the *CBCA*.

4) Corporate Law Reform

a) Introduction

Recently, Industry Canada has been engaged in a wide-ranging consultation process with a view to reforming the *CBCA* for a variety of purposes. As noted above, one of the major purposes is to rationalize the duties imposed on directors by the *CBCA*. Another is to improve the standard form contract function of corporate law by providing default provisions that more effectively reflect the characteristics business people seek in corporations. Related to improving the standard form contract, the reform process also involves a revamping of the unanimous shareholder agreement provisions so they will permit shareholders of closely held corporations to modify the way their corporations are governed to meet more fully their needs and expectations while eliminating unnecessary procedures.[23]

In this section we will briefly survey the reform discussions dealing with directors' liability and unanimous shareholder agreements. Such a

---

21 H.J. Glasbeek, in "More Direct Director Responsibility: Much Ado About . . . What?" (1995) 25 Can. Bus. L.J. 416, questions the significance of this deterrent effect (at 447–51).

22 Daniels & Waitzer, above note 13, refer to the resignations of the directors of Westar Mining Ltd., Canadian Airlines International Ltd., and Peoples Jewellers Ltd. in 1992 (at 43).

23 The Corporations Directorate of Industry Canada has facilitated discussion of reform of the *Canada Business Corporations Act*, R.S.C. 1985, c. C-44, through a series of discussion papers distributed in 1995 and 1996.

review is a useful way to conclude this book not only because it provides an indication of the future of corporate law in Canada but because it recalls some of the problems raised throughout the book and illustrates the relationships of some of the subjects discussed above.

b) Directors' Liability

In its discussion paper on directors' liability,[24] Industry Canada examines the problems with the expanding scope of directors' liability outlined above and provides a set of recommendations which seek to balance the need for adequate accountability of directors to shareholders and other stakeholders with the need to ensure that *CBCA* corporations are able to attract and keep highly qualified people to serve as directors. In particular, the discussion paper considers the desirability of amendments to the scope of the fiduciary duty. For example, it discusses whether the fiduciary duty of directors should be amended to clarify what is meant by the best interests of the corporation: Should corporate law strike a different balance between the interests of shareholders and those of other stakeholders from the one outlined above? Industry Canada noted the unsettled state of the case law on the obligation imposed by the fiduciary duty, especially in the context of hostile takeover bids, as discussed in chapters 8 and chapter 11, but rather than attempt any synthesis or suggest any change requiring the interests of non-shareholder stakeholders to be taken into account, the discussion paper recommended that any development in this area be left to the courts.[25]

The discussion paper recommended that the scope of the defence to allegations of breach of fiduciary duty available to directors under section 123(4) of the *CBCA* be expanded. As discussed in chapter 8, this provision permits directors and officers to rely on financial statements and the statements of certain professionals. Industry Canada recommended that a defence be available in all circumstances in which the director acted reasonably.[26] Such an approach would serve to mitigate the strictness of the fiduciary standard discussed in chapter 7.

The discussion paper dealt with a variety of other issues related to cutting back the effect of directors' liabilities, including recommending the expansion of the indemnification provisions to include the possibility of advancing defence costs[27] and indemnification in investigative, not

---

24   Industry Canada, *Directors' Liability (Canada Business Corporations Act* Discussion Paper) (Ottawa: Industry Canada, 1995).

25   *Ibid.* at 18.

26   *Ibid.* at 25.

27   *Ibid.* at 29.

merely civil, criminal and administrative proceedings.[28] In addition, Industry Canada recommended that the restrictions on the circumstances in which directors' and officers' liability insurance may be obtained be eliminated. Industry Canada concluded that it was more appropriate to let the market regulate the availability of insurance.[29] The discussion paper even contemplated, though it ultimately rejected, a dollar cap on directors' liability.[30] All such changes would directly reduce the disincentive for directors to engage in activity involving risk of personal liability. At the same time, they will blunt the disincentive to engage in activity contrary to various regulatory schemes that have adopted personal liability as a necessary way of ensuring compliance.

Finally, it is interesting that Industry Canada recommended amending the description of directors' power in section 102(1) to bring it into line with our discussion of the role of directors in practice. Section 102 provides that "the directors shall manage the business and affairs of a corporation." In closely held corporations the board of directors is often composed of the shareholders of the corporation who manage the corporation, so this allocation of power may be considered appropriate. In publicly held corporations, however, the board of directors may be said to supervise the management, but it does not manage directly. In order to reflect this basic reality, Industry Canada recommended that the grant of power be amended to add "or supervise the management" of the business and affairs of the corporation.[31]

c) Unanimous Shareholder Agreements

As discussed in chapter 7, in closely held corporations the statutory division of powers provided for in the *CBCA* often will not reflect the true way in which the corporation is managed. Where the same people are the shareholders, directors, and officers, the allocation of distinct roles to each of these classes of participants will be largely irrelevant. The shareholders will manage the corporation directly, allocating powers among themselves as they see fit. If there are outside directors, they are unlikely to exercise any independent oversight of the way the corporation is managed. They are more likely to act merely as advisers, with the true decision makers being those who have an economic stake in the corporation — the shareholders.

---

28 *Ibid.* Indemnification and insurance were discussed in chapter 7.
29 *Ibid.* at 37–39.
30 *Ibid.* at 41–44.
31 *Ibid.* at 44–45.

To facilitate the creation of a structure for closely held corporations which permits shareholders to manage directly, the *CBCA* introduced the unanimous shareholder agreement (the USA), which enables shareholders to assume all of the powers and duties of the directors. Unfortunately, as discussed in chapter 7, the provisions dealing with the USA in the *CBCA* were not sufficiently comprehensive in detailing how this new mechanism for shareholder management would work, with the result that it has not been used as effectively as it might have been. In a recent discussion paper dealing with USAs, Industry Canada considers these problems.[32] In doing so, Industry Canada has sought to balance the desirability of permitting shareholders to design a governance structure that best suits their particular needs with ensuring that the protection for minority shareholders and other stakeholders in the *CBCA* is not compromised. The complexity of doing so is evidenced by the fact that Industry Canada makes no recommendations about solutions to these problems. In this section we highlight some of the major issues canvassed in the discussion paper.

Many of the concerns about the use of USAs relate to the respective roles of the board of directors and the shareholders where the shareholders have assumed the powers of the board under a USA. As mentioned in chapter 7, neither is clear under the *CBCA* at present. If the goal of directors' liability is to reach the real decision makers who influence corporate conduct, then it may be desirable to make certain amendments. One such amendment would be to state expressly that the liabilities of directors, under the common law, the *CBCA*, and other statutes, are transferred to shareholders as is done in the *OBCA* (s. 108).[33] Curiously, the discussion paper fails to address the question of the legislative competence of the federal government to make such a change in relation to liabilities imposed under validly enacted provincial legislation. Another amendment would be to eliminate the need for a board of directors at all, so that no person will be in the untenable position of possibly having liabilities without any authority to take action to prevent them from arising.[34] Doing so, however, might create substantial uncertainty with respect to the legal role of corporate managers: Who is

---

32   Industry Canada, *Unanimous Shareholder Agreements.* (*Canada Business Corporations Act* Discussion Paper) (Ottawa: Industry Canada, 1996) [*Unanimous Shareholder Agreements*]. The Ontario *Business Corporations Act*, R.S.O. 1990, c. B.16 already provides that "the directors shall manage or supervise the management of the business and affairs of a corporation" (s. 115(1)).

33   *Unanimous Shareholder Agreements, ibid.* at 31.

34   *Ibid.* at 39–43. The discussion paper considers a number of options in this regard.

to have the role traditionally associated with the directors? In relation to closely held corporations, where the directors and the shareholders are the same people, it may be a sufficient answer to say that each of the shareholders has this role. In circumstances where the shareholder is a corporation, however, no such easy answer presents itself. In such a case it may be that no human person has responsibility for the duties and liabilities of a director, and the goal of imposing liability personally on the real decision makers, so fundamental to the design of many regulatory statutes, may be defeated.

The discussion paper also considers a related issue raised in chapter 7: Are shareholders who assume the duties of directors bound by all the common law and statutory rules regarding these duties?[35] One aspect of this issue is whether the common law rule, that the decision-making discretion of directors cannot be restricted because directors must always be able to do what they consider to be in the best interests of the corporation in accordance with their fiduciary duty, should apply to shareholders who assume directors' fiduciary duty. Perhaps a more fundamental issue is how the freedom given shareholders to act in their self-interest may be reconciled with a fiduciary duty to act in the best interests of the corporation. The discussion paper raises the possibility that the fiduciary duty of shareholders who have assumed directors' duties could be interpreted less stringently, in a manner similar to the fiduciary duty imposed on partners in partnerships.[36]

Finally, the discussion paper raised another question identified in chapter 7: What should be the procedures by which shareholders exercise their directors' powers?[37] Under the *CBCA* at present, no guidance is provided. Consequently, it is not clear whether the various provisions governing directors' decision making discussed in chapters 7 and 8, such as those regarding dealing with material interests of directors in transactions with the corporation under section 120, and with directors' dissent obligations under section 123, as well as those governing the holding and conducting of meetings, should apply to shareholders when they are acting as directors. Also, it is not clear if there is any need to have annual meetings, since the principal purpose of such meetings is the election of directors.

Reform of the USA provisions in the *CBCA* is fundamentally important to enhancing the utility of the Act for those setting up closely held corporations and, in turn, to improving the marketplace for small businesses

35   *Ibid.* at 31–33.
36   *Ibid.*
37   *Ibid.* at 34–35.

and helping them to prosper. The foregoing discussion illustrates the complex challenges to doing so.

D. SUMMARY AND CONCLUSION

In this chapter, we have looked at the nature of shareholders' interests in the corporation and the ways in which they often conflict with the interests of other stakeholders. The most basic axis of conflict is between the shareholders' interests in having the corporation maximize the financial returns to shareholders and the interests of other stake-holders in having the corporation incur additional costs for the purpose of protecting or advancing their interests. We saw that, for the most part, corporate law, supported by the operation of the marketplace, seeks to protect the interests of shareholders even at the expense of the interests of other stakeholders.

We considered the implications of a model of corporate governance that would require management to take into account the interests of non-shareholder stakeholders. While the wide-ranging social and eco-nomic consequences of corporate decision making may be considered to make such a model desirable, our discussion illustrated the complex and difficult calculus that such a model would involve.

Nevertheless, when we examined two of the dominant trends in corporate governance we saw that, increasingly, directors and officers are being held responsible to various non-shareholder stakeholders through regulatory statutes as well as the judicial development of tort law and the oppression remedy. At the same time, directors and officers are being made more accountable to shareholders as a result of the increasing proportion of shares of public corporations held by institu-tional investors.

Finally, we reviewed some of the issues raised by Industry Canada in the context of the process of reforming the *CBCA*. We saw that the focus of those issues was twofold: to improve the corporate governance struc-ture provided by the *CBCA* by clarifying and rationalizing the duties of directors in light of the real role directors play in public corporations, and to increase the utility of the USA as a mechanism for business people to tailor a corporate structure to meet their particular needs.

FURTHER READINGS

BRITISH COLUMBIA, MINISTRY OF FINANCE AND CORPORATE RELATIONS, *Company Act Discussion Paper* (Victoria: Finance & Corporate Relations, 1991)

BUCKLEY, F.H., M. GILLEN, & R. YALDEN, *Corporations: Principles and Policies* 3d ed. (Toronto: Emond Montgomery, 1995) at 369–73 & 516–62

DANIELS, R.J., & E. J. WAITZER, "Challenges to the Citadel: A Brief Review of Recent Trends in Corporate Governance" (1994) 23 Can. Bus. L.J. 23

GLASBEEK, H.J., "More Direct Director Responsibility: Much Ado About . . . What" (1995) 25 Can. Bus. L.J. 416

INDUSTRY CANADA, *Directors' Liability* (*Canada Business Corporations Act Discussion Paper*) (Ottawa: Industry Canada, 1995)

INDUSTRY CANADA, *Going-Private Transactions* (*Canada Business Corporations Act* Discussion Paper) (Ottawa: Industry Canada, 1995)

INDUSTRY CANADA, *Take-Over Bids* (*Canada Business Corporations Act* Discussion Paper) (Ottawa: Industry Canada, 1996)

INDUSTRY CANADA, *Unanimous Shareholder Agreements* (*Canada Business Corporations Act* Discussion Paper) (Ottawa: Industry Canada, 1996)

MACINTOSH, J.G., "Institutional Shareholders and Corporate Governance in Canada" (1996) 26 Can. Bus. L.J. 145

MACINTOSH, J.G., "The Role of Institutional and Retail Investors in Canadian Capital Markets" (1993) 31 Osgoode Hall L J. 371

Report of the Toronto Stock Exchange Committee on Corporate Governance in Canada: Where Were the Directors? (Toronto: Toronto Stock Exchange, 1994)

"Special Issue on the Corporate Shareholder Debate: The Classical Theory and Its Critics" (1993) 43 U.T.L.J. 297–796

"Symposium: Corporate Governance in Transition" (1995–1996) 26 Can. Bus. L.J. 1–310

ZIEGEL, J.S., *et al.*, *Cases and Materials on Partnerships and Canadian Business Corporations*, 3d ed., (Toronto: Carswell, 1994) at 322–53

GLOSSARY

Affiliated corporations: corporations where one is the subsidiary of the other, both are subsidiaries of the same corporation, or both are controlled by the same person. One corporation is the subsidiary of another if it is controlled by the other. These are the basic and most common types of affiliated corporations. The definitions in the corporate statutes are somewhat broader. "Control" for the purpose of the definition of "affiliate" is legal control: holding voting securities of the corporation which carry more than 50 percent of the votes that may be cast for the election of directors, and where such votes are sufficient to elect a majority of the board of directors. *See CBCA,* ss. 2(2)–(5).

Agency costs: costs arising as a result of someone other than the shareholders being responsible for managing the corporation's business. They include the direct costs associated with directors and officers acting to further their personal interests, in an opportunistic way, at the expense of the corporation, and the related costs that shareholders must incur to monitor their agents in performing their duties for the purpose of guarding against such opportunistic behaviour. *See* chapter 7.

Amalgamation: a statutory procedure by which two or more corporations are combined into one. The rights and liabilities of the amalgamating corporations continue as rights and obligations of the amalgamated corporation. *See* chapter 10 and Short-form amalgamation.

Annual meetings: meetings of shareholders that must be held at least every fifteen months. Annual meetings are identified and defined by the happening of three items of business:

- election of directors;
- receipt of annual financial statements and report of the auditor on such statements; and
- appointment of auditor (unless dispensed with by unanimous agreement of shareholders in certain circumstances).

All other meetings are called "special meetings." To the extent any business other than the three items above is carried on at an annual meetings, it is called an "annual and special meeting." *See* chapter 7.

Articles: the document filed with the Director under the *CBCA* and the statutes modelled after it to create a corporation. They must be filed in the form prescribed by the *Regulations* under the *CBCA* (Form 1), along with a notice of registered office (Form 3) and a notice of directors (Form 6). They set out the fundamental characteristics of the corporation — for example, the class and number of shares authorized to be issued, any restrictions on transferring shares, and any restrictions on the business the corporation may carry on. Once the Director issues a certificate to which the articles are attached, a corporation with the characteristics set out in the articles comes into existence. *See* chapters 3 and 4.

Auditor: the chartered accountant or firm of chartered accountants appointed by the shareholders at each annual meeting to audit the financial statements of the corporation. An auditor must examine and report to shareholders on the financial statements. *See CBCA*, ss. 161–71; *CBCA Regulations*, ss. 44–46; and chapter 7.

Authorized capital: the classes and number of shares of each class a corporation is permitted to issue as stated in its articles. The articles will also set out the rights, privileges, restrictions, and conditions attaching to each class of shares (e.g., the Class A preferred shares are entitled to an annual dividend of $5 per share). The *CBCA* and the other corporate statutes contain certain default provisions that apply if the articles are silent. *See* chapter 6 and *CBCA*, section 24.

By-laws: one way in which a corporation establishes rules for its governance. They may be initiated either by shareholder proposal or by the directors. If a by-law is initiated and approved by the directors, it takes effect immediately, but must be approved by ordinary resolution at the next meeting of shareholders. The main purpose for which by-laws are used in practice is to set out the rules for conducting director and shareholder meetings and to designate and assign responsibilities to offices of the corporation. *See CBCA*, section 103, and chapters 4 and chapter 10.

Capital: generally refers to amounts contributed to a business organization by those with an interest in the residual value of the organization after all other claims have been paid. In relation to a corporation, capital refers to contributions by shareholders. In relation to a partnership, it refers to amounts contributed by partners. Sometimes, however, capital may be used to refer to amounts lent to a business organization as well.

Capital impairment test: a test appearing in many places in the *CBCA* which requires that the realizable value of the corporation's assets are not less than its liabilities and the stated capital of all classes before certain actions, such as declaring dividends, may be taken. *See* chapter 6.

Class of shares: a category of shares designated and given certain rights, privileges, restrictions, and conditions in a corporation's articles, such as dividend entitlements and voting rights. *See* chapter 6.

Closely held corporation: a corporation that has a small number of shareholders.

Co-ownership: a relationship between persons under which they hold title to some property, usually real property, together — for example, as tenants in common. The principal feature of this relationship which distinguishes it from partnership is that the parties' property interests remain separate; each co-owner is free to dispose of his or her interest. *See* chapter 2.

Company: a term that does not have a precise legal meaning. It was the traditional English term to refer to the entity created under English model registration statutes, and it is still used in the U.K. *Companies Act.* Following the English practice, "company" was used in early Canadian legislation and is still the proper term in three provinces: British Columbia, Nova Scotia, and Prince Edward Island. "Company" is also the appropriate term to describe charities or other non-profit organizations incorporated under the Ontario *Business Corporations Act* (R.S.O. 1990, c. C.38). Under the *CBCA* and in the provinces and territories with corporate legislation modelled after it, "corporation" is the proper term. Nevertheless, even in reference to entities incorporated in these jurisdictions, "company" is still used colloquially. "Company" is also used colloquially to refer to a collection of people engaged in any common activity.

Corporation: the entity created under the *CBCA* or any of the provincial or territorial statutes modelled after it. It was adopted from American usage. The term "company" was the traditional English term. *See* Company.

Debenture: the term has no precise meaning. It is sometimes used to refer to a document evidencing a debt obligation (e.g., *Salomon* v. *Salomon & Co.*, [1897] A.C. 22 (H.L.), discussed in chapter 3), but when it is used by bankers it may mean the document evidencing the security rather than the document evidencing the debt. When the term is used by accountants it means an unsecured claim.

Directors: the persons responsible under corporate statutes for managing the business and affairs of the corporation (e.g., *CBCA* s. 102(1)). The directors are elected by the shareholders, and there may be one or more (see chapter 7). If there are more than one, they must act collectively. The "Director" is the person appointed under section 260 of the *CBCA* to carry out the duties and exercise the powers of the Director under the *CBCA*.

Director's resolutions: the means by which directors act. When directors make decisions, they pass resolutions either by voting on them at a meeting or by signing a document expressing the resolution. *See CBCA*, ss. 114 & 117, and chapter 7.

Dissent and appraisal right: the right of a shareholder to have the corporation buy her shares for fair value which arises in certain circumstances prescribed by statute. *See CBCA*, s. 190, and chapter 9.

Dissident proxy circular: the document that must be sent to all shareholders by any shareholder who solicits the votes of shareholders against management if the corporation has fifteen or more shareholders. The form of the circular is prescribed by regulation. *See CBCA*, s. 150; *CBCA Regulations*, ss. 38–41; and chapter 7.

Dividends: payments to shareholders by the corporation. Dividend entitlements may be provided for in the corporation's articles, but whether they are paid is always a matter in the discretion of the directors. *See* chapter 6.

Fiduciary duty: in relation to a corporation, the duty of directors and officers to act honestly and in good faith with a view to the best interests of the corporation. It is provided for in section 122(1)(a) of the *CBCA* and the common law. See chapter 8. Partners also owe each other a fiduciary duty. *See* chapter 2.

Franchise: a purely contractual relationship under which the franchisor gives the franchisee the right to operate a "system" in return for a set of fees. The parties typically provide in their agreement that their relationship does not constitute a partnership or joint venture. The basic terms of the relationship consist of a licence from the franchisor giving the franchisee the right to use its trade-marks and promises to provide certain assistance in running the franchised business, including training. In return, the franchisee agrees to operate the franchised business in accordance with the standards of the franchisor and to pay certain fees based, in part, on the sales of the business. *See* chapter 1.

Fully paid and non-assessable shares: shares with respect to which the consideration must be paid in full before they may be issued, and no further amounts can be assessed after they are issued. *See CBCA,* s. 25(2), and chapter 6.

General partnership or partnership: a relationship that exists when two or more persons carry on a business in common with a view to a profit. A partnership is not a legal entity separate from the partners who make it up, and each partner is fully responsible for all the obligations of the business. *See* chapter 2.

Goodwill: the value associated with a business in excess of the value of its assets. It may exist by virtue of the reputation of operators of the business, the quality of its products, or for some other reason. *See* chapter 3.

Issued capital: the shares of the corporation which have been issued by the directors. *See* chapter 6.

Joint venture: a term used loosely to refer to a wide variety of legal arrangements in which one or more parties combine their resources for some limited purpose, for a limited time, or both. It is not a distinct form of business organization, nor a relationship that has any precise legal meaning. A joint venture may be established, for example, by a contract in which the joint venturers agree that they will do certain things to carry out their common purpose; by two people carrying on business together, in which case the joint venture is a partnership; or by two people forming a corporation to carry out their common purpose. While the legal consequences of a joint venture that is a corporation or a partnership are clear, the legal consequences of a joint venture relationship that is not a partnership or a corporation are not. *See* chapter 2.

Licence: a purely contractual relationship under which one party, the licensor, agrees to permit the other, the licensee, to use something (usually some form of intellectual property such as a patent, trade-mark, or copyright) in return for compensation (usually in the form of a payment based on sales revenues), which is referred to as a royalty. *See* chapter 1.

Limited partnership: a partnership where at least one of the partners, the general partner, has unlimited liability and at least one other, called a limited partner, has limited liability. The liability of the limited partner is limited, typically, to the amount he or she has contributed to the limited partnership. In general partnerships, all partners are general partners in the sense that they all have unlimited personal liability. Limited partnerships come into existence only with a filing made with the appropriate government authority under provincial limited partnership legislation. Limited partners cannot take part in the management of the business of the partnership without losing their limited liability status. *See* General partnership and chapter 2.

Management proxy circular: the document that management of a corporation with fifteen or more shareholders must send to shareholders in connection with shareholder meetings. Its form is prescribed by regulation and includes general disclosure about the corporation as well as specific disclosure about the items of business to be dealt with at the meeting. *See CBCA,* s. 150; *CBCA Regulations,* s. 35; chapter 6.

Memorandum and articles of association: the constitution of a corporation in an English registration model corporate statutes, such as is in force in British Columbia. The memorandum is similar to the articles under a *CBCA* model statute. The articles are similar to a general by-law under a *CBCA* model statute. The memorandum and articles constitute a contract between the corporation and the members. *See* chapter 3.

Minute book: a book in which the records of the corporation are kept. Corporate law requires that certain records be kept, including the articles and by-laws (including any amendments), any unanimous shareholder agreement, minutes of meetings and resolutions of shareholders, and a securities register (*CBCA,* s. 20(1)). It is usual to include minutes of meetings and resolutions of directors as well. *See* Securities Register; *CBCA,* s. 20; and chapter 4.

Obiter **and** *obiter dicta:*   statements made by a judge in the course of giving his or her reasons for a decision in a particular case which are not necessary elements of the reasons for decision. That is, the judge could have reached the decision without making the statements. Under the common law, *obiter dicta* are not binding on courts in subsequent cases.

Officer: a person appointed by the directors to whom certain responsibilities to manage the business and affairs of the corporation are delegated. There are few requirements for officers. In most corporations, the offices are designated in a by-law, and the directors appoint people to fill them by resolution. *See* chapter 7.

Ordinary resolution: a resolution of shareholders passed by a majority of the votes cast by the shareholders who voted in respect of the resolution.

Par value: a provision in a corporation's articles which was intended to represent the issue price of the shares. In many circumstances, however, shares were issued at prices above the par value. Par value has been abolished under the *CBCA* and statutes modelled after it. *See CBCA,* s. 24(2), and chapter 6.

Parent corporation: a corporation which, in relation to another corporation, controls that other corporation. The controlled corporation is a "subsidiary corporation."

Partner: a person who carries on business with another person in a relationship that is a partnership. *See* chapter 2.

Partnership: *see* General partnership and chapter 2.

Pre-emptive rights: rights of the existing shareholders of a corporation to have any shares the directors propose to issue offered first to them, on some basis. Such rights may be set out in the articles or in a shareholders' agreement. *See* chapters 4 and 6.

Private company: defined in section 1(1) of the *Securities Act* (Ontario) (R.S.O. 1990, c. S.5) as a corporation whose articles provide (i) for some restriction on the transfer of its shares, (ii) that the number of shareholders is limited to not more than fifty, exclusive of employees, and (iii) that any invitation to the public to subscribe for its securities is prohibited. "Private company" and "private corporation" are used colloquially and in many places in this book to refer to any corporation that has a small number of shareholders. *See* chapters 4 and 11.

Profits: what is left after all expenses incurred to earn revenue, including operating expenses such as the cost materials and labour, as well as other expenses such as interest on debt and taxes, are deducted from all amounts a business has earned. *See* chapter 2.

Proxy: a document by which a shareholder has designated another person to exercise her votes at a meeting of shareholders. The term is sometimes used to refer to the person who is designated in such a document. Such a person, who is also sometimes referred to as a proxy holder, must act in accordance with the instructions of the shareholder. Until such a document is executed by the shareholder, it is called a form of proxy. *See CBCA*, ss. 147 & 148, and chapter 6.

Public company: a corporation that is not a private company (or corporation). "Public company" and "public corporation" are used colloquially and in many places in this book to refer to corporations whose shares trade on public markets such as the Vancouver Stock Exchange.

Record date: the date for determining who the shareholders are for the purposes of giving notice of a shareholder meeting, paying dividends, or for any other purpose. The directors may set the date. In relation to notice of meetings, if the directors do not set a date, the record date is deemed to be the close of business on the day before the day the notice is sent. In all other cases, if the directors do not set a date, the record date is the day the directors pass the resolution in relation to which it is necessary to determine who the shareholders are. *See CBCA,* s. 134, and chapter 6.

Redemption: the acquisition by a corporation of its own shares pursuant to a provision of the corporation's articles permitting the acquisition. Depending on the provision, redemption may be at the option of the corporation or the shareholder. *See* chapter 6.

Repurchase: the acquisition by a corporation of its own shares pursuant to an agreement between the selling shareholder and the corporation. *See* chapter 6.

Securities: shares or debt obligations, such as bonds, or other claims on a corporation or other business organization. See the definition in *CBCA,* s. 1(1), and section 1(1) of the Ontario *Securities Act,* R.S.O. 1990, c. S.5, s. 2. *See* chapter 11.

Securities register: a record of the securities issued by a corporation in registered form showing the names and latest known address of each person who is a security holder, the number of securities held by each security holder, and the date and particulars of the issue and transfer of each security. *See CBCA,* s. 50(1).

Series of shares: a division of a class of shares. If a corporation's articles permit shares of a class to be issued in one or more series, the directors may designate and assign characteristics to a series of shares which may be different from shares of the same class in other series. In the absence of the creation of a separate series within a class of shares, all shares of a class are equal in all respects. *See CBCA,* ss. 24(3) & 27.

Share: a claim against the corporation issued by the directors in exchange for money, property, or past services, the characteristics of which are defined by the provisions in the corporation's articles creating the class of shares. There are also certain mandatory rules in corporate law about shares, such as the rule that all shares of a class must be treated equally. *See CBCA,* s. 25, and chapter 6.

Shareholder: the holder of a share. For most purposes — for example, giving notice of meetings and paying dividends — the *CBCA* is concerned only with the holder who is registered in the securities register of the corporation, not the beneficial holder of shares. Beneficial holders of shares are entitled to certain protection under the *CBCA* (e.g., they are entitled to claim relief from oppression under section 241).

Shareholders' resolutions: the way in which shareholders take action. Resolutions may be passed by a vote at a meeting or signed by all shareholders. *See CBCA*, s. 142; Ordinary resolution; Special resolution; and chapter 6.

Short-form amalgamation: an amalgamation between certain affiliated corporations which requires only the approval of the directors. A short-form vertical amalgamation may be effected between a corporation and one or more subsidiaries that are either wholly owned by the corporation or where the only shares not held by the corporation are owned by one or more of the other amalgamating subsidiaries. Similarly, a short-form horizontal amalgamation may be effected between subsidiaries that are either wholly owned or where any shares not held by the parent corporation are held by one of the other amalgamating subsidiaries. *See* Affiliate and chapter 10.

Sole proprietorship: a person carrying on business for his own account without adopting some other form of business organization, such as a corporation.

Solicitation of proxies: seeking the votes of shareholders in favour of a resolution or the election of directors at a meeting of shareholders. Under the *CBCA*, management of a corporation with more than fifteen shareholders must solicit proxies. Management is required to send to shareholders a "management proxy circular" in a form prescribed by regulation and a form of proxy so that shareholders can exercise their vote without attending the meeting. Any other person seeking to influence shareholder voting must also send out a circular in prescribed form. *See* Dissident's proxy circular; Management proxy circular; Proxy; *CBCA*, s. 143; and chapter 7.

Special meeting: a meeting of shareholders other than an annual meeting. *See* Annual meeting and chapter 7.

Special resolution: a resolution passed by a majority of not less than two-thirds of the votes cast by shareholders who voted in respect of that resolution, or signed by all the shareholders entitled to vote on that resolution. *See CBCA*, s. 2(1).

Stated capital: the historical total of the value of all the money, property, and past services that have been contributed to the corporation in return for shares it has issued. Each corporation must keep a record of the stated capital for each class and series of shares. *See CBCA*, s. 26 and chapter 6.

Strategic alliance: a term that has no precise legal meaning and is an expression used to refer to a wide variety of relationships involving more or less legal formality and greater and lesser degrees of working together among the alliance partners. A joint venture or partnership may be referred to as a strategic alliance. The term may also be used to describe, for example, an agreement to do research and development together, to market products jointly, or simply to share information. *See* chapter 1.

Subsidiary corporation: a corporation that is controlled by another corporation. *See CBCA,* s. 2(5).

Thin capitalization: a corporation in which shareholders have invested a very small amount in return for shares. Even though most Canadian corporate statutes do not require any minimum capitalization, thin capitalization has been argued to be a ground on which the separate legal personality of the corporation should be disregarded. *See* chapter 3.

Tort: an act or omission giving rise to civil liability. The most important tort is negligence. If a person can prove that the act or omission of another meets the legal standard for negligence, that person will be entitled to compensation from such other person for any loss suffered as a result.

Trade-name: a name used by a business, whether it is the name of a corporation, trust, partnership, proprietorship, or an individual. It includes any name used by a corporation other than its corporate name. *See* chapter 4.

Trade-mark: a mark used to distinguish goods or services as defined in the *Trade-marks Act* (R.S.C. 1985, c. T-13). Trade-marks may be incorporated into trade-names, but need not be. *See* chapter 4 and Trade-name.

Unanimous shareholders' agreement: an agreement among all shareholders of a corporation that restricts, in whole or in part, the powers of the directors to manage the business and affairs of the corporation and includes a declaration to the same effect by a sole shareholder. *See CBCA,* ss. 1(1) & 146(2), and chapters 7 and 12.

Widely held corporation: a term that refers to a corporation that has many shareholders. Usually the shares of a widely held corporation are traded on some form of public market, such as the Toronto Stock Exchange.

Winding up a corporation: the process of gathering in the assets of the corporation, converting them to cash, using the cash to discharge any liabilities of the corporation, and paying out any excess to shareholders before terminating the corporation's existence. Usually, "winding up" refers to this process being carried out under the supervision of a court rather than by agreement of all shareholders. *See* chapters 9 and 10.

TABLE OF CASES

INDEX

ABOUT THE AUTHOR

J. Anthony VanDuzer, B.A., LL.B., LL.M., is a Professor in the Faculty of Law, Common Law Section, at the University of Ottawa where he teaches courses in contracts, business associations, corporate finance, advanced business law, and international business transactions. He has served as an adviser on corporate law to the Department of Industry and as a consultant to the NAFTA Secretariat. Professor VanDuzer has written extensively on corporate law, taxation, international trade, and intellectual property law.